# SOCIAL REPRODUCTION

# Social Reproduction

## Feminist Political Economy Challenges Neo-liberalism

Edited by
KATE BEZANSON
and
MEG LUXTON

McGill-Queen's University Press
Montreal & Kingston · London · Ithaca

ISBN-13: 978-0-7735-3103-1 ISBN-10: 0-7735-3103-3 (cloth)
ISBN-13: 978-0-7735-3104-8 ISBN-10: 0-7735-3104-1 (paper)

Legal deposit fourth quarter 2006
Bibliothèque nationale du Québec

Printed in Canada on acid-free paper

This book has been published with the help of a grant from the Canadian Federation for the Humanities and Social Sciences, through the Aid to Scholarly Publications Programme, using funds provided by the Social Sciences and Humanities Research Council of Canada.

McGill-Queen's University Press acknowledges the support of the Canada Council for the Arts for our publishing program. We also acknowledge the financial support of the Government of Canada through the Book Publishing Industry Development Program (BPIDP) for our publishing activities.

---

**Library and Archives Canada Cataloguing in Publication**

Social reproduction : feminist political economy challenges neo-liberalism / edited by Kate Bezanson and Meg Luxton.

Includes bibliographical references and index.

ISBN-13: 978-0-7735-3103-1 ISBN-10: 0-7735-3103-3 (bnd)
ISBN-13: 978-0-7735-3104-8 ISBN-10: 0-7735-3104-1 (pbk)

1. Women – Canada – Social conditions. 2. Women – Canada – Economic conditions. 3. Sex discrimination against women – Canada. 4. Feminist economics – Canada. I. Bezanson, Kate II. Luxton, Meg

HQ1190.S62 2006 305.420971 C2006–901703–4

---

Typeset in 10/13 Baskerville by True to Type

# Contents

# Preface

This book began as a collaborative project by academics and researchers involved in the Toronto-based Feminism and Political Economy Network. For five years, an informal study group of about fifteen people from the southern Ontario region between Peterborough and St Catharines met monthly to read and discuss new scholarship in political economy and feminist theory. Collectively, participants in the network developed a deeper appreciation of the strengths of a feminist political economy approach in general and the theoretical and explanatory possibilities of feminist conceptualizations of social reproduction in particular.

The circumstances confronting feminists in Canada and in the province of Ontario specifically in the mid- to late 1990s underlined the need for feminist political economy. The Liberal federal government's elimination of the Canada Assistance Plan and its replacement with the Canada Health and Social Transfer in 1994 cut money transfers to provinces and territories and gave them significantly more power to determine which policy areas received funding. The election in 1995 of a Progressive Conservative government under Mike Harris resulted in a dramatic restructuring of Ontario's welfare state, affecting most aspects of social and economic life. The effects of neo-liberal policies and practices at the federal and provincial levels were profoundly gendered. The gains that women had won over the previous twenty years were eroded, and standards of living declined for many women and men, and for poor women in particular. Despite the apparent gender neutrality of neo-liberal policy changes, the cumulative impact was harder on women. In the paid labour force, women's access to jobs, especially well-paid, secure jobs with benefits, is still more constrained than men's; few women earn enough to support themselves and their children.

At the same time, women continue to be primarily responsible for most informal, unpaid caregiving, such as looking after children and providing care to those who need it because they are ill or elderly or live with disabilities. Without adequate social services in areas such as child care or nursing homes, many women have to leave paid employment or at least reduce their hours of employment in order to provide care. As a result, their employment and earning capacities are undermined. When social services are not available, women tend to pick up the work. Their responsibilities for young children mean that many women have to rely on insufficient public income transfers for economic support. Neo-liberal policies in the 1990s exacerbated the tension between paid work and unpaid work, making it harder to balance competing demands.

Participants in the Feminism and Political Economy Network knew that what was happening in Ontario was an example of neoliberalism at work. Similar policies had been implemented internationally by most of the major bodies regulating the global economy, such as the World Bank, the International Monetary Fund, the World Trade Organization, and a range of governments, both national and local (for example, in Britain following Margaret Thatcher's election in 1979, in the United States under Reagan after 1981, and federally in Canada with the election of the Mulroney government in 1984). Although Ontario under Mike Harris, Alberta under Ralph Klein, and British Columbia under Gordon Campbell are the most visible examples of provincial neo-liberal projects, economic restructuring, privatization, and the downloading of care work characteristic of neo-liberalism are present in every province and territory. While each region produces its own specific socio-political and economic dynamics, the general trends are similar. Living through conservative times in Canada and in Ontario, to borrow Sylvia Bashevkin's (1998) phrase, gave participants in the Feminism and Political Economy Network a live example of the perils of ignoring the work of social reproduction. Many of the chapters in this book reflect that perspective.

A goal of the network was to understand the gendered dynamics of neo-liberalism, particularly their impact on women. The network was also committed to exploring the value of the theoretical framework offered by social reproduction to such a project. Individual members of the network developed research projects that examined such questions from a variety of perspectives. We also received a Special Initiative Grant from the Social Sciences and Humanities Research Council of Canada, which allowed the Feminism and Political Economy Network to expand its scope to compare our research with colleagues in other parts of the country. In March 2003 we held a conference at York University called "Rethinking Social Reproduction." Most of the chapters in this book were presented initially as papers at that conference. We thank the SSHRCC for providing us with an opportunity (sadly all too rare in academic life these days) to meet and discuss our work. This book is one result of that initiative. It has been published with the help of a grant from the Canadian Federation for the Humanities and Social Sciences, through the Aid to Scholarly Publications Programme, using funds provided by the Social Sciences and Humanities Research Council of Canada.

All intellectual work is collaborative, and an edited collection such as this one is even more so. As editors, we thank all those involved in the Feminism and Political Economy Network over the years: Sedef Arat-Koç, Barbara Cameron, June Corman, Alice de Wolff, Bonnie Fox, Judy Fudge, Amanda Glasbeek, Marnina Gonick, Kim McIntyre, Haideh Moghissi, Ester Reiter, Pam Sugiman, Tammy Findlay, Katherine Side, and Leah Vosko.

We thank our contributors in particular for their patience and willingness to entertain, on several occasions, suggestions for revisions that would strengthen the collection as a whole. We would also like to acknowledge Philip Cercone and McGill-Queen's University Press for undertaking this project. As well, we wish to thank Cheryl Athersych, Sarah Bezanson, and Ellen Carter for their very able assistance. Our ability to work and the quality of our work is closely related to the social and personal worlds in which we live. We thank friends, family, and colleagues for their support, in particular Jan Campbell-Luxton, Cori Sanders, Jane Springer, Joanne Wright, and the Labour Day Wild Women: Julie McIntyre, Kathy Fox, Cathyann White, Karen Binch, Ester Reiter, and Beth Mair. We also thank some very special children in our lives: Carl, Joshua, Linnea, and Mischa.

# Contributors

SEDEF ARAT-KOÇ was from 1991 to 2005 a professor of women's studies at Trent University in Peterborough, Ontario. She is now with the Department of Politics and Public Administration at Ryerson University in Toronto. Her writing has mostly focused on women, immigration, and citizenship. Her latest book, *Caregivers Break the Silence* (2001), was on the policy impacts of the live-in caregiver program in Canada. Arat-Koc's recent research is on racism in Canada in the post 9/11 context and "whiteness" in Turkey, in relationship to globalization, neo-liberalism, and imperialism.

KATE BEZANSON is an assistant professor in the Department of Sociology and the Social Justice and Equity Studies Graduate Programme at Brock University. She is the author of *Gender, the State, and Social Reproduction* (University of Toronto Press, 2006) and *Public Policy and Social Reproduction: Gendering Social Capital* (forthcoming, Status of Women Canada) along with various policy reports with the Caledon Institute of Social Policy. She is co-author of *Telling Tales: Living the Effects of Public Policy* (Fernwood, 2005). She is co-principal investigator on a three-year SSHRCC-funded project entitled *Ensuring Social Reproduction.*

SUSAN BRAEDLEY, MSW (Laurentian), is a PhD candidate in sociology at York University. Her work on the social relations of care, gender, and the state is informed by her previous career in social work.

BARBARA CAMERON holds a doctorate in political science from the University of Toronto. She is associate professor of political science in York University's Faculty of Liberal and Professional Studies, where her teaching and research focuses on social rights, public policy, and federalism. As a member of the SSHRCC-funded Social Rights Accountability Project, she is working in partnership with the Child Care Advocacy Association of Canada to monitor the negotiation and implementation of intergovernmental agreements related to early learning and child care. Recent publications include "The Social Union, Executive Power and Social Rights," published in the Spring/Summer 2004 issue of *Canadian Woman Studies* , and "Accounting for Rights and Money in Canada's Social Union," in the forthcoming volume *Poverty: Rights, Social Citizenship and Governance.*

MARCY COHEN has worked for the past ten years as the senior researcher and policy analyst for the Hospital Employees' Union. She is currently chair of the board for the BC office of the Canadian Centre for Policy Alternatives and involved in a number of research projects on community health restructuring and health-care privatization. She has a long history of working on community-based research and on women's employment issues.

MARJORIE GRIFFIN COHEN is an economist who is a professor of political science and women's studies at Simon Fraser University in British Columbia. She is currently chair of Women's Studies. She writes in the areas of public policy and economics with special emphasis on issues concerning the Canadian economy, women, international trade agreements, electricity deregulation, and labour. Her most recent publications are *Governing under Stress* (with Stephen Clarkson, ZED Press, 2004); *Training the Excluded for Work: Access and Equity for Women, Immigrants, First Nations, Youth and People with Low Income* (University of British Columbia Press, 2003); and *Global Turbulence: Social Activists' and State Responses to Globalization* (with Stephen McBride, Ashgate, 2003.

BONNIE FOX is a professor of sociology at the University of Toronto. Her research and writing for over twenty years has been on questions central to gender inequality. Currently, she is writing a book on how gender differences and inequalities develop, and are sometimes contested, as heterosexual couples make the transition to parenthood. She is also involved, together with Peggy McDonough, in a study of the effects of workplace restructuring on the health and well-being of municipal workers in the city of Toronto.

MEG LUXTON is a professor of women's studies and social science at York University, Toronto, where she is the director of the Graduate Programme in Women's Studies. She writes about women's work, paid and unpaid, and about international initiatives to measure and value women's unpaid work. She is the author of *More than a Labour of Love: Three Generations of Women's Work in the Home* (Women's Press, 1980). Her most recent book is with June Corman: *Getting By in Hard Times: Gendered Labour at Home and on the Job* (University of Toronto Press, 2001).

LEAH F. VOSKO holds the Canada Research Chair in Feminist Political Economy at York University. Her research focuses on gender, globalization, and labour-market insecurity. She is the author of *Temporary Work: The Gendered Rise of a Precarious Employment Relationship* (University of Toronto Press, 2000) and co-author of *Self-Employed Workers Organize: Law, Policy, and Unions* (McGill-Queen's University Press, 2005). She is also co-editor of *Changing Canada: Political Economy as Transformation* (McGill-Queen's University Press, 2003), co-editor of *Challenging the Market: The Struggle to Regulate Work and Income* (McGill-Queen's University Press, 2004), and editor of *Precarious Employment: Understanding Labour Market Insecurity in Canada* (McGill-Queen's University Press, 2005).

ALICE DE WOLFF is a Toronto-based researcher and activist. She has been active in the women's movement, the labour movement, and international solidarity organizations for over twenty-five years. Since the early 1990s she has focused her efforts on research related to women's paid employment. Her studies have examined the dramatic changes in front-line office work and the growth of non-permanent, precarious work. She has conducted two studies of family-related leave for the Ontario Coalition for Better Childcare and the Ontario Federation of Labour and worked with a wide range of community organizations, community-university research initiatives, unions, and worker organizations.

SOCIAL REPRODUCTION

INTRODUCTION

# Social Reproduction and Feminist Political Economy

KATE BEZANSON AND MEG LUXTON

This collection explores the dynamics of social reproduction around the turn of the twenty-first century in Canada. The concept of social reproduction refers to the processes involved in maintaining and reproducing people, specifically the labouring population, and their labour power on a daily and generational basis (Laslett and Brenner 1989; Clarke 2000). It involves the provision of food, clothing, shelter, basic safety, and health care, along with the development and transmission of knowledge, social values, and cultural practices and the construction of individual and collective identities (Elson 1998; Picchio 1992). The concept of social reproduction builds on and deepens debates about domestic labour and women's economic roles in capitalist societies. Embedded in a feminist political economy framework, social reproduction offers a basis for understanding how various institutions (such as the state, the market, the family/household, and the third sector) interact and balance power so that the work involved in the daily and generational production and maintenance of people is completed.

Social reproduction is dynamic in that most of the work involved in it can be taken up by various actors and institutions. For example, states can underwrite many of the costs associated with providing care to the frail elderly, or such care can be left to the private market to provide for a price and/or to the unpaid labour of family. What is considered socially acceptable for care work will vary culturally and historically, and will reflect the balance of gender, class, and race/ethnic power relations.

Between the mid-1990s and the first decade of the twenty-first century, a neo-liberal order became entrenched in Canada. Neo-liberalism emphasizes "free" markets, decreased state regulation of capital, lower direct taxes, and an approach that sees the individual, rather than the market, as blameworthy for poverty and unemployment (Ferge 1997; Bakker 1996). It represents an ideological shift away from the Keynesian-Fordist consensus, which saw the state playing an active role in market regulation and social provisioning (Bezanson forthcoming; Cameron this volume; Porter 2003; Vosko 2000). Initiatives to implement neo-liberalism resulted in an escalation in the tensions between standards of living and profit-making, as welfare-state supports decreased and labour-market patterns changed.

Despite claims to be pro–free market and anti-regulation, in practice neo-liberal policies tend to concentrate power in the hands of a core group of decision-makers. The federal state and many provinces became less democratic by moving policy and procedural decisions outside debate in elected assemblies (thereby centralizing power) and by devolving and downloading responsibilities for key aspects of social reproduction to lower levels of government (e.g., municipalities) and to individuals (decentralizing blame) (O'Connell and Valentine 1998). Successive federal and provincial governments decreased and/or refused funding to equality-seeking lobby and pressure groups in the 1990s. Simultaneously, major social policy initiatives came to be increasingly determined in closed-door sessions by federal-provincial ministers (see Vosko and Cameron this volume). The result was that democratic process and debate about the future of Canada's welfare state – and about the conditions under which social reproduction took place – were severely constrained.

The redrawn Canadian welfare state allowed provinces to move further toward more punitive, needs- and means-tested welfare states (Peck 2001). Increasingly, battles over social policy became "provincialized," as the federal government withdrew from funding and from setting standards regarding key social entitlements. Neo-liberal provincial governments, especially Ontario's Conservatives and British Columbia's Liberals, overhauled their welfare states. They afforded fewer protections, such as labour-market or environmental regulations, and made other supports, such as social assistance or drug benefits, less generous and less accessible. Social problems and their costs were individualized. This individualization was apparent in a preference for a negative taxation model of social policy delivery in which a tax credit was given to individual households rather than taxes being pooled to provide needed services and supports (see McKeen 2004).

As federal and provincial governments withdrew from their previous roles in social and income support and increased the power of the private market, the work of social reproduction was unequally redistributed across the state–market–family/household–third sector nexus. By default *and* by design, families, particularly the women within them, picked up the work not provided publicly and not affordable personally. Gender, race, and class were central to the neo-liberal project: as economic restructuring and privatization took hold, existing inequalities in income, opportunities, citizenship, and support were exacerbated.

The redistribution of social reproduction across institutions in the neo-liberal period stems from a destabilization of the dominant gender, class, and/or race/ethnic order (see Cameron, Vosko and Bezanson this volume; Fudge and Cossman 2002). Labour markets became more precarious for lower-income workers in particular, and fewer jobs afforded either security or employer supports such as pensions (Statistics Canada 2003c; Heisz, Jackson, and Picot 2002). In female-dominated professions, particularly those in the service sector, women of colour continued to be overrepresented (Teelucksingh and Galabuzi 2005; DeWolffe, Cohen and Cohen, and Arat-Koç this volume). The replacement of a male breadwinner– female carer model with a dual earner–female carer model in Canada resulted in enormous pressures on women particularly to manage paid and unpaid work. Indeed, in 2001 almost 70 per cent of mothers with children under six were in the labour force, and among these, 70 per cent worked full-time (OECD 2005, 70). In the same year, public spending on child care was 0.2 per cent of GDP, translating into 15 per cent of Canadian children under six having access to licensed child care-spaces (OECD 2005, 95).

At the same time as the neo-liberal order in Canada required two earners for most families, the public supports that underwrote some of the work of social reproduction were actively eroded. From health care and education to community services and public transit, public infrastructure was scaled back. New spending in the 2000s has not begun to meet existing needs, and service delivery is increasingly subject to privatization and contracting out (Bezanson and McMurray 2000). Those able to afford market-purchased care-work, such as extended health-care services or live-in nannies, often employed low-paid, precarious women workers, who were often women of colour (see Cohen and Cohen and Arat-Koç this volume). Social reproduction, when valued by the market, is gendered, often racialized, and poorly remunerated.

Where states no longer provided support and where purchasing services on the market was not feasible, the burden of providing additional care and work fell onto families, especially women. In Ontario under the Conservatives (1995–2003), this familializing and individualizing thrust was underlined by a rhetoric about family values and a nostalgic idealization of motherhood and community. As material supports for communities and families were cut, this family ideology blamed families – and mothers in particular — for failing to take responsibility for their members. In fact, a great deal of money was invested in Ontario in centres that encouraged parents to *learn* more about parenting but provided no funds for child-care services (see Vosko this volume). As Fox (this volume) finds, a new ideal of good mothering and intensified concerns about women's devotion to social reproduction were acute in the developing neo-liberal gender order.

Social reproduction involves a huge and complex amount of labour; for the state, then, it also involves exercising social control. Families, and women in them, continued to be subject to active state surveillance while carrying out their unpaid care work. Those caring for elderly parents, for example, were required to meet regularly with caseworkers and to receive suggestions about how they might manage their responsibilities (Braedley this volume). In the absence of public investment in social supports, ensuring that the work of social reproduction is sufficiently completed so that public outcry is minimized requires monitoring, even when no money or support is attached.

Even where measures to reconcile the escalating tensions in social reproduction created by the dual earner–female carer model are in place, more than a decade of neo-liberal governance and an individualized approach to social policy can only begin to mitigate tensions. A framework for a federally funded child-care system is nascent, with new funding beginning to flow by 2005. While crucial to addressing a multitude of issues ranging from child development to family labour-market stresses, it is many years away from being a comprehensive or accessible program (OECD 2004). In the meantime for Canada outside Quebec, centre-based and at-home child care remains low paid for workers and expensive for parents.

This volume shows how an analytical framework based on social reproduction makes possible a range of questions and reveals an array of theoretical assumptions that lead to new ways of understanding women's situation and its relationship to the economy. The authors in this collection employ the term "social reproduction" at different levels of analysis – states, labour markets, families, households, and communities – and in reference to different labours – constitutional negotiations, union organizing, child rearing, adult caregiving – and to different sectors of the population – immigrants, ruling elites, and working and middle classes. They all explore dimensions of the tensions between social reproduction and capital accumulation, showing how such tensions are negotiated and revealing the impact of those negotiations on women. Taking seriously the crucial roles that the institutions of the state, the market, the family/household, and the third sector play in stabilizing the dominant class, gender, and race/ethic order, the authors in this book go beyond the nexus of these institutions to insist on their constant intersection and dynamism. A key insight of feminist political economy offered by this collection is that it is not neutral to shift the balance of work among these institutions; the consequences for individuals and for economies are intimately connected.

The book begins with Meg Luxton's review of the history and development of the concept of social reproduction. While convinced of the theoretical strengths of this concept, Luxton argues that theoretical inconsistencies and confusions inherent in its development, both theoretically and politically, remain in current usages. She calls for a more rigorous interrogation of the concept and a reanimation of the socialist feminist politics that originally produced it.

Barbara Cameron's "Social Reproduction and Canadian Federalism" places social reproduction at the centre of understanding developments in Canadian federalism. Cameron argues that the founding constitution of the Canadian state rests on a fundamental contradiction in the allocation of power and responsibilities between federal and provincial levels of government. Tracing the development of Canadian federalism, which historically placed responsibility for economic development in the hands of the central government and for the social reproduction of the population in the hands of the provinces, she argues that this division of responsibility and power is pivotal to the conflicts that characterize intergovernmental relations in Canada. Distinguishing four periods in Canadian history, she shows that the work associated with social reproduction had to be stabilized in various historical periods so that capital accumulation could continue, forcing the various levels of government to accommodate the needs of accumulation with the standards of living and expectations of the population.

In "Whose Social Reproduction? Transnational Motherhood and Challenges to Feminist Political Economy," Sedef Arat-Koç shows the importance of a perspective that takes account of the global and integrative dynamics of social reproduction. Her study of the experiences of transnational mothering of women who work as nannies in Canadian homes makes transparent the class, race, and gender dimensions of social reproduction: it is at once undervalued and highly valued by states as they mediate the need for two-earner households in North American contexts. It is undervalued in that it is poorly paid, is done by women who have little access to citizenship rights, and is subject to surveillance and control in citizenship terms but not in terms of conditions of work. It is highly valued because foreign domestic workers send large remittances to their countries of origin and are thus an important source of foreign currency. It is also highly valued by the host state because it further privatizes and individualizes the costs of social reproduction; this cost is not borne by the state. Arat-Koç's chapter pushes this dynamic further to reveal the psychological, social, generational, and cultural fallout of mothers working as nannies in other countries. Arat-Koç urges feminist political economy to rethink social reproduction from a supranational vantage point.

The central contradiction between capital accumulation and social reproduction is expressed when workers through their unions try to improve working conditions, pay, and benefits to ameliorate their livelihood, while employers resist and, under pressure to make profits, try to cut labour costs by reducing pay, benefits, and working conditions. The transformation of the Keynesian welfare state since the 1970s and the economic restructuring of most employment in the 1980s and 1990s represent a major challenge to the living standards of the working population. As the chapters by Alice de Wolff (on collective bargaining in Canada in the 1990s and early 2000s) and Marjorie Griffin Cohen and Marcy Cohen (on pay equity and privatization in British Columbia's health-care sector) show, unions have faced difficult challenges when trying to negotiate for measures that recognized the social reproduction responsibilities of their members. Both chapters offer examples of the effects of neo-liberalism on workers, especially in the public sector, and on women's paid and unpaid work. Both show the centrality of women's work to social reproduction and expose the ways in which privatizing social reproduction is central to women's subordination. They also indicate some of the ways that workers have been most effective in winning gains that collectivize some of the costs of social reproduction and help to relieve women of the pressing demands of that work.

The effect of neo-liberalism on social reproduction is illustrated by examining the impact of policies implemented by the Conservative government of Ontario between 1995 and 2003. Vosko, Bezanson, and Braedley consider various aspects of the Ontario Conservative government's approach to limiting the crisis tendencies in social reproduction. Leah Vosko's chapter considers the case study of Ontario's Early Years Centres, exposing them as an example of the individualization and refamilialization of social reproduction. Vosko shows how, by refusing to fund child care and by focusing on tax-based remedies, the Conservatives' Early Years Plan created contradictions that galvanized opposition and subsequent change in social policy. While policy changes in child care emanated from the federal Liberals in 2005, the failure to mediate the child-care crisis in a dual-earner context in Ontario was shaped by the same federal government's early childhood development strategy. Kate Bezanson's chapter exposes the interplay between the restructuring of the welfare state and the capacity of households to manage. It presents findings from a three-year panel study of members of forty-one Ontario households. The study shows that the social, taxation, and fiscal policies enacted during that period were particularly hard on low-income households and on women specifically. The work of social reproduction done by women intensified, and the coping strategies developed by many of those interviewed were unsustainable over the long term. Braedley considers the simultaneous withdrawal of the state from underwriting and supporting the work of caring for frail or ill people and the increased surveillance of those (usually family members) providing unpaid care. Her research suggests that the neo-liberal welfare state in Ontario requires intensified supervision of social reproduction, so that families are compelled to provide unpaid care.

Individuals, as members of families, households, or communities, carry out their responsibilities for social reproduction in ways that are profoundly shaped by familial ideology and class, race, and gender differences, while simultaneously producing and reproducing such ideologies and differences. Bonnie Fox studied new parents over the first year of their child's life. She traces the development of modern practices and ideologies about motherhood, outlining the relationship between capitalism and privatized social reproduction pertaining especially to children. Fox suggests that motherhood as it is currently understood in North America was an "invention" of the middle class in the nineteenth century. On the basis of interviews with new mothers from working and middle class backgrounds, she argues that "good" mothering requires autonomous financial resources and more egalitarian gender relations, and she shows that the existing social relations of motherhood are a source both of women's subordination and of the replication of social class.

The collection concludes with an empirical challenge to the idea that community, family, and friends can make up for cuts in social spending. When state support for social reproduction is cut back, conservative political ideology presumes that families will pick up the slack and that if people need further support, they should turn to friends, neighbours, and their communities. Meg Luxton's study of people who did so following a medical emergency shows how difficult it is for individuals to provide or get access to such informal caregiving. Her findings suggest, in opposition to conservative policies, that the more resources patients have available to them, the more likely they are to have informal support from friends and acquaintances. She also shows that while many people could benefit from such caregiving, prevailing familial and gender ideologies render such relations fragile.

1

# Feminist Political Economy in Canada and the Politics of Social Reproduction

MEG LUXTON

Feminist political economy in Canada has contributed significantly to the development and contemporary use of the concept of social reproduction, especially as it relates to women's paid and unpaid work. In this chapter I argue that the concept of social reproduction offers important tools for analysis and that the implications of such analysis also inspire vital political strategies for human liberation. I do so first by exploring the development of this concept in relation to developments in the women's movement, above all in Canada, and in the tensions arising from different attempts variously rooted in socialist and liberal approaches to political economic analysis. I argue that efforts by feminist political economy to analyze sex/gender divisions of labour and women's work led to three simultaneous conceptual developments: the expanded mode of production model, the sex/gender system, and the analysis of domestic labour as contributing to the reproduction of labour power. These in turn led to contemporary feminist deployments of social reproduction.

Feminist political economy has always been international, and its key concepts have been the subject of international (English-language) theoretical debates. However, their development and deployment in Canada have been particularly important. The analytical rigour of this contribution has been shaped by the politics of the women's movement that informs it, a politics specific to the Canadian context. In particular, the politics of the women's movement in Canada led to the development of a socialist feminist current and, related to it, a feminist political economy whose specific theoretical contribution focused on domestic labour and later on social reproduction. However, that same Canadian context has meant that, given the politics and economics of international formal knowledge production and distribution, Canadian contributions to theory and politics are rarely acknowledged or taken up outside Canada.

I also argue, however, that the potential of the concept of social reproduction has unfortunately been limited by the current political context and recent theoretical tendencies that have reduced and undermined its analytical clarity. Of particular importance, I argue, are the tendency on the part of the broader feminist movement to ignore or deny the salience of class and the tendency of feminist political economy to collapse race and ethnicity into ethnocentrism or class. I urge feminist political economy to rethink its core concepts, especially the possibilities offered by production, reproduction and the sex/gender system for its analysis of gender, race and class, and through those efforts, to animate the social reproduction framework more effectively.

## THE DEVELOPMENT OF FEMINIST POLITICAL ECONOMY

Feminist political economy developed in the early 1980s, out of the engagements between two distinct but related intellectual and political traditions in Canada. One was the new Canadian political economy, itself an integration of liberal political economy, especially as articulated by Harold Innis, and Marxism (Clement 1997, 6–8). The other was feminism, particularly its liberal and socialist currents (Maroney and Luxton 1987, 5). Explicitly interdisciplinary, historical, and comparative, political economy is "the study of society as an integrated whole" that identifies and analyzes "social relations as they relate to the economic system of production" (Drache 1978, 5). It understands society as "a totality which includes the political, economic, social, and cultural, where the whole is greater than its parts" and where these dimensions must be understood in the context of each with the other (Clement 1997, 3). Its broad perspective allows political economy to remain multi-faceted and diverse (Clement 1997, 7) and predisposes political economy to fully integrate the study of women, gender, sexuality, race, and class, as well as other systemic discriminations, such as age and ability.

In practice, however, Canadian political economy has been slow to take up feminist issues and resistant to adopting gender as a key analytical concept, rather than just one topic among many. This complacency has encouraged some feminist political economists to orient their work more closely with other currents of feminist theory and has contributed to an ongoing marginalization of feminism in political economy. At the same time, feminist political economy, like political economy in general, has been slow to acknowledge the importance of racialization and racism. When they are addressed, race and ethnicity, unlike class and sex/gender, are often dealt with as contingencies, rather than as structurally central. As Aboriginal and anti-racist scholars and activists have noted, a failure to theorize race undermines the power and significance of feminist political economy (Carty 1993, 9; Bannerji 1991, 2000; Abel 1997; Dua and Roberston 1999). These indifferences and failures have hampered efforts to theorize the mutual interdependence of economics, politics, racialization, sexuality, and gender that are essential for a comprehensive political economy (Maroney and Luxton 1987, 1997).[1]

Ideally, feminist political economy, like political economy generally, strives "to advance analyses of progressive social change" for economic and social justice (Clement and Vosko 2003, xii). Its anti-racist feminism leads it to seek "a more systematic understanding of how gender, class, race, ethnicity, and ideology intersect within a specific region or nation" and how women "have acted or potentially could act to make their own history" (Connelly and Armstrong 1992, x). Such emphases invite efforts to theorize the relationship between human biology and culture and between social structure and history.

Feminist political economy, shaped by the engagements between its liberal and socialist theoretical roots, has also been shaped by the ways in which its fortunes and capacities are tied to the larger feminist theoretical and political movement of which it is part. While feminism is an international movement encompassing a diverse array of political currents, both its politics and its theoretical developments are shaped by specific national and regional socio-political environments. Canada has, as its leaders justifiably note, "one of the most successful women's movements in the world" (Rebick 2004). Part of its success lies in the fact that "feminists in Canada have been particularly willing to tolerate diversity, understand split loyalties, negotiate compromises as well as engage in common struggles" (Hamilton and Barrett 1986, 4). In that context, as Maroney and Luxton have argued (1987, 8), the Canadian women's movement has produced a particularly well-developed and powerful feminist political economy whose theoretical and political implications are far-reaching.

Revitalised in the late 1960s, the women's movement was significantly shaped by two political features: the form and history of the state and the role of social democracy and socialism in Canada. The particular formation and development of the Canadian state generated at least four relatively distinct currents of women's mobilization. The dominant majority, English-language movement includes a wide range of national and local organizations and individuals. Its most important of many national and binational groups began with the formation in 1965 of the Committee for Equality, a coalition of thirty-two organizations, and later in 1972 as the National Action Committee on the Status of Women (NAC) (Vickers, Rankin, and Appelle 1993; www.nac-cca.ca). The colonization of indigenous peoples and their resistance and struggles for self-determination and recognition of their land claims has produced a range of Aboriginal women's organizations allied in a Native women's movement (Jamieson 1979, Anderson 2001). The existence of Quebec as a distinct nation inside and subordinated to the rest of Canada, with its demands for sovereignty, generated a francophone Quebec women's movement (Dumont et al. 1987). Canada has relied on massive immigration to supply its labour market, but despite a formal commitment to equality, liberal state institutions have been unable to produce equality across race and ethnic differences (Stasiulis 1997). In a context where deep and systemic racism has led to a failure to integrate people of colour and immigrants into full and equal citizenship, women of colour, immigrant women, and women who for reasons of language, religion, ethnicity, national origin, or skin colour are subject to racism, were prompted to challenge the racism of the existing women's movement and, to a certain extent, form a distinct current (Rebick and Roach 1996, 105).

In addition, francophone women outside Quebec organized regionally into independent coalitions and networks (Cardinal and Coderre 1990; Cardinal 1992).[2] Lesbian, bi, and, later, trans activists, facing homophobia in the larger women's movement, organized somewhat separately, while always retaining important links with related groups (Gottlieb 1993; Atlantis 2004). As a result, as Hamilton and Barrett note, "A belief in undivided sisterhood was never very marketable in Canada" (1986, 4). Feminism in Canada has tended to be based on coalitions that recognize different constituencies while working together for particular goals (Vickers, Rankin, and Appelle 1993).

In Canada, unlike the United States, social democratic political traditions remain part of the formal political landscape, giving legitimacy to equality-seeking movements and retaining an openness to socialist politics (Horowitz 1968).[3] Unlike Britain, where both social democracy and socialism were largely based in the organized labour movement, in Canada their base was in broad popular movements, making them more receptive to feminism and anti-racist challenges (Maroney and Luxton 1987, 8). In this political culture, liberal feminism in Canada was open to working with its more radical sisters, and its politics were influenced by the concerns and arguments of a range of other political orientations, including socialism (Hamilton and Barrett 1986, 10; Brown 1989; McPherson 1994). Laura Sabia, a quintessential liberal feminist, member of the Progressive Conservative Party, and president of the Federation of University Women, a liberal feminist group, was instrumental in organizing the 1972 founding conference of the National Action Committee on the Status of Women. She described the importance of broad-based coalitions:

> It brought everybody together. It was just incredible. You had the prim ladies from the local Council of Women, the Councils of Women. You know, those women who legitimately did an awful lot of good work, but did it in the way the government wanted them to do it – nice manners, nice ladies. Then you had the other group who were the Trotskyites and who were just as bold as you could probably do ... they came and screamed and yelled and just did about everything ... They had never come across these women before ... So, in essence, we all learned from each other.[4]

The 1960s women's movement emerged in ideological, political, and theoretical fractures, and its activists and groups learned to work together. A radical left-wing current of the larger women's movement, significantly shaped by socialist feminism, drew inspiration from older socialist and communist movements, especially a commitment to Marxist theory and class politics. The circumstances of its historical reemergence meant that from its beginning socialist feminism was deeply influenced both by the international movements for national liberation from colonialism and for socialism in places such as China, Vietnam, Algeria, Cuba, Nicaragua, Mozambique, and Guinea Bissau and by the related civil rights, Native rights and land claims, anti-racist, and anti-poverty movements for human liberation in Canada and the United States. The women's liberation movement from its inception had a commitment to solidarity with international struggles, a belief that women in capitalist societies such as Canada had much to learn from women in other parts of the world, whose struggles seemed to be more developed, a sense of the importance of respecting and building on differences among women and an orientation to working across lines of division (Adamson, Briskin, and McPhail 1988; Rebick 2005).[5]

For a brief period (from the mid-1960s to the early 1980s) socialist feminism, as a political movement and a theoretical orientation, provided leadership in the women's movement in many countries as well as Canada, especially Britain (Segal 1987; Rowbotham 1989) and Europe (Threlfall 1996), some socialist countries (Molyneux 1994), and many Third World countries (Rowbotham 1992). Typically, its organizational forms and specific actions were locally based, although various international links allowed activists from different regions to meet and occasionally develop shared political interventions.[6] Its theoretical and political publications created an international literature, but inevitably its development was uneven, restricted by language capacities, and tending to reflect the relative strength of national and language-based publishing. General knowledge about socialist feminist politics, for those not directly involved, came to be limited to what was available in print. So for example, while socialist feminist politics was weak in the United States, texts from that country dominate and have come to shape what is typically known as socialist feminism for many readers in a variety of locations, including new generations of scholars in Canada.[7] While the analyses and debates published in French are well read in Quebec, few English-language readers in Canada are aware of them. These readers tend to draw on materials from the United States, Britain, and Australia, while few readers in those countries know anything about Canadian writings or politics (Hamilton and Barrett 1986).

In Canada and Quebec the so-called second wave of the women's movement was significantly shaped by socialist feminism, a politics that continues to inform much of the activist movement and influences academic feminism (Hamilton and Barrett 1986; Luxton 2001). At the same time, the coalition strategy dominating the Canadian women's movement kept socialist feminism receptive to its liberal allies and open to working together on a myriad of issues (Egan 1987). While liberal and socialist feminists united to fight for particular issues ranging from pay and employment equity, access to child care, maternity and parental leaves, citizenship rights for immigrants, and an end to discrimination based on sexual orientation, their underlying differences generated certain tensions, especially related to long-term strategies for change (Prentice et al. 1996).

Adopting the language of socialist and national liberation movements, radical left-wing women activists initially distinguished themselves from liberal equality-seeking feminists by calling themselves the women's liberation movement (not feminists!) (Morgan 1970; Rowbotham 1973). They argued that women are oppressed and subordinated and called for women's liberation (Discussion Collective No. 6 1972). The rather broad and not always precisely defined concept of oppression distinguished the theoretical and political boundaries of these women's liberation movement radicals.

Oppression is the systematic subordination of a recognized social group (e.g., women, Aboriginal peoples, lesbians, and gays) by a dominating group (e.g., men, European colonizers, heterosexuals) and the impact of subordination on the oppressed group. It includes a combination of exclusionary practices that restrict access to economic and social resources (such as education, jobs, property ownership, or formal political power) and enforce restrictions (such as on movement, access to children and residence), ideological discourses that distinguish the oppressed from the dominating groups in ways that affirm the inferiority of the former (through claims about physical, emotional, and intellectual incapacities and derogatory naming) and the myriad ways oppression causes subordinate groups to internalize a false sense of their own inferiority (Fanon 1963; Anderson 2001). Oppression can have many dimensions, such as sexism, racism, or homophobia.

Socialist feminism, which takes its starting point from Marxism's central concepts – class and mode of production – makes a clear distinction between oppression and exploitation. Exploitation "occurs when one section of the population produces a surplus whose use is controlled by another section of the population" (Bottomore et al. 1983, 157). In capitalist societies, exploitation is the central mechanism of working-class oppression based in the relations of production. This penetrating distinction between oppression and exploitation has strategic consequences: class struggle is at the heart of socialist politics. This perspective distinguishes socialist feminism from other currents in the women's movement (Adamson, Briskin, and McPhail 1988).

Liberation, thought of as an opposition to oppression, is perhaps best understood as an ideal which, like democracy, will never be realized, but its fluidity means that it is always open to new content, able to incorporate new concepts as they arise (most recently, for example, trans sex and gender). Sheila Rowbotham (1972, 12–13) articulated the vision: "It is only when women start to organize in large numbers that we become a political force, and begin to move towards the possibility of a truly democratic society in which every human being can be brave, responsible, and diligent in the struggle to live at once freely and unselfishly. Such a democracy would be communism, and is beyond our present imagining."

Liberation is also a somewhat imprecise term used to identify the result of the end of exploitation and oppression. While it drew on eighteenth- and nineteenth-century European calls for liberty and freedom, mid-twentieth-century liberation explicitly articulated the demands and dreams of anti-imperialist struggles by peoples in colonial relations against imperial powers. It was quickly taken up by other political movements, such as the radical wing of the civil rights movement in the United States, international socialist movements such as the Fourth International, and the radical wing of the women's movement. In contrast to both liberal democracy and the socialism of the mid to late twentieth century in countries such as the USSR and China, liberation movements anticipated a radical socialist democracy based on self-determination and an economy in which workers controlled the products of their labours. It articulated an aspiration: an absence of oppression and exploitation and a potential for human individual and collective freedom that could not even be imagined under existing circumstances.

This framework distinguished socialist feminism from the more dominant liberal feminism in several important ways. Liberal feminism's critique of women's inequality and its calls for women's equality produced a strategy based on reforms of institutions and attitudes. Its efforts have led to useful and concrete gains: generally, legal recognition of formal equality with men through, for example, reforms of divorce settlements, challenging discriminatory hiring practices, and strengthening women's control over their bodies. In Canada the Charter of Rights and Freedoms, the decriminalization of abortion, and the recognition of same-sex marriages have all reduced discrimination against women, gays, and lesbians (Razack 1991). As vital and important as these victories are, they have not overturned inequalities, especially in economic power, consumption, distribution, and control. In fact, the impact of neo-liberalism has made life more difficult for the majority of women (Bashevkin 1998; Cossman and Fudge 2002; Cohen and Cohen this volume; Bezanson this volume). Liberal feminist theory has little to offer by way of explanation and no strategic response except to work harder.

Liberal feminism's focus on individuals initially undermined its ability to theorize material relations and social structures. Disturbed by the deeply rooted institutional resistance to change they confronted and challenged by a range of political activists, liberal feminists came to recognize systemic discrimination (Abella 1984) and the existence of other systems of oppression. However, without an analysis of the relations among various systems of discrimination, that recognition too easily becomes a list: for example, gender, race, class, sexual orientation, age, and ability. Individual women's situations are too often understood by adding together the various oppressions. Politically, such an approach is often divisive; it frequently generates complaints from or about groups who are left out, leads to arguments about which discrimination is dominant, and readily degenerates into identity politics.[8] Liberal feminism tends to end up appealing for an elimination of sexism and racism, calling instead for respect for all peoples and an appreciation for diversity that values the existence, appearance, cultural traditions, and practices of all. Furthermore, the underlying assumption of liberal feminism that reform of capitalist societies is possible cannot grasp class structure. Liberal concepts of class remain sociological descriptions of socio-economic status, allowing liberalism to call for an end to classism, a term parallel to sexism and racism which implies that working-class people and their cultural traditions and practices should be accorded greater respect, as part of a larger orientation to respecting diversity.

The Marxist roots of socialist feminism produce a different politics and theory, which start from the conviction that reform of capitalist societies cannot produce liberation. They bring an emphasis on material relations and social structures, modes of production, and a specific concept of class. Arguing that different modes of production are distinguished by the ways in which people produce, allocate, and consume the products of human labour, Marxist theory insists that class is created when the owners of the conditions of production are not also the direct producers; that is, when one class, by virtue of its control over the means of production, can compel the labour of another class and appropriate the wealth produced by the labouring class for its own consumption. From this perspective, the point is not to eliminate derogatory or discriminatory practices by one class against another (as is implied by the term "classism") but to eliminate exploitation and therefore class altogether. Similarly, socialist feminism is skeptical of the term "diversity," arguing instead that while respect for cultural differences is important, the priority is ending the oppression and inequality by which socially identified groups are subordinated. Socialist feminism's critique of oppression and its call for liberation lead to a political strategy based on forming alliances and acting in solidarity with other oppressed groups fighting for liberation, trying to mobilize as many people as possible to resist any oppressive initiatives. The centrality of its class-struggle perspective means that working with and organizing working-class women, is a key priority (Egan 1987; Adamson, Briskin and McPhail 1988; Luxton 2001).

As a result, from its inception, Canadian feminist political economy, while encompassing both liberal and socialist currents, has had a commitment to putting working-class women and their labour at the heart of its analysis (Maroney and Luxton 1987, 1997; Bakker 1989). One of its main preoccupations has been an examination of women's work, both paid and unpaid, of the relationship between the two, and of the ways in which the sex/gender divisions of labour are central to women's subordination (Luxton 1980; Armstrong and Armstrong 1994; Brand 1999). Politically, a trade-union feminism based on the collaboration of the autonomous women's movement and the labour movement promoted a range of policies designed to improve women's economic situation and reduce the oppressive aspects of their dual responsibilities for paid employment and domestic labour (White 1993; Luxton 2001). Analytically, feminist political economy in Canada was in the forefront of theoretical developments relating to women's work, particularly in analyzing women's domestic labour and its relationship to the production of goods and services in capitalist economies (Hamilton and Barrett 1986).

The rapid change in global politics since the 1980s, inspired in part in reaction to the equality demands of widespread mass movements, has challenged the legitimacy of demands for equality, much less human liberation, undermined the organizations that fight for such changes, and eroded the public visibility and effectiveness of feminism (Brodie 1995; Rebick 2005). The rise of neo-liberalism as the guiding framework for the formal policies and practices of the governments of most OECD countries and of key international agencies such as the World Bank and the International Monetary Fund (IMF) imposed structural adjustment programs on most Third World countries and economic restructuring in most welfare-state countries (Bakker 1994). The massive ideological changes that accompanied and legitimized such trends had at their heart a reimposition of inequality and an intensification of women's oppression (NAC 1995). Specifically, neo-liberalism depends on downloading services previously provided by the state onto individuals and families, thereby increasing women's unpaid labour (Day and Brodsky 1998; Bezanson this volume).

Since the 1980s, socialist feminism has been seriously challenged internationally on at least three fronts. First, the collapse of the Soviet Union, the (military) defeat of most socialist projects in countries such as Mozambique and Nicaragua, and the revelation of the oppressive nature of many communist regimes, combined with the apparent strength and power of capitalism internationally, undermined the international socialist movement. Global politics realigned in ways that made the socialist demands of twenty years earlier seem irrelevant. Second, the transformative politics advocated by socialist feminism in the 1970s are too remote from the day-to-day needs of most people to have any widespread purchase in the current climate. A call for the end of capitalism is of little help to workers facing layoffs; the more pragmatic reformist demands for parental leave or an end to compulsory overtime resonate more meaningfully. Likewise, its orientation to anti-imperialism and national liberation struggles limited its attention to racism in its own movement and in its home countries, so that its focus on class failed to address the most pressing issues for many people who face racism more directly in their daily lives (Carby 1982; Joseph 1981; Bannerji 1991, 2000). Finally, the alternatives posed by post-structuralism and postmodernism are both part of a changing political climate that has undermined the popularity of socialist feminism and a reaction against its failure to offer theoretical and political leadership in the areas of concern to post-structuralists and postmodernists.[9] As a result of such challenges to socialist feminism, the utility of its conceptual frameworks and methodological strategies has been debated contentiously, with some arguing that it simply is not adequate for the kinds of political or theoretical tasks people face (Barrett 1991, 1992). In many countries, socialist feminism now has only limited purchase, and its theoretical influence is often muted (Hennessy and Ingraham 1997, 2).

In Canada, despite the decline of the visibility in the organized women's movement, as illustrated, for example, by the apparent demise of NAC in the early 2000s, basic socialist feminist premises still shape much political organizing. The 2000 World March of Women, initiated by the Fédération des femmes du Québec, which took place in over 150 countries, reflected socialist feminist politics in its demands and organizing strategies and mobilized more than thirty-five thousand women to march in Ottawa in the largest feminist demonstration in Canada (Rebick 2005, 246). Its 2005 Charter similarly reflects important socialist feminist principles (Marche mondiale des femmes 2005). The analytical orientation of socialist feminism has had a lasting impact on the development of feminist theory, and it continues to offer significant theoretical contributions to social, economic,and political analyses (Connelly and Armstrong 1992, ix). Some of the most exciting developments, especially in queer theory and anti-racist and post-colonial theory, retain a feminist political economy orientation while challenging it to open up to new areas of analysis (Bannerji 1991; Dua and Robertson 1999). However, those still committed to a feminist political economy approach have tended to move away from the abstract theorizing of its initial phase, concentrating instead on specific case studies (Armstrong and Armstrong 1996, 5–8; Luxton and Corman 2001; Andrews 2003). The focus on women's unpaid work continues, taking on increased importance in light of neo-liberalism's reliance on intensifying it (Fudge and Cossman 2002).

Contemporary feminist political economy has retained many of the analytical strengths of socialist feminism, while also drawing on the strength of liberal feminism's victories, especially in asserting formal equality demands. However, there is a tendency for the radical edge of its socialist feminist current to get blunted, a loss reflected, for example, in the shift of focus from women's liberation to women's equality.[10] Too often, as the key theoretical concepts of socialist feminism become generalized, their potential theoretical rigour has been undermined by rendering them either descriptive or ambiguous, as, for example, when the term "gender," initially coined to permit a more precise distinction between biological and social determinants, became first an alternative to "sex" (e.g., on application forms) and then another word for women (e.g., gender and development) or a way of reducing the attention paid to the specificities of women's oppression (e.g., changing women's studies to gender studies) (Gutierrez 2003).[11]

Nevertheless, Canadian feminist political economy has made impressive contributions to topics such as economic development (Porter and Judd 1999), restructuring (Bakker 1996), labour markets (Fudge and Vosko 2003), state formations and policies (McKeen and Porter 2003), demographics, birthing, and motherhood (Jensen 1986; Maroney 1992; Luxton and Maroney 1992), families (Luxton 1997), health care (Armstrong and Armstrong 1996), and women's movements (Rebick 2005). One of its most significant contributions has been its analysis of the relations between gender and class and its efforts to integrate women's unpaid domestic labour into the theoretical analyses of political economy and, informed by that understanding, to develop a political practice that gives priority to all the activities involved in daily and generational care and well-being of people (Maroney and Luxton 1997, 88–91; Armstrong and Armstrong 2003a, 3).

Stimulated by such concerns, two conceptual formulations – the expanded mode of production, as a corrective to the problems inherent in the widely used production/reproduction model, and the sex/gender system – emerged out of the debates. These formulations led to feminist political economists' efforts to mobilize, first, the concept of domestic labour and later the concept of social reproduction to advance its theoretical contributions. At the same time, many of the tensions inherent in feminist political economy, which reproduce tensions inherent in the differences between its two founding paradigms, liberalism and socialism, have skewed its theoretical development. The challenge for contemporary feminist political economy is to resolve those confusions in ways that strengthen the analytical capacity of its theory.

## MARXISM AND FEMINISM: THEORIZING PRODUCTION AND REPRODUCTION

Marxism, as both a theoretical tradition and an international political movement, was attractive to feminism because it acknowledged women's oppression as a problem, explicitly insisted that it was not universal, and offered a theory of women's oppression that suggested strategic directions for women's liberation struggles. Central to this interest was the key Marxist concept of mode of production, the idea that the ways in which people produce, allocate, and consume the products of human labour are central to shaping their social relations and social organization. According to Marx, the contradictions between the forces and relations of production lead to the historic transformation from one mode into another and underly the dynamic of the capitalist mode of production (Bottomore et al. 1983, 178). The centrality of labour power reinforced recognition that all modes include the production of people, which potentially located women at the centre of theories about modes of production.[12] An early formulation from *The German Ideology* identified Marx's and Engles' main assumptions:

> The first premise of all human history is, of course, the existence of living human individuals ... [Humans] themselves begin to distinguish themselves from animals as soon as they begin to produce their means of subsistence ... This mode of production must not be considered simply as being the reproduction of the physical existence of the individuals. Rather it is a definite form of activity of these individuals, a definite form of expressing their life, a definite mode of life on their part. As individuals express their life, so they are. What they are, therefore, coincides with their production, both with what they produce and how they produce. (Marx and Engels [1845] 1976, 31–2)

They argued that the relationship between the owners of the conditions of production and the direct producers was the key to the organization of any social formation. While they presumed that in small-scale foraging societies ("primitive communism"), no separation existed between the two, so that such societies were egalitarian, they also assumed that the majority of human societies were based on modes of production in which those who owned or controlled the means of production were distinct from, and able to control, the labour of those who were the direct producers. In their detailed studies of the capitalist mode of production, Marx and Engels were primarily interested in its class structure and the class struggles in societies where the capitalist mode of production dominated. In most of this work, they tended to take for granted "the existence of living human individuals." In their discussion of capitalism, for example, they note that the "most indispensable means of production" is the worker and that the "maintenance and reproduction of the working class remains a necessary condition for the reproduction of capital" ([1867] 1976, 718). Noting that "[i]ndividual consumption provides, on the one hand, the means for the workers' maintenance and reproduction; on the other hand, by the constant annihilation of the means of subsistence, it provides for their continued re-appearance on the labour market" ([1867] 1976, 719), they argued that "the capitalist may safely leave this to the workers' drives for self-preservation and propagation" ([1867] 1976, 718). As generations of feminists have noted, the preservation and propagation of the working class involves vast amounts of complex work, mostly done by women. Sexism and a narrow focus on class left gender, and therefore women's domestic work, out of Marx's analysis.

In *The Origin of the Family, Private Property and the State*, Engels took up that absence, elaborating their theory of how sex and class combine in the economy and the state to determine women's oppression. He began with the provocative assertion that social life is determined by both the production of the means of life and the propagation of the species: "According to the materialist conception, the determining factor in history is, in the final instance, the production and reproduction of immediate life. This, again, is of a two-fold character: on the one side, the production of the means of existence, of food, clothing and shelter and the tools necessary for that production; on the other side, the production of human beings themselves, the propagation of the species" (Engels [1884] 1972, 71).

However, Engels failed to realize the implications of his own formulation. He focused on the production of the means of existence, equating it with labour and assuming it was men's sphere of activity. He also equated the propagation of the species with family and assumed it was women's sphere.[13] Changes in modes of production, he argued, occurred with changes in labour and property forms controlled by men. With the emergence of class societies came "the world historic defeat of the female sex" ([1884] 1972, 120). Engels concluded that women's liberation would occur with the elimination of classes, the socialization of women's domestic work, and women's integration into "labour" ([1884] 1972, 138, 221). His work offered exciting insights into the relationship between, and the centrality of, gender and class. Like the earlier works by Marx and Engels, this analysis ignored issues of race and racism and presumed heteronormativity, omissions perpetuated in many of the subsequent feminist efforts to elaborate Marxist theory.

*Production/Reproduction: Dual-Systems Models*

The feminist engagement with Marxist theories of class and particularly with Engels' theory of women's oppression and liberation has generated an extensive literature examining the relationships between gender and class (Vogel 1983; Hennessy and Ingraham 1997). The approach that followed Engels' model most closely postulated a dual-systems model. Drawing on prevailing usages in economics in which production refers to production for the market (a usage informed and replicated by Marxist convention, which uses it to refer to the production of the means of life), some feminists posited a parallel system of reproduction referring to the production of life itself (de Beauvoir 1952, 117; Mitchell 1971). The production/reproduction model is widely used. Reproduction acknowledges and refers to an apparent empirical reality. In almost every society, at least two dominant genders, feminine and masculine, are recognized and anchored by divisions of labour in which specific work is associated with one to the exclusion of the other, where women are typically responsible for child care and much of the work related to feeding, clothing and caring for people, in addition to whatever other subsistence or income-earning activities they may engage in.

In most (but not all) societies, such divisions of labour typically mean that women spend more time working and have less free or leisure time than men. Attempting to explain why such sex/gender divisions of labour frequently correspond to men's domination and women's subordination, many feminists identify patriarchy as a prevailing mode of reproduction based on systemic male domination over women. Kinship and marriage systems subordinate women to the authority and power of fathers, brothers, husbands, and other male kin, restricting their access to property, wealth, and political power and giving control over both their child-bearing capacities and their labour to men.

On closer examination, the production/reproduction formulation retains a theoretical incoherence that creates several serious problems. Like Engels, many feminists tend to equate production, labour, and men with the economy and reproduction and women with the family, even while they recognize women's involvement in subsistence economies or in the paid labour force. That formulation fails to understand the family as both a set of economic relations and a part of the economic workings of society. It also generates conceptual chaos as "reproduction" embodies several overlapping but contradictory meanings, including human biological reproduction, the socialization of children, the reproduction of labour power, and the reproduction of the mode of production or of the society as a whole. Finally, while many have argued that patriarchy (a mode of reproduction) and capitalism (a mode of production) are two separate systems of domination operating in relation to each other (Hartmann 1979) and have described in careful detail the specific forms that women's subordination has taken in different periods of capitalist development (Ursel 1992), they have failed to offer any analysis of patriarchy as a system, leaving the concept problematic and generating even more problematic politics. As Fox notes, "this understanding of patriarchy does not involve a clear specification of its origins, its structure, and its direction. Because the motive force is not specified, the shortest step (usually taken) is to invoke male agency, and by implication, an innate desire for power on the part of men" (1988, 170). As a result, while patriarchy remains a popular shorthand for men's dominance and women's subordination, like mode of reproduction, it lacks analytical utility.

### *The Integrated System or Expanded Mode of Production Model*

An alternative approach argues for a single system based on an expanded concept of mode of production that includes the propagation of the species, particularly the production and reproduction of people on a daily and generational basis (Morton 1972; Beechey 1987, 114; Maroney and Luxton 1987; Smith 1989; Brenner and Laslett 1991). Wally Seccombe, a leading proponent of this approach, argues:

> All human societies are necessarily involved in three interrelated productions: the production of the means of production; the production of the means of subsistence; and the production of labour-power. The reproduction cycle of each is constituted by means of the regular repair and periodic replacement of the productive force in question. Standard Marxist accounts of the mode-of-production concept are confined to the first two "departments." The

> on-going production of labour-power – its daily rejuvenation and generational replacement – is missing. Yet this is primarily what families do: they people societies, restoring their members' energies and replacing worn-out labourers with the 'fresh blood' of youth. The exclusion of labour-power's daily and generational reproduction from the conception of modes of production has made it almost impossible to see families, as labour teams, pumping the life-blood through socioeconomic systems. From a feminist perspective, this tunnel vision is deadly, since the social control of women is based upon the control of their reproductive capacity in a broad range of societies (Seccombe 1992, 11)

In short, the way in which the population as a whole, and a labouring population in particular, is produced is as critical to the organization of any mode of production as the organization of objects (raw materials) and forces of production (tools). Both the production of the means of life and the production of life itself are distinct but interrelated, necessary social processes. But even in this formulation, the term "reproduction" retains some of the conceptual confusion.

First, the concept of reproduction refers to procreation or the propagation of the species, the ways in which any particular society organizes conception, childbirth, and infant viability. The term "reproduction" carries the ambiguities inherent in conception, pregnancy, and birth. On the one hand, once in motion, all three have a life of their own as successful conception, fetal development, the duration of pregnancy, and the processes and outcomes of labour are still significantly beyond the capacity of the participants to affect them. At the same time, they are culturally shaped processes for the woman, the baby, and those around them. In some feminist literature, reproduction is taken to include child rearing and socialization, further conflating the biological and the cultural. Further, many theorists assume that the sexual division in procreation determines the larger sex/gender division of labour, or they argue that men's control over women emerges because of women's essential role as biological reproducers, without showing why women's subordination is either possible or necessary (Firestone 1970). The challenge for social theory is to determine what forces shape the demographics of any particular population and to demonstrate under what circumstances they result in women's oppression or inequality.

Second, in Marxism, "reproduction" is also used to refer to the reproduction of the conditions of social production, to the perpetuation of modes of production. This use of the term assumes that certain relations or processes are core or definitive of a particular mode of production and so must be reproduced in order for social reproduction to occur. The dynamic of the capitalist mode of production is the accumulation of capital, which the capitalist class extracts from the labouring class in the form of surplus value. The prevailing property relations mean that a large segment of the population has no access to the means of subsistence or production. As a result, their only way of making a living is by selling their labour power, or their capacity to work, for a set time on specific tasks in exchange for a wage. Through their work, workers produce goods or services that have a higher value than their wages. That surplus value, which is appropriated by individual capitalists, is used either for their own personal consumption or for reinvestment. In his analysis of capitalism, Marx noted, "Whatever the social form of the production process, it has to be continuous ... When viewed, therefore, as a connected whole, and in the constant flux of its incessant renewal, every social process of production is at the same time a process of reproduction" ([1887] 1976, 711). He summarized the implications of this perspective: "The capitalist process of production, therefore, seen as a total, connected process, i.e. a process of reproduction, produces not only commodities, not only surplus-value, but it also produces and reproduces the capital-relation itself; on the one hand the capitalist, on the other the wage-labourer" ([1887] 1976, 724).

Feminists have asked whether, in this formulation, the production of people is simply assumed or whether it can be understood as part of the core relations that must be reproduced. They have accused Marxism of being sex-blind in failing to delineate the actual socially necessary labour that families, and particularly women, do to ensure the production of people. Feminists have posed several key questions: Under what circumstances does women's child-bearing result in child rearing and other related household and caring work being socially allocated as women's responsibility? Why are women's labour and women's spheres of responsibility so frequently of lower social status that men's, especially when cross-cultural and historical studies confirm the plasticity of gendering: many specific tasks, from weaving to computer programming, change from women to men (or vice versa)? To what extent is the sex/gender division of labour based on women's child-bearing and responsibility for child care a cause or an effect of women's oppression? One answer to such questions was to theorize the existence of a sex/gender system.

### *The Sex/Gender System*

Initially, feminist scholars employed the terms "sex" and "gender" in an effort to provide ways of distinguishing between biological and cultural aspects of human life. Sex referred to material, biological sex differences between women and men (such as genital structure, hormonal patterns, and potential reproductive capacities) and gender to socially or culturally constructed patterns of femininity and masculinity (women wear skirts and like shopping; men wear pants and like football). The relationship between the two, and whether or not such a distinction is even possible, continues to provoke debate. However, gender gradually came to be understood as referring to the historically specific, socially constructed, subject positions, relationships, and language codes by which biological sex differences are rendered materially, culturally, psychologically, and socially significant.

Underlying this effort is a central issue: how to understand "woman." At its simplest, this question asks whether there is in fact anything that can be understood as universal, or common, to all women, and if so, what is its basis, given the enormous historical and cultural diversity and the profound inequalities among women. More importantly, can women have anything in common when some, predominantly white, Euro–North American women of privilege benefit from the subordination and cheap labour of the majority of the world's women? How can the widespread subordination of women in such diverse societies be explained without falling back on biological essentialism? A more complicated version of the question asks what social structures or social systems produce "women." How does a biological female becomes a subordinated woman?

Drawing on Marx, Engels, Freud, and Lévi-Strauss, Gayle Rubin (1975) expands political economy to the unconscious and the sexual-object choice by developing the concept of the sex/gender system. She asks what is required to produce gender, to transform a female into an oppressed woman, or to produce oppressed sexual minorities (158–9). The assertion that "all women are oppressed" recognizes, as Rubin notes (1975, 204), that "[w]e are not only oppressed as women, we are oppressed by having to be women or men as the case may be."

Every society develops culturally specific ways of transforming biological sexuality into products of human activity, organizing identity, desire, and sexuality, and ensuring that biological sexual reproduction occurs on an ongoing basis. This process involves conventions or regulations about copulation, pregnancy and childbirth, and child rearing and social practices about how the child's genealogical status or membership in the society is determined. Typically, it also involves a sexual division of labour at least as relates to infant and child care. Thus a political economy of sex highlights the critical importance for any society of reproducing itself from generation to generation. It also raises questions about whether the existence of (a socially produced gender of) "woman" is necessary for any particular mode of production. Is the existence of woman necessary to the reproduction of existing social relations? How important to any mode of production is the social control (typically by specific categories of men) over women's birthing capacities?

As Rubin and others have argued, one of the strengths of the concept "sex/gender system" is that it "is a neutral term which refers to the domain and indicates that oppression is not inevitable in that domain, but is the product of the specific social relations which organize it" (Rubin 1975, 168; Carby 1982). At the same time, feminist scholars maintain that gender constitutes one of the basic dimensions of all social organization and must be central to any investigation of human activity (Scott 1986; Moore 1988; Laslett and Brenner 1989; Evans 2003). As the ontological basis of gender is embodied in sexual difference, the origins of any gender hierarchy cannot be resolved by theory but require historical answers. There is ample anthropological evidence that sex/gender divisions of labour do not necessarily produce gender inequality. Rather, women's oppression emerges in relation to specific forms of social organization (Leacock 1972; Blumberg 1978; Lerner 1986; Coontz and Henderson 1986). Nor is gender (like patriarchy) an autonomous system with its own dynamic. In fact, recent discussions focusing on gender as a basis of identity politics have tended to be limited to sexual desires and practices, sexualitites and orientation, losing both the material body and the appreciation of its structural relationship to kinship, marriage, and sexuality. This loss of material practices reflects a slide into liberal politics.

However, the strength of a sex/gender system laid a basis for possibilities of linking social organization and subjectivity. Procreation and chid rearing constitute the main processes by which individual gendered subjectivity is produced, resulting in adult sexual identities. As the concept of sex/gender systems insists on historical and cultural specificity, it poses an important question for feminist political economy, especially in studies of capitalist societies. Given that the production of people through childbirth, child rearing, and general caregiving is essential for human survival, why is such work systematically women's responsibility and so often ignored, undervalued, and considered to be distinct from the production of subsistence and wealth? It also invites further questions about the relationship between women's work in the home and other contributions to human reproduction.

### *The Domestic Labour Debate*

In the 1970s, socialist feminists attempting to correct the sex-blindness of Marxist theory with reference to capitalist societies focused on the production of labour power and its market exchange. Observing that an enormous amount of socially necessary labour – unpaid, non-market work – was done in private households, usually by women, they identified it as domestic labour and debated how both the labour and its association with women could best be understood in relation to existing Marxist analyses of labour markets, production, and the accumulation of capital. The extensive literature produced by this endeavour was known as the domestic labour debate (Molyneux 1979; Fox 1980), and theorists from the Canadian left-wing women's movement played a key role in its development and articulation.[14]

The concept of domestic labour began with the recognition that in capitalist societies, the working class depends on more than the wages earned when workers sell their labour power or than the state programs and services often available. In the labour market, people sell their capacity to work, or their labour power, to an employer. During the work process, that capacity or labour power is consumed, and in exchange, workers receive a wage or salary. In their homes and in consumer markets, people use their earnings and their unpaid labour to produce the means of subsistence for themselves and their family members, shopping, cooking, cleaning, and providing care for children, sick, elderly, or otherwise dependent adults as well as the day-today love and support that most people need to give meaning to their lives. Each day the means of subsistence are prepared and consumed, and the capacity to work again is produced. The wealthy can buy such services in the market, from restaurant meals and laundry to sex and nannies, boarding schools or even birthday parties for children, but few workers earn enough even to meet all their needs through the market. Nor can they simply rely on state services to supplement their wages. Even when social democratic welfare states provide extensive services and programs to support the population, they are always based on the assumption that families are available to provide the essentials (Porter 2003).

Throughout the twentieth century in capitalist societies, nuclear families based on a heterosexual couple were the main social form in which people organized their daily and generational reproduction. Typically, men were the primary income earners and women were primarily responsible for child care and household management. By the early twenty-first century, family forms had changed considerably. There were more single-person and single-parent households and more gay, lesbian, and trans parents, and most households of cohabiting women and men relied on the income of both. However, household survival continues to depend on extensive unpaid labour, most of which is still done by women, even when they are fully integrated into the paid labour force, an oppressive reality in most countries (McMahon 1999; Statistics Canada 2000; Bittman 2002).

Socialist feminists argued that domestic labour – required to maintain working-class households and ensure the daily and generational reproduction of labour power – is socially necessary work that is essential to the capitalist mode of production (Morton 1972; Seccombe 1972; Luxton 1980). At the end of the working day, a worker returns home depleted, tired, and hungry. The time off work is necessary as part of the process of replenishing the worker, so that she or he is ready and able to return to work the next day. Similarly, from a social and structural perspective, in raising their children, parents are ensuring the generational reproduction of the working class. This analysis theorized households, families, and kinship systems as crucial relations in any social formation. More significantly, the theoretical advance inherent in this analysis of domestic labour integrated the production of life itself into theories of modes of production (Armstrong and Armstrong 2003a).

Unfortunately, the theoretical gains of this perspective were undermined by initiatives that transformed domestic labour from an analytical category of class analysis to a descriptive term empty of analytical meaning. Many studies of families and divisions of labour used domestic labour to refer to any household maintenance and caring activities that went on in any household, failing to consider how that labour related to the larger economy. Researchers intent on documenting and protesting the exploitative working conditions of domestic servants and particularly the racist, sexist treatment of immigrant women workers used the term "paid domestic labour" to describe their work in other people's homes (Giles and Arat-Koç 1994). Missing from such formulations is an understanding of the importance of the social relations in defining the social organization of the labour. If a working-class woman does certain tasks in her own home for her family, she is doing unpaid non-market domestic labour that contributes to the production and reproduction of labour power on a daily and generational basis. If she does the same tasks in someone else's home for pay, she is a paid employee or wage labourer. The distinction lies in the social relations of the work, not in the tasks themselves or the physical and emotional exertions of the worker. By ignoring the class relationships involved, "domestic labour" lost its analytical power as a way of describing a set of social relations, becoming instead a simple term applied to the performance of a range of tasks.

The domestic labour debate was also undermined by its own tendencies to focus narrowly on technical interpretations of Marxist terminology at a time when Marxism was in decline. However, the political and theoretical questions addressed by the domestic labour debate continued to inform both the politics of the women's movement in Canada and the theoretical debates and research of scholars in Canada. An international feminist movement in which Canadian feminists have played a key role has demanded that unpaid work be measured, valued, and integrated into the economic measuring systems and policies used to regulate international economies (Statistics Canada and Status of Women Canada 1994; Luxton and Vosko 1998). Feminist political economy developed an extensive literature which, based on the analysis of the contribution of domestic labour to the reproduction of labour power, demonstrated the theoretical potential of that approach (Bakker 1989; Bakker and Gill 2004).

Throughout the 1980s and 1990s, as neo-liberal attacks deepened, feminists concerned about domestic labour and its oppressive effects on women made conceptual links with those studying transformations of welfare states and the restructuring of labour markets. Out of that alliance came a recognition that the work encompassed by domestic labour was complemented by related work carried out by state provisions such as health care and education, and both were challenged by related services offered in the market. While Marxist scholars agreed that the state was crucial in producing and sustaining a labouring population through education, training, health care, income security, and regulating labour markets (O'Connor 1974; Hahnel 2005), feminists noted their repeated failure to recognize or deal with gender. Other feminists noted the ongoing failure to deal with issues of racialization and racism, especially in international labour markets. Such sex-blindness and race-blindness mean that political economy, particularly Marxism, has inadequately theorized one of its own key insights about the production of labour power and its market exchange. In contrast, feminist political economy took up the concept of social reproduction as a way of conceiving of how states, markets, and households all interact in the daily and generational reproduction of an international labour force.

## SOCIAL REPRODUCTION

The combination of a single system, an expanded mode of production, and the sex/gender system offered a framework that puts gender at the heart of modes of production, puts biological reproduction and its social and cultural realizations at the heart of social life, and attends to the labour involved in the production of life. But it does so without foreclosing investigation about the cultural forms through which different genders are articulated in any society. This promise is partially realized in the more recent feminist use of "social reproduction."

A central concept for feminist political economy, social reproduction is widely used and frequently cited as a core element of feminist theory more generally. Laslett and Brenner (1989, 382) offer a typical and often-cited definition:

> feminists use social reproduction to refer to the activities and attitudes, behaviours and emotions, responsibilities and relationships directly involved in the maintenance of life on a daily basis, and intergenerationally. Among other things, social reproduction includes how food, clothing, and shelter are made available for immediate consumption, the ways in which the care and socialisation of children are provided, the care of the infirm and elderly, and the

social organization of sexuality. Social reproduction can thus be seen to include various kinds of work – mental, manual, and emotional – aimed at providing the historically and socially, as well as biologically, defined care necessary to maintain existing life and to reproduce the next generation.

This list minimally offers feminist political economy a way of documenting the vast amounts of socially necessary labour as a corrective to other formulations, such as neo-classical economics, which leave that work invisible and unvalued and deprive their own formulations of an analytical tool that can deal with important problems and contradictions in their system (Picchio 1992, 140). However, some important theoretical confusions inherent in earlier uses of the term "reproduction" remain.

By itself, social reproduction offers little more than a fancy term to describe the ordinary activities of daily life. Too often, conventional feminist use of social reproduction still focuses on women's work in the home, leaving vague its relationship to the complementary work (also often done by women for pay) provided by state services such as education and health care or in the market.[15] Even when feminists use social reproduction as a way of conceiving of how states, markets, and households all interact in the daily and generational reproduction of the population, they often retain the ambiguity of the reproduction of the population as a whole and the reproduction of the labouring class. The slippage between the population and the working class reflects a failure to deal with class, a project hampered by the loss of domestic labour as an analytic category. The failure to link the production of life itself and the production of the means of life reduces social reproduction to another term for reproduction in a dual-systems model.[16] Finally, the conflation of a labouring population with the population as a whole, combined with the race-blind tendencies in much feminist political economy, hampers the development of a perspective able to theorize gender, race, and class.

A more rigorous version takes up the analytical framework initially developed by the domestic labour debate. As Picchio argues (1992, 137), "it is not enough to add the process of social reproduction of labour to the economic analysis: it is necessary to define the particular relationship that links production and reproduction." By developing a class analysis that shows how the production of goods and services and the production of life are part of one integrated process, social reproduction does more than identify the activities involved in the daily and generation reproduction of daily life. It allows for an explanation of the structures, relationships, and dynamics that produce those activities.

Starting from the premise that in capitalist societies the majority of people subsist by combining paid employment and unpaid domestic labour to maintain themselves and their households, this version of social reproduction analyzes the ways in which both labours are part of the same socio-economic process. They are interdependent processes of production and consumption that in combination generate the household's livelihood. From this perspective, there is a contradiction between the processes of capital accumulation and those of social reproduction of the labouring population (Picchio 1992). While capitalists strive to extract as much work as possible from their employees in order to ensure the highest possible rates of profit, workers strive to win the highest wages and benefits possible to ensure as high a standard of living as possible for themselves, their families, and their communities. Individual employers have an interest in the processes of social reproduction, regarding not only the cost of wages but also the kinds of employees available to them through the labour market. Everything from formal qualifications, language capacities, and general health, to predispositions toward work determines the quality of labour power available to employers. Individually and in organizations, such as business councils or unions and political parties, employers and workers struggle to advance their interests, demanding state support for the policies they advocate relating to, for example, labour law and labour-market regulations.

As Picchio (1992) has argued, the state and the family are two main sites where the conflicts between the needs of capitalists for profit-making and the living standards of the labouring population are negotiated and taken up as actual struggles that produce results. States play two key roles. First, they regulate and sometimes mediate the relations between labour and capital through a range of laws and policies relating to pro- and anti-natalist policies, immigration, labour laws, health and safety regulations, provision of child care, education, and health care, and environmental protection laws (Clement and Vosko 2003). Second, given the insecurity inherent in the wage system, some states have taken (often limited) responsibility for income security: for example, for the unemployed, low-wage employees, and those with no access to wages (Picchio 1992, 119).

Family-based households produce and sustain their members, ensure that adult income earners are able to return to work, and raise the next generation, particularly through women's unpaid domestic labour: "The family, however defined and composed, functions as an alternator; in the outside world the direction of energy is from the reproduction of persons to the production of commodities (capital accumulation), while in the family this direction has to be reversed – at least apparently – in favour of a more human process whereby the reproduction of persons is the goal and commodity production is the means" (Picchio 1992 , 98). Women's work in the home acts as a residual subsistence labour, expanding or contracting as much as possible to offset the impact of market forces, state practices, or changing family circumstances. Households cannot, however, manage social reproduction on their own, and women's labour in their homes is not endlessly elastic. Without sufficient support, standards of living drop, the most vulnerable households typically collapse, and a crisis in social reproduction is produced.

While markets, states, and families remain the main institutional sites for social reproduction, a range of voluntary associations such as religious, philanthropic, self-help, or activist organizations and informal networks of friends, neighbours, and communities often also play important roles in social reproduction (Statistics Canada 1998a; Brock 2003; Luxton this volume). Such voluntary, non-governmental, and activist organizations often move beyond the direct provision of services to agitate for changes to existing state and/or employer-based contributions to social reproduction, demanding for example, better maternity and parental leaves or improved education and health-care services.

The allocation of responsibility for social reproduction between the different spheres and the standards or quality of life produced vary in different historical periods and in different societies in response to struggles over economic, political, and social priorities (Orloff 1996; Gardiner 1997; Elson 1995; Brenner 2000, 2). Such investigations put issues of imperialism, racialization, and racism at the heart of gender and class analyses. Capitalist development depended on supplies of (reproduced) labour from people who originally lived outside regions where capitalist relations were dominant and on people in and from colonies; the transnational, trans-regional locus of social reproduction and capital's mobility mean that capitalist expansion is foundationally racialized and predicated on differences and divisions.[17]

Tracing the effects of neo-liberalism on labouring populations internationally since the 1970s, feminist political economy has documented their disproportionate impact on women, maintaining or even increasing women's subordination (Elson 1995). Neo-liberal policies, whether as structural adjustment programs in developing countries, or economic restructuring in developed countries assumed that women could intensify their subsistence and domestic labour to offset the cutbacks to social reproduction in both the labour market (with reduced prices for subsistence products, pay cuts, jobs losses, and the expansion of contingent work) and the state (with cuts to welfare payments, education and health care, and new or increased user fees). The more responsibility for social reproduction is imposed on private households, where it is accomplished through unpaid household labour or purchased, the more uneven are its standards and material practices, resulting in growing inequalities of gender, race, and class (Luxton 2002; Neysmith, Bezanson, and O'Connell 2005).

In a country such as Canada, where the labouring population is significantly drawn from immigrants, social reproduction invites an analysis of global patterns of capital development and the systemic inequalities in the global relations of social reproduction by nation, race, ethnicity, and language (Arat-Koç this volume). Since the 1980s, in the context of globalization or more open markets, profit-making by major capitalists is achieved through greater flexibility in production. Reproducing both a labour force and the conditions of production in any particular locale has become less germane to long-term economic growth; so capital, increasingly mobile, has fewer commitments to place. This shift has a profound impact on working-class communities as major employers move, leaving them economically unviable. At the same time, an inability to make a living in their home countries drives millions of people to migrate in the hope of finding better opportunities. This fragmenting of families over national boundaries means that social reproduction is increasingly done across borders (de Wolff this volume). As Sedef Arat-Koç (this volume) has demonstrated, the painful irony for a majority of women migrants is that they end up, despite their qualifications for other employment, working as domestics and nannies for women in the host country in order to make money to support their own dependents in their home country. A social reproduction perspective demonstrates the ways in which capitalism is predicated on racialized divisions, highlights the importance of relations of social reproduction in sites that are outside regions where capitalist relations are dominant, and exposes the dependency of capitalist development on such supplies of (already reproduced) labour.

While the concept of social reproduction generates a deeper more integrated analysis of gender and race, it also opens up the possibilities of a more nuanced analysis of class than that addressed by the current social reproduction literature. Is the oppression of women necessarily produced by the dynamics of the production of labour power? Is it possible to eliminate the sex/gender divisions of labour, and if so, what impact might that have on gender hierarchies? If women and men take equal responsibility for domestic labour and win equal access to jobs and pay in the labour market, will gender inequality be seriously undermined? Can class exist without gender inequalities? Likewise, is the oppression of racialized groups necessary to the class dynamics of capitalism? Can class exist without racism?

The focus on the production of labour power as part of the social reproduction of working-class populations raises questions about the production and reproduction of other classes. What is involved in the reproduction of the capitalist class, and what impact does it have on the dynamics of the social formation as a whole? Practically, the ruling class and elites who own the means of production can buy privacy. There are few studies of upper-class families, and little is known about how the ruling class is reproduced on either a daily or a generational basis, except that the personal wealth of that class means its members can buy most of the needed labour on the market. To what extent are pools of capital still consolidated through marriage or transmitted through kinship-based inheritance? Perhaps of greater social interest is what might usefully distinguish the middle and working classes. Is the production of the labour power of middle-class employees on a daily and generational basis similar to that of workers of the labouring class? In what ways might it be different, and if it is, what, if any, social significance has it? (See Fox this volume.) These questions become even more important as class relationships are increasingly global and profits are less and less tied to actual production (Stanford 1999; Skeggs 2004). Mobilizing social reproduction for an analysis of the ways in which the labouring population is produced, sustained, and reproduced on a daily and generational basis – that is, by retaining the class analysis inherited from socialist feminism – gives feminist political economy the tools to fulfill part of its goal: a way of understanding society from a materialist perspective that puts women, gender, race, and class at the heart of its analysis.

## NOTES

Heather Jon Maroney, June Corman, Bonnie Fox, Kate Bezanson, Jane Springer, and Judy Fudge challenged me to think more rigorously about the questions addressed in this chapter. Their discussions contributed greatly to the ideas presented here. Susan Braedley, Mielle Chandler, and Linzi Manicom read an earlier version of this chapter and gave detailed and helpful comments. I also thank the two McGill-Queen's reviewers for their comments.

1 One of the criticisms often levelled against feminist political economy, especially by postmodernists and post-structuralists, is that it relies on metanarratives, assuming that there is an "explanation that will illuminate *the* conditions that need to be addressed in *specified* ways for *all* women to be free" (Rosenberg 2005, 39–40; italics in original). I think such a critique misrepresents feminist political economy, which, I suggest, argues that any woman's situation can be understood only by locating it in an analysis of society as a totality. Precisely because women are variously located, their conditions are diverse, and both their struggles and their aspirations for freedom inevitably reflect those locations.

2 In 2005 the main organization of francophone women in Ontario was La Table féministe francophone de concertation provinciale, located in Ottawa. I appreciate Jacinthe Michaud's assistance in getting information on francophone women's organizing outside Quebec.

3 Socialist politics in Canada and Quebec were seriously weakened through the 1980s and 1990s, especially in the face of neo-liberal attacks. However, socialism retains a limited legitimacy in the labour movement, the Parti Québécois, the New Democratic Party, and various left-wing groups and movements.

4 Interview with Laura Sabia by Meg Luxton and Shelagh Wilkinson, 14 January 1988, page 60 of transcript.

5 The lack of published material on this political current in part explains the significant misconceptions that are typically made about it. For insight into the politics of this current in Toronto, see the IWD (International Women's Day) *Newsletters* published between fall 1982 and May 1986. In the fall of 1984, several activists who had left IWD started *Cayenne,* a socialist feminist bulletin. The initial editorial committee included Lynda Yanz, Marie Lorenzo, and Christina Mills. The last issue is dated May 1986. Another source is *Rebel Girls Rag,* published by Toronto Socialist Feminist Action. These publications and their equivalents from other parts of Canada should be available in the Canadian Women's Movement Archives at the University of Ottawa or in the Nellie Langford Rowell Library at

York University. For a book discussing these politics, see Adamson, Briskin, and McPhail 1988.

6 Those who were members of parties or movements that were international, such as the communist movement or the Fourth International, had organizational ties with sister organizations in various countries. There were also a range of international conferences, from the more academic International Interdisciplinary Women's Studies Congress (Women's World) which has met every three years since 1981, to the explicitly political European Forum of Left Feminists (ELF), a network of individual women's studies academics and grassroots feminists from most countries of Europe loosely linked through a mailing list and an occasional newsletter. Through this network, the yearly conference on "Migrant Women and Europe" was organized in Amsterdam. In association with ELF, authors Helma Lutz, Ann Phoenix, and Nira Yuval-Davis published *Crossfires: Gender, Nationalism and Racism in Europe* in 1995 (see www.wise.med-inst-genderstudies.org).

7 The evidence for this claim is found in the sources cited in recent Canadian texts that present overviews of socialist feminism. See, for example, Calixte, Johnson, and Motapanyane 2005.

8 Since the mid-1980s, identity politics has emerged as an important political orientation that generates extensive academic work, especially in the United States and to a lesser extent in Canada. Identity politics refers to the organizing by activists who come together around issues based on a shared identity, such as sexual orientation, or membership in racialized, ethnic, linguistic, or national communities, rather than around larger political issues or ideologies. While among feminists such movements emerge in response to the issues faced by their activists, they are often fuelled by activists' anger and frustration that the larger women's movement had failed to take up their concerns. By coming together, activists can sharpen their critiques, develop an analysis of the problems, and determine strategies to resist and fight back. Academically, Judith Butler's *Gender Trouble* (1990) "changed the theoretical landscape of feminist theories of identity and identity politics" (Hekman 2000, 291).

9 Postmodernism and post-structuralism emerged and developed in part in opposition to political economy. The two perspectives not only have different theoretical orientations, but they also have typically addressed different topics, rarely engage directly with each other, and often misrepresent each other's positions. Only a few scholars have worked with both (Weedon 1987). The goal of developing a study of society as an integrated whole is one of the main ways in which political economy is distinguished from post-structural-

ism. Post-structuralists would endorse not ever integrating all factors into one theory but doing the opposite – putting forth only fragments of provisional theorizations, preferably as deconstructions of dominant hegemonic systems. I appreciate Mielle Chandler's comments on this distinction

10 The decline of the radical edge to socialist feminist politics was graphically illustrated by the International Women's Day rally in Toronto in 2004. The slogan of the day was "Because I want to change the world," a vacuous sentiment that glorified "any effort you have made this year to make change." There was no political position about what kinds of changes might be valued by activists struggling to resist American imperialism, capitalist profit-making, men's violence toward women, or attacks on Aboriginal women. There was nothing in the slogan to alert people to the consequences of some of the biggest changes of the preceding year: the war on Iraq, led by US president Bush and British prime minister Blair, or the dramatic growth in wealth of some of the major corporations. In academic milieux, this shift is illustrated, for example, in the name change of the undergraduate course that started as "Women: Oppression and Liberation" and is currently called "Introduction to Women's Studies."

11 The one exception to this trend is the term "social construction," which was initially used as a simple description but has subsequently become identified, especially in the United States, as a theoretical perspective (Hennessy 1997).

12 Different epochs of human history are distinguished by their dominant mode (for example, foraging, horticulture, feudalism, capitalism). While several modes of production can coexist in a particular social formation at any one time, one will typically dominate (the others are usually residual or prefigurative) and so condition prevailing overall economic and socio-political dynamics. In early twenty-first-century Canada, for example, capitalism is the dominant mode, but a few isolated foragers continue to live by hunting and gathering; small numbers of independent producers including family farms, artists, and other craftspeople make goods to sell directly in the market; and workers' non-profit cooperatives perhaps prefigure more widespread collective enterprises.

13 For a detailed critique of Engels' formulation and the problems inherited by feminists who took up his argument, see Maroney and Luxton 1987, 12–17. For other discussions of Engels' impact on feminism, see Kuhn and Wolpe 1978, Sargent 1981, and Vogel 1983.

14 Writing about Britain, Rowbotham (1983, 151) says, "This was the context of what is now referred to as the domestic labour debate. We started off reading Margaret Benston and Peggy Morton." Key texts include Benston 1969; Morton 1972; Seccombe 1974, 1992, 1993; Armstrong and Armstrong [1978] 1994; Connelly 1978; Luxton 1980; and Fox 1980.

15 See, for example, the "Women's Global Charter for Humanity," Supporting Document 1 (Marche mondiale des femmes, 2005:2): "These systems [patriarchy and capitalism] are also rooted in the assurance that women will do the essential work of social reproduction like educating children, caring for intimates, subsistence agriculture, housework, cooking, maintaining clothes, etc., for free."

16 See, for example, Peterson (2002, 1), who "deploys a Foucauldian sense of economies to deny a separation of culture from economy" to bring "the identities, ideologies, and practices of 'social reproduction,' welfare, non-wage labor and informalization *into relation with* the familiar but the now global and flexibilized 'productive economy' of goods and services" (italics in original). However, her analysis does not recognize the processes of production and consumption of labour power in exchange for the means of subsistence that actually link households and workplaces.

17 Linzi Manicom's comments on an earlier draft were particularly helpful here, and I acknowledge her contribution to this section in particular.

2

# Social Reproduction and Canadian Federalism

BARBARA CAMERON

This chapter attempts to demonstrate that the concept of social reproduction offers important insights into the structure of the Canadian federal state and the historical and ongoing conflicts that characterize intergovernmental relations within Canada. As used by feminist political economists, the concept of social reproduction is influenced by, but differs from, that of Karl Marx. In *Capital* Marx argues, "When viewed ... as a connected whole, and as flowing on with incessant renewal, every social process of production is, at the same time, a process of reproduction" [1887, 1954 531). From this general perspective, social reproduction encompasses, first, the maintenance and repair of the means of production (which for Marx includes nature, or what we describe today as "the environment," as part of the instruments of production) and, second, the daily and generational recreation of the population (specifically, the labouring population). Feminist political economists use the term "social reproduction" in the second sense, to refer to the recreation of the population from one day to the next and from one generation to the next. The concept includes but goes beyond physical recreation, in the sense of both biological reproduction and the daily maintenance of the current and future generation of workers. It encompasses as well the transmission from one generation to the next of a historical legacy of skills, knowledge, and moral values. Social reproduction also includes the construction of individual and collective identities and the maintenance across generations of cultures. The term is used in this chapter in the feminist political economy sense (Bakker 2001; Picchio 1992; Ursel 1992).

Feminist political economy sees social reproduction as existing in a contradictory relationship to production. At times, this relationship is depicted in terms of a conflict between two separate spheres, a view that mirrors the separation between the institutions of production and social reproduction in an industrial capitalist society. Instead, this chapter takes the view that production and social reproduction are two aspects of one process of capital accumulation, and the relationship between them is contradictory in the dialectical sense of a unity of opposites. On the one hand, the social reproduction of the working class is a precondition for capitalist production, ensuring a constant supply of labour with the appropriate skills and behaviours. Furthermore, consumption by working-class households is essential to the transformation of the value incorporated in goods and services into new and expanded capital that may be invested back into the ongoing process of production. On the other hand, the more of the social surplus that is devoted to social reproduction, the less there is available for the reinvestment through which capital is further increased or for personal consumption by the capitalist and associated classes. Conflict and compromises around the allocation of resources to social reproduction are central to understanding the relationship among social classes in different periods. These conflicts and compromises take place both within the sphere of production, around wages and working conditions, and at the level of the state, around regulation of the social relations of work and the family, the subsidization or replacement of the wage through income-support programs, or the provision of services to supplement or socialize household labour.

The dialectical relationship between social reproduction and production in the process of capital accumulation means that there are moments when the unity of interests predominate and others when conflict is most evident. Yet unity does not happen spontaneously. State intervention is required to mediate the relationship by containing social conflicts and attempting to reconcile the competing demands of the interdependent systems. In mediating this relationship, the state intervenes to shape and stabilize a particular system of class relationships and, within it, a gender order. The term "gender order" is used by feminist political economists to connote a set of social relations characterized by a sexual division of labour and a gender discourse that support that division. As Brenda Cossman and Judy Fudge argue, "The order is stable to the extent that it has been institutionalized in certain key sites such as the family, the labour market and state policies. For such institutionalization to occur, there must be some fit, however temporary, fragile, and incomplete, between the processes of production and reproduction" (Cossman and Fudge 2002, 7). The relationship between social reproduction and production within the process of capital accumulation is a dynamic one, and while a particular gender order and configuration of class alliances may last for several decades, it is not permanent. In a developed capitalist society, there are constantly tendencies toward destablization and a consequent ongoing need for state mediation. At points of crisis, the system of class alliances, the gender order, and the discourses that support each must be reconstructed, a process that involves social movements as well as the state.

The analysis in this chapter is informed by the political economy insight that political institutions reflect the balance of power – the compromises, accommodations, victories and defeats – among the social forces represented in the process of their creation, the precise shape of these institutions being mediated by the cultural traditions of their creators. Once in place, the institutions provide the framework within which subsequent struggles take place and influence their shape, favouring some interests over others. In this way, political institutions have a relative autonomy until such time as the conflicts among competing social forces become too great and the stability of the system is threatened, requiring new accommodations and occasionally leading to radical changes in political institutions. Feminist political economy situates the role of state institutions, at least in part, in terms of the contradiction inherent in the process of capital accumulation between the processes of social reproduction and production. The contradiction is visible at times of economic crises, in social dislocations of different kinds, and in the struggles of labour, women's organizations, and other social forces around the allocation of resources to social reproduction. It is less visible in periods when a balance, however temporary, has been achieved between production and social reproduction. In analyzing social change, feminist political economy recognizes social reproduction as a terrain upon which political identities may be constructed and political mobilization may occur.

Since the late nineteenth century in Canada, the relationship between labour and capital has been central to the political conflicts and compromises arising from the contradiction between social reproduction and production. Women's organizations have often been allied with labour in demands for state intervention, with the mobilization of women taking place on the basis of their particular location in the system of production and social reproduction. But when the Canadian state was created in 1867, the overwhelming majority of the population was engaged in subsistence agriculture, and the material survival of individuals and communities was considered the responsibility of the private sphere of households or, failing that, charities. Neither labour nor women had yet emerged as influential political forces. Instead, the issue of the state's relationship to social reproduction centred on the cultural survival of a French-speaking Catholic national community in a new country whose population would inevitably be predominantly English-speaking and (it was thought) Protestant. A federal state structure was embraced as a way to reconcile the need for cultural protections for the French Canadian national minority and the requirement of the English Canadian economic elites for a central Canadian state capable of underwriting the costs of continent-wide capitalist expansion.

The central argument of this chapter is that the way that the 1867 constitution institutionalized an accommodation between capital accumulation and social reproduction, which was also a national accommodation, worked as long as social reproduction was primarily the responsibility of private or local institutions. But this original legal structure became more and more strained as the state was increasingly called upon to mediate the relationship between production and social reproduction through regulation and subsidization. With industrialization, new social forces with new political claims and identities, among them labour and women, began to take their place in struggles around social reproduction that intersected with the claims of the French national minority in complex ways. The original legal structure was stretched by means of judicial interpretation, a few constitutional amendments, and, primarily, constitutional and extra-constitutional innovations to respond to these new forces. The cumulative result of this stretching has been growing tensions between the French-speaking national minority and the English-speaking majority, reflected in conflicts between Quebec and the federal government, and the ever-increasing resort to unaccountable intergovernmental arrangements to mediate conflicts around social reproduction.

The examination of Canadian federalism begins with an outline of the division of powers at the time of Confederation to show its contradictory basis. The chapter then traces the stretching of the original division of powers and the consequent tensions through four periods in Canada's development. Each period covers a time when the existing system of gender and class relations was destabilized and/or restabilized, more or less completely, on the basis of a reconfigured relationship between social reproduction and capitalist production. The four periods are the National Policy of 1878 to the Great Depression; the Depression and the search for stablization strategies related to it; the Keynesian restablization; and the turn to neo-liberalism in the second half of the 1970s. For each of the periods, the chapter examines the implications of the federal division of powers for the capacity of the Canadian state to mediate the contradictory relationship of social reproduction to contemporary projects of capitalist expansion. For the second, third, and fourth periods, it explores the ways that this contradictory relationship was reflected in constitutional conflicts between the federal and provincial governments.

## DIVISION OF POWERS AT CONFEDERATION

The primary reason for the creation of a Canadian state in 1867 was to further the capital-accumulation strategy embraced by the English-speaking business interests of Montreal and Toronto after their access to British and American markets was affected by Britain's adoption of free trade in 1848 and the American rejection of it in the early 1860s. The underlying objective of Confederation was to put in place a state structure that would make possible the creation of a continent-wide economy out of scattered British colonies and across a wide expanse of prairie whose main inhabitants were Aboriginal peoples. The new Canadian state would underwrite the costs of constructing the railways, canals and roads that would link the scattered communities, bring settlers to the prairies, transport goods to markets, and spur industrial development in the already established colonies (Creighton 1940). The preference of the dominant capitalist interests was for a state structure modelled on that of Britain, with one elected legislature. However, that model was unacceptable to the political and religious elites of French Canada because it would inevitably make the survival and development of their culture dependent on the goodwill of a legislature representing an English-speaking Protestant majority. A federal state structure was embraced as a way out of a political deadlock between the two groups. Under such a structure, matters related to economic expansion could be assigned to the central state and matters important to French culture given to a legislature controlled by an electorate that was in the majority French-speaking and Catholic.

Even though a federal structure was adopted in order to reconcile French Canada to the Confederation project, the existence of a French Canadian national minority was nowhere recognized in the British North America Act (now the Constitution Act, 1867). An accommodation of this large minority without specifically mentioning its existence was possible because those activities related to the social reproduction of French Canadian society were primarily carried out by private institutions in all the colonies that came together to create the new state. Industrialization was still in the future, and the majority of the population was engaged in pre-industrial forms of capitalist production, primarily subsistence agriculture but also manufacturing, and production was organized through gendered relations of the household or in small enterprises. Social reproduction was considered a matter for the "private sphere" of family, church, and charities and, at times, the local municipal government. In Canada East (now Quebec) the powerful Catholic Church, whose support was required for any political agreement, played the predominant role in moral regulation of the family and other relations but also in the delivery of educational and welfare services. In the English-speaking provinces the Protestant churches were also involved in moral regulation and service delivery, although they were more divided and less monolithic in their political influence. The architects of Confederation could not have imagined that one day the state would have to intervene actively to balance the demands of production and social reproduction and, eventually, to massively subsidize social reproduction. The very idea would have horrified them.

The main logic underlying the 1867 division of powers, then, was that those activities thought at the time to be essential to continent-wide economic expansion, as well as those thought to be inherently national, were assigned to the central state; those thought to be important to the survival of French Catholic culture or that were of a "merely local or private nature" were given to the provincial governments. As there were significant religious minorities (Protestant within Quebec and Catholic elsewhere), the central government was also given responsibility for the protection of their education rights. The economic development powers assigned to the federal government in section 91 of the BNA Act 1867 included a general power over the regulation of trade and commerce and over public debt and property, banking, currency, navigation and shipping, railways, canals, all interprovincial and international transportation, the postal system, the telegraph, inland and coastal fisheries, weights and measures, patents, and copyright. The dreams for capitalist expansion required the appropriation of Native lands in the North-West Territories, which at that time included the area that is now the provinces of Saskatchewan and Alberta. The 1867 division of powers assigned "Indians and lands reserved for Indians" to the federal government, a power that it has exercised historically to destroy the material basis for the social reproduction of Aboriginal peoples. In addition, the preamble to section 91 gave the federal Parliament the power to make "Laws for the Peace, Order, and good Government of Canada" in relation to all matters not assigned exclusively to the provinces. Immigration was made a joint (or "concurrent") power of the two levels of government, with federal legislation having paramountcy in cases of conflict. In section 92 the provinces were given responsibility for such matters as "local works and undertakings"; hospitals, asylums, and charities; "property and civil rights"; and municipal institutions.

Of particular importance to the later development of the Canadian welfare state was the assignment to the provinces of responsibility for "property and civil rights in the province" in section 93(13). This phrase has important historical links with the recognition of the national rights of the French-speaking population of Canada (Hogg 2003, 504), having first appeared in the Quebec Act of 1774 in connection with recognition of the religious and legal traditions of the French inhabitants. There "property and civil rights" referred specifically to the "entire body of private law which governs the relationships between subject and subject, as opposed to law which governs the relationship between subject and the institutions of government" (Hogg 2003, 505). It includes relations within families as well as business and other relationships among individuals, but does not include matters we think of today as civil liberties. The 1867 constitution recognized that in private matters the inhabitants of Quebec would continue to be governed by a body of law rooted in the French civil law tradition, while the rest of the country would be governed by British common law. Criminal law, which is considered public rather than private law, was assigned to the federal government to be in force throughout the whole country. Those economic powers that would otherwise have fallen within the scope of "property and civil rights" but which were thought to be essential to economic expansion were removed from this clause and spelled out as specific powers of the federal government (Hogg 2003, 505). An element of asymmetry was provided for in the never-used section 94, which gave the federal government the power to pass laws to harmonize matters related to "property and civil rights" in the common-law provinces, the harmonization to become effective in a province once the provincial legislature had passed legislation accepting it.

The expectation that the central Canadian state would play an active role through public works in underwriting the costs of constructing a continent-wide market was a departure from the dominant liberal conception of the role of the state at the time. Mid-nineteenth-century liberalism favoured a limited role for the state and a strict delineation of the public and private spheres, and this was certainly the perspective of the domestic agricultural and manufacturing interests, which had long criticized the close ties between business and the state of the Montreal trading interests linked to Britain. However, the British North American colonies in 1867 faced an expansionist power to the south and were not in a position to wait as the economy spread gradually across the continent, on the basis of the surplus generated out of domestic production. Capitalists centred in Toronto and Montreal agreed on the need for a central Canadian state strong enough to pursue economic expansion and to borrow the money on international markets required to underwrite the costs of building railways to link the geographically distant regions of the new country together. The expectations around the provincial state, however, were different. The conception of its role was much more in keeping with the nineteenth-century liberal view, which was that the provincial level would mainly be involved in regulating the private sphere by maintaining the legal framework for the contracts that underpinned family, business, and other relationships. The division of powers around sources of revenue reflected the different expectations about the roles of the two levels of government. The federal government was given the power to raise money "by any mode or system of taxation," while the provinces were limited to levying direct taxes, which at that time meant primarily property taxes, for provincial purposes.

The coexistence of these two conceptions of the role of the state would have seemed natural at the time, corresponding as it did to the dual nature of the economies emerging from colonialism. The dominant section of capital had accumulated its wealth out of the export of staples or raw materials to Britain, and it continued to see its fortunes in terms of the export of staples, now timber and wheat rather than furs, to Britain. It had prospered during the colonial period under a preferential trade regime with Britain and through close ties with the colonial administration and, through these, with the British state. To see its new strategy of accumulation supported by the state, this time a new Canadian state, was not much of a leap for the capitalist elite. Historically, the manufacturing and commercial classes based in Toronto had criticized the close links between the Montreal trading interests and the state. However, the industrialization stimulated by the railways and the prospect of a continent-wide domestic market brought their interests closer to those of their erstwhile foes and created the basis for the Grand Coalition that propelled Confederation. In contrast, the overwhelming majority of the population was engaged in subsistence agriculture, where the basic economic unit was the often isolated household in which productive and property relations coincided with those of the family. The gender order was grounded in the unequal sexual division of labour within the family, which was sustained by laws governing property ownership and inheritance and by religious morality. Within the agricultural household, the formal relations of production and reproduction were patriarchal, with control of the labour of women and children and the products of their labour legally vested in the husband/father (Ursel 1992; Cohen 1988).

Marjorie Griffin Cohen has traced the links between the agricultural household and the staple-exporting economy in nineteenth-century Ontario, arguing that it was this household that produced whatever surpluses of wheat were available for export and during the winter supplied the labour for logging. In return, the household obtained the resources to purchase on the market the manufactured goods, often imported, that it was unable to provide for itself. Very importantly, it was the subsistence production of the household in which women played a central role that sustained the population during swings in external demand so characteristic of international markets for staples (Cohen 1988). In this way, the household was the primary institution for social welfare in periods of market failure at the time of Confederation.

A formula that, for the most part, assigned matters essential to economic expansion to the central government and matters related to the social reproduction of the population (with the significant exception of immigration) to the exclusive authority of the provinces made it possible to accommodate the presence of a large national minority centred in Quebec within a legal framework that assigned the same powers to each provincial government. All provinces were expected to be primarily engaged in providing the legal and institutional framework for commercial, household, and other activities regulated through private contracts or religious teachings and carried out by private institutions (businesses, the family, the church, charities). Within the framework of the French civil code enforced by the Quebec state, private institutions of Quebec society – the churches, the family, and church-run educational and charity organizations – would ensure the cultural survival (and social reproduction generally) of French Canada. If the state were to be involved at all in the provision of support, it would be at the local or municipal level. This was the case in the common-law provinces, particularly Ontario, which had a developed system of municipal institutions. The other major assumption, apart from the identification of social reproduction with the private sphere, was that the cultural survival of French Canada could be separated from control of the economy, which was expected to continue to be in the hands of the English-speaking economic elites (Ryerson 1973, 375).

The premise that social reproduction was essentially a private and local matter began to be tested in the late nineteenth and early twentieth centuries as the effects of industrialization and the extension of the wage relationship began to be felt. As the state moved beyond regulating contracts and private institutions and began inserting itself more directly into private relations – those between worker and employer, parents and children, husbands and wives – and started to deliver services associated with social reproduction, such as primary education, the neat distinction between public and private started to blur and the logic of the 1867 division of powers began to unravel. The identification of social reproduction with the private and local was definitively challenged in the 1930s with the Depression as the need for significant state subsidization of social reproduction became clear, provoking a constitutional crisis. Yet the same developments that blurred the distinction between the public and private also reinforced the importance to the French-speaking national minority of having its own legislature with jurisdiction over matters related to social reproduction. The country's inability to disentangle cultural guarantees for French Canada from notions of what is "merely local or private" and the legal equality of the provinces has brought about an ever-deepening constitutional crisis. Mediating this crisis has been a primary preoccupation of the central Canadian state for the past seven decades. Struggles around social reproduction involving the state in Canada are inevitably caught up in the resulting constitutional morass.

## THE NATIONAL POLICY TO THE GREAT DEPRESSION

The National Policy, which was adopted by the Conservative government of John A. Macdonald in 1878, inaugurated an accumulation strategy based on the development of a domestic manufacturing industry concentrated in central Canada, securing of the Prairies against the threat of American expansionism through settlement and the building of a railway to the Pacific coast, and the creation of an export-oriented wheat economy in the West. The strategy required extensive economic intervention on the part of the central Canadian state in the form of protective tariffs to keep out foreign-produced manufactured goods, massive state subsidies for railway construction, and aggressive immigration strategies to recruit from foreign lands workers for the expanding factories of Ontario and agricultural producers for the West. The rapid pace of industrial expansion and western settlement in this period destabilized the existing system of social reproduction and gave rise to new problems that strained the capacity of traditional institutions of the family, churches, private charities, and local government (Ursel 1992, 62). The disastrous effects of an unregulated wage-labour system on the health and standard of living of the working class were documented by federal investigations into industrial conditions in the 1880s (Guest 1997, 21). There was a cultural dimension to the social dislocation as well. The factory system required the creation of a disciplined working class and increasingly one with minimum levels of literacy. A new working class was being called into existence, primarily through immigration, at the same time as a new nationality was being created in the English-speaking part of the country.

The first wave of feminism in English-speaking Canada played a crucial role in bringing public attention to the effects of the unstable relations of social reproduction and in the political mobilization that resulted in the consolidation of a new gender order, a new set of class relations, and a new sense of national identity for the English-speaking population (Bacchi 1983; Strong-Boag 1976). At the centre of this new order was the ideal of the male-breadwinner family in which the wife/mother operated within a separate but equal sphere to that of the husband/father, with a special responsibility for socializing children and upholding morality within the family and the larger society. Women's sphere was complementary to that of men and was not seen as isolated from public life. Instead, the maternal feminists recognized that the lines between the public and private spheres were no longer sharply drawn and advocated state intervention in employment and family relationships as a means to protect social reproduction. An active role for women in politics, although not necessarily through the ballot box, was justified in terms of women's alleged superior morality and the impact that politics was having on the family. The nascent labour movement, seeking better wages and working conditions through state intervention to limit competition in the labour market, welcomed an alliance with the socially influential women of the capitalist and professional classes who were the activists in the early women's movement. Jane Ursel describes the urban social reform movement as united around a "commitment to stabilizing reproductive relations" and argues that it played an important role in pushing the provincial state into a more interventionist role in regulating and subsidizing institutions of social reproduction (Ursel 1992, 68–9). At the provincial level, family laws reinforced the support obligations of the husband/father, and factory legislation prohibited the employment of children, restricted the employment of women, limited working hours, and imposed minimum safety standards (Fudge 1999). State regulation and support for charitable organizations was increased, and new organizations to regulate reproductive relations, such as the Children's Aid Societies, came into existence. Federal intervention in the employment relationship came with the Industrial Disputes Investigation Act of 1907.

In addition to intervening to regulate relations within business and the family, the state in this period made its first forays into the subsidization of social reproduction. In the late nineteenth and early twentieth century, the federal government aggressively used its immigration power to bring settlers to build the agricultural economy of the West. After the First World War it became directly involved in providing rehabilitation and training for veterans and pensions for veterans and their dependents. The provincial state, too, began to directly subsidize the costs of social reproduction. With the introduction of compulsory public education, an important historical function of the family was socialized. Workmen's compensation, introduced first in Ontario in 1914, provided a state-mandated system of no-fault insurance to provide for the support of injured workers and their dependents and to protect employers from law suits. In 1916 Manitoba introduced the first mother's allowance and state subsidies for homes for the aged, and the other common-law provinces followed with similar measures. In 1927 the federal government introduced its first program subsidizing social reproduction directed at the larger population with the introduction of an old-age pension, a measure that supplemented market income by providing a means-tested benefit at the age of seventy to British subjects residing in Canada (Guest 1997, 77).

During this period, state involvement in social reproduction, except for the Old Age Security Act, did not stretch the 1867 division of powers. It was developments in the courts rather than legislatures that had the greatest long-term consequences for federal-provincial relations. As the state intervened to regulate or subsidize social reproduction in ways not foreseen in 1867, the courts were increasingly called upon to decide which level of government had responsibility for a new area of social reproduction. While the judges in Canada sometimes recognized the national dimension of matters such as labour relations, the Judicial Committee of the Privy Council in Britain (the highest court of appeal for Canada until 1949) continued to see the new responsibilities of the state in social reproduction through the prism of private contracts and private social relations. As a consequence, the courts opted to classify many new matters under the "property and civil rights" power of the provinces, rather than choosing the "trade and commerce," "peace, order, and good government," or other powers assigned in 1867 to the federal government. A casualty of this approach was a Canada-wide system of collective bargaining when the courts ruled in 1925 that the federal Industrial Disputes Investigation Act, 1907, did not apply to municipal employees or to any industries within provincial jurisdiction ([1925] A.C. 396).

## THE DEPRESSION AND THE CRISIS OF SOCIAL REPRODUCTION

The mass unemployment and widespread destitution of the 1930s destabilized the system of class relations and the gender order centred on the ideal for all social classes of the male breadwinner–dependent wife model. The crisis strained the capacity of the traditional institutions of the family, churches, private charities, municipal, and even provincial governments. As the depression deepened, it gave rise to the mobilization of the unemployed in direct confrontations with capital and the state. The increased political organization of the working class was reflected in the emergence and rapid growth of the Co-operative Commonwealth Federation, the increased membership of the Communist Party, and the expansion of industrial unions. The collapse of markets for commodities (including labour) was compounded by the problem of drought on the Canadian Prairies. There was widespread disillusionment with capitalism, experimentation with new ideologies, and a search for alternative strategies. The strategies advanced – from socialization of the means of production to Keynesian techniques for managing supply and demand in the economy – recognized the failure of unregulated capitalist markets and presupposed active intervention on the part of the state.

With the deepening economic crisis and the ineffectiveness of state repression in stopping working-class organization, important sections of the political elites began to recognize the necessity of a new kind of state intervention in labour and other markets, and liberal intellectuals started to embrace Keynesian economic theories that centred on using the state to manage the relationship between the supply of goods and services and the demand for them through government expenditures to maintain the purchasing power of the population during times of economic downturn and to finance public works projects. In the midst of the Depression and in the last year of his mandate, Conservative prime minister R.B. Bennett – known to the unemployed as "Iron Heel Bennett" – underwent something of a political deathbed conversion, and in January 1935 his government introduced into the House of Commons a package of legislative measures that amounted to Canada's version of the American New Deal.

The "New Deal" legislation that related directly to social reproduction included the Employment and Social Insurance Act, the Minimum Wages Act, the Limitations of Hours of Work Act, and the

Weekly Rest in Industrial Undertakings Act. The first of these was directed at establishing a system of unemployment insurance and unemployment services across the country; the other three were aimed at bringing the country's practices with respect to minimum wages and hours and days of work in line with Canada's obligations under the 1928 conventions of the International Labour Organization. The legislation involved a significant expansion of the role of the central Canadian state in economic and social life, provoked controversy in Bennett's own party, and brought the federal government into conflict with the provinces, particularly Ontario and Quebec. The legislative package did not save Bennett's government, and the 1935 general election brought the Liberal Party into office. The new prime minister, William Lyon Mackenzie King, had questioned the constitutionality of the measures as leader of the opposition, and once elected, he referred the legislation to the Supreme Court of Canada for an advisory opinion on whether or not it fell within federal jurisdiction.

Drawing on precedents from the previous period, the court found that the legislation was in "pith and substance" an insurance measure and, as such, fell under the "property and civil rights" power of the province ([1937] 1 D.L.R. 684). The court was evenly split on the three pieces of legislation related to the conventions of the International Labour Organization ([1936] S.C.R. 461). However, when the Supreme Court's decision was appealed, the Judicial Committee of the Privy Council in Britain maintained that the federal government's newly acquired capacity to enter into international treaties independent of Britain did not mean it could use that power to enact legislation that would otherwise fall within provincial jurisdiction ([1937] 1 D.L.R. 673). The federal executive (Cabinet) has the authority to enter into treaties, but when legislation is required to implement the provisions of a treaty, it must be enacted by the legislature (federal or provincial) that has the responsibility for that particular matter under the constitutional division of powers. Minimum-wage and hours-of-work legislation in most industries fell to the provinces under their powers over "property and civil rights" and "matters of a merely local or private nature," and so it was up to the provinces to decide whether or not they would introduce legislation to meet the terms of the ILO conventions. The federal government could only legislate measures to conform to the conventions for those industries for which it was specifically assigned responsibility. As a consequence of this judgment, there is a two-step process involved in Canada's commitment to international human rights treaties, such as the Convention on the Elimination of All Forms of Discrimination against Women. The federal government has the constitutional authority to sign, but the provisions of the agreements only become part of Canadian law if implemented by the legislature having jurisdiction for the matter in question, which is often at the provincial level.

The court decisions compounded the crisis of social reproduction by transforming it into a constitutional crisis. In the wake of the decisions of the Judicial Committee of the Privy Council, Prime Minister King appointed the Royal Commission on Dominion-Provincial Relations (commonly known as the Rowell-Sirois Commission) to address these interrelated crises (Canada 1940). Reporting in 1940, after the Second World War had begun, the commission outlined a comprehensive program to remove the constitutional obstacles to managing the relations between production and social reproduction. At the centre of this program was a proposal to realign federal and provincial powers so that the federal government would assume responsibility for the maintenance of the standard of living of the "employable" unemployed and the provinces would retain responsibility for the "unemployables"(Canada 1940, 128).

The commission assumed that the "unemployable" element of the population would be small, as the central Canadian state would now take responsibility to maintain high levels of employment. In the process, it would be maintaining the wage as the main way to access subsistence for the majority of the non-agricultural population. The commission advocated a program of contributory unemployment insurance with an additional program of unemployment aid, financed out of general government revenue, for those unemployed workers not covered for one reason or another by the social insurance program. Regarding other social insurance programs, the commission recommended that the federal government have responsibility for seniors and the provinces for health insurance.

The gender order underlying this proposal was founded on the male breadwinner–dependent wife and children model. The commission assumed that the husband/father would be the breadwinner and his wage would support an economically dependent wife/mother and their children. This model was similar to the male breadwinner–dependent wife ideal of the earlier period, with the difference that the commission envisaged large public subsidies from the federal state to make this ideal a reality for the working class as a whole. The federal government's responsibility was to manage the economy in order to maintain the male wage, either by keeping rates of unemployment low or, in periods of higher unemployment, by replacing the male wage through benefits paid under a social insurance program. Within this framework, responsibility for the economic well-being of wives and children was subsumed under the federal responsibility for the employable section of the working class. The commission's preferred approach was for social insurance to cover both the wage earner and his dependents. Yet it recognized that not all women and children would be able to access subsistence through a male wage. In its memorable words, "there would always be a residue of widows, deserted mothers and orphans to be provided for. These would remain a provincial responsibility" (Canada 1940, 35). These unfortunate, husbandless mothers would be the responsibility of the provinces, along with other sections of the "unemployable" population.

## KEYNESIAN STABILIZATION

The post-war era in Canada saw the stabilization of a class and gender order based on Keynesian strategies of capital accumulation. At the level of the national economy, this process involved regulation of the domestic market to ensure sufficient demand for domestically produced goods. Maintaining the purchasing power of households was key to this approach, and women's role as managers of household consumption was prized. Internationally, the strategy involved the regulation of the world economy under the leadership of the United States through trade agreements and international institutions such as the World Bank and the International Monetary Fund. The gender order underpinning this strategy was the same as that outlined in the Rowell-Sirois report and was captured in the concept of "the two person-unit" approach to social insurance, articulated in British and Canadian post-war social welfare reports and endorsed by the *Final Report* of the federal government's Subcommittee on Post-War Problems of Women in 1943. This approach "treats a man's contribution as made on behalf of himself and his wife as for a team, each of whose partners is equally essential and it gives benefits as for the team" (Canada 1943–44, 28). In the view of the subcommittee, this conception was even more relevant to Canada than to Britain because of this country's large agricultural population. "In this occupation, wives are directly contributing to and actually sharing the husband's occupation, while among urban wives, the function is rather that of managing, housekeeping, caring for the well-being of the family, and saving" (Canada 1943–44, 28).

The role of the central state in managing the relationship between production and social reproduction required by Keynesianism brought the federal government into conflict with successive Quebec governments. In the 1950s Quebec opposition to federal social welfare initiatives was led by the conservative, nationalist Union Nationale government of Maurice Duplessis, which rejected both the Keynesian view of the role of the state generally and the post-war role assumed by the federal government. The conservative nationalist perspective was comprehensively elaborated in the 1954 report of the Quebec Royal Commission of Inquiry on Constitutional Problems, commonly known as the Tremblay Commission (Kwavnick 1973).

As with the Rowell-Sirois Commission, the vision of federalism outlined in the Tremblay report was connected to a very specific conception of the appropriate gender order. The report began from a conservative Catholic notion of society as composed of an organic hierarchy of institutions with the family as the most fundamental institution. The report argued that, based on the principle of subsidiarity, responsibilities should be assigned to the most basic institution capable of fulfilling them and only assumed by the next higher institution when necessary. As applied to the role of the state, this concept meant that the state should leave the welfare of members of society to the family and the church and confine its role to providing the financial support necessary to allow these institutions to carry out their responsibilities. As applied to federalism, it meant that the federal government should hand over the taxing power that it had assumed during the Second World War to the provincial government so that it could provide the necessary support to non-governmental organizations. This organic conception of federalism was identified with the French Canadian Catholic world view, and the notions of the role of the state in the Rowell-Sirois Commission were seen as typical of an English Protestant view.

The church remained in control of education and the social welfare system in Quebec until 1960. But with the Quiet Revolution, liberal elites with an agenda of modernizing Quebec society assumed office in the province, and the state rapidly and decisively replaced the Church as the main protector of culture and aspirations. In a very short period,

Quebec went from being the province that relied most heavily on non-governmental (in this case church) organizations in the delivery of social welfare to the one with the largest role for public institutions. Yet, while they had fundamentally different views from the conservative elites on the state-market-family-voluntary sector/charity relationship, the liberal elites shared their view of the role of the federal government in social programs. They too considered matters of social reproduction as vital to French Canadian cultural survival and as falling within the exclusive jurisdiction of the provincial government. Thus federal intervention in these matters is not simply a matter of overstepping the legal boundaries in the constitution; it is a threat to the very cultural survival of French Canada and a reneging on the agreement that underlies the Canadian state. This view applies to taxation as well as to spending: both should be limited to financing the specific responsibilities assigned to the federal government under the 1867 division of powers.

The opposition of Quebec to the expansion of the federal role was the central dynamic in federal-provincial relations with respect to social programs in the period of expansion of the welfare state, as it is today. From time to time, Quebec is joined by other provinces, particularly the wealthier ones, but this opposition is of a different kind and degree from that of Quebec. For Quebec, the opposition is profoundly rooted in a historical defence of a minority national culture and in a deep, society-wide consensus about the importance of maintaining the protections given to that culture when the Canadian state was created. When English Canadian premiers invoke the "exclusive powers" of the provinces to counter federal initiatives, it is often to defend particular capitalist interests located within their borders, as conservative governments in Ontario, British Columbia, and Alberta did on behalf of the private insurance industry during the lead-up to the introduction of medicare (Shillington 1972, 160; Taylor 1978, 376). More often, it is to ally temporarily with Quebec in order to wring more money or better conditions out of the federal government. Once this tactic has succeeded, they generally abandon Quebec, whose opposition continues on principle. Provincial governments in the English-speaking provinces can often count on their citizens to support their demands for more federal money for provincial programs and their criticisms of federal cutbacks. No provincial government outside Quebec has the support of the electorate to challenge the very existence of a federal role in social programs.

The consequence of Quebec opposition, supported on a number of issues by governments of the wealthier provinces of English Canada, was that the federal government failed in its attempts to bring about a modernizing of the division of powers between the federal and provincial governments in the post-war era. The neat division of responsibilities envisaged by the Rowell-Sirois Commission was not implemented or even very seriously entertained. In two areas, formal constitutional amendments were agreed to: unemployment insurance and pensions. A 1940 amendment made unemployment insurance the exclusive responsibility of the federal government under a new section 91 (2A) of the constitution. In 1951 the constitution was again amended, this time to make pensions a joint area of responsibility, with the provincial legislation having primacy in cases of conflict. In 1964 another amendment expanded the pension power to encompass survivors' benefits. Other than these formal amendments, the main instrument for the expansion of the post-war welfare state under federal leadership has been the federal spending power. This power, which is not spelled out explicitly in the constitution, has been defined as the capacity of the federal Parliament to transfer or lend its funds to any government, institution, or individual it chooses, for any purpose it chooses, and to "attach to any grant or loan any conditions it chooses, including conditions it could not directly legislate" (Hogg 2003, 166).[1]

The first use of the federal spending power for social programs was the 1927 program of old-age pensions, which was cost-shared between the federal and provincial governments. It was exercised in the 1930s to transfer money from the federal to provincial and municipal governments to finance "relief" for the unemployed. The Family Allowances program was an example of the use of the federal spending power to transfer resources to individual Canadians. Direct funding to women's services and women's organizations (once more generous than it is today) came under the federal spending power. The federal spending power is the constitutional basis for the federal contribution to the provinces for medicare, as it was for the Canada Assistance Plan (the framework for income support and services for low-income Canadians before it was abolished in the 1995 budget). Another example of the exercise of the federal spending power in the area of social policy is the federal loan/grant program for post-secondary students. While recognizing the need for a special arrangement for Quebec, the child-care movement in English Canada, as represented by the Child Care Advocacy Association of Canada, calls for an ambitious exercise of the federal spending power to create a country-wide system of child care, with the costs shared jointly by the federal and provincial governments and with conditions attached to the federal transfer to ensure quality. All these matters fall within the "exclusive" jurisdiction of the provinces. Federal involvement is only possible through the federal spending power.

A federal spending power is common to all federations. What is unique about Canada is the extent to which it has been relied upon as an instrument to achieve the expansion of social rights at the level of the central state. The exercise of this power was and remains one of the most hotly contested issues in Quebec-Canada relations. Through the means of its spending power, the federal government was able to finesse the limitations placed on its role in social reproduction by an outdated, yet politically unchangeable, constitutional division of powers, as well as the differences between Quebecers and other Canadians about the appropriate roles for the federal and provincial governments in social programs. As a consequence, the exercise of the federal spending power must be seen as contradictory. On the one hand, it was the instrument for the expansion of social rights on a Canada-wide basis in the period after the Second World War. On the other, it provided a means for the imposition on Quebec of an English Canadian view of social citizenship and the role of the central Canadian state in constructing it.

## NEO-LIBERAL DESTABILIZATION

The Keynesian welfare state in Canada reached its highest point in the early 1970s, with the extension of unemployment insurance in 1971 to encompass most of the working class and the full indexing of the then universal programs of Old Age Security and Family Allowance to inflation in 1973 and 1974. The class compromise inherent in Keynesianism, which involved working-class support for capitalism in exchange for the promise and in many cases the reality of an ever-increasing standard of living, was beginning to be seen as too restrictive for capital. Not only was the cost of socializing reproduction high, but the historically unprecedented levels of security enjoyed by working people contributed to labour militancy and limited capital's flexibility in introducing changes in work processes and the organization of production. As a consequence of the post-war period of capitalist expansion, the largest corporations had outgrown the domestic market and Keynesian strategies for economic regulation. They sought new markets for goods and services in other countries and new opportunities for capital investment, both internationally and within the public and quasi-public sector, such as health services. Competition from the now reconstructed economies of Europe and Japan, combined with advances in science and technology, at once accelerated and facilitated the drive to replace Keynesianism with a new strategy for capital accumulation.

In the search for an alternative to Keynesianism, the political elites at the level of the central Canadian state initially swung back and forth between policies of accommodation, attempting to enlist labour's participation in corporatist or "tripartite" bodies, and coercion, introducing wage controls, using the courts to limit labour's capacity to strike (Panitch and Swartz 2003), and cutting back on social entitlements. During the 1980s, however, political and economic elites increasingly coalesced around a strategy of unilaterally breaking the social contract by rolling back the costs of social reproduction, as reflected both in the wage packet and in social programs, and limiting the power of organizations representing those social groups whose interests are most strongly linked to social reproduction, particularly labour and women. In the middle of the 1980s, the Royal Commission on the Economic Union and Development Prospects for Canada (the Macdonald Commission) played the same role in elaborating a new strategy for economic and political regulation for the dominant Canadian elites as the Rowell-Sirois Commission had done at the beginning of the Keynesian era (Canada 1985). While many of its recommendations were not implemented in the form proposed, significant ones were, and the others formed the basis for negotiations around attempted compromises among various sections of the elite.

At the centre of the Macdonald Commission proposals was a shift away from Keynesian approaches to regulating the relationship between capital accumulation and social reproduction through managing the balance between aggregate supply and demand in the economy. Instead, the focus in the report was on the use of monetary tools (interest rates, the supply of credit) to manage the economy. The shift is reflected in a redefinition of unemployment as a problem with the supply of labour (the characteristics and behaviour of the unemployed), rather than the demand for labour (the lack of jobs). As a consequence, the commission shifted the focus for government away from the creation of employment to influencing the behaviour of the unemployed through economic coercion, or what was euphemistically described as removing the "disincentives" to work allegedly inherent in existing social programs and state regulatory measures. In effect, it advocated a shift away from employment to what later came to be described as "employability." Severe cutbacks and even the elimination of the unemployment insurance program were central to its vision of the future. It proposed the eventual replacement of the Canada Assistance Plan, and possibly unemployment insurance as well, with a minimal income-support program, the Universal Income Security Program, that would effectively act as a subsidy for low-wage employers and eliminate the need for minimum-wage legislation (Canada 1985, 2: 542, 811). The commissioners recommended devolving the delivery of social services to voluntary organizations, which are "less bureaucratic and potentially more responsive structures" than government, although governments would retain a supervisory and funding role (Canada 1985, 2: 807). They acknowledged that the current system of daycare drives the majority of Canadian parents into the unsupervised private sector but cautioned that "Canadians must consider carefully whether or not we wish our governments to spend more public funds on providing day care services" (Canada 1985, 2: 813).

The effect of the federal policies since 1985 has been to begin to put in place a new "employability model" of the welfare state, based on a specific conception of the state-family-market-voluntary sector relationship (Porter 2003, 212; Cameron 2002). Within this model, the role of the state is no longer to manage the relationship between social reproduction and capital accumulation to ensure a national market for domestically produced goods but to lower the costs of labour and the expectations of the population with respect to living standards in line with the regional and global expansion strategies of the dominant sections of capital. This process requires removing barriers to the free movement of capital, goods, services, and, to a lesser extent, labour through trade and investment agreements such as the Canada-US Free Trade Agreement and the North American Free Trade Agreement and increasing the "flexibility" of labour through deregulating employment standards, outsourcing production, and eliminating social programs and other protections that provide some insulation for workers from the pressures of competitive labour markets. The virtues of service delivery through the voluntary sector are extolled, and nonprofit organizations are brought into a "partner relationship" with the state in which they are turned into subcontractors for the delivery of government programs and placed in competition for contracts with commercial operators eager to have their profits subsidized by government grants (Shields and Evans, 1998). A limited form of employment equity, which permits the full utilization of skilled human resources, is consistent with this model and is considered preferable to pay equity, which the Macdonald Commission described as administrative wage-setting (Canada 1985, 2: 636).

Implicit in the employability model of the welfare state is a new gender order characterized by continuing inequality between men and women in the workforce and in the home and a marked polarization among women with respect to opportunities and resources. With the erosion of a male wage high enough to support a wife and dependent children, the model assumes the labour-market participation of virtually all women, including those with young children, but on terms of inequality with men. The consequences for women are contradictory. While women's new labour-market position holds the promise of increased economic autonomy, they have been drawn into the labour force without the services being put in place to replace their labour in the home. In the name of deinstitutionalization and moving services closer to the community, the labour associated with social reproduction is increasingly off-loaded onto the non-waged labour of family members and individuals. The result is tremendous stress for families and for women in particular. In the absence of public services to replace the domestic labour of women, the greater equality of opportunity for a small stratum of more professionally trained or highly skilled women is being subsidized by the growing army of low-paid, precariously employed women engaged in child care, cleaning, or food preparation in the growing service sector. Often employed on temporary or casual employment contracts, workers in the domestic and personal services industries are disproportionately drawn from communities of colour or recent immigrants (Arat-Kroc this volume).

The creation of the employability model of the welfare state was brought about through the actions of the state as well as of corporations. The federal government used the same instruments to roll back the Keynesian welfare state as it did in its expansion: its exclusive jurisdiction over unemployment insurance, shared jurisdiction over pensions, and federal social transfers to individuals and, particularly, to provincial governments. Following the logic, if not the exact detail, of the Macdonald Commission, Conservative and Liberal governments decreased entitlements to unemployment insurance so that the proportion of the unemployed who actually got to collect benefits declined from 74 per cent in 1990 to 39 per cent in 2001 (Canadian Labour Congress 2003). Just as the federal spending power was crucial to the construction of a Canada-wide system of social welfare, in this period it became a primary instrument for its deconstruction. Stephen McBride has used the term "negative spending power" to characterize the federal government's role as it used reductions in transfers to the provinces to bring about a restructuring of social entitlements (McBride 2001, 141). These cuts, begun in 1977 under the Liberal government of Pierre Elliott Trudeau when block funding was introduced for health and post-secondary education, were continued under the Conservative government of Brian Mulroney and became particularly severe under the Liberal government of Jean Chrétien after 1993. In addition, the 1995 budget, brought in by Finance Minister Paul Martin, went farther than the proposal of the Macdonald Commission by abolishing the Canada Assistance Plan and with it the right to assistance based on need, without putting in place a new program for the long-term unemployed.

By cutting its social transfer to the provinces at the same time as it was off-loading the cost of supporting the unemployed onto provincial welfare rolls, the federal government effectively undermined the system of intergovernmental relations. Unilateral changes in funding arrangements, such as the imposition of a cap on the federal transfer for social assistance to Ontario, Alberta, and British Columbia in 1989, broke the contract, both explicit and implicit, underpinning federal-provincial relations. This breach occurred at the very time that Quebec-Canada relations were severely strained by the patriation of the Canadian Constitution in 1982 over the strenuous objections of the Quebec National Assembly. The amendments to the Constitution at that time ignored Quebec's historic demands for recognition of the unique responsibility of its legislature for the protection and advancement of the culture and social institutions of French Canada. They reduced the collective demands of Quebec to the matter of individual language rights in the Charter of Rights and Freedoms, which was consistent with the preference of then prime minister Pierre Elliott Trudeau, an opponent of Quebec nationalism, and effectively enshrined the principle of "provincial equality" in the constitutional amending formula (McRoberts 1997; Hurley 1996, 297).

The concept of provincial equality was quickly embraced by provincial governments, particularly Alberta, and extended beyond the amending formula to all matters of federal-provincial relations. It is compatible with a neo-liberal agenda of weakening the power of the federal government. Given the historic and continuing position of Quebec governments of all political stripes that social programs are the exclusive jurisdiction of the provincial government, it ensures that any response to ongoing Quebec concerns will result in a provincialization of responsibility for social reproduction. It also creates a constitutional straitjacket that dooms attempts to reconcile Quebec to the 1982 constitutional amendments, as was evident in the failure of the Meech Lake Accord and the Charlottetown Agreement. These two constitutional proposals combined a symbolic recognition of Quebec's distinctiveness with the extension to all provinces of the powers historically demanded by Quebec, including the right to opt out of national cost-shared programs with compensation. Linking the recognition of Quebec to measures that would weaken the federal role in the rest of the country undermined the support that socially progressive English-speaking Canadians might otherwise have had for an accommodation of Quebec and made it impossible for the political elites to forge an alliance capable of carrying the amendments. The consequence of two failed attempts at constitutional change was an embitterment in Quebec-Canada relations.

The response to the crisis in Quebec-Canada relations was a new elite strategy for managing intergovernmental relations in the era of neo-liberalism: "constitutional change by non constitutional means" (Lazar 1997). This strategy involves an extension of the concept of provincial equality and of the practice of executive federalism – the "eleven white men meeting behind closed doors" criticized by women's organizations during the Meech and Charlottetown discussions. Maintaining publicly that the last thing Canadians wanted to hear about was constitutional change, federal and provincial governments began to put in place new rules and institutions to govern relations among themselves. The main instrument of this new approach to Canadian federalism is the multilateral intergovernmental agreement, which is analogous to international treaties in the area of trade. These agreements, whether the Agreement on Internal Trade or the Social Union Framework Agreement, contain rules and procedures governing relations among the parties and provide for institutions to resolve intergovernmental disputes among them and to monitor observance of the mutual commitments (Doern and MacDonald 1999). In the new era of federalism, the social union is not a relationship between the state and citizens possessing social rights but one among governments possessing jurisdictional powers. These agreements or accords are negotiated in secret by the executive branch, represented by Cabinet ministers or senior public servants at the federal and provincial levels of government. Unlike the basis for intergovernmental agreements around social programs in the Keynesian era, the statutory basis for these new agreements is weak or non-existent. This characteristic gives great flexibility to the executive branch and makes it difficult for legislatures and the courts – the two institutions in our system whose role it is — to ensure the accountability of Cabinet ministers and public servants. Canadian federalism is increasingly run as a rolling set of deals among executive branches at the federal and provincial levels of government (Cameron 2004b).

While these new arrangements are presented as bringing harmony to fractious relations among governments, many are centrally concerned with managing conflicts around social reproduction, including what are essentially class conflicts about the allocation of resources to social reproduction and national conflicts between Quebec and English-speaking Canada around the appropriate roles of the federal and provincial governments (Cameron 1999). Some social policy analysts see the possibility of a new political space being opened up for civil society organizations in monitoring accountability under the agreements (Jenson, Mahon, and Phillips 2003). At the moment, however, the effect of the new rules, institutions, and practices around intergovernmental relations is to remove decisions about social programs almost entirely from the more public arena of legislatures to private negotiations among senior public servants and Cabinet ministers. In place of accountability to legislatures, which was already weak enough in the Canadian system, a new form of public accountability is being promoted, centring on performance measures and periodic reports to the general public. In practice, responsibility is diffused, the division of responsibility among governments is less transparent than in the past, and organizations advocating state support for social reproduction are even more excluded from decision-making concerning social programs than they were in the past (Cameron 2006).

## CONCLUSION

At the time of Confederation, the conservative political and religious elites of Canada East (now Quebec) were the one social force organized on the terrain of social reproduction, and their political mobilization influenced the structure of the Canadian state. Federalism provided protections for the French Canadian national minority through a division of powers that assigned to all provinces responsibility for matters that were "merely local or private nature." This accommodation worked in 1867 because social reproduction in a society on the verge of industrialization was still primarily the responsibility of institutions in the "private sphere" of family, church, and charity or of local government. Industrialization gave rise to new social forces organized around issues of social reproduction, including labour and women. Over the years, their struggles have taken place within the framework of a division of powers grounded in the conception of social reproduction as "local and private," forcing this framework to stretch to accommodate growing state intervention in mediating the contradictions between production and social reproduction and in the process shaping the organization and strategies of labour, women and other groups.

Yet the ways that the social relations of class, gender, and nation are linked through the constitutional division of powers around social reproduction mean that stretching the original framework constantly gives rise to new contradictions. In the Keynesian era, a class compromise involving mediation by the central Canadian state of the relationship between production and social reproduction and based on the male-breadwinner model provided three decades of relative stability. Yet at the same time it aggravated the relationship between Quebec and the rest of Canada and eventually was unable to reconcile popular demands for women's equality and greater social equality generally with strategies for capital accumulation. The current neo-liberal "employability model" of the welfare state is based on a growing social polarization and will give rise, over time, to increasingly sharp conflicts over the allocation of resources to social reproduction. The removal of issues centrally related to social reproduction from the legislative to the intergovernmental arena allows political elites temporarily to mediate class and national conflicts related to social reproduction, but it will increasingly be challenged on democratic grounds. The current accommodation is therefore unstable, providing opportunities for intervention by social movements.

There is a tendency in Canada outside Quebec to see constitutional debates as unrelated to day-to-day struggles and for more recent immigrant communities to view them as ancient battles between the British and French having no relevance to their lives. As former Quebec premier Jacques Parizeau once put it, these debates feel like one long trip to the dentist. The problem with this attitude, as this chapter has tried to show, is that struggles for social equality at the level of the state, which centre on social reproduction, invariably get tangled up with the constitutional division of powers. It was easy enough – even if unjust – for Canadians outside Quebec to ignore that province's concerns about the federal role in social reproduction during the 1950s, when the Union Nationale was clearly a drag on social advance, and even during the 1960s, when the federal state was using its spending power to expand social rights. Indeed, during the Quiet Revolution of the 1960s the competition between the federal and Quebec states concerning jurisdiction over social programs tended to encourage their expansion.

But the embrace by political and economic elites of neo-liberalism introduces a new dynamic into intergovernmental relations as elite strategies of limiting the role of the state in social reproduction through provincialization dovetail with historic Quebec demands for control by the Quebec National Assembly over all matters related to social reproduction. Social movements in Quebec and English-speaking Canada are united in their opposition to neo-liberalism but divided in their response to it by differences over the appropriate role for the federal government. Moving beyond the current impasse will require agreement on a political alternative that fully recognizes the rights of the French Canadian national minority while delinking them from a constitutional framework that treats Quebec as a province like the others and social reproduction as a matter that is "merely local or private."

## NOTE

1 The federal claim to a spending power is derived from powers specifically enumerated in the Constitution Act, 1867, including the power to levy taxes by any method, to legislate in relation to public property, and to appropriate federal funds (Hogg 2003, 164). As it has been interpreted by the courts, the spending power allows the federal government to spend but not legislate in areas of exclusive provincial jurisdiction. The key distinction here is between, on the one hand, compulsory regulation, which can only be done by the level of government with the legislative authority, and, on the other, spending, lending or contracting, which imposes no obligations on the

recipient or obligations that are voluntarily assumed. In this context, voluntary means that the recipient cannot be obligated to accept the money offered, although if the offer is accepted, the money can come with conditions attached. If a matter falls within provincial jurisdiction, a federal law cannot compel an individual, organization, or government to accept money, follow a particular policy, or respect standards. But it can make money available to these same individuals, organizations, or governments and require that the recipient respect conditions set out in the federal law. The federal government can use the carrot of money but not the stick of compulsion in matters within provincial jurisdiction. An important corollary to the distinction between compulsory regulation and a non-compulsory transfer is that the only mechanism the federal government has to enforce conditions (or "standards") is to withhold money if the conditions are not met.

# 3

# Whose Social Reproduction? Transnational Motherhood and Challenges to Feminist Political Economy

SEDEF ARAT-KOÇ

The phrase *vagabond capitalism* puts the vagrancy and dereliction where it belongs – on capitalism, that unsettled, dissolute, irresponsible stalker of the world. It also suggests a threat at the heart of capitalism's vagrancy: that an increasingly global production can shuck many of its particular commitments to place, most centrally those associated with social reproduction, which is almost always less mobile than production ... Insisting on the necessity of social reproduction provides a critical arena, as yet undertheorized, within which many of the problems associated with the globalization of capitalist production can be confronted.

Cindi Katz (2001, 709–10)

One of the greatest achievements of feminist political economy has been to talk about social reproduction, to make visible and to problematize what would otherwise be invisible or seemingly trivial to the economy, to society, and even to (liberal) feminist theory. One of the purposes of this chapter will be to explore another layer of invisibility, to uncover the cases and the ways in which social reproduction takes place transnationally.

Feminist political economy studies social reproduction in the family-market-state nexus. Most theory assumes that this relationship takes place at the nation-state level. However, we are living in a world where social reproduction is increasingly taking place at a transnational level.

Although there are many ways in which such transnationalization of social reproduction occurs, one of the most glaring example is the experience of transborder, transnational families.

This chapter focuses on the experiences of migrant domestic workers in Canada with transnational mothering to see how their experiences of social reproduction can inform feminist political economy. To understand social reproduction, it is necessary that one go beyond the individual worker and her conditions here and now in Canada and look into her family relations transnationally.

In some ways, social reproduction occurring in a trans-regional, transnational scale is nothing new. Hontagneu-Sotelo and Avila (2000) suggest that contemporary "transnational motherhood" continues a long and dirty legacy of people of colour being admitted to some countries only through coercive systems of labour that do not recognize family rights. These systems have historical roots and close parallels in slavery, contract labour, and migrant labour systems such as those in South Africa under apartheid and in the US South involving Mexican workers, which were all "organized to maximize economic productivity and offered few supports to sustain family life" (Hontagneu-Sotelo and Avila 2000, 292). In Canada we have the precedents of Chinese families that were separated for thirty years or longer – between 1918 and 1947, when the Chinese Immigration Act completely banned all Chinese immigration, including those involving family reunification – and the residential school system, which systematically disabled First Nations people from providing nurture and culture for their children.

What *is* new and of growing significance for recent history, however, is the size and nature of the migrant labour force. There are currently 175 million people in the world who reside outside their country of birth (United Nations 2002). Many of these people do not have citizenship status and rights in the country of residence. In fact, there is evidence that with accelerating globalization of the economy, which creates a "push" factor in migration, there is also a tightening of borders in most advanced industrialized countries. In Saskia Sassen's frequently cited words, economic globalization is "*denationaliz(ing)* national economies," whereas immigration is "*renationalizing* politics" (Sassen 1996, 59; emphases mine). As a result, much recent migration is undocumented. What is interesting is that despite the tightening, even militarization, of borders and anti-immigration measures introduced in many countries, the numbers of migrants continue to climb rapidly. It is estimated by the US Census Bureau, for example, that the number of undocumented migrants in the United States increased from 3.5 million in 1980 to 8.7 million in 2000, despite the fact that around 2.7 million foreigners were legalized in 1987–88 (Adams and Liu 2001).

In recent decades we have witnessed a "feminization" of international labour migration. Men predominated in labour migration in the immediate post–Second World War period, but now half the world's legal and undocumented migrants and refugees are believed to be women (Ehrenreich and Hochschild 2003, 5). An International Labour Organization (ILO) report published in 1996 described the feminization of international labour migration as "one of the most striking economic and social phenomena of recent times." Making this phenomenon especially notable has been migration out of Asian countries that involved women migrating alone, as "autonomous, economic agents" in their own right (cited in Kempadoo 2004, 471).

Women migrants from several countries outnumber men. In Third World countries that rely on export-oriented development, female, as opposed to male, workers are especially encouraged to migrate, as women are thought to be more reliable than men in sending remittances, rather than spending their money on themselves (Ehrenreich and Hochschild 2003, 7). Female migrant workers, who typically send from half to nearly all of what they earn, not only ensure social reproduction for their families but also finance the specific economic development regimes of their countries. In 1994, remittances from foreign domestic workers were the third largest source of foreign exchange for Sri Lanka. In that year 84 per cent of Sri Lankan workers in the Middle East were women. They saved over 90 per cent of their earnings and remitted almost all these savings home (Samarasinghe, cited in Momsen 1999, 9).

Many women who are part of recent international migration are migrating precisely to fulfill reproductive roles for the "host" society. Whether they work as maids, nannies, caregivers for the elderly or the disabled, or sex workers, they are doing "women's work." The irony is that among those involved in transnational migration, it is specifically those who migrate to provide reproductive labour who are unable to care for their own children since they arrive as either temporary or undocumented workers. In both situations they lack rights to bring their children with them. "The ties of transnational motherhood suggest simultaneously the relative permeability of borders as witnessed by the maintenance of family ties and the new meanings of motherhood, and the impermeability of nation-state borders" (Hontagneu-Sotelo and Avila 2000, 292).

In some cases, states not only deny family rights but also are explicit in their denial of reproductive rights to migrant domestic workers. In Singapore, for example, Filipina domestic workers are required by the government to take pregnancy tests every few months. If a woman is found to be pregnant, her work permit is deemed null, and she is required to return home (Human Rights Internet 2003).

In the first part of this chapter I summarize research results from the experiences of migrant domestic workers in Toronto, Canada, with transnational mothering. In the second section I raise some questions and make some analytical observations about what insights we might gain about social reproduction from the transnational mothering of some women. In the final section I discuss the possible contributions a transnational perspective can provide to feminist political economy.

## TRANSNATIONAL MOTHERHOOD FOR MIGRANT DOMESTIC WORKERS IN CANADA: RESEARCH RESULTS

In 2000 Fely Villasin and I did research among domestic workers in Toronto. This involved questionnaires, individual and group interviews with domestic workers and immigrant service providers, and archival research at a Toronto organization promoting domestic workers' rights, INTERCEDE. I reviewed case files and telephone logs of INTERCEDE from 1992 to 2000.

Canada, which receives significant numbers of immigrants every year, has created a multi-tier system for different groups of immigrants. Whereas business people and professionals can enter as "independent class" immigrants and enjoy many of the rights and freedoms of citizenship, except the franchise, some groups of workers, including domestic workers, are denied significant rights and liberties, including the right to live with their families and the freedom to choose their jobs and employers. Canada uses a point system to determine who can qualify to enter the country in the first tier of the immigration process. The official justification given for the denial of entry to domestic workers in this category has to do with the low number of points given their work (as well as the education and the work experience of the worker) under the system. The history of the temporary-worker programs for domestic workers, however, reveals that the reasons may have a lot to do with the political will to create a flexible and vulnerable group of workers doing reproductive work.

The Live-in Caregiver Program (LCP), like all the previous immigration programs for domestic workers since 1970, is built on the premise that foreign domestic workers who arrive in Canada are – or should live as – single people. In reality, a significant proportion of domestic workers have children. Fifty-two per cent of respondents to our survey in 2000 admitted to having children.

The status of foreign domestic workers as single, unattached individuals is ensured through the treatment of domestic workers as temporary labour – as opposed to immigrants – as well as through the live-in requirement. Canada, along with western European countries and the United States, refuses to sign the International Convention on the Protection of the Rights of All Migrant Workers and Members of Their Families, adopted by the UN General Assembly in 1990. Canadian immigration regulations, as well as individual employers, assume that there is an incompatibility between this type of employment and the workers' parenting responsibilities. During the interviews a domestic worker explained that her employer did not allow her visiting daughter to stay in her house and the employer warned, "Don't forget you are working." Sometimes the worker herself internalizes the notion of incompatibility between worker status and parenting imposed by the state and the employer. One of the respondents to our questionnaire replied to the question "If you have children, did they come to Canada with you?" in the negative, explaining that she "did not come to Canada as an immigrant but as a worker" (Arat-Koç with Villasin 2001, 21, 22).

The LCP program allows domestic workers to apply for permanent resident status after two to three years of live-in service under temporary work permits. However, from the time of their arrival in Canada, it takes, on average, three to five years and often longer for domestic workers to sponsor their families. For many domestic workers, Canada is not necessarily the first country they go to on a temporary work permit. When several years of work abroad is combined with an average of three to five, sometimes up to seven, years of waiting in Canada, the experience and the impact of separation are profound for domestic workers and for their families.

Both in the societies that foreign domestic workers come from and in Canada, there are powerful ideologies surrounding motherhood that often glorify it and strongly emphasize maternal responsibility for children and even criminalize maternal neglect. In recent years, fundamentalist discourses prevalent in many societies and neo-liberalism in state policies have increased the emphasis on maternal responsibility, both ideologically and practically. In some cases, migrant female workers have come from countries where they are exposed to contradictory messages. In the Philippines, for example, migrant workers are hailed by the state as "national heroes" (Rodriguez 2002) for their contributions through remittances; at the same time they are cast as negligent mothers by media that sensationalize the suffering of children in transnational families (Parrenas 2003). In addition to the experience of separation, therefore, the social, cultural, and ideological meanings attached to the mother-child relationship affected migrant workers.

In our research we found that it was not just powerful feelings of responsibility and guilt that made family separation painful for migrant domestic workers. It was also deprivation of their own needs for intimacy and support. One of the respondents to the questionnaire expressed with eloquence what being with her family meant to her: "One of the sweetest things in life is to be near or close to your loved ones ... to share with them whatever life could bring in today and in the future" (in Arat-Koç with Villasin 2001, 24).

While domestic workers who were in bad or abusive relationships felt liberated when they left their countries, others mourned the loss of intimate ties. The impact of being deprived of close relations, if these are working, supportive relationships, can be devastating for anybody. The impact can be even more significant for immigrants who are in the process of adapting to working and living in a new country. During the interviews, Edna regretted being separated from her husband. She said that the deprivation of "emotional and physical contact" caused her loneliness and depression. Another domestic worker summarized the effects of separation from her common-law spouse as a feeling of "... emptiness in the sense that [there is] no one who would comfort you when you have a problem or giving reassurance when you are down" (in Arat-Koç with Villasin 2001, 29).

For most migrant domestic workers, the decision to leave their children was an extremely painful one. In addition to handling practical questions regarding whom to leave their children with and whether the children would be safe, well-cared for, happy, and healthy, domestic workers had to deal with heart-wrenching feelings during separation from their children. During her interview one domestic worker, Amor, described the time she bid her children goodbye and boarded the bus to Manila: "I could not walk up the bus, the driver had to carry me up. I was so weak and faint – leaving my kids and not knowing how long it would be before we could be together again." When she took her seat on the plane and was struck by the reality of separation, she "cried, and laughed and wailed like a madwoman" (in Arat-Koç with Villasin 2001, 26).

Even though migrant workers were very aware of the significance of their remittances for their children's upkeep and future, they experienced a profound sense of guilt, anxiety over the well-being of the children, and a sense of sadness, loss, and loneliness: "My life will not be complete. A part of me will always be missing, wondering about how my child is doing" (in Arat-Koç with Villasin 2001, 26). These mothers constantly worried about their children. They tended to blame themselves when the children were maltreated, got into trouble, or did badly in school. Even when there were no apparent problems, they felt anxiety about the unknown. One domestic worker said that her biggest regret was that she would "not know what is going on inside" her children and that she could not share "their troubles and triumphs" (in Arat-Koç with Villasin 2001, 27). Most mothers tried to maintain a good long-distance relationship with their children by spending large amounts of time on the telephone.

Our surveys and our interviews with domestic workers, as well as with professionals dealing with immigrants' health, revealed serious physical and mental health problems associated with separation from family. Complaints ranged from chronic stomach pain, muscle tension (specifically in the neck and shoulders), sleep problems, and frequent headaches to severe anxiety and depression. Describing the effects of separation on herself, one of the respondents to the questionnaire wrote about "a gap, depression, frustration and loneliness." Another domestic worker dealt with similar feelings by "always wanting to keep [herself] busy because [she] always felt sad if [she was] not doing something" (in Arat-Koç with Villasin 2001, 27).

Mothers often assumed that the separation affected the children negatively, that they "felt as orphans," deprived of love of their parents. "The effect of separation on my children was overwhelming. [They] felt insecure and unprotected while I was away. The trust on me as a parent was totally diminished by the time we got together in Canada" (in Arat-Koç with Villasin 2001, 28). Some children were too young when the mothers left to know or remember them. Older children might be angry and resentful toward the mother, who, they thought, had betrayed them. Some children appreciated the economic necessity and the sacrifice but had deep feelings of longing and sadness. Other studies confirm this pattern. Rhacel Salazar Parrenas, who interviewed children of migrant domestic workers in the Philippines, reports on the profound sense of loss. When she asked Ellen, who was ten when her mother left, how she felt about the children in her mother's care in New York, the girl responded:

> Very jealous. I am very, very jealous. There was even a time when she told the children she was caring for that they are very lucky that she was taking care of them, while her children back in the Philippines do not even have a mom to take care of them. It's pathetic, but it's true. We were left alone by ourselves and we had to be responsible at a very young age without a mother. Can you imagine? (Parrenas 2003, 42)

Even as she experienced a sense of loss, Ellen was not unaware of her mother's dedication and commitment:

> I realize that my mother loves us very much. Even if she is far away, she would send us her love. She would make us feel like she really loved us. She would do this by always being there. She would just assure us that whenever we have problems to just call her and tell her ... And so I know that it has been more difficult for her than other mothers. She has to do extra work because she is so far away from us. (Parrenas 2003, 43)

Parrenas's research makes it clear that the children of transnational mothers who had positive surrogate parental figures and open, regular communication with their mothers were able to resolve the emotional challenges and focus on school. Even the well-adjusted, though, suffered the loss of family intimacy (Parrenas 2003). It was not unusual for some children to deal with feelings of loss and longing by emotionally withdrawing from the mother. Two of the respondents to our questionnaire who were still separated from their children said: "I think they do not miss me anymore or I don't exist. They don't care if I call or write to them." and "They hardly know me ... Even in my vacation in the Philippines, I could feel the gap between us" (Arat-Koç with Villasin 2001, 28, 29).

Parrenas's interviews of children at the other end of the transnational family relationship reveal the psychology of emotional withdrawal. Eighteen-year-old Theresa said:

> Telephone calls. That's not enough. You can't hug her, kiss her, feel her, everything. You can't feel her presence. It's just words that you have. What I want is to have my mother close to me, to see her grow older, and when she is sick, you are the one taking care of her and when you are sick, she is the one taking care of you. (Parrenas 2003, 50)

Jeek was eight when his parents left for New York. More than eight years later, he was still unable to join them. The distance of the relationship made him cynical about the benefits of sharing problems and emotions:

> I talk to my mother once in a while. But what happens, whenever she asks how I am doing, I just say okay. It's not like I am really going to tell her that I have problems here ... It's not like she can do anything about my problems if I told her about them. Financial problems, yes she can help. But not the other problems ... She will try to give advice, but I am not very interested to talk to her about things like that. (Parrenas 2003, 45)

Providing for and improving the life chances of their children was the main factor behind the decision of transnational mothers to leave, but they wanted to parent their children in more ways than just financially. During the interviews, some migrant workers expressed feelings of hurt that their children had started seeing them merely as providers (Arat-Koç with Villasin 2001, 29).

It is not only women with children or married partners who have suffered family separation as a result of immigration regulations for domestic workers. Most people have close and meaningful relationships with people they see and are attached to as "family," such as parents, siblings, other relatives, same-sex partners, or intimate friends. As several participants in our research argued, one of the major problems with the Canadian immigration department's approach to family reunification has been the fact that the concept of "family" it uses imposes a narrow, Eurocentric, and heterosexist definition of the nuclear family that fails to resonate with definitions in the migrant worker's personal life, society, or culture.

Problems did not end if or when families were reunited. When children met their mothers in Canada, they often met as strangers. Most mothers found it very hard to help their children get over feelings of abandonment. They also found it difficult to undo the distance that had developed between themselves and their children: "The children

I take care of give me a hug as soon as I come to work, and hug me goodbye when I leave. They are much more affectionate than my own children who have joined me" (in Arat-Koç with Villasin 2001, 33–34).

In addition to problems in establishing trust, love, and intimacy, mothers found it difficult to establish authority over their children. As mothers tried to fulfill their new maternal role, some children resented, resisted, and rejected this, questioning where their mother had been all these years and what right she had to control their lives (Arat-Koç with Villasin 2001, 34).

The difficulties in re-establishing parent-child ties sometimes lasted many years, sometimes never ended. In addition to the challenges of re-establishing authority, intimacy, and trust, mothers were confronted with the anger of children who were having difficulties adjusting to life in a new country. Feeling powerless about imposed emigration, the children tended to blame their difficulties on the person who seemed to be responsible for making this decision. One domestic worker related a moving story of how her kids were "brainwashed" against her and how she has often "fe[lt] alone against the world," despite all the efforts she put into providing for them and sponsoring them to Canada. It took five years before her children even "began to understand" her. Still, she admitted: "It is really hard for us to get reunited with them after a long time of separation" (in Arat-Koç with Villasin 2001, 34).

As a result of the difficulties during separation, as well as the challenges faced after reunification, most migrant domestic workers in our research experienced forced family separation as a form of abuse that emotionally scarred those involved for a long time, if not permanently.

## ANALYTICAL QUESTIONS AND OBSERVATIONS

What do the experiences of migrant domestic workers as transnational mothers teach us about relations of social reproduction? What additional insights does a transnational perspective on social reproduction provide us which we would not have with analyses at the level of the nation-state?

One of the greatest theoretical advantages of socialist feminist over liberal feminist theory has been to show the ways in which women (and men) are not abstract, rational, and atomistic individuals but embodied beings constituted through social relations. In socialist feminist theory, women and men are embodied by relations of power based on gender, class, and race. The question we may pose in relation to transnational motherhood is whether an analytical framework that assumes embodiment by gender, race and class is enough.

In a different context, Gayatri Spivak pointed out the shortcomings of "focusing on the migrant as an effectively historyless object of intellectual and political activism" (Spivak 2000, 354). She argued that one could not simply treat the postcolonial migrant as a "blank slate," pretending that she could be analyzed simply within a class-gender-race calculus that begins and ends in the First World metropolis. The theoretical challenge at this juncture is to see the migrant as a historied subject and in her connectedness to her history, family, and home country, while avoiding essentialist conceptualizations of these forms of connectedness.

As early as the 1970s, political economists explored questions of how migrant labour benefits capital as well as the welfare state in receiving countries and how it also may serve to divide working-class struggle. They demonstrated how denial of social citizenship to migrant workers and their separation from family creates the possibility of paying only for the daily reproduction of workers as they actively worked, while transferring the responsibility and costs of their families' as well as their own upkeep during times of unemployment, sickness, disability, and old age on to the home country (Burawoy 1980; Castles and Kosack 1973; Gorz 1970).

The literature on the political economy of migrant labour can teach us a lot about social reproduction. To make sense of transnational motherhood, however, we may need additional theoretical insights and tools, as most of the women involved are doing reproductive and, specifically, care work. The implications of transfer of social reproduction in this case cannot simply be measured economically, in terms of its implications for capital and the welfare state.

Some writers mention the emergence of a "care deficit" in advanced industrialized countries when the accelerated movement of women into the labour force since the 1960s was followed with the failure of governments to provide public child care, on the one hand, and further cuts to public services and programs, on the other (Ehrenreich and Hochschild 2003). While Third World countries respond to this "deficit," they do not do so because of a surplus of care. Rather, what the families, the communities, and the countries experience is a "care drain" (Hochschild 2003; Parrenas 2003).

A feminist political economy of transnational motherhood needs to clarify where it stands on motherhood. Feminists, socialists or not, do not believe motherhood and parenthood to be natural relationships.

We do not glorify motherhood or assume mothers are the only or the best caregivers for children. As socialist feminists, we further believe that child care should not be a private responsibility of the mother or of the family, but that society and the state should at least share in the work, cost, and responsibility of raising children.

If socialist feminist theory (like most other feminist theories) denaturalizes motherhood and emphasizes collective responsibility for children, how do we articulate a critical position in relation to the forced imposition of transnational motherhood? The answer depends on how the position is framed – in essentialist glorification of motherhood or every mother's right to choose her own parenting arrangements.

> While demanding the right for women workers to live with their children may provoke critiques of sentimentality, essentialism, and the glorification of motherhood, demanding the right for women workers to choose their own motherhood arrangements would be the beginning of truly just family and work policies, policies that address not only inequalities of gender but also inequalities of race, class and citizenship status. (Hontagneu-Sotelo and Avila 2000, 292)

Theory concerned with inequalities of race, class, and citizenship status, as well as gender, cannot go in the direction of *naturalizing* forced separation, while it *denaturalizes* motherhood. This, however, might be precisely what liberal feminist theory does through its notion of the atomistic individual and its fetishization of "choice" in contract relationships. In contrast, socialist feminists interrogate the relationships of inequality, power, and force involved in "choices" made in contract.

Shellee Colen's concept of "stratified reproduction" is useful in demonstrating and making sense of inequalities in social relations of reproduction. Stratified reproduction is a concept that shows how "reproductive labour – physical, mental, and emotional – of bearing, raising and socializing children and of creating and maintaining households and people (from infancy to old age) is differentially *experienced, valued and rewarded.* (Colen 1995, 78; emphases mine). Colen talks about how "physical and social reproductive tasks are accomplished differentially according to inequalities that are based on hierarchies of class, race, ethnicity, gender, place in a global economy, and migration status" (78). The concept is useful in helping us to ask who is normatively entitled to be a parent, a caretaker, or to refuse child bearing or rearing, to have others give care for her children. It also helps us to ask who can "give nurture or give culture (or both)." "Stratified reproduction" describes "the power relations by which some categories of people are empowered to nurture and reproduce, while others are disempowered." The concept helps us to identify "the arrangements by which some reproductive futures are valued while others are despised" (Ginsburg and Rapp 1995).

The concept can help to highlight not just the economic obstacles but also the various social, political, and policy systems that disable transnational mothers as well as other groups of women, such as poor single mothers or Aboriginal mothers separated from children by residential schools or child welfare agencies, from nurturing their children. It demonstrates not only how some mothers are unsupported and underserved by the state but also how they may also be over-regulated as mothers. The concept of stratified reproduction helps feminists to articulate demands, not of only women but also of their children, for equality and a decent life.

It is important to remember that any application of the concept of stratified reproduction to transnational mothers – or any other group – needs to employ the concept not just as one of inequality but also in *relational* terms, focusing on what production and reproduction of one form of stratification means for others. Employment of domestic workers, often as caregivers, brings together women who, despite the significant class differences, share a common condition: they both experience their paid work as incompatible with their reproductive roles and responsibilities. For both, social reproduction has to be hidden (either at home or in the country of origin) as a condition to secure and keep present employment.

Despite significant increases in women's participation in the labour force, there have been hardly any changes in organization of paid work and expectations of the workplace in most countries that accommodate this reality. According to ILO reports, people in the United States worked much longer hours in the 1990s than in the 1970s (Ehrenreich and Hochschild 2003, 8). For the employers of domestic workers, it is often the neo-liberal ethics and expectations of the contemporary workplace for many professionals, while for the domestic worker/caregiver, it is the requirements of live-in arrangements and immigration restrictions associated with temporary or undocumented status, which force both groups of women to tuck their maternal roles neatly away, out of sight and out of mind, from the market and the society they are living in.

Another common condition for both groups of women is that they have to raise their children in societies where child care is seen as an individual parental responsibility and where the state refuses any substantial role in social reproduction. For both the employer and the employee, the employment arrangement is a private solution to a private problem. For the domestic worker, it is a private solution to the problem of poverty and economic underdevelopment. For the employer, it is a private solution to care and domestic needs.

While both the employer and the employee are likely to be citizens of states that do not accept substantial public responsibility for social reproduction, employers who are citizens in receiving countries can at least theoretically make demands and claims on the welfare state, whether they are listened to or not. Migrant workers, on the other hand, are stateless in terms of their (in)ability to make claims on either state. Even though sending countries can, at least theoretically, negotiate basic rights for their citizens living in other countries, they are often reluctant to do so for fear of losing trade or risking remittances from the receiving countries (Pettman 1996, 191).

We can say that migrant domestic workers, who often lack citizenship rights, are the ideal subjects of a neo-liberal state since they are workers whose social reproduction is not just privatized in the home but can be totally hidden, with the economic, social, and psychic costs transferred to a different location and state. With their lower wages, longer working hours, and lesser ability than citizen workers to negotiate working conditions, they are also the perfect workers who can help to conceal their employers' social reproductive needs.

Migrant domestic workers can be considered the ideal subjects of a neo-liberal state for concealing not just their own reproduction but also the needs and dependency of their employer. In many liberal societies, middle-class women's exercise of citizenship rights, their access to the public sphere as men's equals, has been achieved only on the condition that their labour-market participation resembles that of men. "In order to participate *like men* women must have workers who will provide the same flexibility as wives, in particular working long hours and combining caring and domestic chores"(Anderson 2000, 190).

What makes a female employer of a migrant worker appear manlike and "independent" – that is, of family responsibilities – in her own workplace is precisely her dependency on an invisible worker. Migrant workers are ideally suited to support this type of labour-market participation, since they can be (made to be) more flexible than citizen workers. Such flexibility is made possible by the vulnerability of the –

migrant or undocumented – non-citizenship status, often associated with a lack or near impossibility of asserting labour rights. "The fact that employers are citizens and the workers are not citizens formalizes their unequal power relations – even outside of the employment relationship, workers and their employers are not equal before the law" (Anderson 2000, 193).

Flexibility is also made possible by the "extra time" that migrant workers, with no family rights of their own in the country of immigration, can spare for their employers. Employers show a preference for workers with such legal status precisely because "migrant care workers can give the best possible care for their employers' families when they are free of care-giving responsibilities to their own families" (Parrenas 2003, 54). In Canada since the 1970s, the expectation of such flexibility and availability has been formalized through immigration programs that require migrant domestic workers to live with their employers.

Reliance on such flexible domestic help enables some women to participate equally in the labour market without any significant pressure being put on them to fight for a transformation of gender relations in the home and of the relations in the larger society between production and social reproduction, the state and civil society, and public and private spheres. Instead of being transformed, those relationships are merely reproduced with only some changes in the cast.

> Not only do migrant domestic workers, documented or undocumented, contribute to the state, they are also providing the welfare that is the social right of citizens, but to which many of these workers, however, necessitous, have no right. By providing welfare, one of the crucial social rights of the citizen, they are helping to give meaning to the notion of citizenship status, while themselves being denied any of its rights. (Anderson 2000, 191)

Earlier I said that both the employer and the employee in a paid domestic labour relationship often have to hide their reproductive responsibilities to secure or keep their respective employment arrangements. While both the employer and the employee may share this condition, their relationship to each other is one that clearly emphasizes the social reproduction needs of one and denies those of the other.

The weakness of the welfare state and the absence or inadequacy of socialized child care explains much about the choice for some women to employ domestic workers, but this choice is also based on some class privileges that employers can enjoy by hiring vulnerable, underpaid, and flexible migrant workers. In addition to the advantages of flexible time, such workers provide luxuries to employers that would otherwise be well beyond their reach. As Bridget Anderson (2001) points out, domestic work is not only about "caring," which is socially necessary work. It "is also concerned with the reproduction of life-style, and crucially, of status." Domestic work reproduces not just people but also class subjects. While "[w]e need to accommodate the raising of children, the distribution and preparation of food, basic cleanliness and hygiene ... [n]obody has to have stripped pine floorboards, hand-wash only silk shirts, dust gathering ornaments" (Anderson 2001, 6).

The choice to hire domestic workers rather than use child-care centres is also connected to middle-class fears of public spaces and institutions and middle-class assumptions about children's needs. As some sociologists have pointed out, there is a recent cultural obsession with security in many countries, especially in the United States, predating fears that resulted from the attacks of 11 September 2001. A sense of insecurity is displayed with everything from "nannycams" and child monitors to the widespread use of security cameras in all types of public spaces (Furedi 2002; Katz 2001).

We accept the reality of transnational motherhood precisely in an environment of obsession with security, an increased sense of the vulnerability of children, and greater emphasis on the needs of "the child" in social and public policy. The irony of the obsession with security, as with social reproduction, is that it is often the relatively most secure whose needs for security, as well as quality social reproduction, become most visible and most clearly articulated. Clearly, response to risk, insecurity, and vulnerability are determined by class, race, and global inequalities. As the state downloads more and more responsibility on parents, as responsibility for social reproduction is more and more privatized, the sense of risk and insecurity in society increases.

## NOTES TOWARD A FEMINIST, ANTI-RACIST, TRANSNATIONAL POLITICAL ECONOMY

Globalization corresponds to specific restructurings of social reproduction. Feminist political economy demonstrates the havoc caused in people's lives by such restructuring through neo-liberalism in advanced industrial countries and structural adjustment policies in the Third World. Feminist research in Canada has documented the various social consequences of economic restructuring and the neo-liberal restructuring of the welfare state: increased economic insecurity for the vast majority of the people; loss of or diminished access to social assistance on the part of the working class and the poor; forced movement into "workfare" or into the labour force by single mothers with no corresponding support in the form of socialized child care; losses of public sector jobs for women – where they were highly represented; increased privatization of responsibility and increased domestic work for women with cuts and/or closings in education, health care, and care of the elderly and the disabled. This documentation amounts to no less than a powerful demonstration of the *unsustainability* of neo-liberalism.

While studies at the level of the nation-state are valuable in advancing a critique of neo-liberalism, I would argue that a transnational perspective would not only add new insights to this critique but also raise further productive questions regarding the unsustainability of the global order we are living in. The case of transnational motherhood demonstrates the increased racialization and transnationalization of reproductive work. The case stands as an extreme example of the inequalities and injustices of *stratified reproduction*, of *who* is reproduced *how*. At the same time, however, the case is also useful as it exposes the myths of independence and "self-sufficiency" on which neo-liberalism heavily relies. Stories of transnational mothers lay bare and crystallize the relations of *dependence* that both the individual employers of migrant workers and First World states are involved in.

Canada, as an imperialist and settler society and one that, like the United States and Australia, continues to rely on immigration, has never been "self-sufficient" in social reproduction. For Canada, immigration has historically been essential to meet labour-market needs – for capital to reproduce itself. In addition, it has recently been defined as essential to sustaining the welfare state. With demographic realities of a low birth rate and a rapidly aging population, immigration is seen as "fresh blood" that would enable and improve the capacity of the Canadian welfare state to continue to offer social security.

There are several potential political implications of introducing a transnational perspective in political economy. Acknowledgment of the dependency of advanced capitalist nations on the rest of the world – for not only reproduction of capital but also social reproduction – urges us to ask whether the question of rights and entitlements can be limited to the level of the nation-state. There are proposals that encourage a post-national reconceptualization of rights.

Rethinking social reproduction in transnational dimensions helps to crystallize the inhumanity of capitalist reproduction on a global level. As Cindi Katz argues, it is by looking at social reproduction, especially in its global connections, that we can most effectively expose "the vagrancy and dereliction" of capitalism as an "unsettled, dissolute, irresponsible stalker of the world" (Katz 2001, 709).

In its invisibility, transnational motherhood can help to hide the problems of the organization of the family, the economy, and the state under neo-liberalism. By making it visible, feminist political economy can help to force a rethinking and re-envisioning of the relations between/among the family, the economy, the community, the state, and the world. We may contemplate what is wrong with a world in which we talk about "care deficits" or unaffordability of social programs in the midst of levels of wealth unprecedented in human history; a world that creates "care deficits" in countries both importing and exporting migrant workers; where the paid caregivers are people who are themselves denied caring for and being cared for by their own families; where "independence" and "self-reliance" are fetishized as social possibilities and qualities of ideal workers and citizens as long as they involve an absence of demands on the workplace, the community and the state, but can hide dependence on the invisible work of gendered, racialized others. We may contemplate the *possibility* and *desirability* of long-term survival in such a world. Through such contemplation, we may be compelled to envision new relations in, between, and among the family, economy, community, state, and world.

There are signs that such envisioning is already taking place. As Alice de Wolff (this volume) demonstrates, in the 1990s and early 2000s Canadian public sector unions have developed and struggled for positive strategies in response to the growing tensions between paid employment and other life responsibilities. Campaigns for reduced work time, leaves for caring work, more-inclusive benefits, and workplace-based child-care programs have helped to address work-life tensions, educate the larger public, and provide some concrete solutions. De Wolff argues that the gains are limited, both because the benefits do not reach beyond union membership and because they have taken place in a context of reduced government social spending and economic restructuring. Despite their limitations, however, these campaigns have been politically significant as they have offered healthy collective alternatives to the individual solutions to work-life tensions that neo-liberalism forces.

# 4

# Bargaining for Collective Responsibility for Social Reproduction

ALICE DE WOLFF

Since the 1970s women in the paid workforce have increased their demands on employers, unions, and governments to implement policies and practices that make it easier for women to manage the competing demands of both employment and their caring responsibilities. Strong, activist women's committees in unions across Canada have worked on bargaining and campaign strategies that focus on the importance of minimizing conflicts between women's "double day" of paid employment and social reproduction, especially unpaid caring work at home. As women have entered the paid workforce in greater numbers, more women have become union members, more male union members have partners and daughters who are employed, and more men are under pressure to take on domestic responsibilities. Unions have had to pay attention to concerns that have come to be called "work-life issues."

Activists in most of Canada's large unions have conducted hundreds of work-life education sessions, changed the priorities and structures of their unions so that members' life responsibilities are taken into account, and have mobilized public campaigns for child care, parental leave and health care. Many have confronted employers at the bargaining table and on picket lines about maternity leave, parental leave, flexible work hours, and limitations on overtime. Activists have made important gains, even in the decade following the mid-1990s, when employers concertedly reduced wages and benefits, governments reduced public services, and both governments and employers attacked unionized workers. Their efforts have created a much broader understanding in the labour movement and amongst the general public of the importance of addressing work-life tensions and have had a direct impact at bargaining tables and in changing public policy.

This chapter first draws on government and government-supported surveys to outline how work-life tensions have grown from the mid-1990s. It then describes labour-movement activists' bargaining and campaign successes in the context of these growing tensions. My observations about union strategies are based on a review of a wide range of collective agreements and union campaign materials, meetings with committees affiliated with the Ontario Federation of Labour and the Canadian Labour Congress, and participation in regional and national union conferences (de Wolff 1994, 2003). Activists generally concentrate much of their energy and strategizing on making changes to their own collective agreements, but they also offer a tremendous amount of support and encouragement to others who are working on similar issues with other employers, in other unions, or in other parts of the country. Their local and collective strategies have created notable bargaining and campaign successes since the early 1990s, including compressed work schedules and reduced overtime, employer-paid supplements for thirty-five-week parental leave, benefit coverage for same-sex spouses and non-kin relationships, workplace-based child-care programs, and workplace-based violence against women programs. These gains suggest that even in a hostile economic and political climate, strategic bargaining, well-timed public campaigns, work with coalitions, and strategic use of the human rights systems and the courts have made significant differences in the lives of a great many workers.

As more and more women with family responsibilities have moved into the Canadian labour force and as their activism has raised the profile of work-life issues, government policy-makers and managers have been under pressure to develop responses. The federal government has supported social policy research and "work-life balance" policy approaches since the United Nations Year of the Family in 1994 (Social Development Canada Web site). While the initiatives have created a higher profile for these issues, they are not unproblematic. The balance promoted by government is a hypothetical "win-win" situation where "by reducing work-life struggles, individuals can enjoy a healthier lifestyle while improving productivity at work." (Social Development Canada Web site). It suggests that workers can negotiate their needs from an equal position with employers, and it under-represents the economic power that employers have in the employment relationship. The promise of greater productivity is not, however, accepted by all employers. Even the government recognizes that after a decade of promotion, "there remains a need to provide information to convince employers of the need for and the benefits of taking action" (Social Development Canada 2002). "Work-life balance" is often promoted as an achievable, long-term state, even though most working people experience their life and work arrangements as constantly changing and very rarely satisfactory. Further, many activists have recognized the limitations of the notion of "family" embedded in most policy and have actively campaigned to ensure that "work-life" measures cover all employees' significant relationships, whether they are with kin relations or others (de Wolff 2003).

## GROWING WORK-LIFE TENSIONS

A number of studies have found that tensions between paid employment and other life responsibilities grew during the 1990s and early 2000s in Canada. Higgins and Duxbury's (2001) survey of over 14,500 employees found that 58 per cent of workers experienced high levels of work-family "overload," compared to 47 per cent in 1991. A Conference Board of Canada study also reported an increase in the percentage of employees experiencing moderate to high work-life stress from 27 per cent in 1988 to 46 per cent in 1998 (McBride-King and Bachmann 1999).

The increased tensions that workers are dealing with are related to a constellation of social, economic, and political changes that have intensified since the 1990s. Obviously, the most dramatic is the labour-force participation of mothers (and fathers) of young children. Many women seek paid employment because economic independence is a central component of their identity and because it provides the basis for healthy relationships with other people both in and outside the paid workplace. Increasingly, however, the decision to work for pay is not really a choice – one income is no longer enough to support most households. In 1996 women's earnings contributed at least half the income in 25 per cent of households in Canada and between a half and a quarter in every second household in the country (Statistics

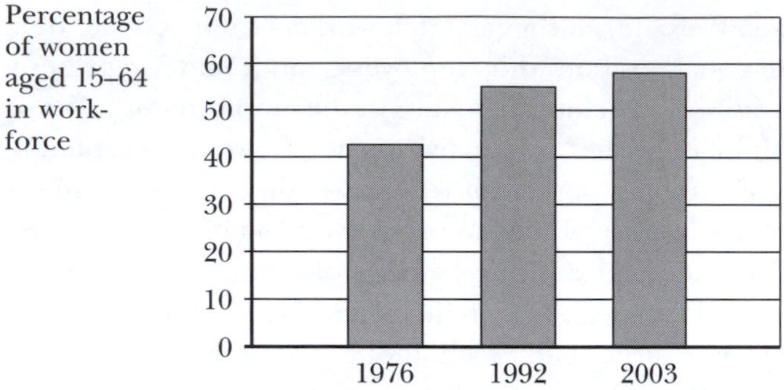


Fig. 4.1 Women's workforce participation, age 15–64, Canada, 1976–2003
SOURCES: Advisory Council on the Status of Women 1994; Statistics Canada 2004.

Canada 1998b). The same Statistics Canada study estimated that in 1996 the number of two-parent households living below the poverty line would increase by 300 per cent without women's incomes. In fact, the Canadian economy is now organized so that it relies on the labour of most adult women and men. Figure 4.1 shows that 61.6 per cent of women between the ages of fifteen and sixty-four were in the paid workforce in 2003, a significant increase from 45 per cent in 1976.

Figure 4.2 illustrates an even more dramatic increase in the labour-force participation of women with young children. In 2002, 80.7 per cent of women whose youngest child was between six and fifteen years of age were in the labour force, as were 73.4 per cent of women whose youngest child was between three and five years and 65.8 per cent of women whose youngest child was less that three years old (Friendly, Beach, and Turano 2003). At the same time, women are having children later in their lives: women in their thirties and older accounted for 32 per cent of live births to first-time mothers in 1999, more than double the proportion in 1983 (Statistics Canada 2001a). These demographic changes reflect the kinds of tensions workers experience trying to manage both paid employment and family life. In most cases, women's need to get established in the labour market and their concerns about ensuring a sufficient and secure income to support a child combine to delay the birth of their first child. The demands of paid employment and the costs of child care are likely contributors to the decline in the average number of children born to Canadian women: it was 1.5 in 2003, the lowest in Canada's history (United Nations Development Program 2003).

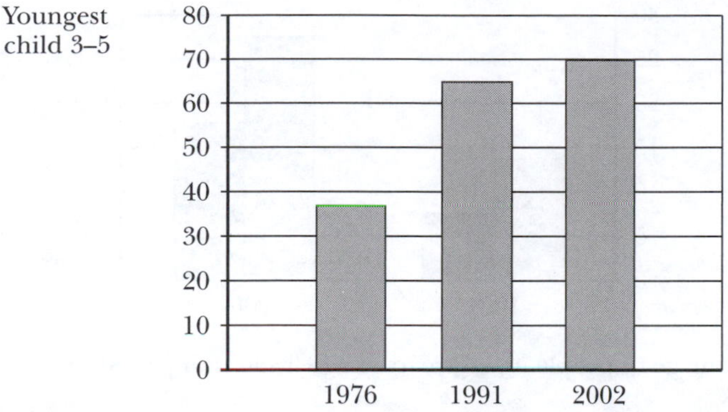


Fig. 4.2 Women in the workforce in Canada with children aged 3–5, 1976–2002 (percentage)

SOURCES: Advisory Council on the Status of Women 1994; Friendly, Beach, and Turano 2003.

Women's labour-force participation and the importance of their income to their households have not been met by more equality in the sharing of unpaid work in the home. Women still carry most of the responsibility for housework, child care, and care for the sick or elderly. The 2001 census indicates that while the proportion of men who did absolutely no unpaid housework declined between 1996 and 2001, women still put in the longest hours (Statistics Canada 2003d). In the same period the number of men who spent up to fifteen hours each week looking after children increased slightly (Statistics Canada 2003f), and more men have become involved in caring for seniors (Statistics Canada 2003e). Women, however, are still doing most of the housework, child care, and elder care.

At the same time, responsibilities at home have become more complex and demanding. Schools are requiring more involvement and resources from parents. Children are staying at home longer, as illustrated in figure 4.3. In 1985 young people's transition from high school to employment took an average of six years; in 1998 it took an average of eight years (Bowlby 2000). It is tougher for young people to launch themselves into the labour market and become economically independent than in the 1980s and 1990s, and consequently, parental responsibilities are lasting longer.

Changes to health-care services mean that family members are expected to provide more complex treatments at home and to coordinate health-care providers and even health-care administrative (see

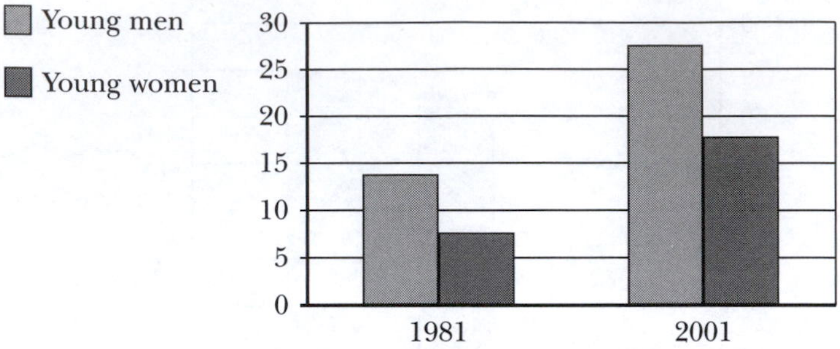


Fig. 4.3 Percentage of people 25–29 years of age living with parents in Canada, by sex

SOURCE: Statistics Canada 2003g.

Luxton this volume; Armstrong et al. 2002). As life expectancy increases, family members, usually women, are also expected to provide care and oversee the lives of elders who are living longer.

Other changes that create tensions in the lives of working people relate to the composition of the workforce – its increased age, its growing mobility, and the greater numbers of immigrants. In 2001 the average age of workers in Canada was 37.6 years, a significant increase from 29.6 years in 1981. The average age of the workforce is projected to increase to 41 years in 2011 (Malatest 2003). As the workforce ages, more workers face an array of age-related difficulties ranging from health concerns to discrimination at work based on their age. Many laid-off older workers have serious difficulties finding new jobs. In response to changes in the labour market, many Canadian workers move to new communities in order to find work. Between 1996 and 2001, over three and a half million people, or about 12.8 per cent of the population, moved to another municipality in the same province, and just under a million, or 3.2 per cent, moved to another province or territory (Statistics Canada 2002b). The proportion of immigrant workers who have been in Canada ten years or less increased from 6 to 7.9 per cent in 2001 (Statistics Canada 2002a). While moving is itself disruptive and often increases the pressures and demands on all household members, such mobility also means that a growing group of workers are simultaneously cut off from established support networks while managing extended caring responsibilities across great distances and national borders (see Arat-Koç this volume). The added costs and stresses of long distance care impose additional burdens on such workers.

Finally, major changes in the labour markets and in most workplaces have increased the pressures on workers. Governments maintained the legislated minimum leaves for Canadians at an international low throughout the 1990s and early 2000s. In comparison with workers in all countries in the European Union, many Canadians have between thirteen and nineteen fewer statutory public holidays and annual vacation days each year (de Wolff 2003). Throughout the 1990s there were major layoffs in many industries, especially in manufacturing, traditionally the best paid and most secure jobs (Luxton and Corman 2001). Fear of layoffs and wage cuts created a climate in which many employees were increasingly nervous about their own welfare. At the same time, through the 1990s and early 2000s, most employees experienced an increase in employers' expectations and hours of work. A Canadian Union of Public Employees study found that more than four of every ten employees (43 per cent) reported that their workload had increased between 1999 and 2001 alone (EKOS 2001). When these workers described the factors that contributed to the increase, 72 per cent said they had more responsibilities, 61 per cent were working with new technologies, 60 per cent experienced greater demand for their services, and 54 per cent were in departments that had experienced staff cuts. Julie White's study for the Communication, Energy and Paperworkers Union indicates that one in five Canadian employees (19.8 per cent) worked an average of nine hours overtime per week in 2001 (White 2002). Another study estimates that just under half (46 per cent) of those working overtime hours are paid and that the other half are making "donations" to employers – 1.17 million workers "donated" an average of 9.2 hours a week to their employers in 2000 (Higgins and Duxbury 2001). This study indicates that non-profit employers are the recipients of the most unpaid "donated" hours.

Further, a large proportion of the workforce have working schedules that make it difficult for them to manage employment, child care, school, and home care. Non-standard employment relationships have grown since the early 1990s. In 1995, 45 per cent of earning couples with children under age sixteen included at least one partner who worked a non-day shift (Johnson 1997). In 2002 just over one-third of the workforce were in temporary or part-time jobs or were solo self-employed. The growth of precarious forms of employment has been led by part-time temporary jobs and low-paid solo self-employment, which have the most unpredictable schedules and most precarious incomes (Vosko, Zukewich, and Cranford 2003).

Union activists have argued that work-life tensions have visible effects on the job, an argument that has been supported in a number of studies. Higgins and Duxbury (2001) found that job satisfaction and company loyalty were two casualties: employees with high levels of work-life stress were less satisfied with their jobs, and fewer were committed to their employers, compared with workers who had lower work-life stress. They estimated that work-life conflict cost employers $2.7 billion in lost time as a result of work absences in 1997. The health effects of work-life tensions are similar to any type of stress: workers who report high levels of work-life tension experience burnout, higher rates of absence from work, and more visits to medical practitioners. In an earlier study the same researchers (Higgins and Duxbury 1999) estimated that extra visits to physicians among Canadians working under high work-life conflict conditions cost the Canadian medical system an estimated $425.8 million in 1997. These authors also point out that workplace conflicts and absences lead to a significant loss of skills and a reduced labour supply. The Conference Board of Canada found that because of work-life stresses, over one-third of employees had turned down or did not apply for a promotion, one-quarter had not accepted or not applied for a transfer, 17 per cent had difficulty attending meetings after business hours, 16 per cent had not been available for training after hours, 16 per cent seriously considered leaving their current job, and 14 per cent had already left one job because of work-life problems (McBride-King and Bachmann 1999).

## BARGAINING AND CAMPAIGNS

Collective bargaining constitutes one of the few forums where people actually sit down face-to-face to negotiate forms of collective responsibility for the increasingly difficult issues relating to employment and social reproduction. Bargaining affects the working conditions of approximately one-third of women (32.0 per cent) and men (32.3 per cent) in the Canadian workforce, a drop from 35.2 per cent of women and 43.2 per cent of men in 1988 (Jackson and Schetange 2003). Most unionized workers are in the public sector: in 2002, 75.8 per cent of the public sector was unionized compared with 19.6 per cent of the private sector (Jackson and Schetange 2003). As table 4.1 illustrates, collective bargaining makes a significant difference in wages, particularly for women, and it has narrowed the wage gap between men and women.

Table 4.1 Union impact on wages and wage gaps

| | *Average hourly wage* | | |
|---|---|---|---|
| | *Men* | *Women* | *Women as percentage of men* |
| All employees | $19.38 | $15.82 | 81.8 |
| Union | $21.43 | $19.52 | 91.1 |
| Non-union | $18.40 | $14.08 | 76.5 |

SOURCE: Jackson 2003.

Table 4.2 Union impact on benefit coverage (percentage)

| | *Medical plan* | *Dental plan* | *Life/disability insurance* | *Pension plan* |
|---|---|---|---|---|
| All employees | 57.4 | 53.1 | 52.5 | 43.3 |
| Union | 83.7 | 76.3 | 78.2 | 79.9 |
| Non-union | 45.4 | 42.6 | 40.8 | 26.6 |

SOURCE: Jackson 2003.

Union members are also much more likely to have benefits, as illustrated in table 4.2. Union activists are proud of the difference that they make for their members, but many have not limited themselves to improving the conditions of their members only. They have conducted education and lobbying campaigns intended to improve the working and living conditions of all workers.

The labour movement has a long tradition of insisting that employers have some responsibility for ensuring that employees are healthy enough to work and able to care for their dependents and educate their children. Throughout the early part of the twentieth century, unions fought for the "family wage," arguing that workers could not be expected to be settled in their work if they were not earning enough to keep their families fed and healthy. That argument was, of course, based on the presumption that the "worker" was a man and that women at home provided full-time, unpaid caring labour which was largely invisible as an economic contribution. As women moved into the paid labour force in larger numbers in the 1970s, women activists, particularly those in the public sector, began to demand job-protected maternity leave and other accommodations that ensure that employed women are not penalized or discriminated against because of their reproductive responsibilities. They also argued that employer-based benefits and programs can be offered in ways that encourage more equal sharing of those responsibilities between men and women.

Unions use a range of resources and strategies to influence working conditions and government policies. The strategy most popularly associated with unions – the withdrawal of labour from the workplace in a strike – is employed only after many other efforts have failed. The Canadian Labour Congress and the regional federations of labour have considerable research and education capacity through their staff, have large information and action networks, and are able to represent the interests of large numbers of workers to policy-makers. Members of unions that are affiliated with each federation meet regularly to develop broad labour-movement policy and strategies and to initiate or guide lobbying and campaigns. Individual unions and their locals bargain directly with employers, but they also have significant research, education, and advocacy capacities.

The labour movement has used a combination of strategies to make it possible for members to more easily handle their life responsibilities. Larger public and private sector unions have continually put pressure on larger employers to set new "best practices" for employers. The classic example was reached in 1981 by the Canadian Union of Postal Workers, which found that there was no alternative but a strike to achieve paid maternity leave for its women members. It was the first national union to achieve this goal, and it set a precedent that cleared the way for similar agreements in other public and private sector workplaces across the country. Unions have successfully used human rights tribunals and the courts to establish that certain employer practices discriminate against women because of their reproductive responsibilities and against gays and lesbians and their partners. Even as the federal government has abandoned most of its responsibility for influencing labour markets and standards to the provinces, unions have still been able to pressure it to use its remaining policy mechanisms, most particularly Employment Insurance (EI), to put pressure in turn on provincial governments. Many unions have found that the most effective strategies are developed when they work in coalitions with other unions and with community-based groups.

As the tensions between demands at work and caring responsibilities increased through the 1990s, activist arguments and strategies changed in response. Most large unions and federations had women's committees by the end of the 1980s. Women activists can take substantial credit for building more democratic structures and encouraging cultures of inclusion in most unions. Many unions, federations, and labour councils have added advisory committees for workers of colour, youth, people with disabilities, Aboriginal people, and gay, lesbian, bisexual and transgendered workers. These new committees and new activist leaders have conducted educational and political campaigns, encouraged new involvement among the membership, changed who is in leadership positions and on bargaining committees, developed new policies, and redirected organizing priorities.

Because women continue to be most affected by work-life tensions, women's committees and women activists still take the lead on work-life issues. They have, however, broadened their demands beyond those relating to pregnancy, childbirth, and formal equity, developing arguments and strategies that address the concerns of women and men at all life stages and in all forms of family and household arrangements. Activists have mobilized their unions to support broad-based campaigns for a national child-care program, recognition of same-sex partners and marriage, health care, home care, increased minimum wage, extended job-protected leaves in employment-standards legislation, and, most recently, reforms to Employment Insurance to expand eligibility for, among other benefits, maternity, parental, and compassionate leaves.

In general, the gains have been uneven and tend to be specific to each broad industrial or service sector. Many employers have attempted to or have successfully rolled back previous gains, putting many unions in a position where they must choose between salary increases, job security and increased benefit deductibles, increased work days per year, pay cuts for sick and other leaves, cuts to vacation and other leaves, and reduced seniority rights (see Cohen and Cohen this volume). There have, however, been victories.

Employers in the private sector have been more likely to agree to compressed work schedules, longer vacation, and limits to overtime, rather than workplace programs and work-life related leaves. In the public sector the federal government has agreed to supplement EI benefits up to full salary for its employees who are on parental leaves. Unions have negotiated longer work-life-related leaves and the inclusion of non-kin relationships in relevant collective agreements with provincial governments and non-profit employers. The more expensive programs, such as workplace-based child care, are harder to find: there were approximately 340 workplace-based child-care programs across the country in 2001 (Barbeau 2001). They exist in large and medium-sized workplaces in the public and private sector, in workplaces that include auto manufacturers, Canada Post, Revenue Canada, and the National Film Board. Finally, some of the most significant successes have been the result of cross-sectoral campaigns and have resulted in longer legislated leaves and a broad definition of family and non-kin relationships that affect workers in all sectors.

### *Reducing Work Time*

While gender equality both at home and at work is crucial, many activists have recognized that when almost all adults are in paid employment, there is simply not enough unpaid time and energy in most households to handle life's day-to-day demands, and certainly not enough to handle the more intensive demands of birth and early childhood, illness, disability, relocations, caring for seniors, and death, even if they are equally shared between men and women. "It doesn't matter how well you manage that whopping great increase in the family work load: it will always be too much" (32 Hours 2000).

Some activists take the position that employers' primary work-life responsibilities are to design jobs that are doable within the hours employees are paid, to prevent job tensions from disrupting employee's personal lives, and to make hours of work sufficiently flexible to accommodate employees' life responsibilities. This approach targets hours of work, job security, excessive and unpaid overtime, and health and safety and speaks to both male and female employees.

In 1999 the Canadian Labour Congress adopted a policy that states: "Canadians want to work to make a contribution to society and to develop their own skills and capacities. But jobs can't swallow our lives. We want laws and policies that reduce the hours and stress of work" (32 Hours 1999). That year the congress launched a countrywide education and lobbying campaign to shorten hours of work. Many activists' interest in shorter hours of work had been encouraged by the Saskatchewan Federation of Labour's efforts in the early 1990s to promote employment-standards legislation that provided protections for part-time workers. In the mid-1990s two activist groups, 32 Hours and the Shorter Work Time Network, had formed, and their research, education materials, and policy recommendations influenced the formal labour movement. This broad network of activists campaigned for legislated shorter working hours and employees' right to choose shorter working hours and limits to overtime. In 1999–2000 they began to highlight the work-life stress and progressive family policy connections (32 Hours 2000).

It cannot be claimed, however, that public campaigns and bargaining efforts have decreased hours or increased protections for workers. Rather, they are holding off a concerted push by employers to increase hours of work and just-in-time human resource management strategies. Employers' interests are perhaps best illustrated by Ontario's 2001 employment-standards legislation, which made it possible for employees to "agree" to a sixty-hour workweek at regular rates of pay. Employers have resisted increases in the numbers of workers who can refuse overtime. The right to refuse overtime was included in only 31 per cent of collective agreements in both 1988 and 1998 (Rochon 2000). The types of arrangements that have increased are those most likely to be acceptable to or introduced by employers. These include the right to time off instead of overtime pay (in 34 per cent of agreements in 1988 and 40 per cent in 1998), compressed working time (in 15 per cent of agreements in 1988 and 20 per cent in 1998), and job-sharing (in 6 per cent of agreements in 1988 and 10 per cent in 1998) (Rochon 2000).

Since its formation in the early 1992, the Communication, Energy and Paperworkers Union (CEP) has been particularly active in reducing hours at work, limiting excessive overtime, and establishing schedules that create longer periods of time away from the job. "Shorter hours of work is about being against the extended, flexible hours, lean and mean philosophy of business corporations. For our members, more time off is about better health, safety and improved family and social life. More broadly, it's about less unemployment, jobs for young people and a better community life" (Communications, Energy and Paperworkers 2004). Several CEP locals have managed to create regular three-day weekends by reducing the hours of work each week and limiting overtime. Others have either shortened shifts for more flexible personal time or lengthened and clustered shifts for longer stretches of time away from work. White (2002) describes several victories, starting with one mill workers' local in Quebec that negotiated a thirty-six-hour workweek in 2000, the lowest of any mill in the country. Another local in Ontario went on strike for six months over excessive overtime. Workers had been averaging between three hundred and four hundred hours of overtime a year, and they recognized it was taking a huge toll on their health and on the well-being of their households. Their employer eventually agreed to hiring eleven new workers, reducing mandatory overtime, and reducing unpaid on-call hours. Still other locals have refused to work overtime until members who were laid off are rehired. White (2002) observes that because many of this union's members are mill workers in smaller towns, they have been able to see the concrete improvements that shorter hours make in the local economy and social relations of their communities.

The Canadian Union of Public Employees has found that some smaller employers, in joint committees with the union, are prepared to re-examine workloads and review whether jobs are actually doable within the agreed working hours. It and other unions have negotiated workplace surveys of the work-life needs of their members and have used these to open up problem-solving discussions with their members and with employers. The United Steelworkers of America Canada has recognized that despite its best efforts at the bargaining table, all of its members and their households do not have access to full benefits. It has begun to establish its own member/employee assistance program, notably by opening non-profit dental clinics in Ontario communities.

A number of unions, including United Food and Commercial Workers, Canadian Auto Workers, United Steelworkers, Hotel Employees Restaurant Employees, International Ladies Garment Workers Union, and Service Employees International Union, have initiated organizing campaigns that focus on youth and immigrant workers. They have recognized that many younger and immigrant workers labour shorter hours as part-time and temporary employees and that their shorter-hours jobs should not be treated differently from full-time jobs in terms of pay and benefits. The Public Service Alliance of Canada recognizes that some part-timers choose to handle their work-life stress by working less than full-time and that they deserve equivalent benefits to full-time workers (Public Service Alliance of Canada 2003).

### *Leaves for Caring Work*

One of the most dramatic changes in the period between 1990 and 2004 was the introduction of legislated and publicly supported parental leaves for the birth or adoption of a child and compassionate leaves when family members are critically ill. In the early 1990s these leaves tended to be short and had a variety of names, including paternal, family and adoption leave. They were available to workers covered by only 7 per cent of collective agreements (Rochon 2000). Activists, particularly those in the federal public sector, kept up a consistent pressure until 2000, when the federal government introduced thirty-five weeks of EI benefits for parental leave for qualified employees. The EI fund is the one of the federal government's most effective mechanisms for influencing provincial and territorial labour-market policy and legislation, and the Liberal government used it as a component of federal "family policy" to establish benefits for thirty-five weeks of paid parental leave in 2000 and six weeks of compassionate leave in 2004. Changes to provincial and territorial legislation have followed, protecting anyone who takes these leaves from losing her or his job.

The EI benefits for these leaves are not what activists demanded. The number of working hours needed to qualify excludes the growing numbers of women who work part-time, in temporary jobs, or on contract, and the benefit rate is low – only 55 per cent of weekly insurable earnings. These requirements have meant that only 61 per cent of new mothers were eligible for maternity and parental leave in 2002 (Marshall 2003). The Canadian Labour Congress launched a campaign in 2003 to broaden the use of the EI fund. The campaign promotes it as a women's work-life issue and demands a minimum qualifying period of 360 hours of work within the previous fifty-two weeks and a benefit rate of 66 per cent (Canadian Labour Congress 2005b).

Unions have turned to employers to provide a "top up," or supplement to EI benefits, for workers who are on parental or compassionate leave. Many employers have agreed to do so for seventeen weeks of maternity leave, but it is proving much more difficult to get agreements for the longer thirty-five weeks of parental leave. The Public Service Alliance of Canada broke through this impasse in its 2003 negotiations with the federal government: its agreement now includes a supplemental benefits plan for parental leave. Activists have also begun to insist that employers encourage fathers to take parental leave; men made only 3 per cent of parental leave claims in 2000 and 10 per cent in 2002 (Marshall 2003).

Bargaining committees and women's advocates have been creative about a wide variety of other leaves that would assist with caring responsibilities beyond maternity and infancy. Family, emergency, compassionate, relocation, spousal union, and bereavement leaves have all been designed to assist with particularly demanding moments in employees' lives. Unions continually point out that when these leaves are not available, employees squeeze the time they need to handle children, family, household, and friends' illnesses, celebrations and emergencies from their vacation time, sick time, or unpaid leave, which in turn takes a toll on employees' ability to manage their own health and energy.

### *Inclusive Benefits*

Larger unions and labour federations have been integral to the fight for human rights for gays, lesbians and transsexual and transgendered people. In the workplace this means preventing harassment and discrimination and ensuring that leaves and benefits are broadly defined so that same-sex spouses are treated in the same manner as heterosexual spouses. The movement has been remarkably successful in getting Canadian governments to legally recognize all aspects of same-sex partnerships, including the right to marry.

In 1994 the Canadian Labour Congress (CLC) convention adopted a policy statement on sexual orientation calling for action to confront and eliminate discrimination against lesbians, gay men, bisexuals, and transsexuals in the labour movement, in the workplace, and in society. This was a response to the work of a strong group of activists, and it laid the groundwork for the formation of Solidarity and Pride committees in the CLC, provincial labour federations, and most large unions. Unions had begun to take their frustrations with bargaining to human rights tribunals, to the courts, and to the streets before the CLC convention. In 1991 Canadian Auto Workers members filed human rights complaints against Canadian Airlines and Air Canada for their refusal to extend benefits for same-sex partners (Canadian Auto Workers 2004). In 1995 the Public Service Alliance of Canada filed similar human rights complaints against the Treasury Board (Equality for Gays And Lesbians Everywhere 2005). In 1998 the Canadian Union of Public Employees (CUPE) won a ground-breaking Ontario Court of Appeal decision that expanded the definition of spouse and survivor benefits in the Income Tax Act (Hurley 2005). Union activists have consistently coordinated their bargaining, education, and court challenges with broad coalitions, including Canadians for Equal Marriage, the Quebec Coalition for Same-Sex Relationship Recognition, and Equality for Gays And Lesbians Everywhere (EGALE). These are all coalitions of individuals, family members, community groups, unions, and social justice organizations. As a participant in many coalitions, CUPE has educated both community partners and employers about work-life issues and has even developed a corporate code of conduct that details acceptable employee treatment for the growing number of employers that want to participate in Pride Day events across the country.

In 1996 the federal government amended the Human Rights Act to include sexual orientation as a prohibited ground of discrimination, and in 2000 Parliament passed Bill C-23, the Modernizing Benefits and Obligations Act, which amended sixty-eight federal statutes to provide same-sex couples with equal rights and responsibilities as heterosexual couples (Hurley 2005). In 2003 and 2004 provincial courts in most provinces upheld the ruling that those rights and responsibilities included marriage, and in 2005 the federal Parliament passed Bill C-38, legalizing same-sex civil marriage in Canada. Activists in both the public and private sectors continue to push to have pensions, spousal leaves, and benefits for same-sex partners included in a wide range of collective agreements. These coalitions have used a particularly effective combination of tribunals, courts, and bargaining, setting precedents in different jurisdictions and industries and organizing celebrations and demonstrations to create one of the most significant social changes of the early twenty-first century.

### *Employer-Based Child Care Programs*

Labour-movement activists have been central to national and regional campaigns advocating early childhood education and care across the country. They have been part of regional and national coalitions, in particular the Child Care Advocacy Association of Canada.

Activists in Quebec lobbied for years for licensed, accessible child care. In 1997 the Parti Québécois government agreed to pay costs above fees of $5 a day for regulated child-care services for all four-year-olds, for these services to be extended to children of all ages by 2002. Between 1998 and 2001 the province increased the number of regulated spaces by 57,400 (an increase of 69.7 per cent) and committed $2.24 billion (Tougas 2002). After the Liberals formed the government in Quebec in 2003, they increased the fee limit to $7 a day and threatened to reduce services. This government has also prohibited home-based child-care workers from joining a union or bargaining collectively.

Activists outside Quebec can claim cautious success in moving the federal government toward establishing a national child care program. The federal Liberal Party promised a national child-care program during the 1993 election campaign, but did nothing about it until 2003, when $935 million was allocated to start a negotiating process with the provinces. Activists have demanded a contribution of at least 1 per cent of gross domestic product, or $10 billion, with even larger amounts in the initial years. This would be an equivalent investment to that of most European Union countries and could build a system capable of handling the large numbers of children who currently have no access. Activists point out that the international standard for public education and care is changing and that Canada is falling behind. Most European countries and some US states are beginning to provide public education programs for children from the age of three (de Wolff 2003). One study indicates that while the proportion of children of employed mothers who are in regulated care increased from 13.1 per cent in 1994 to 17.9 per cent in 2001, 2.7 million children are still without regulated care (Friendly, Beach, and Turjano 2003). It will take more than $935 million to provide them with regulated education and care.

Workplace-based child-care programs have almost doubled since the early 1990s. There were 338 employer-based child-care centres in Canada in 2000, up from 176 in 1991 (Barbeau 2002). These services, however, were available to only 6.1 per cent of full-time and 4.6 per cent of part-time employed women and 6.6 per cent of full-time and 5.3 per cent of part-time employed men (Comfort, Johnson, and Wallace 2003). Two large unions, the Canadian Union of Postal Workers (CUPW) and the Canadian Auto Workers (CAW), have won landmark agreements with employers. They have recognized the limitations of local child care, particularly with a large employer, and have used these agreements to develop programs that not only serve their members but are also integrated with public programs.

In the early 1980s the CUPW women's committee set its sights on workplace child care. The committee successfully added child care to the union's priorities, and in 1987 it won a mediation/arbitration decision that committed the employer to a joint child care study.

The study formed the basis for a 1991 agreement to create a joint child-care fund, with the employer contributing $200,000 every quarter to a maximum of $2 million. The joint decision-making did not work well, and after some struggle, the union won full control of the fund in 1995. Another group of Canada Post workers, who are represented by the Union of Postal Communications Employees, went on strike in part over the issue of creating a child-care fund for their members in 1999. The two unions now work together on furthering the child-care initiative and have added a child-care centre in Fredricton to CUPW's previous eleven community-based child-care centres. The fund supports services in non-profit centres to accommodate parents' irregular hours, supervised care in members' homes, short-term emergency care, after-school and summer programs for school-age children, and information and financial support for children with special needs (Canadian Union of Postal Workers 2003).

The CAW won its first child-care agreement in negotiations with Ford, Chrysler, and General Motors in 1987. This agreement established funding to create the Windsor CAW Community Child Care and Development Services, which includes spaces for infants and children whose parents work extended hours in that city. In 1999 the union expanded the existing child-care benefits by negotiating a $10-a-day subsidy for employees in all locations for full-time child care and $5 a day for part-time child care in licensed, non-profit child-care programs. The agreement also includes the provision of another $150,000 a year to enhance existing licensed services by extending hours and adding infant care.

The efforts of both unions have created a blend of workplace and public services. The automakers now contribute approximately $15 million per agreement to the public system of licensed, non-profit centres, establishing a new and direct interest on the part of employers and CAW members in public child care and the creation of a national child-care program. Even the best-designed workplace programs cannot be a substitute for universal programs and cannot provide adequate services for workers in all locations and all shifts or for infants or all children with disabilities. Consequently, the CAW took a further step in its 1999 bargaining and negotiated a public letter from DaimlerChrysler to the prime minister in support of a national child-care program.

### *Domestic Violence*

Since the early 1980s, union women's committees have worked with women's organizations across the country to mobilize Take Back the Night rallies and support for local crisis lines and shelters. In the early 1990s several unions took this process further and began to conduct educational campaigns about how domestic violence can cause some of the most dramatic work-life tensions. They educated workers and employers about the signs of abuse that can show up at work, the needs of women in abusive situations, breaking ranks with male members who are violent, and workplace accommodations that can support abused women (Ontario Federation of Labour 1997). Some accommodations can be remarkably simple: in one instance a union encouraged the employer to move the work station of a woman who was being stalked so that she was not visible from a public window. In 2002 the CAW won a ground-breaking agreement with Daimler-Chrysler that introduced women's advocates in large plants. This program selects and trains local union members as women's advocates who are paid for a term to counsel, refer, and negotiate workplace accommodations for members who experience harassment and domestic violence.

### *Work-Life Issues and Service Workers*

In the absence of universal public sector child care and full public health and home care, many working adults deal with their work-life tensions by turning to growing numbers of private caregivers or non-profit and private sector service organizations. This is how many working adults experience the "market" solution to policy absences and program cuts, and it is creating a new set of social inequalities. Workers in health-care, child-care, home-care, domestic, laundry, and food services are disproportionately ethno-racial minority and recent immigrant women. Their working conditions are generally poorer than most – they are often poorly paid, have few benefits, and are precariously employed. And they must regularly negotiate exploitive employee/service provider relationships between themselves and the women and men who hire them.

Most service workers are not unionized, but several unions are actively organizing in these sectors. For instance, over many years the Canadian Union of Public Employees has represented a significant number of child-care workers and has been a leader in the campaign for a national child-care program. The Manitoba Government and General Employees Union has initiated an innovative process that is intended to bring non-profit boards together with the government to form a sector-wide bargaining process in that province. Unions and advocates for regulated early childhood education and care have worked for a number of years to establish the Child Care Human Resource Sector Council. It opened in 2003 with a mandate to improve the sector's ability to attract and keep qualified workers and to ensure the work that they do is valued.

Working conditions for home-care workers are similarly poor and undervalued. The Service Employees International Union, the Canadian Union of Public Employees, and the Newfoundland and Labrador Association of Public and Private Employees are among several unions that have recently made explicit efforts to unionize home-care workers.

## CONCLUSION

Union activists have successfully used a variety of strategies to win progressive agreements that help workers manage their work and life responsibilities. This chapter has provided an overview of unions' successes in reducing time at work, introducing paid parental and caring leaves, extending benefits to same-sex spouses, developing workplace child care, and creating anti-violence programs.

The most successful initiatives have tended to rely on larger unions pressuring governments and large private sector employers to be model employers. Activists have then been able to use these precedents to push for legislation and programs that establish similar standards in all workplaces. Ongoing reductions in government spending and in the public sector and the reorganization and restructuring of large manufacturers are, however, warning signs that this strategy may not continue to be effective. Attacks on public programs are in part attacks on the equity and work-life agreements won by public sector workers (see Cohen and Cohen this volume). Program cuts and privatization not only make services less available to all Canadians, but they also jeopardize working conditions and existing collective agreements and make it very difficult for public sector unions to negotiate new protections. Further, activists have recognized that even the larger and carefully planned workplace programs, such as the CAW and CUPW child-care funds, are limited and cannot replace a quality, public program. Workers in smaller workplaces, particularly non-profit social service workers, home-care workers, and educators, have found that the several rounds of restructuring and cuts to public spending that have occurred since the early 1990s have left very little room to maintain basic benefits, let alone negotiate significant improvements. These observations suggest that future collective labour-movement strategies must address the realities of smaller workplaces and at the same time continue to build broad-based support for stronger public sector programs that will effectively reduce the work-life tensions of all employed people. The efforts of union activists since the 1970s demonstrate that support for caring for relations, friends, and communities should not be a privilege available only to some but, rather, that support for working people should be delivered through public programs and available to all.

## APPENDIX: LARGE CANADIAN UNIONS

*Canadian Auto Workers (CAW)* The CAW is best known for representing workers in auto manufacturing, the airline industry, and hospital services. In 2002 it had 260,000 members, a quarter of whom were women. Members were organized in 280 locals and 2,107 bargaining units. They work in several industrial sectors: 54 per cent in manufacturing, 16 per cent in transportation, 26 per cent in services, and 4 per cent in primary industries.

*Canadian Labour Congress (CLC)* The CLC is the countrywide body that represents the majority of unionized Canadian workers. Its primary purpose is to pursue social and economic justice for working people. It's affiliates include over a hundred unions – the majority of national and international unions in Canada – twelve provincial and territorial federations, and 137 district labour councils. Together, these organizations represent 2.5 million unionized Canadian workers.

*Canadian Union of Postal Workers (CUPW)* CUPW members are employed by Canada Post and include full-time, part-time, and temporary letter carriers and postal clerks, coders and manual sorters, wicket clerks and lead-hand wicket clerks, stores persons, vehicle mechanics, mail handlers and mail dispatchers, electricians, electronic technicians, and inside assistants. A new unit of over six thousand rural and suburban mail carriers joined in 2004.

*Canadian Union of Public Employees (CUPE)* CUPE is Canada's largest union, with more than half a million members across Canada. It represents workers in health care, education, municipalities, libraries, universities, social services, public utilities, transportation, emergency services, and airlines. CUPE members are service providers, white-collar workers, technicians, labourers, skilled trades people, and professionals. More than half of CUPE members are women. About one-third are part-time workers.

*Communications, Energy and Paperworkers Union of Canada (CEP)* CEP represents workers in pulp and paper mills; telephone companies; the oil, gas, chemical, and mining industries; the print media, radio, and television; hotels and transportation. It was formed in 1992 through a merger of three smaller unions, and by 2002 it had grown to a membership of 150,000.

*National Union of Public and General Employees* (NUPGE) NUPGE is a family of fifteen unions that together form the second largest union in Canada. Most of its 337,000 members deliver provincial public services, but it also has a growing number of members who work in the private sector.

*Public Service Alliance of Canada (PSAC)* The PSAC represents 150,000 members who work for the federal government or its agencies as immigration officers, fisheries officers, food inspectors, customs officers, and others. PSAC members also work in the private sector in women's shelters, universities, security agencies, and casinos. In the North, the PSAC represents most unionized workers employed by the governments of Yukon, Nunavut, and the Northwest Territories and some municipalities.

*Service Employees International Union (SEIU)* The SEIU has 80,000 members in Canada. It represents workers in home care, homes for the aged, hospitals, nursing homes, retirement homes, and emergency services. It also represents workers in manufacturing, auto parts, building maintenance, food and laundry services, social services, the travel industry, and other areas.

*United Steelworkers of America (USWA).* The USWA has 190,000 members in Canada, about 65,000 of whom are employed in the steel industry and in mining. The others are in every sector of the economy, from factories to offices, hospitals, university campuses, hotels, warehouses, bakeries, banks, transportation, and communication, and many other fields. More than 20 per cent of Canadian Steelworkers are women.

# 5

# Privatization: A Strategy for Eliminating Pay Equity in Health Care

MARJORIE GRIFFIN COHEN
AND MARCY COHEN

Historically, women working in the health-care sector have experienced considerable wage discrimination. The struggle of health support workers to redress those gender-based wage gaps has spanned several decades and in the last thirty years, has proved remarkably successful. Pay-equity gains in this sector not only raised the wages of women workers but, just as importantly, have affirmed the value, skills, and responsibility involved in the work they perform.

In the absence of legislation as exists in most other Canadian provinces and territories, pay equity in British Columbia has been achieved primarily through the efforts of unions and the requirement, introduced by the New Democratic Party (NDP) government of the 1990s, that pay equity in the public sector be addressed primarily through raising wages of low-wage workers. However, pay-equity gains, along with the long-held understanding that women and men performing the same work should be paid equally, are being reversed through privatization. On 28 January 2002 British Columbia's Liberal government passed legislation (Bill 29, The Health and Social Services Delivery Improvement Act) that unilaterally altered signed collective agreements between health-care employers and unions and removed essential provisions related to job-security protection and contracting out. The legislation's goals were very explicit: to provide new investment and business opportunities for private corporations in the health-care sector and to reduce compensation for health-care support workers. These changes cleared the way for government and its health authorities to privatize health-care support work in hospitals and long-term care facilities and to lay off thousands of health-care support workers across the province. The effect on wages and conditions of work have been stunning: wages in the areas that have been privatized have been cut almost in half, and most benefits have been either eliminated or drastically reduced.

In British Columbia the health support sector covers virtually all non-medical work performed in hospitals, long-term facilities, and community settings. The occupational classifications include cleaners, laundry workers, food-service workers, nursing assistants, licensed practical nurses, technical, trades, and information systems workers, security staff, and clerical workers. The overwhelming majority of these are women, many of whom are the primary wage earners for their families. A high proportion are older, visible minority, or immigrant women. This chapter will show how the BC government's actions to facilitate the privatization of health-care support work not only undermine these equal-pay wage gains but place many of these women workers and their families in precarious economic circumstances. As a result, their capacity to ensure their own and their family's long-term social reproduction is jeopardized.

The new low-wage precedent for "women's work" in the health-care sector will in all likelihood have ramifications for women working in similar public and private sector jobs throughout British Columbia and across Canada. Traditionally, the public sector has taken the lead in recognizing the value of women's work and providing women with fair compensation for their labour. In British Columbia this recognition was particularly important because of the absence of pay equity legislation. As this chapter will show, the bargaining route has been especially successful in bringing about more equity in wages in the health sector, particularly in comparison to what was achieved through a legislated route in Ontario. But it also raises significant questions about the effectiveness of strategies to achieve pay equity and whether it is possible to maintain these gains without strong legislation.

It is also important to situate the changes in British Columbia in the context of shifts that are occurring throughout the country, for while events in the province can be attributed to a government that has little sympathy with women's issues in general and pay equity specifically, the privatization effort cannot be attributed to that factor alone. Rather, it is a result of a variety of both federal and provincial initiatives that ultimately serve to undermine the advances of women.

This chapter focuses on social reproduction of women's work from two quite distinct points of view. First, it deals with the ways that pay-equity gains have contributed to the economic security and stability of the families of the women who work in health support occupations. Second, it examines the actual content of the work performed, which is seen as very similar to household labour – caring, cleaning, laundry, and food preparation. A close examination of the working conditions, technical skills, and experience required in a health support occupation in a hospital suggests that this work is significantly different from household labour. And yet it is the assumed similarity between the two, in the past and now once again, that is contributing to the undervaluing of health support work.

## PAY EQUITY

The undervaluation of women's labour, particularly in areas where it closely resembles domestic work, is both well documented and acknowledged by governments. According to the BC government's 2002 Pay Equity Task Force, "there is no dispute that substantial sex-based wage disparities (also referred to as gender pay gaps) exist in British Columbia and across Canada, or that they adversely affect women in a number of ways" (Iyer 2002, i).

The feminist revival of the 1970s made "equal pay for work of equal value" (or pay equity, in current parlance) an important issue for very good reasons. Most provinces in Canada had laws on the books from the 1950s stating that employers had to pay women the same as men when they did the same work. However, these laws had little effect on changing the entrenched practice of paying men higher wages than women. This was because employers tended to segregate work into male-specific and female-specific jobs, which allowed them to continue the practice of paying less for women's jobs.

In contrast, pay-equity initiatives and laws that were first initiated in the 1970s focused on the value of the work performed and demanded that if the value of the work performed by a woman is the same as the value of the work performed by a man, they should be paid equally. By evaluating work on the basis of the knowledge, skills, effort, responsibility, and working conditions required to do a job, comparisons between different kinds of work can be made, making it possible to determine where wage inequalities exist.

The idea of pay equity, or "equal pay for work of equal value," is really nothing new. Early in the twentieth century, it was a feature of the Treaty of Versailles, which became the basis for its inclusion in the Treaty of Rome and which, in turn, established the European Union's approach to pay equity. The International Labour Organization (ILO) drew up a convention on pay equity in 1951, which was signed by Canada. And in 1977 Canada included equal pay for work of equal value in the Canadian Human Rights Act. It is also the law in Quebec (1975), Ontario (1987), Manitoba (1985), New Brunswick (1989), Nova Scotia (1988), Saskatchewan (1997), and Yukon.

While the term "pay equity" focuses on wage differentials between males and females doing comparable work, it can also it can also provide for the examination of other areas where different treatment in compensation seriously disadvantages women. Women in public sector employment in particular have benefited by the inclusion of benefit packages in pay-equity considerations (i.e., pensions, sick leave, medical and dental coverage, disability provisions, and vacation pay) that go beyond minimum employment standard regulations (Akyeampong 2002).

## PAY EQUITY IN BRITISH COLUMBIA

Pay equity is the law in most jurisdictions in Canada, but it is not the law in British Columbia. This discrepancy is surprising because for most of the 1990s an NDP government was in power, and NDP governments are generally more associated with women-friendly legislation than are other governments. While some form of pay-equity legislation had been established in most other provinces by the early 1990s, lack of public support and the complications arising from pay-equity legislation in Ontario led the new NDP government to a prolonged "study" of the issue. The result was an approach to pay equity that focused on the wages of all low-wage workers and the introduction of pay-equity guidelines in the public sector. In 1995 the government introduced the Public Sector Employers' Council Pay Equity Policy Framework. It was a proactive policy requiring all public sector employers to develop pay-equity plans and to file these plans with the government (Iyer 2002, 43).

The measures to both raise the pay for low-wage workers and institute pay equity within the public sector had a significant impact on the wage gap between males and females in that sector. But when the government realized it was about to lose the election in 2001, the "framework" agreement's inability to protect women's wage gains in the long run pointed to the real problem with the lack of legislation. Women within the party urged some kind of legislative action quickly. Ultimately, and very late in its term, the NDP government passed an amendment to the Human Rights Code to add a pay-equity provision.[1] This amendment was never implemented because one of the first acts of the new Liberal government was to repeal the legislation. However, in an attempt to show that they were doing something, the Liberals created a task force to study pay equity for the private sector.

The results of this task force were very disappointing for pay-equity advocates. Its recommendations were decidedly against pay-equity legislation; instead it called for "equal pay for equal work" (something that had been in effect since 1953) and "study, education, industry participation, and voluntary measures over a period of time" (Iyer 2002: 100).

Historically, because of the absence of legislation in British Columbia, many individual trade unions, particularly those representing women in the public sector, specifically bargained for pay equity (Fuller 2001: 7). In the health-care sector, the Hospital Employees' Union (HEU) represents more than 90 per cent of hospital support workers in British Columbia in hospitals and long-term facilities and is the union that has been most affected by the Liberal government's privatization initiatives. It is a trade union with a long history of fighting for wage equality, using several different negotiating strategies over time to advance that goal. The first steps toward pay equity were made in the 1960s when wage rates for similar jobs were standardized across the province and discriminatory "male" and "female" job classifications were eliminated (Fairey 2002; Webb 1994). These changes were important, but they were not sufficient to end the bias against female-dominated jobs. During the first half of the 1970s, HEU pursued several different strategies in its efforts to achieve pay equity including bargaining, human rights complaints, representations to government, and arbitrations. Of particular significance was a human rights complaint filed on behalf of radiology attendants at Vancouver General Hospital, which was ultimately upheld by the Human Rights Commission. Bargaining successes included winning equal pay for specific

Table 5.1 Gender-based wage differences, 1991 and 2001 (wages in female-dominated jobs as percentage of value of comparable male work)

| | Gender-based wage differential (percentage) | |
|---|---|---|
| *Job classification* | *1991* | *2001* |
| Housekeeping aide | 16 | 3.7 |
| Nursing assistant | 29 | 11.0 |
| Food service worker | 10 | 0.2 |
| Laundry worker | 14 | 1.9 |
| Clerk II, medical records | 14 | 1.1 |

SOURCE: HEU pay-equity plan.

classes of workers (i.e., between female practical nurses and male general orderlies) and a specific monthly anti-discrimination adjustment for the more than eight thousand hospital workers earning less than the rate for cleaners.

These initiatives were largely stalled in the mid-1970s and 1980s with the imposition of, first, federal and then provincial wage controls. Once again the union shifted tactics, focusing the struggle for pay equity on the establishment of a broad classification system that would establish hospital wage rates comparable to those in similar classifications in the provincial public service.

In 1991, after twenty years of concerted efforts by HEU to reduce the wage gap between men and women, differentials of between 10 and 29 per cent remained (see table 5.1). On the heels of pay-equity gains in the direct public service, the union launched a major strike in 1992 to make pay equity a reality in health care. The primary demands were related to closing the gender gap. They included a general neutral base rate for all workers, to be established at the male entry-level rate; across-the-board, rather than percentage, wage increases; an elimination of all incremental steps; an industry-wide pay adjustment for all hospital workers as a recognition that even men in the sector were underpaid because the work had been undervalued; and comparability with the provincial government union. Supplementary demands included on-site child care, paid maternity leave, and a ban on wage reductions resulting from pay equity for any employee. As a result of that strike, 90 per cent of HEU's membership received pay-equity increases on top of general wage increases. Although this achievement did not establish full pay equity, it was a solid beginning that was gradually improved upon throughout the 1990s. As part of this agreement, a Job Value Comparison Plan was established with the provision that up to 1 per cent of payroll per year would to be allocated for pay equity until equity was achieved.

The agreement did not, however, change the fact that only after very long and protracted arbitration did the union succeed in raising the rates of health-care worker job classifications to rates that were similar to provincial government employees. And by 2001 the wage differentials for comparable male and female work in the health-care sector had declined significantly (see table 5.1).

It is notable, as other studies have shown, that collective bargaining proved more effective in achieving pay-equity gains for hospital support workers than did legislation in Ontario (Stinston 1999; Fairey 2003). A comparison with hospital workers in Ontario shows that pay-equity adjustments in British Columbia are greater in all categories, ranging from changes of two and a half times greater for food service workers to ten times greater for nurse aides. And the overall average improvement for hospital support workers in British Columbia is almost five times greater than in Ontario (Fairey 2003). Perhaps the most significant difference between the two is the fact that while pay-equity adjustments greatly reduced the differential between the low and high wage earners in health support occupations in British Columbia, in Ontario it increased the differences – women at the top of the wage scale received larger pay-equity settlements than women at bottom of the wage scale (Stinson 1999, 67–72; Fairey 2003, 9). For the general population of workers who are not unionized, however, the existence of equal-pay legislation is probably important in reducing wage inequalities. In this regard, it is interesting to note that in 2001 the wage gap between male and female workers working full-time, full year, in Ontario and British Columbia was virtually the same, with females earning about 71 per cent of what males earned (Statistics Canada 2001b). However, comparisons of this type should be viewed with some caution because the results may be influenced by different factors, including the age of the workforce, type of industries, and rates of unionization (Drolet 2002).

## HOSPITAL SUPPORT WORKERS

Hospital support work is primarily women's work, and the union representing support workers is primarily a women's union. Eighty-five

Table 5.2 Ethnicity, gender, and age (proportion of BC population and HEU membership)

| *Category* | *BC* | *HEU* |
|---|---|---|
| Visible minority | 19% | 27% |
| Immigrants* | 20% | 31% |
| Women | 50% | 85% |
| Average age of workers | 39 yrs | 47 yrs |

SOURCE: McIntyre & Mustel Research
*This category designates people born outside Canada.

per cent of HEU's 46,000 members are women. It is also a union that represents a larger proportion of immigrant women, visible minority women, and older women than is present in British Columbia's overall working population (McIntyre and Mustel 2002) (see table 5.2). These groups are recognized as being especially disadvantaged in the labour force and therefore most likely to benefit from pay-equity initiatives. Pay-equity adjustments have enabled these workers to achieve reasonable incomes, job security, and benefits that they would not likely have achieved in comparable private sector work.

As a result, even though this is a predominately older female workforce, it shares many characteristics typically associated with primary male wage earners. The majority of HEU members with families are dependent exclusively on the HEU-negotiated extended benefit plan coverage (68 per cent), and close to a half (48 per cent) are dependent solely on HEU pension entitlements. In other words, many HEU members are either sole-support parents or live with partners who do not work in jobs with extended health and/or pensions benefits. In fact, when asked about the security of their partner's employment, only 18 per cent of HEU members living with an adult partner reported that their partner's work arrangements were "very secure."

The availability of steady work at reasonable wages combined with benefits, including pensions, has provided a stable workforce for the hospital sector. Two-thirds of HEU members are employed full-time, and all workers tend to stay at their jobs for lengthy periods. Full-time employees have held their jobs for an average of 11.6 years, while part-time employees have been in the same positions for an average of 6.1 years. In addition, over 50 per cent have one or more dependent children, and one-quarter support dependent adults. These membership characteristics indicate that the BC government's decision to nullify the HEU contract will leave many women workers and their families in precarious economic circumstances, without the means to ensure their own and their families' long-term social reproduction.

## THE BACKDROP TO PRIVATIZATION

Privatization is an important policy objective of the Liberal government in British Columbia and is based on an ideology that assumes that privatization will be effective in stimulating business activity in the more "efficient" private sector and reducing government expenditures. The imperative to reduce government expenditures in the province stems from the accumulation of a rather substantial budget deficit that is largely a result of a dramatic decrease in income associated with tax cuts. Immediately upon taking office the Liberals cut taxes by $2 billion a year, benefiting mainly those in upper income brackets.

While ideology and money problems are factors that alone could have brought about the changes that are occurring for hospital support workers in British Columbia, there is more behind them than just a provincial government that is unsympathetic to trade unions and the principles of pay equity. The overall "conditioning framework" that makes privatization of women's work possible has more widespread roots in Canada.

Probably most significant has been the federal government's reduced financial commitment to health care. Federal cash transfers to the province have decreased from a high of 47 per cent of hospital and physician expenditures in 1977 to a low of less than 15 per cent in 1999 (Romanow 2002, 67). According to the Romanow Commission on health care in Canada, "the federal government has successfully moved the risk of growing health expenditures to the provinces," both through its reductions in cash and through the elimination of an escalator factor when the Canada Health and Social Transfer (CHST) was established (Romanow 2002, 67). Also significant has been the expansion of the provincial health-care system to cover some drugs, home care, and other services for an aging population, without a commensurate expansion of coverage and funding under the Canada Health Act.

In any discussion of the dismantling of pay equity, it is important to understand that it is not just the actions of the immediate jurisdictions that are responsible. While the local health authorities are the front-line activists in the privatization process, they are responding to pressure put on them by the province's funding. The provinces get away with privatization because the federal government, in its mania for budget surpluses and its indirect approval of privatization initiatives, is complicit. All levels of government, then, become allies in the downward spiral of women's wages.

## UNPRECEDENTED PRIVATIZATION INITIATIVES

In 1995 the Fraser Institute, a right-leaning think tank, published a slim five-page "study" comparing the costs of ancillary support services in hospitals – cleaning, laundry, food services, trades, and clerical – to "hospitality" services in hotels, arguing that hospital support workers are overpaid (Ramsey 1995; Cohen 2001). This line of reasoning has since been taken up by a number of very influential people in the media and in the BC Medical Association, who have argued that high wages for "non-professional" and "non-essential" health support workers are starving "the acute care system of health system resources" that should be going to direct care and professional services (Palmer 2001; Courtice 2000).

The Fraser Institute "study" and the support it garnered set the stage for the Liberal government to introduce legislation to facilitate the privatization of hospital support services. In January 2002, nine months after taking office, the Liberals introduced Bill 29, which unilaterally altered collective agreements negotiated between employers and workers in the health and social service sectors. This legislation removed key rights and protections for about 100,000 health-care workers during the life of the contracts. In particular, it eliminated HEU members' ability to "follow the work" should it be contracted out to a private employer, facilitated hospital and long-term care centre closures, and made the privatization of support services within the health-care sector much easier to achieve. By voiding the employment security and no-contracting-out provision of the health and social service collective agreements, this legislation made it possible for employers to easily lay off employees and to restructure the workplace with an entirely new workforce paid at much lower rates and with far fewer benefits.

While government intervention in labour relations has a long history, legislation aimed at altering collective agreement provisions is rare, and where it does occur, it is usually limited to changes in compensation rates (Rose 2003, 15). In an affidavit submitted on Bill 29,

Joseph Rose, a professor in the Faculty of Business at McMaster University, noted only three other occasions in Canadian history where governments infringed on statutory or collectively bargained job-security provisions. In all of these cases, government interventions were intended "to limit or foreclose" future bargaining on job security; they did not "void collective agreement provisions during their term" (Rose 2003, 17). In this respect the provisions of Bill 29 are unprecedented.

As a result of the scope of Bill 29 and its impact on a vulnerable group of women workers, HEU and the other unions affected by the bill launched a Charter of Rights court challenge under three provisions of the Charter: equality rights (section 15), freedom of association (section 2), and security of persons (section 7). This challenge was turned down by the Supreme Court of British Columbia in September 2003 and by the Appeal Court of British Columbia in July 2004, but the unions have taken the case to the Supreme Court of Canada. In April 2005 that court agreed to hear the unions' argument in relation to charter violations, and the case will come before the Supreme Court of Canada in February of 2006.

A recent Supreme Court of Canada decision, acknowledging the validity of pay-equity claims by public sector workers in Newfoundland may significantly help the case of the BC unions ([2004] 3 S.C.R. 381, 29). In the Newfoundland case, the pay-equity claim was recognized as an appropriate response to gender discrimination under section 15 of the Charter. However, the government was exempted, under section 1 of the Charter, from having to pay the claim because of the fiscal crisis in the province and legislative agenda to address that crisis ([2004] 3 S.C.R. 381, 2–3). The BC government has not submitted arguments or evidence based on the "ability to pay," and therefore an exemption on financial considerations is unlikely to apply. A positive ruling by the Supreme Court that not only recognizes occupation-based gender discrimination as a violation of equality rights under the Charter but also acknowledged the right of union members to be compensated for their loss of income would be very important in entrenching pay-equity rights in Canada.

## THE RATIONALE FOR PRIVATIZATION OF HEALTH SUPPORT SERVICES

With Bill 29 in effect, health authorities, primarily in the Lower Mainland, initiated plans to privatize most or all of their housekeeping, security, laundry, and food services work. By June 2004 more

Table 5.3 Wages, minimum wage, and housing cost comparisons, 2001–2002 (BC's percentage above other provinces)

| | *Ontario* | *Alberta* | *Canada* |
|---|---|---|---|
| Housing costs | 12.6 | 33.5 | 26.3 |
| Median wage (full-time) | 3.8 | 11.8 | 9.1 |
| Median wage (part-time) | 15.4 | 35.6 | 10.5 |
| Minimum wage | 16.8 | 35.6 | 24.6 |

NOTE: See appendix 1 for detailed figures for dollar amounts and percentages for all provinces and sources for figures.

than eight thousand HEU members were affected, most of them women from immigrant and visible minority backgrounds. The largest outsourcing contracts, for housekeeping and food services, were given to the three largest multi-national service corporations in the world – Compass, Sedexho, and Aramark. None of these corporations is Canadian; all operate internationally with head offices in the United States, Britain, or France and have reputations for poor labour relations and/or union-bashing (Walker 2002a, 2002b, 2002c).

According to the health authorities, the primary reason for contracting out health-care support services is to save money on labour costs in response to reductions in funding from the provincial government and in particular its refusal to fund negotiated wage increases for a unionized health-care workforce. The provincial government and the health authorities argue that health-care support workers in British Columbia are considerably more expensive than hospital workers in other provinces. This claim is true, but as tables 5.3 and 5.4 show, while the wage rates in British Columbia are higher, they are in line with the province's higher general labour costs and higher cost of living. For example, while a hospital cleaner in British Columbia was paid almost 9 per cent more than an equivalent hospital employee in Ontario, housing costs are more than 12 per cent higher in BC than in Ontario (see tables 4.3 and 4.4). Similarly, while a dietary aide in British Columbia was paid 29 per cent more than her counterpart in Alberta, BC housing costs were 34 per cent higher.

Neither the relationship between prices in different provinces nor consideration of support workers' wages in British Columbia relative to other public sector workers was a compelling argument for the government when the need to save on labour costs arose. While the case has been well made that neither doctors' nor nurses' wages should fall

Table 5.4 Interprovincial wage comparisons of hospital workers' wages, January 2003 (BC's percentage above other provinces)

| *Job category* | *Ontario* | *Alberta* | *Canada* |
|---|---|---|---|
| Cleaner | 8.9 | 34.7 | 31.5 |
| Cook | 14.8 | 26.8 | 28.7 |
| Laundry worker | 11.2 | 45.1 | 31.5 |
| Dietary aide | 5.0 | 29.0 | 27.4 |

NOTE: See appendix 2 for details and complete interprovincial comparison in dollar amounts and percentage differences from British Columbia's rates, including wage rate sources.

– and in fact should be increased – in order to protect the integrity of the jobs themselves, a similar argument fell on deaf ears when it came to hospital support workers.

The very nature of the work – "housework" – enables those trying to "fix" the health-care system to see those who do this work as dispensable. This attitude is, surprisingly, even the position of the Romanow Commission report, *Building on Values: The Future of Health Care in Canada.* It is surprising because this is a report that has been applauded for the strong position it takes against the privatization of health care. Yet it makes exceptions. According to the report,

> It is important to distinguish between two types of services: direct health care services such as medical, diagnostic and surgical care; and ancillary services such as food preparation, cleaning and maintenance. An increasing proportion of ancillary services provided in Canada's not-for-profit hospitals are contracted out to for-profit corporations. Canadians seem to find this role for private sector companies acceptable. (Romanow 2002, 6)

With no substantive research evidence to back up its claim, the report goes on to say that because the quality of these services is relatively easy to judge, privatization of the services can therefore easily be evaluated and, presumably, kept under control (McFarlane and Prado 2002). The commission also assumes (incorrectly and again without evidence) that health-care facilities can easily change suppliers if the latter perform badly. For these reasons, and presumably to save money, the commission felt that "a line should be drawn between ancillary and direct health care services and that direct health care services should be delivered in public and not-for-profit health care facilities" (Romanow 2002, 7).

This conclusion is unfortunate and it reflects a point of view that sees certain types of work currently being performed within medical establishments as not integral to the success of health-care performance. While this chapter cannot document the extent to which ancillary health-care services directly contribute to the successful operation of the health-care system, it is an issue that has gained considerable attention with the increased spread of antibiotic-resistant organisms, or AROs (Cohen 2001; Rampling et al. 2001; Ayliffe, Babb, and Taylor 1999; Dancer 1999). For example, preventing the spread of inflections of this type, including SARS, requires highly professional cleaning related specifically to hospitals (*Taipei Times* 2003). Other kinds of support work within hospitals, such as plumbing and electrical work, laundry work, clerical work, and dietary work, are also specialized and require workers who are specifically trained for employment in a hospital setting. The assumption that any contractor can immediately provide a work crew to do the jobs at very low wages (as is the case in BC) indicates that the work requirements are not well understood. In fact in Britain, where the contracting out of cleaning services was the norm in the 1990s, many hospitals are now bringing services back in-house for exactly these reasons. Problems arose with sub-optimal levels of cleanliness, rapid turnover of staff, and deterioration in infection control standards (Perry 2003).

## THE IWA AND THE MULTINATIONAL CONTRACTORS

As already noted, under the provisions of Bill 29, multinational companies bidding for health support service contracts were not required to hire HEU workers or recognize the union's successorship rights. To even further limit the possibility that HEU would organize these workers, the multinationals took the unprecedented step of approaching a number of other trade unions to offer them "voluntary recognition agreements."[2] In such agreements the terms and conditions of employment are established by mutual consent between the union and the company prior to the hiring of the workforce. The overwhelming majority of BC Federation of Labour affiliates recognized HEU's right to organize this work and refused to cooperate with the outside contractors. There was, however, one notable exception, Local 1-3567 of the Industrial, Wood and Allied Workers of Canada (IWA).

This local has signed "voluntary recognition agreements" with each of the three largest private service providers – Sedexho, Compass, and Aramark. Up to this point the IWA had been primarily a male union with no experience in the hospital sector. Its main role had been to represent workers in forest industries, who are overwhelmingly male. In this respect, the IWA's experience with women's issues has been very limited.[3]

The agreements signed by IWA Local 1-3567 are quite similar. They were all signed prior to the start date of the contracts between these multinationals and the health authorities and before HEU members were laid off their jobs. It is worth examining one of the agreements in detail because they could become a template for future privatization in British Columbia and elsewhere. If these agreements are allowed to stand, they demonstrate quite clearly the very rapid changes in wages and working conditions that may occur through privatization and the ways in which a trade union with no commitment to women's issues may take advantage of the situation to expand its membership.

On 17 July 2003, Local 1–3567 signed a "partnership agreement" with Aramark (Aramark and IWA Local 1–3567 2003). Thirteen days later Aramark was awarded the housekeeping contract for the Vancouver Coastal Health Authority (covering all sites from Powell River to Vancouver, including the Vancouver General Hospital, UBC Hospital, Lion's Gate Hospital, St Paul's Hospital, and many long-term care and smaller acute care hospitals). Throughout the fall of 2003, Aramark recruited new employees through job recruitment fairs. Employees hired at these fairs were required to sign a union card with the IWA as a condition of employment. As a result, by year's end approximately 950 HEU housekeepers in the Vancouver Coastal Health Authority lost their jobs to a new workforce hired under the terms of the IWA "voluntary recognition agreement." The new workers had no opportunity to choose their union or to have a say in the terms of the agreement itself. The contract established substandard wage rates that the IWA would not have tolerated for its core, male membership.

The severe wage reductions contained in the Aramark-IWA contract are clearly unorthodox, if not exploitative, particularly for workers in a province with such high costs of living. For example, wages for housekeepers (cleaners) have decreased by 44 per cent from what had

Table 5.5 Interprovincial wage comparison

| *Company* | *Cleaner $ per hour* | *% more than health authority* |
|---|---|---|
| IWA-Aramark Van Coast Health Authority | 10.25 | |
| BC's health support subsector | 18.32 | 44.0 |
| Alberta | 13.60 | 24.6 |
| Saskatchewan | 13.22 | 22.5 |
| Manitoba | 12.74 | 19.5 |
| Ontario | 16.82 | 39.0 |
| Quebec | 14.29 | 28.2 |
| New Brunswick | 12.73 | 19.5 |
| Nova Scotia | 11.92 | 14.0 |
| Prince Edward Island | 13.40 | 23.5 |
| Newfoundland | 12.28 | 16.5 |
| National average (union) wage rate 2003 | 13.93 | 26.4 |

been bargained under the HEU contract, which is in turn 26 per cent lower than the national average for this work (table 5.5). Under these new rates, British Columbia will drop to the lowest pay scale in the country – not by a few percentage points but by substantial amounts (between 14 and 39 per cent lower than anywhere else in Canada). Even relatively low-wage provinces such as Newfoundland, Prince Edward Island, and New Brunswick pay considerably more an hour than the wages negotiated under the Aramark-IWA contract (table 5.5). These wages are so low that they place the purchasing power of housekeepers, for example, at about what it was thirty-five years ago. It is estimated that it is thirty years since a member of HEU earned the equivalent of what the IWA-Aramark contract pays workers.

This development represents a tremendous loss for women's work by any standards. It is even more disturbing when one compares the wages negotiated by the IWA under the Aramark contract to current wages for the same occupations under a standard IWA contract for male cleaners. Under the IWA Master Agreement (2000–03) janitors are paid $21.92 an hour, which is 2.1 times more than the wage rate negotiated for hospital cleaners. In this context, the Aramark-IWA agreement is not only a setback for pay equity; it is also a complete rejection of the concept that women and men should be paid equally for the same work, an understanding that has been in place in Canada since the 1950s. Even as far back as the IWA Master Agreement of

Table 5.6 Measuring the current value of past HEU housekeeping wages

| | *HEU housekeeping wage* | *In 2002 dollars* |
|---|---|---|
| 1954 | 0.83 | 5.88 |
| 1964 | 1.15 | 6.98 |
| 1968 | 1.76 | 9.35 |
| 1974 | 3.53 | 13.46 |
| 1984 | 9.48 | 15.59 |
| 1994 | 14.90 | 17.32 |

NOTE: See appendix 3 for more details.

Table 5.7 Private sector wage comparison: service occupations pay rate comparison, 1 January 2003

| *Union and employer name* | *Housekeeping aide/cleaner* |
|---|---|
| CEP pulp & paper master | 21.92 |
| IWA Master Agreement 2000–03 | 21.92 |
| BCGEU – Coast Canadian Inn | 14.47 |
| CAW Local 3000 – Pacific Palisades | 15.29 |
| CAW Local 4234 – Coast Inn & Ramada Hotel | 13.21 |
| HERE Local 40 – Hyatt Regency Vancouver | 15.02 |
| HERE Local 40 – Westin Bayshore Hotel | 15.42 |
| Aramark | 10.25 |

note: Top step rate used.

1983–1986, wage rates for cleaners were not as low as what has been negotiated for the women working for Aramark. In the mid-1980s, almost twenty years ago, the IWA negotiated $13.48 an hour for its janitors (male) – $3.23 an hour more than it has been willing to negotiate for its cleaners (female) today (see table 5.6). As table 5.7 shows, the wage rate negotiated with Aramark is also substantially lower than current wages for these categories of work in British Columbia's hospitality sector.

There are other ways that the Aramark-IWA contract is a setback for the rights of women workers. As stated earlier, hospital support workers made important advances in the 1960s that standardized wage rates throughout the province. Under the new contract, standard wages can now be ignored at the employer's discretion. The employer is not only paying housekeepers different wage rates (article 13, section 1) but is specifically allowed, at its "sole discretion," to raise the wages for individual workers. Historically, this is the type of activity that has undermined women's wages, particularly in circumstances where the employer wants to reward certain workers or punish others, or when an employer simply has a "preference" for some workers over others.

While the reduction of wages to about half of their existing levels is the most dramatic and obvious change under the IWA-Aramark contract, additional concessions to the employer radically change other aspects of compensation for health-care support work. The contract eliminates many of the hard-won gains that are significant for all employees but are particularly important for keeping women workers out of poverty, both when they are working and when they retire. The following are some of the most consequential changes to working conditions and benefits that occurred when the work shifted from a HEU contract to the Aramark-IWA contract.

*Pensions* The HEU contract provides for pensions for all full- and part-time regular employees. Employees and the employer both contribute to the plan. The Aramark-IWA contract has no pension plan.

*Vacations* The HEU contract provides twenty days' vacation, and after five years of service, one day is added for each year of additional service. The Aramark-IWA contract offers no more vacation than is mandated under the Employment Standards Act – two weeks after one year and three weeks after five years (Aramark and IWA Local 1-3567 2003, 7).

*Parental Leave* HEU has provisions for seventeen weeks of paid parental leave and up to forty-two weeks of unpaid parental leave. There is no right to paid parental or maternity leave under the IWA contract.

*Benefits* Under the HEU contract, all employees, regardless of hours worked, are eligible for benefits. Under the Compass-IWA contract, employees who work less than twenty hours a week on a regular basis are not eligible for benefits. The HEU contract provides benefits for medical and dental expenses, long-term disability, injury on duty, vision care, and pharmacare. The premiums for these benefits are fully paid by the employer. The Aramark-IWA contract does not offer long-term disability or injury-duty benefits. For benefits that are included, the employee pays 50 per cent of the premiums (19).

*Sick Leave* Under the HEU contract, all regular full-time employees receive 1.5 sick-leave days a month and can accumulate sick-leave benefits up to 156 days. Sick time is pro-rated for part-time employees. Under the Aramark-IWA contract employees receive 10 days of non-cumulative sick leave a year (19).

*Scheduling and Hours of Work* Under the HEU contract employees must be given fourteen days' notice of schedules. Scheduling preferences are based on seniority and position. If for some reason fourteen days' notice is not given, overtime pay is required. In addition, hours of work cannot be changed without following a process of notice and consultation outlined in the collective agreement. The Aramark-IWA contract states that the employer "does not guarantee hours of work to any employee and reserves the right to schedule work, including overtime work" (6).

*Transfer between Work Locations* Under the HEU agreement the transfer of employees to new locations is based on seniority and negotiated with the union. Under the Aramark-IWA agreement the employer has the sole discretion to assign people to various locations.

Taken together, these changes in benefits and working conditions make work in hospitals and other health-care facilities significantly more precarious. Workers cannot count on a specific number of hours of work a week, and they cannot be sure of when the work will take place. This is an intolerable work situation for all workers, but it is particularly hard on women and men who have family obligations.

## THE IWA AND THE UNION MOVEMENT

The relationship between Aramark and Local 1-3567 of the IWA, as established through this "voluntary recognition agreement," sets an alarming precedent for employer-union collusion in the organizing of British Columbia's health-care workers. At the Vancouver Coastal Health Authority, the "partnership agreement" between Aramark and the IWA was in place before the employees had worked a single day, and as a result, there was no opportunity for members to decide on their union representation or vote on a collective agreement. In addition, in the "statement of partnership" at the beginning of the agreement, the commitment of the IWA goes well beyond what is normally negotiated in a collective agreement. In that statement the IWA accepts "joint responsibility for the profitability and competitiveness of ARAMARK" (Aramark and IWA Local 1-3567 2003, 1).

Traditionally, trade unions in Canada are independent of employer or government influence. In stark contrast to those countries where "company unions" or employer-dominated unions are typical (such as Mexico), Canadian workers have had the right to choose their own union. They have also had a say in setting the terms and conditions of their collective agreements. Exceptions to this pattern exist in the building trades and in forestry work, where work is short-term and specific trade unions have long-established records in protecting workers' rights in these industries. In these limited cases, setting up a "voluntary recognition agreement" between the employer and the trade union before the work actually begins protects workers from having to build a union from the beginning each time a new short-term job begins. In fact, it guarantees them the wages and benefits already standard in the sector. But this is a very different circumstance from the work in hospitals, where voluntary recognition agreements are undercutting wages in an established sector and where an ongoing work relationship with a different union already exists.

Not surprisingly, HEU has worked through its national union, the Canadian Union of Public Employees (CUPE), to lodge a complaint against IWA Local 1–3567, for violating the constitution of the Canadian Labour Congress (CLC). The complaint is based on article 4, section 4, of the constitution, which states that "each affiliate shall respect the established work relationship of every other affiliate." And, "No affiliate shall by agreement or collusion with any employer or by exercise of economic pressure, seek to obtain work for its members as to which an established work relationship exists with any other affiliate, except with the consent of such affiliate" (CLC 2005: 12).

On September 17, 2003 impartial umpire Victor Pathe found that IWA Local 1–3567 had violated the CLC constitution. In his decision he notes that "many of the IWA actions complained of occurred while the HEU members were still performing the work, and in all cases the one year right of rehire had not elapsed and there is therefore an employment relationship and an established work relationship" (Pathe 2003, 11). Following this decision, the president of the CLC, Ken Georgetti, wrote to the president of the IWA, Dave Haggard, giving him until 2 October to reply in writing about "what steps" he would take "to come into compliance with the CLC Constitution" (Georgetti 2003). The deadline passed with no response from the IWA. Ironically, on 6 October 2003 the *Financial Post* reported that contract negotiations between the coastal forestry locals and the IWA were deadlocked over the issue of contracting out of tree-fallers' jobs (Greenwood 2003).

Because the IWA continued in violation of the CLC constitution, the CLC applied first-level sanctions on 26 March 2004. However, these sanctions did not stop the IWA local (referred to now as the United Steelworkers of America Local 1–3567) from negotiating new voluntary recognition agreements with the multinational companies. In September 2004 a settlement was finally worked out between CUPE and the United Steelworkers, which still gave Local 1–3567 some leaway to organize health support workers on Vancouver Island. The delays in reaching this settlement and the limitations of the settlement mean that terms and conditions of the voluntary recognition agreements are the starting point for any first-contract negotiations with the newly contracted-out workforce.

Circumstances finally began to shift back in HEU's favour with the BC Labour Relations Board (BCLRB) decision of 20 May 2004 (BCLRB decision, no. B173). The board ruled that the voluntary recognition partnership agreement between Aramark and the IWA was invalid specifically for the reasons stated in this chapter: that the workers had no opportunity to select their union or vote on the terms and conditions of the collective agreement. This ruling left HEU free to represent this workforce once again. Because HEU did not acknowledge the validity of the voluntary recognition agreements, it had begun a grassroots member-to-member organizing drive as soon as the new workforce was in place. The organizers hired by HEU were themselves laid-off support workers who were representative of the ethnic composition of the new workforce. Their success in organizing translated into several application for certification with the BC Labour Relations Board. In all but one very small unit, HEU has won the certification votes with support from 76 to 100 per cent of the new workforce. By July 2005 it had organized three thousand contract workers in the Lower Mainland employed with the three multinational companies and was in first-contract negotiations with these companies (Hospital Employees' Union 2005). In other words, HEU is now following a two-track strategy, negotiating for higher wages and working conditions, on one hand, and continuing to oppose privatization and argue that services should be brought back in-house, on the other.

## IMPLICATIONS FOR PATIENTS

In British Columbia's health sector, the availability of steady work at reasonable wages, combined with pension and other benefits, has built a stable workforce that contributes positively to the overall quality of care patients receive. One of the strongest arguments against privatizing work in hospitals and long-term care facilities is the potential it has to adversely affect health care outcomes for the province's population as a whole. This is largely due to the new conditions of work, which will in all likelihood compromise the quality of the work performed. Hospital cleaning is a good example. Because of the special requirements and dangers inherent in a hospital setting, this type of cleaning requires a level of knowledge and skill that is acquired through years of on-the-job experience as well as special training (Cohen 2001). Such training is not typically offered by the private sector, and a workforce destabilized by low wages and working conditions is unlikely to build specialized knowledge over time. This was the case in Scotland, where the auditor general noted that under privatized conditions, "hospital cleanliness was adversely affected by poor staff retention and problems recruiting staff" (Auditor General of Scotland 2000, 2).[4]

The extremely low wages being offered by the IWA-Aramark contract are almost guaranteed to ensure that few employees remain in the job very long. Under this contract, a housekeeper will earn from $10.25 an hour with no guarantee of full-time work. If an employee manages to work thirty hours a week, her yearly earnings would be $15,980. If she works forty hours a week, she would earn about $21,315.

These are extraordinarily low wages for workers anywhere in the country, but they are particularly problematic in British Columbia, where living costs are high. Examinations elsewhere of the relationship between wage levels and turnover rates confirm what most people would suspect: very low wage work has much higher turnover rates than does work that is well paid. In the health-care sector this is especially true. In California, for example, where the hourly average wage for nursing assistants is about CDN $11.56 (US$7.50) an hour, the turnover rate is close to 80 per cent (California Advocates for Nursing Home Reform 2001). In Alberta the direct relationship between wage and turnover rates was established by the experience with community-based rehabilitation staff. For people who earned less than $10,000 a year, the turnover rate was about 200 per cent. When workers earned between $15,000 and $20,000, the turnover rate decreased to 32 per cent, but if they earned between $35,000 and $40,000, the turnover rate declined to 11 per cent (Sonpal-Valia 2001, 1).

The turnover rates in hospitals and long-term care facilities, coupled with the fewer numbers of people employed and the unstable conditions of their work, will likely have an impact on the quality of the work performed. Adequate health care is as much an issue of cleanliness as it is of direct patient care. This link between cleanliness and care is increasingly understood by hospital administrators, particularly as it relates to the greater risk of hospital-acquired infections (Murphy 2002). With the proliferation of new drug-resistant infections, hospital cleanliness has been the first line of defence. In Britain, serious problems have arisen with cleanliness in hospitals following the contracting out of publicly run services to private contractors (Perry 2003). The attempt to reduce costs through privatization resulted in reduced staff levels and an overall deterioration in cleaning levels (Dancer 1999). Similarly with food services, higher costs and poorer nutrition have been attributed to the contracting out of food service production (Singleton 2000).

## CONCLUSIONS

Achieving pay equity in the health-care sector not only raised the wages of women workers but affirmed the value, skills and responsibility involved in the work they performed. It also reflected recognition on the part of employers, through a series of negotiated agreements and arbitrations, that this work commanded wages equal to comparable work performed by both males in the hospital sector and other employees working directly for the provincial government.

It would be tempting to believe that because this goal was achieved through negotiated contracts, pay-equity legislation is unnecessary. Legislation might be unnecessary when governments are responsive to the concept of raising the wages of low-wage workers and to the idea of equal pay for work of equal value. But since no government can guarantee how long it will survive, protecting workers with legislation is a very important tool to support contract negotiations. While any legislation can be undone by future governments, it is somewhat easier to nullify trade union contracts than it is to set aside legislation.

Claims that the women who do health-care support work receive excessive wages are subjective and unproven. As this chapter has shown, these wages can only be considered excessive if they are compared to discriminatory wages; they are not excessive when compared to the wages paid to men for similar work or to the wages of other workers in the public sector.

The major changes to health-care support work in British Columbia means that the province is at the very bottom of the scale when it comes to compensation for women's work in the health-care sector. The pay-equity gains won for women who did hospital support work were remarkable but fair. It appears that this very success has attracted the government's ire and has encouraged it not simply to reduce wages but to reduce them to a point where they are the very lowest for this category of work in the country.

The BC Liberal government's actions, which have set aside pay-equity gains for women in traditionally low-wage categories, provide a precedent that will have repercussions beyond health-care workers. When public sector wages and conditions of work deteriorate significantly, as they are doing in this case, they set an example for the private sector. If the government reduces women's wages, it sends a signal to the private sector that it too can set aside arguments for decent wages for women's work. Actions to roll back pay-equity gains, begun by the government in British Columbia, could spread and become endemic across the country.

British Columbia has been condemned by a United Nations committee report on discrimination against women. It specifically noted the high poverty rates for single mothers, Aboriginal women, and women of colour and the negative impact government cuts were having on women and girls. The privatization initiatives, such as the ones in health care, appear to deepen an already disturbing trend. Not only will women's wages in some sectors deteriorate relative to men, but they are also likely to exacerbate an already large and growing gap between different classes of women workers (Jackson 2003).

## APPENDIX ONE: AN INTERPROVINCIAL COMPARISON OF WAGES, MINIMUM WAGES, AND HOUSING COSTS

| | Original data | | | | BC's percentage above other province | | | |
|---|---|---|---|---|---|---|---|---|
| *Province* | *Median wage FT* | *Median wage PT* | *Minimum wage* | *Housing cost*[a] | *Median wage FT* | *Median wage PT* | *Minimum Wage* | *Housing Cost*[a] |
| BC | $18.17 | $10.50 | $8.00 | $1,538 | 0.0 | 0.0 | 0.0 | 0.0 |
| Alberta | $16.25 | $ 9.25 | $5.90 | $1,152 | 11.8 | 13.5 | 35.6 | 33.5 |
| Saskatchewan[b] | $15.00 | $ 8.05 | $6.35 | $ 980 | 21.1 | 30.4 | 26.0 | 56.9 |
| Manitoba | $14.50 | $ 8.53 | $6.50 | $1,022 | 25.3 | 23.1 | 23.1 | 50.5 |
| Ontario | $17.50 | $ 9.10 | $6.85 | $1,366 | 3.8 | 15.4 | 16.8 | 12.6 |
| Quebec | $15.71 | $10.00 | $7.00 | $ 995 | 15.7 | 5.0 | 14.3 | 54.6 |
| New Brunswick[c] | $13.27 | $ 7.25 | $6.00 | $ 891 | 36.9 | 44.8 | 33.3 | 72.6 |
| Nova Scotia[c] | $13.73 | $ 7.69 | $5.80 | $ 891 | 32.3 | 36.5 | 37.9 | 72.6 |
| PEI[c] | $12.26 | $ 8.00 | $6.00 | $ 891 | 48.2 | 31.3 | 33.3 | 72.6 |
| Nfld | $13.39 | $ 6.75 | $5.75 | $ 891 | 35.7 | 55.6 | 39.1 | 72.6 |
| Canada | $16.65 | $ 9.50 | $6.42 | $1,218 | 9.1 | 10.5 | 24.6 | 26.3 |

SOURCES: Wages data from the Labour Force Historical Review 2001 (R) CD-ROM, Statistics Canada, Ref: 71F0004XCB. Minimum wages are from CCH Canadian, *Canadian Labour Law Reports*, effective July 2002. Housing cost data are from Carlos Leiato, Housing Affordability Index (RBC Financial Group, Economics Department, June 2002).

NOTES:

"Median wage" for full-time (FT) and part-time (PT) workers reflect the median wage of all workers (both sexes) over age fifteen in all industrial sectors.

[a] Housing costs are monthly.

[b] Saskatchewan figures are an estimate based on the report's bar charts.

[c] Atlantic housing costs are aggregated. One figure corresponds with all Atlantic provinces.

# APPENDIX TWO:
## INTERPROVINCIAL COMPARISON OF SUPPORT WORKERS' WAGE RATES, 1 JANUARY 2003, AND ARAMARK GROUP/IWA

Non-patient areas at VGH (with province as the denominator)

| | | *IWA/Aramark Vancouver Coastal Health Authority* | *BC* | *Alberta* | *Sask* | *Manitoba* | *Ontario* | *Quebec* | *New Brunswick* | *Nova Scotia* | *PEI* | *Nfld* | *National average wage rate 2003* |
|---|---|---|---|---|---|---|---|---|---|---|---|---|---|
| Cleaner | Hourly Rate | 10.25 | 18.32 | 13.60 | 13.22 | 12.74 | 16.82 | 14.29 | 12.73 | 11.92 | 13.40 | 12.28 | 13.93 |
| | % Difference with BC | | 44% | 24.6% | 22.5% | 19.5% | 39% | 28.2% | 19.5% | 14% | 23.5% | 16.5% | 26.4% |

SOURCES:

BC: Health Services and Support Facilities Subsector Collective Agreement, expires 31 March 2004.

Alberta: average of CUPE Multi Employer Agreement, expires 31 March 2004.

Saskatchewan: average of CUPE Sask and SEIU Saskatoon; both agreement expire 31 March 2004.

Manitoba: weighted average of these CUPE hospitals: Brandon, Central Region, Concordia, Grace, 7 Oaks, RDF, Health Sciences Centre (4yr and 26 mo agreements, expiring 30 April 2006 and 3 June 2004).

Ontario: average rates of Ontario CUPE (OCHU) and Independents (source: SALAD, CUPE research).

Quebec: CUPE (Quebec Federation of Labour) master collective agreement, expires 30 June 2003.

New Brunswick: average wage of the NB/CUPE Hospital Agreement, expires 30 June 2003, and NB/CUPE Nursing Homes Agreement, expires 15 October 2004.

Nova Scotia: CUPE rates: clerical, service, and healthcare agreements, expire 31 March 2004.

PEI: average of CUPE Master (expires 31 March 2004), IUOE 942 Master (expires 31 March 2003), and PEI Public Sector (expires 31 March 2003); Care Aide and LPN Rate ends 31 March 2003.

Newfoundland: CUPE/NAPE and Hospital Boards, expires 31 March 2004.

## APPENDIX THREE: MEASURING THE CURRENT VALUE OF PAST HEU HOUSEKEEPING WAGES

| *Year* | | *HEU hskpg wage (dollars)* | *Today's value of wage (dollars)* | *HEU kitchen wage (dollars)* | *Today's value of kitchen wage (dollars)* |
|---|---|---|---|---|---|
| 1954 | 16.8 | 0.83 | 5.88 | 0.95 | 6.73 |
| 1960 | 18.5 | 0.98 | 6.30 | 1.04 | 6.69 |
| 1964 | 19.6 | 1.15 | 6.98 | 1.27 | 7.71 |
| 1968 | 22.4 | 1.76 | 9.35 | 1.89 | 10.04 |
| 1972 | 26.1 | — | — | — | — |
| 1976 | 37.1 | 4.92 | 15.73 | — | — |
| 1980 | 52.4 | 7.37 | 16.68 | — | — |
| 1984 | 72.1 | 9.48 | 15.59 | — | — |
| 1988 | 84.8 | 10.93 | 15.29 | — | — |
| 1992 | 100 | 13.78 | 16.34 | 13.78 | 16.34 |
| 1996 | 105.9 | 15.93 | 17.84 | — | — |
| 2000 | 113.5 | 16.80 | 17.55 | — | — |
| 2002 | 118.6 | 17.77 | — | — | — |

NOTES: In 1974 the hours of work decreased to 37.5 hours/week from 40 hours/week.
In 1993 the hours of work decreased to 36 hours per week.
Prior to 1964 a "housekeeper" was called a "maid" and is now classified as BMW1.
The starting first-year rate was selected for the wage rates.
118.6 is used as the CPI reference for years 1971–2002 because the CPI nos. used are local (Vancouver). 119 is used as the CPI reference for calculating 1954–70 as the CPI nos. used are national (CDN).

## NOTES

1 Many voters understood this move as an attempt to convince women that the NDP would be better than the Liberals, but it was seen as a rather cynical attempt on the part of the NDP to bring in legislation that it should have passed much earlier in its mandate.

2 Trade unions that have been approached to enter into a "voluntary recognition agreement" in the hospital sector include the BCGEU, UFCW Local 1518, Hotel and Restaurant Employees' Local 40, United Steelworkers, CAW, SEIU, and RWU. None of these trade unions agreed to do this.

3 At the IWA's national convention in 2000, the existence of a Women's Committee was recognized for the first time by the constitution. Until 2002, when a woman became the first president of a local, Local 324 in Manitoba, no woman had ever been elected to a position that would entitle her to serve

on the National Executive Board. While a resolution was passed at the 2002 convention related to women, it was an organizational type of resolution. None dealt with substantive issues that are significant for women, such as pay equity or child care. The Women's Committee's objectives for 2000–01 were also related to IWA organizational goals; what is conspicuously absent from these goals is any recognition of women's issues that should be included in bargaining. The IWA Web site address is http://www.iwa.ca/hubpage.htm.

4 The auditor general found that the average staff turnover was higher among external contractors (40 per cent) compared with in-house staff (23 per cent).

# 6

# Crisis Tendencies in Social Reproduction: The Case of Ontario's Early Years Plan

LEAH F. VOSKO

In May 2001, in the face of growing emphasis on "the child" in social policy discourse and design, Ontario's minister responsible for children unveiled a new set of initiatives on early childhood development. Responding to escalating tensions in social reproduction, Ontario's first Early Years Plan included a range of programs targeting "children [zero to six years], caregivers and their parents" (Ontario 2002, 1). Its stated aim was to ensure that children are "physically and emotionally healthy, safe, secure and ready to learn," so that "they become responsible and contributing citizens" (1–2). The creation of Early Years Centres was a vital pillar of the Early Years Plan. These centres were to serve as clearing houses for community service and program information and to provide direct services "such as expert advice on parenting, information on developmental milestones, and organized programs and activities for parents and children" (4). Other initiatives under the Early Years Plan included programs promoting healthy pregnancy, birth, and infancy, parenting and family supports, and community supports. Yet the Early Years Plan was silent on the question of child care, a glaring omission given that the federal-provincial Early Childhood Development Agreement (ECDA, 2000) named child care a priority and given repeated calls by municipalities and child-care advocacy groups for increased funding for regulated child care in Ontario. The Early Years Plan thus symbolized a shift away from a model of policy design and delivery underpinned by a conception of early childhood development that recognized community responsibility for children (albeit limited) toward a more individualized and privatized model (Eichler 1997; Luxton and Vosko 1998).

This chapter pursues an analysis of the policies and practices emanating from Ontario's Early Years Plan from its inception in 2001 to 2005, with particular attention to the creation of Early Years Centres. I argue that the Early Years Plan exacerbated inequalities in the provision of early childhood development programs and services in Ontario by creating Early Years Centres targeting narrow constituencies of children, parents, and caregivers and, at the same time, failing to support high-quality, accessible, regulated child care in the province. The Early Years Plan represented one province's effort, a province led by a Conservative government at the inception of the plan, to mediate escalating tensions in social reproduction through a strategy of individualization, reprivatization, and familialization. By overtly neglecting child care, however, Ontario's Early Years Plan opened space for opposition and thereby positive material changes in this area: it galvanized criticism at the provincial and municipal levels, especially after a new provincial Liberal government came to power in 2003, as well as at the federal level, after a minority Liberal government joined forces with the New Democratic Party to pass the federal budget in 2005. The case of Ontario's Early Years Plan thus illustrates the paradoxical nature of crisis tendencies in social reproduction and the responses they engender.

The chapter unfolds in four parts. Part one defines some core concepts and develops the notion of "crisis tendencies" in social reproduction, with attention to both the Canadian situation and Ontario's effort at mediation in the 2001–05 period. Part two traces the evolution of federal-provincial collaboration on social policies centred on 'the child' with an emphasis on the federal-provincial Early Childhood Development Agreement (2000), which enabled the Early Years Plan to emerge by virtue of the unprecedented autonomy it granted to provinces and territories in funding, designing, and delivering early childhood development programs. Turning to the case study, part three examines Ontario's approach to the early years, sketching the evolution of the Early Years Plan and investigating the funding, design, and operation of Early Years Centres first under a Conservative and subsequently under a Liberal provincial government. The chapter concludes with a synthesis of Ontario's interventions into early learning and child care, highlighting the paradox underlying the Early Years Plan and identifying signs of positive change as well as persistent pitfalls.

## CONCEPTUAL BACKDROP

Ontario's Early Years Plan represents a state-driven effort to address crisis tendencies in social reproduction whose parameters are changing in the face of fundamental shifts in the gender order. Social reproduction[1] refers to the social processes and labour that go into the daily and generational maintenance of the population, and it is intimately linked to gender relations. In capitalism there is a tendency toward the separation of the site of procreation and daily and generational maintenance (the household) from "productive"[2] relations (waged work); in practice, this means that social reproduction is not directly structured by employers but is typically organized and performed in households by primarily women. This separation of production from social reproduction gives rise to an essential contradiction – the conflict between the standard of living of the workers[3] and the drive to make profits (McDowell 1991; Muszynzki 1996; Picchio 1992). The state's role is particularly crucial in mediating this contradiction or, put differently, limiting persistent crisis tendencies in social reproduction (Picchio 1992; Ursel 1992).

Crisis tendencies (Connell 1987, 158) are "dynamics which have the potential to transform and thus change in fundamental ways the conditions of future social practice." They are ever-present – and they hold both pitfalls and opportunities – but two broad sets of developments are fuelling their growth in Canada in the early twenty-first century (Vosko 2002b). First, dramatic shifts are occurring in the gender order, a historically constructed pattern of relationships between men and women, and hence in the gender regimes[4] of the institutions that give it shape (e.g., "the family," the labour market, and the state) (Connell 1987; see also Bezanson this volume). The gender regime inside "the family," for example, is transforming in myriad ways. The male breadwinner–female caregiver model no longer dominates even at a normative level, and multiple-earner households, where several household members are engaged in precarious employment, are gaining ascendancy (Fudge 1997; Vosko 2002b). A declining birth rate is accompanying this trend.[5] Changes in the structure of emotional attachment that challenge entrenched modes of organizing social reproduction also characterize the shifting gender regime inside "the family"; the growing legitimacy of same-sex partnerships is a case in point. The second broad set of developments relates to the decline of the Keynesian welfare state, and it entails the simultaneous withdrawal and reconfiguration of collective responsibility (Vosko 2002a). The Early Childhood Development Agreement (2000) represented an example of reconfiguration promoting highly uneven early childhood development services and programs at the provincial and territorial levels.[6]

States respond to tensions in social reproduction in various ways. Like crisis tendencies themselves, efforts at mediation are inherently neither regressive nor progressive. Still, the neo-liberal character of the federal government at the time that the Early Childhood Development Agreement was reached shaped efforts at mediation, as did the presence of a Conservative government in the province of Ontario, where social policy restructuring was characterized by both an emphasis on "self-sufficiency" and "independence" or *individualization* through waged work and an emphasis on conservative "family values" (Vosko 2002a). While the province's tax-based child care and child benefit policies reflected the government's commitment to achieving self-sufficiency through waged work and thereby individualization, Ontario's Early Years Plan resonated with the conservative family-values dimension of provincial social policy and thereby reprivatization and familialization, two aspects of privatization identified and defined by Fudge and Cossman in the introduction to their volume *Privatization, Law, and the Challenge to Feminism* that I employ in this case study. According to Fudge and Cossman (2002, 20), reprivatization is a process whereby public services – in this case child care and certain dimensions of early childhood development programs – are "reconstituted as private, that is, as more appropriately located in the private spheres of the market, the family, and/or charity."[7] Familialization, in turn, involves a process where public services are shifted to their "natural" location in the family (Fudge and Cossman 2002; see also Brodie 1994; Philipps 2002). An exploration of the Early Years Plan in operation, Ontario's first official plan under the banner of pan-Canadian social policy renewal around "the child," reveals the mutually reinforcing character of these strategies.

## FEDERAL-PROVINCIAL POLICIES TARGETING CHILDREN: LOCATING THE EARLY CHILDHOOD DEVELOPMENT AGREEMENT

In federal and provincial social policy, the renewed emphasis on "the child" dates to the mid-1990s, when the federal government replaced the Canada Assistance Plan (CAP), a system of federal-provincial cost-sharing for social policy, including for child-care services for "families in need" or "likely to become in need," with the Canada Health and Social Transfer (CHST), which rolled federal transfers for social assistance, health, and post-secondary education into one block grant. The CHST entailed retrenchment as a result of inadequate levels of block funding and reconfiguration as a result of the degree of autonomy granted to the provinces and territories in spending and policy design (Bashevkin 1998; Boychuk 1998; Vosko 2002a). It amounted to a movement away from the moderate Keynesianism of the early 1990s to a neo-liberal emphasis on employability and the devolution of federal responsibility for services. For example, the federal government spent $724 million annually on child care alone at the height of funding in the early 1990s, but federal funds earmarked for child care ended in 1996, resulting in the reduction or elimination of direct funding to child-care programs in most provinces (Boismenu and Jenson 1998; Doherty, Friendly, and Oloman 1998; White 2002, 106).[8] Whether separate health and social transfers, which came into effect in 2004, mitigate or exacerbate retrenchment or promote transparency, the explicit goal of such measures remains an open question.

At the same time as the CHST emerged, the federal government and the provinces reached agreement on two principal means through which the federal government would provide significant funds to the provinces to support children, an initiative involving increased tax-based benefits to low-income families and an early childhood development initiative: the National Child Benefit Supplement (NCBS) and the Early Childhood Development Initiative (ECDI).

On the tax side, introduced in 1997, the NCBS was constructed as a supplement to the basic benefit under the Canada Child Tax Benefit (CCTB) for low-income families. The only proviso that the federal government attached to the NCBS was that it be used to support low-income families, although provinces and territories were granted leeway in defining such families as broadly (or as narrowly) as they saw fit. The NCBS was organized around the following federal-provincial agreement: as the federal benefit increased, provinces and territories were permitted to decrease the benefits for social assistance recipients in the same amount. Where provinces opted to adopt this strategy, this clawback was to be made across the board for parents on social assistance by treating the NCBS as income to be deducted from their welfare entitlement. Provinces could then channel the funds accrued into supports for low-income families generally, with the objective of lowering the so-called welfare wall that inhibits social assistance recipients' movement into the labour force (Boismenu and Jenson 1998).[9] In exchange for increased payments to parents from the federal government through the supplement, provinces and territories agreed to direct the money subtracted from the provincial/territorial welfare cheques to support low-income families; however, they had complete control in determining the form of this support (e.g., income supports or services) (Canada 2002c). Notably, the government of Ontario neglected to use this discretion to augment child-care provision in the province, expecting children of parents in precarious jobs to be cared for by their neighbours and thereby heightening contradictions between policies directed at encouraging self-sufficiency through waged work (a goal of the federal government in crafting the NCBS) and those fostering reprivatization and familialization (e.g., Ontario's Early Years Plan under the ECDI, described below).

On the early child development side, initiated in 2001, the ECDA was nested in the Social Union Framework Agreement, 2000 (SUFA), a framework agreement between the federal government and every province and territory (save Quebec) that embodied collaborative federalism in that it advanced the principle that the federal government should not intrude into areas of provincial jurisdiction without provincial consent. Substantively, the ECDA provided the blueprint for carrying out the National Children's Agenda (NCA 1999), a federal-provincial agreement (also accepted by every party except Quebec) whose premise was that "what happens to children when they are very young shapes their health and well-being throughout their lifetime ... [and that] healthy children grow into healthy, successful adults, who will shape the future" (Canada 1997).

The ECDA set out four program areas for "investment in children": healthy pregnancy, birth, and infancy; parental and family supports; community supports; and early childhood development, learning, and care. Through its Early Childhood Development Initiative, the federal government contributed funds (a repackaged mixture of preexisting and new money amounting to $23 billion over the first phase of the initiative) to four sets of programs in accordance with the priorities of the ECDA as well as transfer payments. Federal support went into the following areas: early childhood development programs for children and families at risk, especially for at-risk Aboriginal children living off-reserve; social, health, and economic programs for First Nations and Inuit children and families; research, information, and education; and early childhood development–related income support measures (Canada 2002b, 5–6).

The federal government also committed itself to providing $2.2 billion in transfer funding to the provinces and territories over the five years, beginning with a transfer of $300 million in the first year of the ECDI (2001/02) and rising to $500 million by the fifth year (2005/06) (Canada 2004). Yet provincial ECDI transfer dollars contributed only marginally to the costs of delivering services in the four core areas. For example, the first year's total federal funding allocation under the ECDI was about the same as the federal government was spending on child care alone when the CAP ended in 1995 and the ECDI gave provinces complete discretion over their funding allocation (Rothman 2001, 92). It was "designed to allow provinces to pursue different children's policies based on ideology and financial resources, not to 'ensure access to basic social programs of reasonably comparable quality,'" as the SUFA provides (Friendly 2001, 80).

The ECDI only required that provinces and territories and the federal government invest in the four areas and report annually on their investments. No further direction was given on the implementation, design, or substance of early childhood development programs and services. One outcome was that some provinces used a portion of their allocation to enhance regulated child care (e.g., Newfoundland, Nova Scotia, New Brunswick, Manitoba, and Saskatchewan),[10] while others (e.g., Ontario) did not allocate any funds to child care. Predictably, therefore, the introduction of the ECDI corresponded with a decline in total funds going to child care in Ontario from $564 million in the early 1990s to $470 million in 2001 (Friendly, Beach, and Turiano 2003). This decline resulted in a $19 million drop in total provincial funding for regulated care between 1998 and 2001 alone (Friendly, Beach, and Turiano 2003, 11). Despite the significant numbers of children under twelve with mothers in the labour force (1,325,400 in 2001) and the high percentage of single mothers receiving social assistance and/or living below the low income cut-off, recurring funding for wage grants and regulated child care for those enrolled in employment programs or Ontario Works also dropped precipitously over this period (Friendly, Beach, and Turiano 2003). In consistency with the NCBS, the ECDI gave provinces and territories the leeway to craft initiatives with vastly different emphases, including, in the case of Ontario, early childhood development initiatives fostering individualization, reprivatization, and familialization.

## ONTARIO'S APPROACH TO THE EARLY YEARS

Ontario's response to the ECDI was framed by, on the one hand, provincial tax-based measures targeting "families with children" and, on the other, initiatives in early childhood development dating to the Conservative government's rise to power in the mid-1990s. The province's early childhood development strategy between 2001 and 2005 mirrored the federal approach, although with a more conservative family-values cast.

On the tax side, with the election of a provincial Conservative government, benefits to low-income families became more targeted by the late 1990s. For example, the province introduced the Ontario Child Care Supplement for Working Families in 1998, a tax measure that used funds clawed back from the NCBS to provide modest child-care support through the tax system. But this tax-based benefit was closer to a targeted work and training income supplement than a genuine support for child care since eligibility was contingent on labour-market earnings or participation in training and since families could receive the supplement whether or not they had any child-care expenses (Ontario Coalition for Better Child Care 2003, 7). Following a similar logic, the province also amended the Day Nurseries Act in 2000 to allow child-care fee subsidies to flow directly to parents "in need" to enable them to pay for unregulated programs after an independently commissioned study found a shortage of child-care spaces to be a major obstacle in job placement under Ontario Works (Vosko 2002a).

In line with the NCA, the province also developed "new" approaches to early child development in this period. The roots of the Early Years Plan date to 1999, when an early years study commissioned by the province tabled its recommendations, when the government announced five demonstration projects experimenting with early childhood development programming, and when the Early Years Challenge Fund (which later became a key component of the Early Years Plan) was established.

*Reversing the Real Brain Drain: Early Years Study* (1999), prepared by Margaret McCain and Fraser Mustard, was foremost among these initiatives. This report provided a blueprint for improving early child development programs and services in Ontario. It advanced a rationale for "investing" more public funds in children aged zero to six based on neuroscientific research on early childhood development and socio-economic factors pertinent to development (McCain and

Mustard 1999, 122). The report's recommendations were too numerous and too complex to detail here; however, they included recommendations for wide-ranging initiatives to support early child development, from increased parental and maternity leave and benefits and "family-friendly" workplaces to tax incentives for community information networks. One of the report's main proposals was the creation of Child Development and Parenting Centres sensitive to local needs and cultural and linguistic diversity and responsive to the "*child care* needs of parents at home full-time, and those who are employed in the workforce on a casual, part-time or full-time basis" (McCain and Mustard 1999, 160; emphasis added).

Ontario's approach to the early years between 2001 and 2005 took some of these proposals forward but in a different direction from what its authors intended.[11] For example, the province launched Ontario's Promise in November 2000. Inspired by Colin Powell's "America's Promise," this initiative promoted public-private partnerships and volunteerism as a means of fulfilling five promises to children – a healthy start, an adult who cares, safe spaces to learn and grow, the tools to succeed, and a chance to make a difference. Shortly thereafter Ontario also introduced the Early Years Plan.

## *The Early Years Plan*

Although it spent $162 million on early years programming in 2000/01, Ontario first tabled its Early Years Plan only in November 2002.[12] Drafted to fulfill the federal government's basic requirements for securing funding under the ECDA, this report set out the Early Years Plan in a single paragraph. It asserted: "Ontario's Early Years Plan builds on existing partnerships, programs and services to improve the foundation for lifelong health, well-being and learning of children. The focus is on Ontario's 850,000 children from the prenatal period to age six, and their parents" (Ontario 2002, 1).

At an aggregate level, Ontario directed the bulk of its funding up to 2002 to the first three areas identified in the ECDA. For 2001/02, the largest funding allocation went to programs devoted to strengthening early childhood development, learning, and care, followed by those promoting improved parenting and family supports. Funds to programs directed at healthy pregnancy, birth, and infancy included supports for pre- and postnatal health initiatives, such as programs for pregnant women with addictions and children with fetal alcohol syndrome. Funds for strengthening community supports included mainly research initiatives, such as a perinatal and child health survey and "the collection and analysis of data needed to track progress in improving early years programs and undertake future planning" (Ontario 2002, 3). The third group of programs fell in the category of improving parenting and family supports. This group included support for programs for children with developmental disabilities and other health-related problems (e.g., services for children with autism) and programs tied to social assistance, such as the Learning, Earning and Parenting Program of Ontario Works. Funding to Early Years Centres and the Early Years Challenge Fund also fell into this group.

In 2001/02, funding allocated to these two related initiatives under the ECDI amounted to $45.6 million ($30.2 million for Early Years Centres and $15.4 million for the Early Years Challenge Fund), 40 per cent of the total annual funding allocated to the province (i.e., $114 million). In February 2003, in the wake of the federal budget and Ontario's reluctant participation in a new multilateral framework for early learning and child care, the province announced that it would provide $46 million in supplementary funding to Early Years Centres that were either in existence or through the approval process administered by the Ministry of Community and Social Services, funds previously unspent under the ECDI (Ontario 2002–03).

### *The Early Years Centres*

Ontario's Early Years Centres were designed to be "one-stop shops" where parents or caregivers were to either be referred to or provided with services to support them in their parenting roles (Canadian Child Care Federation 2001a, 35–6). They were created to promote parental responsibility and individualized care by parents or caregivers. After a short demonstration project phase, forty-two centres opened in 2001/02 and a further sixty-one opened by the end of 2003 (Ontario 2004, ii). In initiating the Early Years Plan, the province aimed ultimately to establish one Early Years Centre per riding; these entities could or might not be new sites but were to pull together existing facilities. Some Early Years Centres developed under the plan were new entities. Others were located in schools. In still other cases, existing family resource centres and child-care resource centres became either Early Years Centres or "satellites," raising concern over their long-term capacity to deliver services, such as assistance in finding child care, consistent with their original mandate (Moody 2002). For example, in one riding in Niagara (Erie-Lincoln), a family resource centre (Port Cares in Erie-Lincoln) became an Early Years Centre, and in another (St Catharines) the Walker YMCA became host to a centre.

*The Charity-Driven Funding Model*

Early Years Centres initially received $500,000 annually for providing "core services," and after February 2003 each centre received supplementary funding of $250,000 annually for the remainder of the ECDI (Ontario 2002, 8–9). At their inception, centres were expected to seek support for their remaining services, and they were eligible for funding from municipal and federal governments and private sponsors as well as provincial funding through Ontario's Promise and the Early Years Challenge Fund.

Many Early Years Centres acquired supplementary funding indirectly from the Early Years Challenge Fund, through community-based projects falling under their auspices. The Early Years Challenge Fund was a prototypical example of reprivatization, whereby supports formerly provided directly by the state are located in the sphere of charity. It operated on a match-funded basis by funding 'new' community initiatives on the assumption that they would ultimately self-fund (Ontario 2002, 2). It provided up to $30 million dollars annually to community-based projects to match funds (direct funding or in-kind contributions) from business, community organizations, and other levels of government. Notably, the fund matched "market rates" for professional services, space, and equipment but only $12/an hour[13] for volunteer work of any sort. To receive funding, a community group had to develop a project fulfilling the priorities of a local Early Years Action Plan and, ideally, associated with the work of an existing centre. Early Years Challenge Fund projects also had to deliver services to children aged zero to six and their families, secure matching funds and written confirmation of community contributions, name a lead agency in an incorporated body, provide services eligible for funding, establish partnerships with other agencies, and provide "accessible and barrier free" services (Ontario 2002, 3).

Since the Early Years Challenge Fund provided one-time-only funding, applications also had to demonstrate how programs would become autonomous (e.g., through user fees). The province also required "sustainability plans" addressing how services would be integrated with other initiatives under the ECDI, describing fundraising plans, and listing partnerships. The Early Years Challenge Fund provided seed funding for community projects for an average of only two years.

Initial program guidelines cast United Way agencies and the Canadian Centre for Philanthropy as suitable community or non-profit sector partners. Consequently, initiatives formerly funded by Children's Services had to seek support from registered charities, agencies, or private sector sponsors. Communities also had to find institutional homes for their initiatives in agencies deemed to be suitable by the province, such as service clubs, church groups, private sector groups, resource programs (e.g., family resource programs), libraries, and non-profit organizations (Ontario 2002, 8).

Of the over 526 projects funded under the Early Years Challenge Fund between 2000 and 2006, none received funding for regulated child care.[14] Many such projects delivered parenting and caregiving programs (e.g., training fathers in early child development and parenting issues and providing workshops for seniors who are caregivers), literacy and numeracy workshops (e.g., providing resources to francophone families for the development of early literacy and numeracy for children with special needs), and prenatal, birth, and postpartum services. For example, projects funded by the Early Years Challenge Fund in Peel Region ranged from "Parenting Education for Punjabi Fathers," delivered by Family Services of Peel Region and the "raise a reader" program at the Brampton Four Corners Library, to a twenty-six-week program for parents to learn employment skills, delivered by Pathway Non-Profit Community Development Inc. at the Arbour Mills Parent-Child Centre (Peel Early Years 2003). To receive funding through the Early Years Challenge Fund, all projects were required to fall under one of its three programming streams: community (i.e., projects with a local focus), Aboriginal, or francophone (Ontario 2001, 26; Ontario 2002, 6).

## *"For Parents/Caregivers and Their Children": Early Years Centres in Operation*

While Early Years Centres often served as venues for specialized programs funded through public-private partnerships, the province's use of core funding through the ECDI shaped their design. All centres were required to have the same name, signs, and visual identity. All centres reported to the minister of Community, Family and Children's Services and operated along a common administrative structure. Each centre was led by a volunteer "community champion," a leader in early years services in the community who was nominated by the community and approved by the ministry. In plans for Early Years Centres, the role of the community champion was to organize and lead a community-planning process and to create a steering committee of community partners charged with creating a centre in consultation with the ministry. Planning involved identifying a site for the Early Years Centre (as well as a lead agency), outlining capital costs, defining services to be delivered, and devising a coordination structure. Upon approval by the ministry, Early Years Centres normally operated in or in close proximity to a lead agency, but they were governed by an autonomous steering committee headed by the local community champion.[15]

All Early Years Centres were required to employ a literacy specialist and staff to monitor and gather data on early years initiatives,[16] and each centre was mandated to deliver the following "core services":

- early learning activities
- parenting resources and training
- pre- and postnatal resources and information
- information about and links to other local early years services
- the services of early literacy specialists to work with early years practitioners and community organizations to promote literacy
- outreach services
- a speakers' bureau
- volunteer coordination services

Centre staff were also required to gather data and monitor the effectiveness of the community's early years services as well as their impact on the province's child development outcomes (Ontario 2001, 6).

Rather than respond to population- and community-specific needs, Early Years Centres were designed to meet the needs of the "whole community." According to the "Guidelines for Communities," meeting the needs of the "whole community" amounted to the application of an aggregate approach; all Early Years Centres were to deliver the identical set of core services on the basis of identical resources (Ontario 2001, 26). Their hallmark was standardization, where the norm of the service recipient was narrowly conceived around the white, English-speaking male breadwinner–female caregiver household. The design of the Early Years Centres thus contrasted sharply with the proposals of the *Early Years Study*. McCain and Mustard (2002,

32) made the following statement in responding to the creation of these centres: "The Early Years Centres put in place by the provincial government do not adequately embrace concepts set out in the report. They are more centrally accountable to the government public service than their communities … [Centralized control] does not readily enable communities to build ECD and parenting centers and runs the risk of bureaucratic programming which we, in our report, said should be avoided." The *Early Years Study* called for universal accessibility to centres – not a standardized approach – supplemented by targeted programs funded by the Early Years Challenge Fund or other parts of the ECDI (e.g., programs for children with autism).

With the exception of a few francophone centres and centres providing programming for aboriginal communities, Early Years Centres operated in English. Accessibility was equated narrowly with geography: the "one centre per riding" model took neither varying population density nor demographics into account, with significant consequences for large urban centres. At the same time, despite the call by McCain and Mustard (1999, 176–7, 180) for operating hours suitable for parents engaged in paid work, many Early Years Centres ran their main programming during the standard workday. Some provided programs for households with multiple earners, but these were treated as "special programs," suggesting that these household forms are in some way exceptional. Programs operating outside the standard workday included those for fathers, such as "Saturday morning fathers breakfast/playtime" (Simcoe North) and "Dads 'n' Fun for children 0–6 years," an evening fathers' group (North Bay). Two assumptions underpinned such programs: that most children aged zero to six live in nuclear families where only one parent is engaged in paid employment and where the other parent cares for the children at home and, second, that the role of the parent in the labour force is to assist with early learning, parenting, and care, while the primary (read female) caregiver is responsible for early childhood development.

This effort at mediating crisis tendencies in social reproduction embraces familialization with a racialized and gendered twist. In the development phase of the Early Years Plan, the province acknowledged that a large segment of children in the target population for Early Years Centres (i.e., children aged zero to six receiving individualized care) were cared for by either non-parent relatives or paid caregivers. For this reason, most Early Years Centres provided caregiver drop-ins as well as caregiving classes, including drop-ins for grandparents, such as the Barrie Early Years Centre's "Grands, Parenting Again Support Group."

Together with the Ontario Child Care Supplement for Working Families, this type of programming was designed to supplement individualized (and unregulated) child-care provision of various sorts (paid and unpaid). Moreover, the approach to early childhood development focused on educating parents and caregivers to be *better* parents and caregivers, rather than on delivering programs to children collectively (see also Fox this volume). In the final phase of implementing the Early Years Centres, the target audience grew to include child-care providers, including those working at institutionally based daycare centres and those running home daycares; however, child-care providers were primarily offered the use of equipment and resource-borrowing privileges, where centres include resource libraries that provide curriculum kits and other information on programming.

An inventory of programs offered at Early Years Centres between 2001 and 2005 reveals strategies of individualization and familialization – in particular, informed "curriculum design." Services offered by most centres fell into three areas: health promotion, parenting and caregiving, and child development. Health promotion programs included breastfeeding clinics and supports, cooking classes for parents, and dental checkups for children. Individual and "family" health and nutrition was the principle focus of these initiatives, rather than community health and well-being. Parenting programs, in turn, covered topics ranging from "stress relief" and literacy and numeracy training for parents and caregivers to workshops on sibling rivalry and baby massage. Finally, child development programs addressed behavioural issues and emotional expression. Core programs and services took the nuclear family as the central unit of daily and intergenerational reproduction for facilitating early learning and development and the primary locus of care.

While a broad notion of community health and well-being was absent in core curriculum, community commitment was central to the coordination of Early Years Centres from their inception. They were designed to be run by volunteers – the community champion was expected to be a volunteer responsible for a volunteer steering committee and coordinating volunteer services in early childhood development in a given riding. The centres were thus positioned as hubs of gendered volunteerism.

## *The Place of Child Care*

The absence of high-quality, accessible, regulated child care in Early Years Centres as well as in the broader vision of early childhood development programming in Ontario's Early Years Plan under the ECDA was striking. Where child care was made available at Early Years Centres, it involved short-term child-minding, normally by volunteers. In some instances, child care was available on site, but in such instances it was a product of initiatives outside the Early Years Plan. For example, some Early Years Centres operated in schools that had daycare facilities, and others operated in non-profit or even public agencies providing child care, but neither core funding nor the Early Years Challenge Fund supported child-care provision. Ontario went on record for its commitment to an "integrated early childhood development strategy," but in practice, this strategy did not take child care to be integral to early childhood development. Rather, the ideal place of early childhood learning was assumed to be the nuclear family and its class- and "race"-mediated forms.

This neglect of child care in the Early Years Plan did not go unchallenged, however. The City of Toronto called on the province to increase funding for child care and to facilitate the democratic administration of funding from the ECDI. For example, in December 2001, Toronto City Council adopted the following recommendations of the city's Community Services Committee: "that the City request the Federal Government to: (a) in future, attach genuine criteria on the use of funding installments under the Early Childhood Development Fund Initiatives, in order to prevent misuse of such funds by the provincial government (b) transfer funds directly to municipalities with child care services and family resource centres" (Toronto 2001, 14). Concerns about accountability and locally appropriate programming lay behind these requests. When provincial officials were developing the Early Years Plan, city officials were concerned about its implications for Toronto's Children's Strategy. From the outset, Toronto indicated that it would only agree to the ECDI if the province recognized and fulfilled the city's needs for increased child-care funding and its existing child-care plan and children's strategy and if it developed clear guidelines for community organizations. Yet when the province tabled the Early Years Plan, the city discovered that the plan not only removed municipal autonomy while increasing municipal responsibility but failed to address low levels of child-care funding. Toronto City Council also criticized the province for failing to fund a sufficient number of Early Years Centres to serve its population, for designing centres as replacements for some long-standing family resource programs, and/or for narrowing the mandate of family resource centres, especially their child-care-finding services. Indeed, City Council minutes and *Toronto's Report Card on Child Care* (2002) drew attention to the misfit between the standardized approach of the Early Years Centres and Toronto's needs, given the city's population size and demographics.

The province largely failed to respond to the city's concerns in 2001/02, leading the municipality to escalate its campaign. In August 2002 City Council provided extensive data on Toronto's unequal share of Early Years Centres based on a per capita funding formula. It also demonstrated that none of the programs funded under the Early Years Plan were those identified as priorities in Toronto's Action Plan for Children or its Children's Services Plan. One of the city's most vehement objections to the Early Years Plan revolved around the province's failure to use the ECDI to fund any of Toronto's First Duty projects. Operating in the 2002–05 period at five sites across the Greater Toronto Area, First Duty projects were among the clearest examples of integrated early childhood development service and program delivery in existence during the ECDI. Bringing together child care, early child development programs, literacy training, health promotion, and parental supports, they drew on existing community resources, linked institutions such as family resource centres and schools, and were supported by public-non-profit sector partnerships (Toronto First Duty Research Team 2004). First Duty projects aimed to provide early childhood development programs appropriate to communities – defined broadly to include high-quality, accessible, regulated child care – and they were endorsed by, among others, Margaret McCain (Coffey and McCain 2002, 26). From their inception, the main challenge faced by First Duty projects was the need to rely on a significant amount of time-limited charitable funding. Toronto First Duty's support of collective child care, its broad vision of community, its rejection of standardization, and its discomfort with a heavy reliance on unpaid volunteers clearly influenced the failure of the Challenge Fund to support this initiative.

In its Moving Forward Action Plan as well as in the *Report Card on Children* (2002), Toronto criticized the province for its failure to support such integrated initiatives as Toronto First Duty, the disproportionate support for Early Years Centres and their standardized design, and the constraints embedded in the criteria for receiving support through the Early Years Challenge Fund. The city stated boldly:

Ontario's decision to fund the Early Learning Centres as its sole early childhood development initiative while refusing to increase funding for child care is contradictory. Combining these centres with a stable, properly funded child care system would make them more valuable to families. By not integrating the Early Years Centres with licensed child care, the Province has made its own initiative less effective and has ignored the advice of its own experts, Fraser Mustard and Margaret McCain. (Toronto 2003a, 13)

In 2003 city officials reported further that regulated child care was in crisis in Toronto. Between 1999 and 2002 the province had cut the annual base funding for Toronto's regulated child-care programs by $11.8 million (an accumulated impact of over $35 million), leaving the city with its lowest number of subsidized child-care spaces since 1992 (Toronto 2003a, 13). The city compensated for the provincial funding cutback (of $11.8 million annually). However, child-care spaces were still lost. The municipal funding available was insufficient to meet the growing demand and the increasing costs of child-care provision resulting from inflation, provincial pay-equity obligations (which were passed on to the city and which most centres had to meet by increasing fees to unsubsidized clients), and the maintenance of physical infrastructure. At a time when the waiting list for subsidized care was approximately 15,000 in Toronto in 2002 (this figure represented 13.6 per cent of the city's children living below the low-income cut-off), the city lost 1,616 subsidized spaces in 2002, and it lost a further 1,800 in 2003 (Toronto 2002, 17, 38; Toronto 2003c).[17] A major survey conducted by the city in 2003 found that "the preferred choice of most families who require child care outside the home is licensed care ... only 10 per cent of families using informal care would continue to do so if they had another choice" – strong criticism of the province's resort to tax-based initiatives for low-income families, such as the Ontario Child Care Supplement for Working Families (Toronto 2003b, 3–4). Backed by these data, the City of Toronto condemned the province for failing to recognize the dominance of multiple-earner households, the high concentration of the province's population in its urban centres, and the varying demographics of Ontario's population. The official position of the City of Toronto revealed further that, ideologically, the Early Years Plan was at odds with any notion that high-quality, accessible child care is good for children childhood development and for communities.

## *Opportunities in a Period of Crisis*

Despite the protestations of municipalities such as Toronto, the Early Years Plan remained in operation until 2006, and it had lasting effects on the provision of early childhood development programs (Ontario 2004). Crisis tendencies do, however, afford opportunities. In 2003 Ontarians elected a Liberal government after nearly a decade of successive Conservative governments. Shortly thereafter, a minority Liberal government also came to power federally.

Displeased with the highly variable usage of ECDI monies and responding to sustained pressure from the child care movement, the City of Toronto, and developments in Quebec, the federal government that year imposed greater discipline on provinces and territories in introducing new funds through the federal budget. The 2003 federal budget included a $935 million increase in funding targeted specifically to regulated child care over five years. The Multilateral Framework on Early Learning and Child Care (2003), which fell under the SUFA, grew out of this promise. Agreed to by all the first ministers responsible for social services (save Quebec), its objective was to promote early childhood development and to support the participation of parents in employment or training by improving access to affordable, high-quality early learning and child-care programs and services. The agreement identified regulated early learning and child care programs for children aged zero to six years as the two key areas of "investment." It was remarkable not only in its identification of child care as a priority area but in its specification that child-care programs funded under this umbrella be regulated. To make its objectives clear to provinces and territories failing to use its ECDI transfer dollars to maintain pre-CHST child-care funding, the agreement articulated several principles and provided examples of how they should be interpreted. The principles underpinning the agreement were that child care be available and accessible, affordable, high-quality, inclusive, and flexible (i.e., allowing for parental choice). Examples of initiatives that supported affordability and accessibility noted in the agreement were enhanced fee subsidies and increased child-care spaces respectively.

The identification of regulated child care as a priority area for the federal government was a direct response to Ontario's conduct under the ECDI. However, partly to persuade the province to sign on to the multilateral agreement, the definition of regulated care grew weaker and weaker as the agreement evolved. In the final analysis, it defined regulated programs as "programs that meet the quality standards that are established and monitored by provincial governments," giving the provinces and territories significant discretion in defining regulated child care (Canada 2003, 1; see also Chow 2003). Two other key weaknesses characterized the agreement. First, it lacked enforcement mechanisms; if a province or territory failed to comply with its terms, the only option for the federal government and the other provinces and territories was to introduce tougher controls in the next round of negotiations. Second, it extended minimal funding to provinces and territories, even relative to the ECDI. When the multilateral framework was introduced in March 2003, the federal government announced that it would provide $900 million dollars over five years to support provincial and territorial investments in early learning and child care. In the subsequent Budget in 2004, the federal government provided an additional $150 million over five years. Ontario's share of funding under the multilateral framework was $9.7 million in 2003/04,[18] $58.2 million in 2004/05, $87.4 million 2005/06, $116.8 in 2006/07, and $136.6 in 2007/08 (Canada-Ontario 2005). Until 2005, Ontario used its funding exclusively to restore child-care facilities, that is, to repair facilities, furnishings, and equipment at child-care centres rather than to expand the availability of subsidized child care (Ontario 2005).

The Multilateral Agreement on Early Learning and Child Care nevertheless represented the architecture for a national child-care strategy for future governments to build on.[19] Despite its weak definition of regulated child care, the lack of enforcement mechanisms, and the limited degree of funding, it signified a renewed commitment of the federal government to funding social services, specifically services for children, and it set the stage for more significant commitments to child-care services by the federal Liberals in the 2004 election campaign and the 2005 federal budget.

Changes subsequent to the Multilateral Agreement on Early Learning and Child Care validate this claim. Although they reinforced the model of collaborative federalism embraced under the ECDI, federal interventions in the Throne Speech of October 2004 and the federal budget of 2005 offered meaningful substantive responses to the child-care shortage in most provinces and territories. In the 2005 budget, the government committed $5 billion to build a framework for an early learning and child-care initiative with the provinces and territories over a five-year period (Canada 2005, 5–6). Of this $5 billion, $700 million was earmarked for third-party trust, for provinces and territories to draw on, on a per capita basis, in 2005–06 while a framework was devised; however, like the ECDI, no accountability or monitoring mechanisms were attached to this trust. Another $100 million was earmarked for First Nations living on reserves, and yet another $100 million allocated to research. The budget also promised provinces and territories that they would receive a total of $650 million for early learning and child care in 2006–07 and $1.15 billion in successive years through 2009/10 (Canada 2005, 5–6). This future funding was conditional on the creation of a common federal-provincial/territorial framework for the provision of early learning child care (Canada 2005). In the interim, however, a coalition between the federal Liberal government and the opposition New Democrats allowed the 2005 federal budget to pass by a narrow margin (a development critical to making child care a funding priority), enabling the federal government to negotiate bilateral agreements with various provinces and territories, including Ontario.

In spring 2005 the governments of Canada and Ontario negotiated Moving Forward on Early Learning and Child Care, an agreement in principle on early learning and child care. The articulation of several common principles and the commitment to a "shared national vision for early learning and child care" were noteworthy in this agreement (Canada-Ontario 2005, 3). Indeed, the parties committed to "incremental, predictable, and sustained investments" in quality, universally inclusive, accessible, and developmental early learning and child care (Canada-Ontario 2005, 3). Under this agreement, the quality principle was designed to be sufficiently broad to enable Ontario to use funds to support, among other things, developmentally appropriate programs for children and to strengthen and enhance provincial regulation and monitoring of early learning and child care (Canada-Ontario 2005, 4). The principle that early learning and child care must be "universally inclusive," in turn, was defined rather generally, allowing the province to use federal monies to, among other possibilities, strengthen programming and supports for children's cultural, linguistic, and/or special needs and supports for developmental education (Canada-Ontario 2005, 4). Similarly, the principle of accessibility, as articulated in the agreement, was expansive enough to allow the province to allocate funds to develop "innovative approaches to service provision in rural and underserved areas" and "flexible approaches that address a range of family and employment circumstances," in addition to enhancing operational funds and/or fee subsidies, a long-standing priority for child-care advocates (Canada-Ontario 2005, 4). Finally, through the developmental principle, the agreement permitted Ontario to use federal funds to strengthen the learning and developmental components of early learning and child care through creating safe, secure, nurturing, and stimulating early learning environments (Canada-Ontario 2005, 4).

In return for federal funds, bilateral agreements, such as the agreement in principle between Canada and Ontario, required provinces to contribute funds for regulated early learning and child care. In the case of Ontario, the provincial government committed to "develop and enhance its regulated early learning and childcare system" toward achieving three objectives (Canada-Ontario 2005, 5). Its first objective of measurable and demonstrable improvements in the quality and developmental component of early learning and child care amounted to a commitment to develop an integrated early learning program for young children, strategies to improve quality in early learning and care settings, and the establishment of a college of early childhood educators to develop and monitor professional standards. Its second objective of better access to early learning and child care that is universally inclusive entailed commitments to increase the availability and affordability of regulated early learning and child-care spaces and to address the child-care needs of Aboriginal and francophone children in the province. Finally, its objective of improving services in French for francophone children involved a broad commitment to support French language and culture in Ontario.

To fulfill these objectives, the province agreed that funds provided by the federal government would be invested in regulated early learning and child-care programs and services for children aged zero to six, although the agreement maintained a watered-down definition of regulated programs. At the same time, signaling a significant advance, the federal government and the province concurred on a common definition of early learning and child-care programs and services eligible for funding: "those supporting direct care and early learning for children in settings such as *child care centres, family child care homes, preschools and nursery schools*" (Canada-Ontario 2005, 5; emphasis added). Simultaneously, in accordance with the federal government's requirement for provincial/territorial action plans and annual reporting, the province announced its Best Start Plan.

Ontario's response to developing integrated, accessible early learning and child-care services for young children, the initial Best Start Plan introduced in 2005 aimed ultimately to provide care and learning supports for children aged zero to twelve. However, in its first phase (i.e., its first five years), it was designed to target children aged three to six exclusively. In addition to activities such as creating neighbourhood "early learning and care hubs," a chief objective of the plan was to establish integrated early learning and care programs for children in preschool and junior and senior kindergarten through providing "wrap around" child care from September to June. Despite the success of pilot projects such as Toronto First Duty, funded initially for a three-year period ending in 2005, the Best Start Plan did not envision seamless programming, effectively supporting fragmented care. As the Ontario Coalition for Better Childcare (2005, 2–5) observed, the plan also retained the user pay/subsidy distinction, was silent on the needs of children aged zero to three and six to twelve, neglected to introduce protections against the expansion of commercial child care, and did not articulate the four interrelated principles named in the federal-provincial agreement in principle. Furthermore, it made no mention of the provincial Liberal government's pre-election commitment to allocate funds remaining under the ECDA to regulated child care (Ontario Coalition for Better Childcare 2005, 5).

On the positive side, developments in 2004 and 2005, especially the 2005 federal budget, amounted to federal-provincial agreement on some common principles. Still, several cautionary notes merit emphasis. Agreements in principle, such as the one signed by the governments of Canada and Ontario, amounted neither to the creation of a pan-Canadian child-care system based on quality, inclusivity, universality, accessibility, and developmental programming nor to a plan for a provincial child-care system of a smaller scale, although the gradual creation of a pan-Canadian system remains a central objective for child-care advocates (Child Care Advocacy Association of Canada 2005). Such agreements also failed to guarantee publicly provided and delivered services and programs, another long-standing goal of the child-care movement.

Reflecting collaborative federalism, the form of the federal-provincial agreements that emerged in 2005 resembled those negotiated under the ECDA. They did not address provincial accountability sufficiently; in them, provincial governments agreed to abide by common principles but they were required only to report to citizens and not to

Parliament. As Cameron (2004a, 3) demonstrates, "intergovernmental agreements are useful as a preliminary to legislation and in the past bilateral agreements between the federal and a provincial government have been important instruments for implementing legislation. They are not, however, a substitute for legislation. The problem with intergovernmental agreements is that they are simply political accords ... that can be broken more easily than they are made."[20] What is thus required, according to Cameron, is a Canada Child Care Act akin to the Canada Health Act. The case of the ECDA, especially the Early Years Plan that materialized under the ECDI in Ontario, gives credence to this argument. Like their counterparts under the ECDI, agreements in principle announced in 2005 required provinces to table early learning and child-care plans, not to demonstrate how public funds were used to support long-term goals. Moreover, they failed to deliver funding sufficient to build a child-care system over the long term, deficiencies that only federal legislation could remedy. In many ways, the promise of an infusion of funds into early learning and child care by the federal government and the provinces from 2005 to 2010 represented a positive step in the provision of child care. But the medium of change – that is, channelling change through federal-provincial framework agreements – left considerable discretion to provinces and territories. Despite a commitment to increased money for child care and the establishment of common principles, arguably monumental gains, striking similarities characterized the political accords that emerged in 2005 and the ECDI. These similarities are notable given that the ECDI paved the way for provincial/territorial early years plans with vastly different emphases. They illustrate vividly that who is in power provincially shapes implementation profoundly in the absence of clear federal standards.

## CONCLUSION

The state's power to mediate crisis tendencies in social reproduction holds both opportunities and dangers (Connell 1987, 158). Like crises themselves, efforts at mediation are neither inherently progressive nor inherently regressive. Ontario's Early Years Plan nevertheless represented a troubling response to the crisis tendencies in social reproduction in the province, one that was fuelled by individualization, reprivatization, and familialization and that took sharp expression in the child care crisis. The neo-liberal cast of the Canadian state shaped Ontario's post-CHST early childhood development strategy, and collaborative federalism allowed the Early Years Plan to flourish.

The Early Years Plan and its central components materialized through openings at multiple levels within the Canadian state. At the level of federal-provincial/territorial policies targeting children, decentralization – first through the CHST (and later the CST and the CHT), the SUFA, and the ECDA – amounted to a lack of standards. In the arena of early childhood development, this absence allowed provinces and territories to institutionalize individual 'choice' through the extension of tax-based benefits to families with children and to shift formerly public responsibility for early childhood development programs and services onto households, under-resourced communities, and charities. At the level of provincial-municipal relations in Ontario, standardization in the delivery of early childhood development programs cultivated programs, services, and institutions that generated particular outcomes, such as Early Years Centres dependent upon volunteers and charitable funding and all its implied obligations. Finally, at the level of communities (defined geographically), the very structure of Early Years Centres defied an inclusive notion of "community" and opposed a conception of early childhood development that recognized community responsibility for children. In these ways and at these multiple levels, the Early Years Plan endorsed a highly individualized and privatized model of early childhood development services and programs.

Yet, beginning in 2003, openings for contesting Ontario's effort to mediate crisis tendencies in social reproduction surfaced. Toronto City Council (2003a, 13), for example, proved correct in its observation that "by not integrating the Early Years Centres with licensed child care, the Province has made its own initiative less effective." More broadly, Ontario's Early Years Plan was shown to be at odds with dominant trends: labour-market conditions and fundamental changes in the gender order in 2001–05 period meant that women were in the labour force in growing numbers and, at the same time, more and more households deviated from the white, Canadian-born, male breadwinner–female caregiver norm. Tax-based remedies did not resolve crisis tendencies in social reproduction. Their capacity to foster "self-sufficiency" and "independence" through paid work among people with young children in the face of a dearth of child care in Ontario proved limited. Nor did Early Years Centres that targeted narrow constituencies of children, parents, and caregivers offer a viable solution to the child-care crisis.

The key for feminists is to use the case of Ontario's Early Years Plan, as well as the set of contradictions it unleashed, and similar case studies strategically. The key is to use the paradoxical developments that exacerbated tensions in social reproduction in Ontario under the ECDA to reject privatized remedies aimed at mediation. The grounds for this rejection are straightforward, so commonsensical that federal and provincial policy discussions echoed them increasingly after 2003, as crisis tendencies mounted in Ontario and elsewhere: early childhood development programs that encompass (and indeed augment) genuinely high-quality, universal, accessible, and developmentally oriented public, regulated child care are central to maintaining a viable process of social reproduction in the long term and to raising healthy capable children in the short term.

## NOTES

This chapter is the product of a research project on "Rethinking Feminization: Gendered Precariousness and the Crisis in Social Reproduction" made possible by support from Social Sciences and Humanities Research Council of Canada grant no. 410–2000–1362.

I thank Barbara Cameron for her helpful feedback on an earlier version of this chapter, Kayla Scott and Tammie Hyde for their able research assistance, and the volume's editors, Kate Bezanson and Meg Luxton, for their comments and their leadership in producing this volume.

1 This definition of social reproduction is drawn from Fudge and Vosko 2003.
2 I place the word "productive" in quotation marks here to acknowledge that some authors speak of three *departments* of production in response the false narrowing of the economic in political economy of the mid- to late-twentieth century (see, for example, Seccombe 1974).
3 The standard of living of workers is always historical, moral, and institutional and not determined via the price mechanism of the market exclusively (Picchio 1992).
4 The gender regime in a given institution is a synthesis of three structures – the division of labour, power, and cathexis (Connell 1987, 98–9).
5 In Canada the fertility rate has decreased steadily in the last thirty years. It declined from 2.12 to 1.52 between 1971 and 1999. Moreover, in Ontario it declined steadily between 1999 and 2004; there were nearly 3,000 fewer births in 2003/04 than in 1999/2000 (Statistics Canada 2005a).

6 An example of withdrawal is where patients used to be able to remain in hospitals or long-term care facilities for months and even years (see Braedley this volume).

7 To be clear, many of the services addressed in this chapter, such as child care, were never fully public. Hence, while I follow the spirit of Fudge and Cossman's definition of reprivatization, I view broader processes of privatization to be central to it.

8 Similarly, under the CHST, block transfers were stable to 1999/2000, but provincial/territorial social assistance expenditures declined everywhere except in the Yukon between 1996/97 and 1999/2000 (Vosko 2002b, 35).

9 Following the introduction of the NCBS, provinces proceeded in the following ways. Some adhered to a self-sufficiency model, some delivered the NCBS through social assistance and clawed it back (Prince Edward Island, Ontario, Manitoba – for children over 7 – Alberta, and the three territories). Others delivered it through social assistance but did not claw it back (New Brunswick and Manitoba). Still others introduced income-tested child benefits outside social assistance and clawed back the NCBS provided through these programs (British Columbia and Saskatchewan). The remaining group had income-tested child benefits outside social assistance yet did not claw back the NCBS (Newfoundland, Nova Scotia and Quebec).

Quebec was never an official participant in the NCBS. However, it adjusted the Quebec Family Allowance for increases in the NCBS supplement. With the increases in the federal benefit in July 1998 and July 2000 and the clawback in July 1999, Quebec adjusted the family allowance, essentially clawing it back. With the increase in the NCBS in July 2001, however, the province did not claw it back. (For an extensive discussion of the Quebec case, see Baril, Lefebvre, and Merrigan 2000, 7).

10 The Parti Québécois government in Quebec used federal transfer monies to fund $5 per day child care in 1997. The subsequent Liberal government raised this amount to $7 per day in 2004.

11 The plan deviated so dramatically from the recommendations contained in *Reversing the Brain Drain* that McCain and Mustard produced a highly critical follow-up study three years later (McCain and Mustard 2002).

12 Ontario failed to table an Early Years Plan and a breakdown of provincial ECDI initiatives in fall 2001, and in the *Federal/Provincial/Territorial Early Childhood Development Agreement: Report on Government of Canada Activities and Expenditures, 2000–2001*, there was scant mention of early childhood development programs in the province. Consequently, federal and provincial governments established guidelines requiring all governments to report annually on their progress in enhancing early childhood development programs and services on the basis of a shared framework of principles, beginning in 2002.

13 This was the dollar amount in 2002, the last amount available publicly.

14 Some child-care centres did, however, receive program-specific funding through the Early Years Challenge Fund.

15 In a city such as Toronto, the three entities involved with each centre also interacted with a regional administration, which assigned quadrant co-chairs for subregions, and area-wide planning bodies.

16 These employees are funded separately and operate under separate guidelines set by the Ministry.

17 The relationship between the availability of subsidized child care and the province's self-sufficiency objective is clear: in 2002, over 40 per cent of subsidy users (6,500) were households led by an employed single parent with average annual earnings of $20,684.

18 This figure is relatively small since the province required an additional $96 million just to restore regulated child-care funding to 1995 levels.

19 Indeed, its champions made this acknowledgment. The federal Cabinet identified and debated many of the weaknesses observed here and anticipated the two principal objections (one related to federalism and the other ideological) of the provinces – that some parties to the ECDA would not support the targeted use of funds for child care based on the perception that the federal government was trespassing on provincial jurisdiction and that a national child-care strategy would be perceived by some provinces as "anti-family" (Human Resources and Development Canada 2003, 4). Yet Cabinet ministers decided to set these issues aside in favour of advancing an agreement since most provinces were already expending considerable funds on quality, regulated child care and since "good parenting is made easier by supportive communities" (Human Resources Development Canada 2003, 4). They put forward this architecture on the understanding that if unanimous agreement could not be reached, the federal government would pursue bilateral or federal-provincial and federal-municipal agreements designed to benefit communities in the participating jurisdictions (Human Resources and Development Canada 2003, 4).

20 For a history of Canadian federalism as it relates to social reproduction, see also Cameron in this volume.

# 7

# The Neo-liberal State and Social Reproduction: Gender and Household Insecurity in the Late 1990s

KATE BEZANSON

In May 1995 a majority Progressive Conservative government was elected in Ontario, one of Canada's wealthiest provinces; it was re-elected in 1999.[1] Adopting a neo-liberal economic approach, this government dramatically overhauled Ontario's welfare state.[2] The Progressive Conservatives enacted major changes in most areas of public life by focusing on decreasing taxes, reducing the debt and deficit (although these rose under their watch), decreasing government provision of social services and income supports, and reducing the role of government in regulating capital, especially by weakening labour-market protections. The period of Conservative rule in the province also saw a redesign of legislative practices which resulted in less consultation and the transformation of some legislative items into regulations not subject to review or debate (Bezanson and Valentine 1998; Bezanson 2006). Despite a booming economy in the second half of the 1990s, income inequalities grew in this period (Bezanson and McMurray 2000; Yalnizyan 1998). The tenure of the Conservatives was marked by a pitched political struggle between liberal individualism and welfare-state collectivism. This struggle hinged in part on reconfiguring the distribution of the work of social reproduction among the market, welfare state, family/household, and third (not-for-profit) sector. Individuals felt the brunt of this shift in responsibility.

This chapter offers a case study of neo-liberal welfare-state restructuring as experienced by members of forty-one households in Ontario. It is based on intensive interviews with them conducted every eight months between 1997 and 2000.[3] The study revealed that incomes and social supports from market and state sources were insecure or diminishing.[4] For those with low incomes, in particular, the available sources of formal and informal inputs into social reproduction, along with various state protections, decreased or were restructured. These conditions tested the capacity of members of households – women in particular — to manage and maintain standards of living. The neo-liberal framework adopted by the Conservatives presumed that the family/household would internalize and harmonize for its members the conflicts of income and labour-market insecurity, including a lack of welfare-state supports for care work or a lack of resources to purchase care. Contra this assumption, the case study found that the gendered work of social reproduction done in families/households did not automatically act as a shock-absorption mechanism to stabilize crises and manage insecurity. The relationship of family/households to markets and the state was complex and conflictual. By examining multiple social policy changes *over time,* the study revealed the dynamics and limits of this way of organizing social reproduction.

This chapter offers three important findings about social policy and social reproduction in Ontario. First, women and men had different experiences of neo-liberal economic changes because of existing divisions of labour and the gendered assumptions built into restructuring. Patterns of refamilialization (that is, pushing social reproduction onto family/households) and defamilialization (that is, elevating the individual citizen-worker and making women more like men) competed for primacy in this period. Second, the effects of neo-liberal social policy reorientations on people's lives are cumulative and compounding. Finally, the coping strategies that those with low incomes were able to employ were not sustainable.

The chapter begins by exploring sites of mediation of the tensions inherent in social reproduction. It then provides an overview of the range of alterations to Ontario's welfare state under the Progressive Conservative leadership of Mike Harris. After providing a brief sketch of the methodology employed in the case study, it then presents the results, examining the experiences and survival strategies of members of predominantly low-income households as they struggled with major changes in income and social service supports.

## MEDIATING TENSIONS IN SOCIAL REPRODUCTION

Social reproduction involves a range of activities, behaviours, responsibilities, and relationships that ensure the daily and generational social, emotional, moral, and physical reproduction of people. It includes, among other things, how "food, clothing, and shelter are made available for immediate consumption, the ways in which the care and socialization of children are provided, the care of the infirm and elderly and the social organization of sexuality" (Laslett and Brenner 1989, 382–3). The work involved in social reproduction is extensive, undervalued, and largely invisible. While there is nothing inherent in this work that requires it to be done by women, its organization and carrying out is highly gendered in most societies. As feminized work that takes place predominantly in private homes, it is largely unseen and unaccounted for in systems of national accounting (Waring 1988; Luxton 1998). As feminized work, it is likewise undervalued socially and underpaid (and often racialized) when it is commodified (Armstrong and Connelly 1999).

Social reproduction occurs in all economic systems. In capitalist systems, the imperative of production for profit stands in conflict with needs related to social reproduction (Picchio 1992). This tension between capital accumulation and social reproduction requires mediation. Several avenues are available: the work involved in caring for and maintaining people can be shifted to private homes; it can be taken up by states to different extents; it can be taken up by the private market to provide at a price; or it can be taken up by voluntary, religious, or other third-sector organizations. Existing forms of social stratification and inequalities in power are ready conduits for the direction that mediation takes in a given period. Degrees of political mobilization and/or the orientation of particular governments can reroute the state–household–market–third-sector circuits of mediation. In short, social reproduction is politically, socially, and culturally determined (Picchio 1992). That the family/household intensifies its social reproduction labour in a period of economic retrenchment reflects negotiation and mediation, rather than an *automatic* adjustment to external demands.

The work that is done in the home and in neighbourhoods as a privatized "labour of love" underwrites much of the work done in the sectors of the market and the state. Because the work of social reproduction relies on access to particular items (food and food production, shelter, time, clothing, and other socially and historically determined needs), the inputs into social reproduction in capitalist economies generally come from some kind of exchange. Social reproduction thus depends on income, which typically comes in the form of wages, government transfers, access to arable land and/or resources (such as fish). The insecurities inherent in the labour market and, to some extent, in other forms of access to money are absorbed and mediated at the household level. The conditions under which social reproduction can take place are also mediated in capitalist economies by the regulations and limitations that states place on capital. Thus the state plays a central role in structuring the *inputs* into, and *conditions* of, social reproduction in its approach to regulating the labour market, by providing income support and by underwriting child, elder, and dependent care (see Cameron this volume). The neo-liberal character of the Progressive Conservative regime in Ontario in the second half of the 1990s encouraged a non-standard labour market, decreased access to public social and income supports, and limited care support.

## CONSERVATIVE ONTARIO, 1995–2000: A NEO-LIBERAL EXPERIMENT

Among the most notable elements of the agenda of the Conservative government of Ontario was its stated emphasis on decreasing the size and scope of government itself.[5] In a sense, the provincial government viewed itself as the "anti-government" government. The concept that government itself over-regulates business and individuals is common among proponents of neo-liberalism. The Ontario government borrowed heavily from other models of sub-national and national state restructuring, such as the examples of Thatcher in Britain, Reagan in the United States, and especially the experiments in the 1990s of workfare-driven social policy in Wisconsin and New Jersey (see Bashevkin 2002; Vosko 2002a).

The Ontario Conservatives enacted legislation that reduced the size of some parts of the government itself (cutting jobs and agencies), shifted many of the costs and delivery of key social policies (such as social assistance and child care) to municipalities to deliver, pursued the wholesale privatization of government agencies, and significantly reduced its involvement in regulating industry. These changes occurred at the same time as the government pursued significant decreases in the rates of personal income tax. Premier Harris claimed that his overall vision was to "run the government more like a business" (*Toronto Star*, 5 April 1996, A1).

Within just its *first* year in office, the provincial government cut funding to almost every ministry and agency (a $5.5 billion cut was announced for the 1995–96 fiscal year), cut funding to not-for-profit agencies, and declared a moratorium on non-profit housing.[6] Policy changes were immediately enacted regarding social assistance rates, cohabitation while receiving social assistance, waiting periods for social assistance, youth social assistance, and the introduction of a "welfare fraud" hotline. In order to meet its targets for reductions in spending and shifting costs to other sectors, including the private sector, the provincial government enacted a series of legislative changes that gave authority to ministers, third agencies, and the Management Board Secretariat to restructure or eliminate agencies, ministries, and government bodies.[7] The dramatic redesign both in servicing and staffing levels and in decision-making authority were first, necessary steps toward implementing the Ontario Conservatives' version of neo-liberal governance. One of the main ways to redesign control and decision-making came through a series of legislative changes found in omnibus legislation.[8]

Despite confrontation, resistance and strikes, the Conservative government redesigned and reregulated most areas governing the conditions of paid work (including introducing work for welfare), union legislation, income support, housing support, education, health care, and child care (on early childhood initiatives, see Vosko this volume). In short, the state took an active role in reducing the extent to which it would shield citizens from the risks of capitalism. Further, it focused on increasing community-based supports, which resulted in caregiving work being shifted out of institutions such as hospitals and onto individuals in families or to the private sector (Bezanson and Noce 1999; Armstrong et al. 2001). Among other changes, the Conservatives rewrote the Employment Standards Act, reorganized Worker's Safety Insurance, eliminated employment equity, rewrote the landlord-tenant act, and enacted major changes in education, social assistance, health care, and training. It thus shaped the contours of the labour market in the province in favour of lower wages and fewer restrictions on industry, while making non-wage supports and services more restrictive.

## THE CASE STUDY: METHODOLOGICAL CONSIDERATIONS

The study on which this discussion is based is a three-and-a-half-year household-based panel study.[9] Between 1997 and 2000, four rounds of in-depth interviews (a total of 158 interviews) with a total of 127 members of forty-one households were conducted.[10] The study shows the multiple unequal effects of dramatic policy, program, and taxation change on households from a range of ethnic, religious, and geographic backgrounds. It also reveals how individuals within households (predominantly women) picked up – or failed to pick up – the shortfall produced by the dramatic reductions in public services. The experiences of the various households illustrate the impact of the neoliberal restructuring experiment that took place in Ontario between 1995 and 2000, a process that dramatically altered the scope of the welfare state, labour-market protections and conditions, and the capacities of people to manage and plan their lives.

The selection of households was purposive rather than representative. Longitudinal research is able to "distinguish transitory and persistent phenomena ... and allows the researchers to take into account the timing (in terms of age, or life-course stage) and the duration of conditions and experiences, both of which are crucial for understanding social continuity and change" (Scott 1995, 61). While the sample size of forty-one households from across the province provided a clear picture of the effects of particular policy initiatives on different groups of people, the longitudinal model was in this case limited by not being representative of the population as a whole. However, the panel-based design (involving intensive repeat interviews with the same household participants), when combined with policy, statistical and economic analysis, provided a strong basis for understanding the dynamics of economic and social policy restructuring on a broad cross-section of income groups across Ontario (see Neysmith, Bezanson, and O'Connell 2005).

Interview questions were in-depth, semi-structured and open-ended. After each round of interviews, the concerns identified by households about policy changes were reviewed, and specific questions about policy areas that many households had in common were developed for the next round. The policy areas addressed in detail included health, employment, income, education, citizen engagement, and voting practices. In this way, household experiences fed the policy-analysis process. Specific policy questions about people's concerns allowed for a more nuanced understanding of the consequences particular legislative or regulatory action or inaction had, cumulatively, on participants.

A template reflecting the diversity of Ontario's population was created to guide the purposive sample; it, however, was only a guide since household configuration, income, and location changed over time as people moved, were married, or, in one case, died (see appendix B).[11] Template characteristics included household income; geographic location; household structure (two-parent, single-parent, single people, housemates, couples, or multi-generational kin group); sources of income (employment, social assistance, retirement funds, Employment Insurance, or rental income); and other characteristics, such as race and ethnicity, physical disability, sexual orientation, housing status, age, and gender (McMurray 1997). Sixty per cent of the households met the Statistics Canada definition of low income at the time of the first interview in 1997.[12] Thirty-seven per cent were middle-income, and two per cent were high-income. A little over half of the households were in the Greater Toronto Area at the time of the first interview.

While the study incorporated households from all income categories, the findings reported in the next section of the chapter outline the income and support constraints for *all* participant households and then highlight in-depth the experiences of members of the *lowest-income* households. There are two key reasons for this focus on low income. First, the effects of policy changes enacted in the province were borne significantly by those with the lowest incomes. Social class was central to the Conservative's "Common Sense Revolution." From major changes to social assistance including the introduction of work for welfare, to a decrease in labour-market protections and a frozen minimum wage, to changes in rental-housing protections and new costs in education and health care, social policy reorientations affected the bare bones of getting by (income, job protection, rent, and so on). Second, women are disproportionately represented among interviewed household members who were poor, and this trend bears out in national statistics. This overrepresentation of women in the low-income category is intimately tied to their responsibility for social reproduction. The external supports for and conditions of this work were undermined in this period. The Ontario case study suggests that the restructuring imperative of the late 1990s was

Table 7.1 Household Income Sources

| *Income Source* | *Variations* |
|---|---|
| Wages/salaries | salaried employment<br>hourly waged employment<br>self-employment<br>cash work |
| Federal transfers | Employment Insurance<br>Canada Child Tax Benefit<br>Canada Pension Plan<br>Old Age Security<br>scholarships |
| Provincial transfers | Ontario Works<br>Ontario Disability Support Program<br>workers' compensation<br>Aid for Children with Severe Disabilities<br>Ontario Student Assistance Program<br>scholarships/grants |
| Private sources | child support<br>rental income<br>Registered Retirement Savings Plan (RRSP)<br>loans or gifts<br>private pensions |

at best indifferent to the impacts on the poor and at worst assumed that poor women could stretch their unpaid labour indefinitely to make up for shortfalls in state mediation. Women's strategies were short-term and usually unsustainable.

## SOCIAL REPRODUCTION AND STANDARDS OF LIVING

### *Circumscribing the Inputs into Social Reproduction: Income Insecurity*

The retrenchment of Ontario's welfare state rested on exacerbating social-class divisions and prioritized income from wages as the only legitimate form. The ascendancy of the liberal individual in political and policy discourse is at odds with the experiences of those interviewed. The income stories from the case study suggest that the state plays a large role in structuring the conditions and levels of income available to people. While the wage relationship is a determinant of standards of living, other income sources provide crucial inputs into

Figure 7.1 Household income sources, 1999

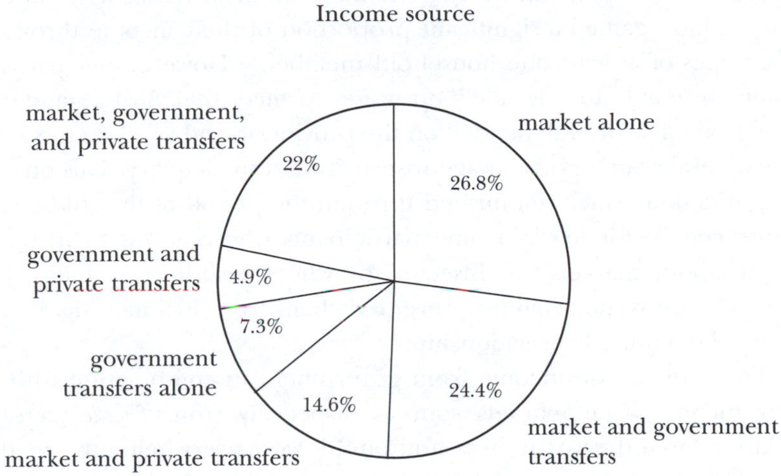


social reproduction. As table 7.1 shows, there were twenty different income sources under four main categories.

As figure 7.1 illustrates, most households (thirty of forty-one) had income from more than one source. Ten combined wages with some form of government transfer.[13] Six had income from wages and private sources (such as child support or rental income). Three had income from government transfers alone, while two had income from private sources and government transfers. Finally, nine had income from wages, government transfers, and private transfers. A focus on income from wages alone occludes other important sources of income, the relationships among sources of income, and the role of the state in labour-market insecurity.

The combined income sources did not translate into income security. Three-quarters of the members of the forty-one households reported that their household incomes had either dropped or were stagnant between 1995 and 2000. At least three factors account for this finding: the labour market was shifting toward non-standard work; public income transfers decreased or became more difficult to access; and labour-market protections and supports were weakened. For the low-income households in the study, these trends exaggerated existing income inequalities.

Over 90 per cent of adult participants in this study worked for pay at some point between 1995 and 2001, and 68 per cent had employment as their *main* source of income in 1999.[14] While participants' job types, characteristics, pay, time requirements, and relative security varied widely, most gained a significant proportion of their income through the wages of at least one household member.[15] However, few participants were able to rely solely on wages to meet their living-standard requirements. Many depended on the provincial, and to a lesser extent the federal, state to offset wage insecurity and inadequacy. This offsetting function, which diminished through the period of the study, was more central for lower-income participants whose access to income from labour markets was insecure or whose health, age, ability, or unpaid care responsibilities prevented them from maintaining a sustained labour-market relationship.

Those reliant on income from government in combination with a low income from markets sources, especially from *female* wages/ salaries, fared the worst; these households were overwhelmingly made up of single mothers.[16] Of the eight households in which the most significant source of income came from a government transfer, women headed six.[17] These households were the poorest in the study. The male participants receiving government transfers included a man with AIDS receiving a small public disability pension and income support from a provincial disability support program, and a senior citizen receiving a small public pension and age-entitlement transfer. Nonetheless, for most low-income households, whether or not they had wages, mixed income sources and supports from programs, transfers, and tax credits played a significant role in overall household income.

Participants also had income from other sources, including from non-resident family members or investments. The availability of indirect social spending initiatives (usually targeted programs based on income), such as subsidized child care or subsidized housing, were also significant factors that assisted poorer households to maintain a minimal standard of living. Indirect or direct access to assets was almost always tied to social-class location or to having a parent who had a standard employment relationship with a relatively secure income. Access to assets based on social relationships (such as a parent owning a home into which an adult child moved) or ownership of assets such as a car (which could be used as collateral for loans) were important factors in alleviating income shortages or stretching small incomes. The presence or absence of a *social* package (benefits, compassionate leave, paid maternity leave, and so on) accompanying a wage bundle was a determining factor in who fared well or poorly in a context of socio-economic change.

For those households with low incomes (predominantly headed by women), managing various income sources was a constant struggle. The presence of young children often predicted the incidence of poverty. The absence of active full-time child-care responsibilities for young children was a factor that differentiated households with income from wages alone from those with mixed income sources.[18] Those households with income from wages and private sources included one member who was working in a well-paid professional or semi-professional job; three were couples, and two were single or female headed. Those with incomes from government and private sources were again female-headed households, with income from social assistance and/or the Child Tax Benefit and child support. Those with the most mixed income sources were almost all women who combined paid work with a variety of arrangements to maximize household incomes. Seven of nine had children in their homes.[19]

Interpersonal household relations were a chief factor affecting household members' access to income. A key element in lifting medium- and low-income female-headed households into higher income categories was a relationship with a wage-earning man. Gender composition in households was not the only characteristic affecting income status. Race and ethnicity clearly affected income too: five of the seventeen low-income households were composed of people of colour or First Nations, while only four of twenty-three households were composed of people of colour or First Nations in the middle-income category.

Household interviews confirmed national data, which showed that full-time work is often subject to insecurity or is contractually limited. Twenty-five per cent more of the individuals interviewed were working for wages in 1999 than in 1997, but almost 35 per cent of them were employed in non-standard jobs or had multiple jobs. Almost half of all those interviewed had changed jobs since 1997 (see appendix C). Many of those who went through job transitions during the period of study were only able to find part-time, short-term, or contract work. Most non-standard work for women was in part-time employment, while men were equally represented in part-time and self-employed work arrangements. Further, most part-time employment was involuntary (see Noce and O'Connell 1998).

Income from multiple sources became more insecure and precarious following social and economic restructuring, while new demands and eligibility restrictions in social programs made budgeting difficult. Increasingly inaccessible or inadequate benefits associated with public income-transfer programs meant that last-resort programs could not sustain households. Despite increases in tax credits related to children, only one woman moved up in income categories, and this was because she married a man with a high wage. The erosion of the supports, such as education, training, and health care, that can assist households in moving out of poverty meant that low-income spells lasted longer.

Insecurity in access to the means of subsistence affects and is affected by the ways in which the work of social reproduction done in families is able to absorb the shocks of changes in income or adjustments in social spending. Changes in social policies affected the work of social reproduction in households providing insight into how households managed in the "new" Ontario.

### *Circumscribing the Inputs into Social Reproduction: Social Policy Retrenchment*

As participants tried to manage their incomes in an increasingly insecure labour market and social-transfer environment, they had to contend with the erosion of the complementary supports of the welfare state. The need for social services, when these are cut, eliminated, or simply not provided, does not disappear, but its provision is often shifted onto the work of (usually) women in households, who may or may not have the time and energy to cope with all the extra work. The extent to which people can take up these tasks depends on their income, their ability to navigate complex social service structures, and their own social support networks. Participants developed coping strategies in order to manage income insecurity, revealing the interdependent relationship between production for profit and social reproduction; for low-income households with multiple policy area attachments, coping strategies were often short-term and usually not sustainable.

Major changes to social policy areas (such as health care, education, housing, transportation, child-care, and social assistance) had a significant effect on many participant households.[20] Budget cuts and restructuring to key policy areas meant that costs associated with these services shifted across the state-market-household sectors. In each of the policy areas, social service redesign and social spending reductions meant an increase in unpaid work for women and/or a reprioritizing of household expenses to meet new ones. Women also lost paid positions in the public sector, a sector that historically offered women room for advancement and moderate rates of unionization. Participants in this study did not experience policy changes as discrete categories in their lives; such changes interacted with one another and participants scrambled to adjust to new time and money demands in response. Central policy areas common to most participants included health and education. Highlighting these two policy domains shows the linkages among public policies, labour-market insecurity, and household coping options.

Health care was perhaps the most obvious policy area in which changes to spending visibly translated into shifting the costs of care either to the household or to the private market sector. Cuts to hospital budgets (and in some cases, the elimination or merger of particular hospitals), fewer nurses, long waiting lists for specialist care, restructuring of community-based care budgets,[21] under-regulated retirement and nursing home facilities, the delisting of services covered by the provincial health plan, and a large population with no access to drug, dental, or vision insurance have meant that the task of providing care and support to an ill person and the associated costs are increasingly individual or household responsibilities.[22] Paid work in the care segments of the health sector remained feminized and racialized, and increased demands were placed on workers to manage the effects of the dramatic overhaul of this social policy area. The aging of Ontario's population was beginning to put an additional strain on already depleted health-care resources and increased demands on children, particularly daughters, of those older persons requiring care (see Braedley this volume). In many cases, new or increased demands on women to care for elderly parents came at the same time as they were managing their own children.

For example, Cheryl, a mother of two young boys who lived with her spouse, Paul, in a medium-sized southern Ontario city, found herself also providing care for her elderly parents. In 1998 she described her stress and fatigue levels as extremely high. "Last week I told Paul that I'd had enough," she explained. "I said I just can't take care of you, my mother and my father, the cat and the kids". For some participants such as Cheryl, shifting the work of caring for people onto the household meant that labour-market relationships and personal relationships were strained or dissolved, while for others, the caring work fell through the cracks and did not get taken up, leading to increased health-care needs, costs, and intervention.

The restructuring of the health-care sector along the lines of efficiency and cost reduction did not mean that the need for services for those who were ill or recuperating disappeared.[23] Household experiences revealed that, as services were reduced, the responsibility was shifted both onto women to pick up the slack and onto the private market sector to be provided at cost to those who could pay. Because it was almost exclusively women who managed their own, their children's, and sometimes their spouse's health-care needs, it was generally women who navigated the health-care system. Women also were responsible for administering medications and, increasingly, using technical machinery at home to do so.[24] For example, Anne, a mother of four, noted that she had to keep track of thirteen different medications, along with administering asthma medication through a machine. In addition to managing her children's health-care needs at home, she had to spend the night in hospital with them if one was sick because the staffing levels were insufficient to care for a child overnight. The work done by women both in unpaid caring labour and in formal care work (such as nurses) intensified in response to the emerging crisis in health care in the province. Class therefore emerged as a central determinant in who would have access to quality and quick care. Those with the money to purchase additional services or supports and those with the knowledge and skills to advocate for better and quicker services fared comparatively better.

As with health care, many participants had some relationship with the education sector as it was radically reorganized in the late 1990s.[25] A number of participants had a child attending a primary, secondary or post-secondary institution. Sometimes they themselves were enrolled or hoped to enrol in an educational institution. Several were employed in some capacity in the education field and experienced changes in their daily work. Household experiences with changes in the education sector revealed that new costs emerged in this area, and the demands placed on households, in particular on, women, were significant. Education and training are intertwined with labour-market policy, and policies related to education affected the ability of participants to take up opportunities or increase their skill levels vis-à-vis the labour market.

School boards were amalgamated into large boards, and the role of trustees was dramatically reduced. Parent councils were given a much greater role in the running of school boards. Many participants, especially those with non-standard labour-market relationships, noted that they wanted to be more involved in the administration and planning of their children's education but lacked the time to attend parent council meetings. Others noted that the councils had little or no decision-making ability and no impact on policy. For example, Ray, who lived in northern Ontario, saw the parent councils as organizing vehicles for school fundraising activities. In effect, the introduction of mandatory school councils, under the guise of giving parents more control in education, resulted in the paid work of trustees being converted into the unpaid work of unelected people with the time and resources to serve on school councils (O'Connell and Valentine 1998). Dehli (1994) found that parent activists and council members were likely to be women who were not in the labour force.

In primary and secondary education, then, parents were increasingly called upon to make up for funding and institutional reorientation by increasing their time commitments in their children's schools through councils and fundraising activities. They spent more for basic supplies and services, while advocating and navigating their way through a restructured education system to get services for children who did not fit into the standardized education model. For parents with low incomes or with children with special needs, meeting these demands was stressful and difficult.[26] In some cases, new costs or time demands could not be met, resulting both in children not being able to fully participate in school activities and in parents feeling excluded from decision-making opportunities in their children's lives.

At the level of post-secondary education, cuts in transfers to universities and colleges translated into higher tuition fees for students. These new costs and debt loads reduced the accessibility of post-secondary education for many students and put increased demands on parents and students to find money for educational opportunities.[27] For those low-income participants receiving social assistance, changes to the program's funding for education and training meant that many had to take out student loans in order to participate in educational upgrading at the college and university level. For women raising children alone, this requirement effectively barred them from obtaining training that would move them out of a low-wage category.

Funding to programs, including English as a second language (ESL), was reduced, and adult and ESL programs were predominantly utilized by women. A survey by the Ontario Secondary School Teachers' Federation found that among adult students, 63 per cent were female, 16 per cent had disabilities, 53 per cent needed additional assistance with English as a second language, and 48 per cent received social assistance (Ontario Secondary School Teachers' Federation 1998). In post-secondary and adult education, then, increased costs associated with tuition and student loans together with cuts in programs themselves made education inaccessible for many students. In addition, restrictions and waiting lists for programs such as child-care and transportation subsidies made enrolling in programs more challenging for those receiving social assistance. The individualizing of post-secondary educational costs for people with disabilities increased already steep barriers to educational and job advancement.

As the welfare state was restructured and social services moved toward increasingly minimal provision, participants juggled the greater demands on them to take up costs and care work no longer provided. As these responsibilities were shifted onto households, women in particular took them up, in large measure because the gender division of labour within the home and in the workforce placed the management of households on them. How did people in households cope? The combination of more-insecure income sources and an increasingly inaccessible and ungenerous social support network placed disproportionate demands on those who were already stretched. The work of putting together a living is starkest when we consider the ways in which, in this context of restructuring, households manage or fail to manage their members' care.

## *Social Reproduction: Coping with Income Insecurity and Social Service Restructuring*

Because states have a significant role in offsetting or off-loading the high costs of social reproduction onto, or away from, households, social policies and labour-market regulations significantly affect the abilities of household members to manage and maintain their standards of living. Generally, it was women within households who managed the work of transforming income sources so that expenses were met.[28] The experiences of the lowest-income households reveal that the process of social reproduction involves a huge amount of labour, a complex division of labour, and enormous resources.[29] For the low-income participants in the study, the work of transforming income to meet the needs of household members, including preparing them to attend school or go to work, was the flexible element of managing of their living standards. Participants managed their income and social service insecurity, as well as increased personal costs, through a variety of means.

In low-income households many combined different strategies. The main strategies they identified were the following:

- doing without basic goods
- moving to cheaper housing or sharing housing
- going into debt
- borrowing from or relying on gifts and in-kind support from family and friends
- selling household goods, crafts, and other handmade items
- increasing time spent growing, shopping for, and preparing foods
- bartering
- developing detailed budgets
- increasing labour-market participation
- using food banks or requesting support from not-for-profit agencies or other services

Those who did without basic goods in the face of income shortfalls described going without food, making impossible decisions about whether to buy groceries or shoes, not filling prescriptions or sharing medication, going without a telephone or transportation, sharing winter boots, coats, and prescription glasses, and giving up all social activities outside the home. They risked their health and endured social isolation or ridicule along with endless tension within their households.

In all of the eight low-income female-headed households, the most flexible item in their budget was food. The women in these households said that they curbed their own consumption so that children would have enough to eat. They described the dilemmas they faced every day, trying to feed themselves and their children. In 1999 Jenny, a single mother receiving social assistance, described some of the consequences for her and her children of doing without basic goods:

> The last time I bought myself clothing would have been in 1995 and that would have been maternity clothing. I can't buy anything because if I do, I won't have

enough money for bills or groceries. The kids always need stuff, and that's [my priority]. Sometimes I can find something [for them] in a second-hand store which is really cool. There's a lot of things that you cannot do because of your financial situation. Like, we can't go to church every Sunday. I would like to but I'm thinking I don't have any clothes to wear there. My kids don't have any clothes. Like, are we going to show up in our grungy clothes to church?

Teresa, who received Ontario Disability Support because of her physical disability and multiple health needs, said on a number of occasions that she had been faced with the choice of feeding herself or meeting other basic needs. "Some of my medications they [social assistance] don't cover, and I have to pay for them myself, which they don't take into consideration … Groceries [are hard] because I only have $40. I needed new shoes this month. My choice was: do I get new shoes or do I get groceries? So I got new shoes. I'm relying on the food bank this month because I had to get new shoes." Teresa says that she often feels that she would be better off dead than living as she is: "Many times, I shouldn't say this, but many times I wish that I was dead, because I can't handle the stress of all these things that are happening. And things happen all the time." Compounding Teresa's difficulties were her special dietary requirements, which she could not meet through the food bank. In the last round of interviews, she confided that she was eating only one meal a day because she could not afford more of the nutritious foods she needed.

Many participants noted that, because of a lack of money for food, they increased the amount of time they spent growing (where possible), buying, and preparing foods. One participant began to make bread as a way to offset costs, in part because flour was one of the things that was readily available at food banks. For a while, before her relationship with her neighbour deteriorated, she was able to store her bread in her neighbour's deep freezer. Another woman was retired but working part-time to supplement her pension as a result of increases in her property taxes.[30] She shopped very carefully, bought day-old products, and relied on friends to drive her to discount grocery stores. She also began a small garden. Christopher and Janet, a couple in southeastern Ontario, worked on the parents' family farm on a weekly basis both to help the aging parents and to get meat and vegetables for their large household. These kinds of informal supports bolstered the capability of households to manage short-term difficulties in social reproduction, but they did not provide long-term solutions.

Many participants attempted to increase their incomes by selling household goods or making and selling items informally, while others went deeply into debt or bartered for needed goods. Some sold various household items in order to get enough money to cover basic food costs. Some regularly pawned and then repurchased household goods in order to get through a month. However, buying back items usually meant purchasing them at a marked-up price. One participant reported selling her children's swing set one month in order to purchase diapers and milk for her daughter. An artist living with his partner in northern Ontario sold his tools in order to meet unexpected veterinary costs. One woman bought fabric and made angels at Christmas in order to buy small gifts for her granddaughter. Another painted and tried to sell cards, while a third made curtains or covers. One participant tried making and selling East African foods. Making and selling goods as a source of income was, however, generally insecure and required capital outlays that were not always feasible.

High debt loads were common among low-income households. Many had student loans that they were trying to pay off; some were considering defaulting. Others owed back taxes. Single mothers, in particular, who had relied on social assistance at some point in the last ten years discovered that one of the strategies of the Conservative provincial government in its cost-saving efforts was to reopen old files and claim that former recipients had been overpaid and owed the province money. Suddenly, these women faced new debts, and most could not afford to challenge the charges. Michelle, in the Greater Toronto Area, was bulldozed by a letter she got from social assistance, saying she owed it $70,000. She had received assistance occasionally when she was between contract jobs and ineligible for Employment Insurance. Because her income was so low, she continued to be eligible to have some of her children's medical costs covered through social assistance while she was working. Information about the disposal of Michelle's broken-down car was said to be missing from her file. Social assistance officials determined that she was retroactively ineligible.[31] Michelle explained:

I thought it was a mistake! I have not received social assistance in quite some time. But Community and Social Services said to my MPP's secretary that it's not a mistake, it is correct. They were saying that it was too late to appeal it. They said that they're going to send it to the collection agency which would seize all my income ... the child tax credit or any of my income tax. I'm just barely making $19,000 a year. In that thirty-day period which they gave me to respond to the letter, I was calling the welfare office. I was calling my previous worker and there was no information given out to me. The last result I've got is that they're thinking of giving us a review to open the case, because there was so little information on why they claim that I owe them $70,000.

Other households had credit card debts or owed family members money. Many lived on overdraft at the bank. Some were financing part of their children's university or college education on credit cards.

Antonio was juggling helping his daughter with her university tuition fees and trying to repay his own large student loan. In order to manage his debt load, he was forced to take a minimum-wage job outside his field of training. He said: "This is the promise I got with this company: my boss will make the student loan payments for me. He will pay the monthly payments. I owe $200 a month, so this makes a big difference. That's why I stay. I cannot work in the field I trained in because I owe money for that training. But this is the only way I can manage because wages in other jobs are not enough to pay off the debt."

Some people swapped child care or shared costs. Tensions arose, however, if one person was not able to reciprocate. As relationships deteriorated, in part as a result of the constant pressures of small incomes, participants lost a central source of support in their lives. Josie, a grandmother raising her two grandchildren, said that accepting care forced her into relations of obligation with kin whom she sought to avoid: "If I have a family member that is going to come and help, you can be guaranteed that you will have their kids to babysit after ... No thanks." One participant who was a home-daycare provider, bartered in a more formal manner. She swapped child care for veterinary bills as a way to offset unexpected costs related to her dogs. A community worker in southeastern Ontario made use of a community local exchange program to get services such as plumbers, but found that she did not have many of the skills or the time to reciprocate in the program.

As a response to their limited inputs into the work of social reproduction, many low-income households attempted to increase their formal labour-market participation. A single mother tried to earn back the amount that was cut from social assistance through a telemarketing job, but she was laid off after a short time. A full-time student and parent first worked cleaning houses as a way to make extra income when she was receiving social assistance; later she got a part-time, seasonal job as a bus driver. Another participant managed to coordinate child care with her partner by working nights in a telemarketing company, but her hours and income were unpredictable.

Another strategy was to borrow money or rely on gifts. Three-quarters of the members of the forty-one households said that they were providers or receivers of support from non-cohabitating kin. While this strategy worked for some, especially if they had a family member who had assets, most had members of their extended kin and social networks who were in similar financial situations. In every case, *significant* sums of money were borrowed only from family members or partners; no one cited borrowing from friends. The remaining household participants sought support from formal sources, such as not-for-profits, government sources and churches. Leo, a seasonal textile worker whose wife, Maria, was a full-time teacher, noted that he preferred to borrow from the bank rather than muddy familial relationships with financial matters. The effect of borrowing money from kin affected people's relationships, often negatively, and in many cases left them feeling "like a charity case" (as one participant put it) because they were unable to reciprocate.

When Sabrina was laid off from her job in social services in the initial round of cuts to social spending in Ontario in the mid-1990s, she exhausted all other income sources and then received social assistance. After her termination, she struggled to pay for necessities such as groceries and rent. Her long-time friend and roommate decided to increase her share of the rent and utilities to offset Sabrina's income drop. Sabrina's parents were retired and on a fixed income, but they agreed to cover her student loan. The network of supports she had in place largely offset the financial setback of losing her job. She was well educated with strong professional skills; therefore her support network viewed her financial situation as an anomaly resulting from a provincial government bent on shrinking public services. Participants with education and/or job skills and social networks with assets were able to borrow money more readily because their positions were seen as short-term. For those with long-term needs, borrowing money tended to drain relationships.

Another common household strategy involved reducing costs by moving to cheaper accommodation or by sharing housing. In some cases, sharing a home worked out well for participants. However, economic need often damaged central relationships in people's lives. Moving to a new area in order to cut housing costs isolated individuals from community supports and friends, especially if they could not afford transportation costs for visits. Recent immigrants, in particular, faced social and cultural isolation if their moved away from their communities. Most low-income participants moved – sometimes often – in order to keep costs down, but such transience made it harder to access main supports.[32] Many people sought rent-geared-to-income housing, but the province restructured and retreated from all social housing, making extensive waiting lists even longer.

Having a parent or other family member willing to share an asset such as a house greatly helped several participants, although in all cases, parents were not wealthy to begin with.[33] Six households gained access to their current homes because of their parents. In three cases, parents split their homes so that each family had a separate living space. In one case, the woman's parents owned but did not live in the home; Jessie and Mark moved in and contributed to the mortgage. In the other two cases, mothers, daughters, and grandchildren shared homes.[34] In four cases, adult children moved in with parents to meet costs. Denzel, a young man who struggled with a series of low-paying jobs, periodically lived in a small apartment with his mother and siblings while trying to find affordable housing. At the time of the last interview, he was living in a room in a converted college residence and working full-time.

Relying on family to offset low incomes for housing had the same kinds of potential pitfalls as borrowing, and the strategy was often not sustainable. The experiences of two households with sharing housing are illustrative of the limitations of a reliance on family as a long term strategy. Jackie's and Ashley and Rosa's stories show two different outcomes of relying on family for support but reveal similar stresses. While extended kin relationships do not have the same legal support obligations as are associated with couple and child relationships, they nonetheless reflect the familialization thrust of the Conservative government of the late 1990s. These stories also demonstrate that households use a range of strategies to manage social policy and income changes.

Jackie was in her mid-thirties and lived in a medium-sized city in southeastern Ontario. She worked half time for a small not-for-profit agency and shared a home with her three children and her mother, Edith. When we first met in 1997, Jackie's son, Angus, was not yet a toddler. Her daughter Kerry was fourteen years old. Jackie had divorced Kerry's father many years before because he was violent. In 1999, after a brief reconciliation with Angus's father, she gave birth to a second daughter. Jackie managed on her part-time income because she received a partial day-care subsidy and shared costs with her mother.

Maintaining a good relationship with her mother, Edith, was a constant struggle. While the strategy of sharing a home in order to keep housing costs lower was helpful financially, it caused deep fractures in Jackie's and Edith's relationship and was a source of constant stress for them both. Jackie felt that she and her children were a burden to her mother, but they had few other housing options. In 1997 Jackie and Edith were trying to maintain separate spaces while living in the same house. They shared the kitchen, the laundry facilities, and the yard, but had separate phone lines. Jackie, Angus, and Kerry were living in the basement, while Edith used the rest of the house. By early 1998 they gave up this division when Angus was diagnosed with asthma and allergies and could no longer live in the basement. As a result, Jackie and Edith both had significantly less personal space and time. Jackie intensified her unpaid work as she attempted to make up in labour the income she could not contribute to the house. She said: "My mother complains about the house, that the roof needs doing, it needs painting, the furnace is old, the windows need to be replaced, the rug needs replacing. It just gets right on top of me, and I have no escape. I don't know where to channel it. I have no money or time to go work out at a gym. But I have to manage. I have to be healthy for Kerry and Angus. I have to [provide a good home]."

Both Edith and Jackie needed a car, and so they shared a used car. Edith had increasingly severe arthritis, and Kerry had a physical disability that limited her capacity to walk. Jackie contributed to paying off the loan they got for the car, but Edith paid the insurance and maintenance. Jackie would have preferred to find other housing for her family. However, Kerry would not be able to get around the city if they moved, because Edith would keep the car, and Jackie could not afford to buy and maintain one on her own.

Ashley and Rosa's story shows that the more people are required to depend on just one or two others, the more their relationship is at risk. It also demonstrates how the stigma typically associated with receiving social assistance not only can erode recipients' self-esteem but also can alienate them from their family and friends. Ashley, a woman in her mid-fifties, lived in a southeastern Ontario town in the early 1990s.[35] When it became clear that she would not find employment there, she moved to the Greater Toronto Area, where she found full-time but low-paid employment. Her thirty-three-year-old daughter, Rosa, became pregnant and, because of complications with her pregnancy, could no longer hold down her full-time job. Ashley then lost her job because of funding cutbacks at a community agency. Rosa applied for social assistance and was enrolled in a full-time upgrading program, while Ashley continued to look for full-time employment. Out of financial necessity, they decided to pool resources and move in together.

Embarrassed by their situation, Rosa and Ashley tried to keep their financial status to themselves. They were hurt by the lack of understanding of their family members, particularly Rosa's three siblings. They felt judged for their failure to find good jobs, for their sparse living quarters, and for their inability to entertain. This humiliation was compounded by their feeling victimized by public hostility to the poor and those on social assistance. Isolating themselves from others, including other family members, only made them more dependent on each other. As their economic situation deteriorated, their utilities were cut off, they bought cheaper cuts of meat and produce, and increasingly they had to go without to make ends meet. Mother and daughter were forced to rely on each other more, pooling resources and even sharing personal belongings such as a single pair of winter boots. Their experience as they increasingly confronted the need to ask family for financial aid highlights the difference between entitlements and charity. Ashley had no difficulty accepting her non-resident partner's offer to extend his employer's medical and dental coverage to her. Neither she nor her partner had to justify their request for it. In contrast, when Ashley and Rosa had to ask Rosa's siblings for help, they both felt ashamed.

Feeling burdened, resentful, and overwhelmed by their debt load, Ashley and Rosa saw their relationship begin to fray. By the third interview, they were no longer living together, and each accused the other of not carrying her weight. Ashley describes the final days of their shared living arrangement:

> I told Rosa, I said I just, I can't take it any longer, and I couldn't take her any longer. We were just arguing and it was like very tense. She [Rosa] wasn't paying her fair share. All of my money was going, all of the food I was buying. I ended up paying most of the ... bills ... I didn't have the money. From about the sixth of the month I would pay all the food from there. Where the heck was her money? I don't know. I was paying all of it, and I'm not going to not buy food. If I put one thing down [in the cellar] it was gone. It was like a very stressful situation, extremely stressful.

Rosa also attributed their break-up to strained finances:

> It's almost like a married couple, when money and stuff comes into play. That's the big, that's one big argument, do you know what I mean, and it gets worse, money always gets worse. The payments ... it was just like trying to dodge, and trying not to get caught, give them a rubber cheque. I think that was the proverbial straw.

After a bitter parting of ways, Rosa rented the basement of her sister's home. While the arrangement was mutually beneficial in terms of reciprocal child care, Rosa hid her financial situation from her sister. Her sister was oblivious to Rosa's frequent use of food banks or her need to pawn personal possessions to make the rent. In fact, her sister was so unaware of Rosa's financial situation that she asked Rosa to act as co-signer for a mortgage.

Ashley moved back to her former home in a southeastern Ontario town and applied for social assistance. Her partner and her mother paid her property tax arrears, but she still feared her home would be taken away from her if she was forced to stay on social assistance. These experiences undermined her confidence and her ability to make positive changes in her life. Family relations were fraught with conflict, and for a period of months Ashley did not have any contact with her children.

The examples of Ashley and Rosa and Jackie and Edith show the dangers of forcing people to rely on family, especially for housing. Ironically, the government policy of encouraging people to rely on family and friends instead of state services serves to disrupt those relations and threatens to erode the support such networks could provide.

The coping strategies that households employed to maximize resources directed to social reproduction were in most cases short-term or unsustainable. Doing without basic goods, whether by restricting food or limiting personal sundries, affects nutrition and health. Increasing social isolation resulting from a lack of money for leisure, transport, or child care contributes to augmenting vulnerability and illness.

Strategies such as moving homes, moving in with others, or borrowing were not sustainable measures for many households. The changes to rent control legislation in Ontario made rental housing increasingly unaffordable and housing conditions questionable.[36] Sharing a home or relying on a family member who had one was a mixed strategy. For one household, it allowed members to run a daycare in a good-sized home with low rental payments. For others, the strain of sharing a parent's home while all were in difficult financial situations strained key supports in their lives and often left them in tight financial situations. Making family the main source of support can compromise household cohesion, including between spouses, for individuals. Because reciprocity is difficult for many on low incomes, participants who borrowed money or shared homes felt indebted, and the relationships they had with family members often became strained. They were left with few options for additional needed moneys. Some sold household goods or tried to work informally, but again, these strategies did not offer sustainable solutions to their income shortfalls.

Changes in labour-market regulation resulting in increased insecurity in job tenure and access to income combined with a vilification of social assistance recipients, altered the supports and resources available to households to convert into the products of social reproduction. Female household members in particular devised and implemented survival strategies for their families by increasing the amount of time they spent on main activities in order to maximize household resources. In the experiences of participants, then, there was a relationship between cutting social spending, reregulating the labour market, and increased unpaid work for women.

## CONCLUSION: A GENDER DIS/ORDER?

The neo-liberal regime that emerged in Ontario sharpened the contradiction between the pursuit of profit and the work of social reproduction.[37] The state in this Canadian province mediated this friction through mechanisms such as legislation that deregulated capital controls and privatized key sectors and through centralization of decision-making authority for areas such as health care and education. It simultaneously increased its surveillance of the poorest members of society – women in particular. The result of this mediation was to shift increasing amounts of responsibility for provisioning away from the state's purview and onto families/households.

Neo-liberal governments individualize problems in meeting standards of living. The household is assumed to absorb the shocks of economic adjustment and to be the safety net of last resort (Elson 1998). The capacity of the household to compensate for malfunctions or decisions elsewhere in the economic system is not without limits; the household "can be undermined by lack of resources, insecurity and demoralization; and in return it will be unable to supply ... the demand, the labour, the intangible social assets that the public and private sectors need to reform" (Elson 1998, 199). Demoralization results from, among other things, an assumption that little work or investment is required to maintain what Elson terms intangible social assets at the household level, including a sense of ethics, citizenship, communication, and uncodified social norms (Elson 1998, 200). An examination of the shift in state form in a Canadian context and its effects on individuals in households over time reveals that a neo-liberal model of accumulation requires states to mediate the work of social reproduction, intensifying demands on the household to serve as an alternator for adjustments related to standards of living. The case study described here demonstrated that cumulative reductions in regulations on capital and in social spending, coupled with increased surveillance of the poorest citizens, result in degrading household infrastructures (Little 1998; Mosher 2000). Over the long term, these trends have multiple consequences, including a labour force that is less equipped and less healthy and in which norms necessary for circuits of communication at the meso- and macro-levels are poorly developed.

Three main conclusions emerge from the study. First, at the level of individual households, decreased support for and increased work in the tasks associated with social reproduction intensified the strain on women, in particular, to develop strategies to maintain standards of living. Women and men had different experiences of neo-liberal economic changes because of existing divisions of labour and the gendered assumptions built into restructuring. Refamilialization and defamilialization patterns competed for primacy in this period as families/households tried to absorb additional social reproduction responsibilities while managing more-insecure labour markets. Second, the effects of multiple social policy reorientations on people's lives were cumulative and compounding. Social policies and labour-market protections and conditions *interacted* in the lives of members of households, circumscribing the inputs into and conditions of social reproduction. Resistance was complicated by such vast change happening so quickly and on so many fronts. Finally, the strategies that those with low incomes were able to employ were not sustainable. The emerging neo-liberal gender order in Ontario is one in which the work of social reproduction continues to be organized predominantly via women's unpaid labour; the context, however, has shifted to a dual earner–female carer model with few state supports.

# APPENDIX A: DETAILED HOUSEHOLD INCOME SOURCES, 1999

| *Income source*[1] | *# of households (out of 41)* | *Household structure* | *Male market or cash income (including private pensions)* | *Female market or cash income (including private pensions)* | *Children present* | *Income level* |
|---|---|---|---|---|---|---|
| Income from market alone | 11[2] | 2 lone-father households<br>3 single men<br>4 opposite-sex couple households<br>1 housemate household<br>1 mixed-generation household | 9 of 11<br>(1 does not contain a male member) | 6 of 11<br>(5 do not contain female members) | 4 of 11 | 1 high income<br>9 middle income<br>1 low income |
| Income from market and government transfers | 10 | 1 lone mother<br>7 opposite-sex couple households<br>1 same-sex couple (HIV/AIDS)<br>1 single male | 9 of 10<br>(1 does not contain a male member) | 7 of 10<br>(2 do not contain female members) | 8 of 10 | 6 middle income<br>4 low income |
| Income from market and private transfers | 6 | 1 same-sex couple<br>2 opposite-sex couples<br>3 single females[3] | 3 of 6<br>(2 do not contain a male member) | 5 of 6<br>(1 does not contain a female member) | None present | 5 middle income<br>1 low income |
| Income from government transfers alone | 3 | 1 lone mother<br>1 opposite-sex couple<br>1 single woman with severe disability | None | None | 2 of 3 | All low income |
| Income from government and private transfers | 2 | 2 lone-mother households | None | None | 2 of 2 | Both low income |

APPENDIX A – (*continued*)

| *Income source*[1] | *# of households (out of 41)* | *Household structure* | *Male market or cash income (including private pensions)* | *Female market or cash income (including private pensions)* | *Children present* | *Income level* |
|---|---|---|---|---|---|---|
| Income from market, government and private transfers | 9 | 5 lone mother households<br>1 opposite-sex couple household<br>1 single-female household<br>1 retired opposite-sex couple<br>1 three-generation household | 3 of 9 | 9 of 9 | 7 of 9 | 3 medium income<br>6 low income |

[1] Income from market sources refers to wages and salaries as well as net income from self-employment. Government transfers include all social welfare payments from federal, provincial, and municipal governments, including Child Tax Benefits, Old Age Security and Guaranteed Income Supplements, Spouse's Allowances, Canada and Quebec Pension Plan benefits, Employment Insurance, workers' compensation, training allowances, veterans' pensions, social assistance, and pensions for the blind and persons with disabilities. While Statistics Canada also includes refundable tax credits and the Goods and Services Tax credits as income, I have chosen here not to include the GST as a government income transfer. Most low-income households that file tax returns receive very small amounts. Private transfers include alimony and child support payments, annuities, superannuation, scholarships, and other items not included in other categories (Statistics Canada, 2000: 146). I note here that the Ontario Student Assistance Plan is included as a private transfer, as it is in fact a loan that is repaid with interest.

[2] Included in this calculation is one participant whose main income was from wages/salaries, but who also relied on undeclared cash gifts from family periodically.

[3] One woman receives an indirect male wage from child support payments for her co-resident adult child.

## APPENDIX B
## HIGH-MIDDLE-LOW: INCOME BY HOUSEHOLD UNIT, 1999[1]

High-income household (1 household)

| *Household income and location* | *Name* | *Household composition* |
|---|---|---|
| $250K Toronto | Sara and Anand | 2-parent household of 4 - mother, father, and 2 children; ages 38 and 39, children are 5 and 8 |

Middle-income households (23 households)

| *Household income and location* | *Names* | *Household composition* |
|---|---|---|
| $23K Toronto | Denzel | single; age 28 |
| $29K Toronto | Liz | single – lives alone; age 56 |
| $40K Toronto | Carl | now single – rents apartment with brother; age 36 |
| $23.5K Toronto | Rosie and Bob | couple (+adult son, who pays rent); ages 62 and 68 |
| $36K mid-sized northern Ontario city | Lisa and Ray | 2-parent household of 4 – mother, father and 2 children; ages 46 and 40, sons are 16 and 13 |
| $56K Greater Toronto Area | Maria and Leo | 2-parent household of 3 – mother, father, and 1 son (+ 1 away); ages 53 and 54; son is 25 |
| $102K Toronto | Melanie, Heather and Ron | 2-generation household of 3 – mother, daughter, and daughter's partner; ages 53, 31 & 29 |
| $45K $11K $22K Greater Toronto Area | Josie Rebecca and Frazer* | 3-generation household of 7 – mother, daughter, and partner, 4 children;ages 50, 26, and late 20s; children are 8, 6, 4, and 4 months |
| $27K mid-sized northern Ontario city | Jessie and Mark | couple – no children; ages 34 and 33 |

APPENDIX B – (*continued*)

| *Household income and location* | *Names* | *Household composition* |
|---|---|---|
| $37K Mid-sized southwestern Ontario city | Monica and Randy | blended household of 5 – mother, father and 3 children; ages 35 and 33; children are 16,10, and 8 |
| $26K Ottawa | Jerry | lone-parent household of 2; age 26; daughter is 4 |
| $50K Mid-sized northern Ontario city | Pamela and Bert | 2-parent household of 3 – mother, father, and 1 child (+1 away at university); ages late 40s/early 50s; sons are 28 and 18 |
| $63K Mid-sized southeast Ontario city | Janet and Christopher | blended household of 5 – mother, father, and 3 children (+2 more on weekends +2 away); ages 42, 49; children are 19, 17, and 14 |
| $41K Toronto | Aida and Xavier | 2-parent household of 3 – mother, father, and 1 daughter (+ 2 away); ages 49 and 45; daughters are 26 and 28, son is 21 |
| $32K Greater Toronto Area | Gary | lone-parent household of 2 – father and 1 child; age 38; daughter is 16 |
| $87K Small northern town | Barbara and Adam | household of 4 – lone parent with 2 children and new partner; ages 30s/40s; daughters are 18 and 17 |
| $25K $47K Toronto | Sabrina and Elizabeth | housemates; ages 34 and 36 |
| $103K Toronto | Frank and Michael | Couple – no children; ages 39 and 41 |
| $43K Greater Toronto Area | Denise and Rick | blended household of 5 – mother and father with 3 teens (+2 away); ages 41 and 46; children are 19, 17, and 16 |
| $101K Ottawa | Angie and Travis | blended household of 5 – mother, new partner, her 2, and his 1 child (+ 1 lives away); ages 36, 40s; her sons are 16 and 14 |
| $48K Small southwestern Ontario town | Christine and Dwight | 2-parent household of 3 – mother, father, and child; age mid-30s and 38; son is 14 |

APPENDIX B – (*continued*)

| *Household income and location* | *Names* | *Household composition* |
|---|---|---|
| $72K Small southwestern Ontario city | Cheryl and Paul | 2-parent household of 4 – mother, father, and 2 children; ages 49, 51; sons are 17 and 14 |
| $60K Ottawa | Victoria | lone-parent household of 2 – mother, 1 daughter (+1 away); age 49; daughter is 20 |

*Frazer moved out of the household in mid-1999. He continues to pay a small amount of child support.

Low-income households (17 households)

| *Household income and location* | *Names* | *Household composition* |
|---|---|---|
| $19K mid-sized southeastern Ontario city | Anne | lone-parent household of 5 – mother and 4 children; age 29; children are 10, 9, 6, and 4 |
| $13K Small southeastern Ontario town | Ashley | single – boyfriend joins her on weekends; age 59 |
| $22K Toronto | Amy | lone-parent household of 4 – mother, 3 children; age 29; children are 14, 8, and 6 |
| $15K Toronto | Julie | Single – lives alone; age 37 |
| $18K Toronto | Richard and Henry | couple; ages 52 and 44 |
| $18K Greater Toronto Area | Veronica | lone-parent household of 3 – mother and 2 children; age 31; children are 9 and 6 |
| $8K Toronto | Teresa | Single – lives alone; age 33 |
| $14K Toronto | Samantha and Nathan | 2-parent household of 4 – mother, father, and 2 children; ages 17, 20; children are 3 and 1½ years |
| $11K Toronto | James | Single – staying with a friend; age 29 |
| $19K Toronto | Sadan | lone-parent household of 6 – mother and 4 children (+ 1 who lives away); age 42; children are 23, 16, 13, 9, and 3 |

APPENDIX B – (*continued*)

| *Household income and location* | *Names* | *Household composition* |
|---|---|---|
| $20K Toronto | Rosa | lone-parent household of 2 – mother and 1 child; age 35; daughter is 5 |
| $13K Toronto | Kate | now 1-parent household of 3 – mother and 2 children (+1 lives away); rents house with sister; age 30; children are 9 and 4 |
| $22K Mid-sized southeastern Ontario city | Jackie | lone-parent household of 4 – mother and 3 children; age 36; children are 17, 3, and 2 mos. |
| $12K Toronto | Patrick | single – lives alone; age 35 |
| $16K Mid-sized southeastern Ontario city | Jenny | lone-parent household of 5 – mother and 4 children; age 30; children are 11, 8, 4, and 3 mos. |
| $21K Toronto | Natalia and Antonio | 2-parent household of 4 – mother, father, and 2 children (+1 lives away); ages 42 and 38; children are 13 and 9 |
| $18.5K Toronto | Michelle | lone-parent household of 3 – mother and 2 children; age 43; children are 10 and 8 |

[1]Where income is not pooled in households, the earnings for each person are listed. This is the case, for example, with Sabrina and Elizabeth, who are housemates, and with Josie, Rebecca, and Frazer, who are mother, adult daughter, and adult daughter's partner.

# APPENDIX C
# JOB STABILITY AMONG INDIVIDUALS IN HOUSEHOLDS, 1995–99

| *Job experience* | *Number of adults* | *Characteristics* | *Assessment of job experience* |
|---|---|---|---|
| In same job | 19 | mostly medium incomes<br>mostly full-time<br>predominantly 2-parent households | 5 positive<br>8 negative<br>3 same<br>3 uncertain |
| One job change | 12 | low and medium incomes<br>one high income<br>mix of full-time, part-time, and moved into retirement<br>mix of 2-parent and lone-parent households | 5 positive<br>4 negative<br>3 uncertain |
| Two or more job changes | 26 | low and medium incomes<br>mix of multiple, part-time, and full-time<br>mix of households: singles, couples, 2-parent, and lone-parent | 9 positive<br>13 negative<br>4 uncertain |
| Didn't work | 6 | more low than medium incomes<br>mix of households: singles, couples, 2-parent, and lone-parent | |

SOURCE: Bezanson and McMurray 2000, 13

## NOTES

1 The Conservative government was in power in Ontario until the autumn of 2003. Mike Harris stepped down as premier in April 2002 and was replaced by Ernie Eves. The bulk of the changes to the various policy areas were put in place in the first five years of their mandate.

2 While this chapter is concerned mainly with the policy changes enacted by the ruling Conservative party in Ontario in the second half of the 1990s, the federal context set the stage and in many ways mirrored the Ontario experience. In 1990 a cap on the Canada Assistance Plan (CAP) was introduced. The CAP, a federal transfer to provinces for social assistance, was 50–50 cost-shared between the federal and provincial governments. In 1995 the Canada Health and Social Transfer replaced the cost-sharing formula, and eligibility and level of benefits were left to the provinces to determine. It rolled social assistance, health, and post-secondary transfers into a block transfer (see Brooks and Miljan 2003). The 2000 Social Union Framework Agreement further entrenched provincial discretion. Changes at the federal level, including significant retrenchment in social spending in areas of federal jurisdiction and reductions in transfers to provinces, circumscribed many of the options available to provinces.

3 Members of households were asked questions about income levels, income sources, and expenses for the period 1990–2000. Particular attention was given to income sources and changes in income levels from 1995 onward. They were also asked to reflect on changes in social policy from 1995 onward. Thus, although actual interviews took place between 1997 and 2000, the data collected on household incomes (and expenses), along with experiences of social policy change, covered a longer period of time.

4 Daly and Lewis (2000) and Pierson (2000) wonder why European welfare states have remained resilient in the face of concerted assaults on them through the last two decades. Ontario's experience raises similar questions: why, despite dramatic restructuring, tax cuts, and funding cuts, does a safety net of sorts remain? Pierson suggests that "institutional stickiness" is in part to blame. Political mobilization and legal challenges have played a role in Ontario. Sylvia Bashevkin notes that the moderate successors to harshly neoliberal regimes have enacted some of the deepest changes to redistributive social policy. Ontario's experience under the Progressive Conservatives suggests that for the poorest members of society, the "safety net" and educational and training structures that might have levelled the labour-market and opportunity playing fields have been deeply eroded. The welfare state that

remains is one that predominantly supports the middle class and a dual breadwinner–female caregiver norm.

5 While the Conservative provincial government claimed that it was reducing the size and scope of government, caution must be taken in accepting this claim. The concentration of executive power, coupled with extensive re-regulation of particular sectors of the economy, indicated that government itself had not decreased its scope but, rather, had shifted its regulatory energies.

6 While $5.5 billion in cuts were announced for the first fiscal year of its mandate, the full amount was not cut during this time period but, rather, spread over the next three years. In his 1996 budget, the finance minister announced plans to cut government spending on programs, staffing, and services in order to meet a balanced budget goal for the fiscal year 2000/01 (Ontario Ministry of Finance 1996). The major announcement in this budget, however, was the government's plan to cut personal income taxes by 30 per cent over three years and its plan to cut payroll taxes for business.

7 For example, the minister of health was given authority under the Savings and Restructuring Act (1996) to eliminate hospital boards, take over hospitals, shut them down or merge them, and decide what services should be provided (Bezanson and Valentine 1998).

8 The Conservative provincial government enacted a series of Red Tape Reduction Acts (following a Red Tape Commission), along with eight bills governing various ministries entitled Government Process Simplification Acts (S.O. 1997, ch.36 and 39; S.O. 1998, ch. 38; S.O. 1999, ch.12; S.O. 2000, ch. 25). Nine Red Tape Reduction bills were initially tabled in the 36th parliament (September 1995–September 1999). Three major omnibus acts, all entitled "An Act to reduce red tape, to promote good government through better management of Ministries and agencies and to improve customer service by amending or repealing certain Acts and by enacting new acts," or the Red Tape Reduction Acts (Bill 25, 1998; Bill 11, 1999; and Bill 119, 2000) for short, were ultimately proposed and passed, amalgamating a massive series of regulatory changes and amendments in areas ranging from the Sheep and Wool Marketing Act to the Marriage Act to the Ministry of Health Appeal and Review Boards Act. In total, eight new acts were enacted through these massive pieces of legislation (Environmental Review Tribunal Act, S.O. 2000, ch. 26, sch. F; Wine Content and Labelling Act, S.O. 2000, ch. 26, sch. P; Enforcement of Judgments Conventions Act, S.O. 1999, ch. 12, sch. C; Settlement of International Investment Disputes Act, S.O. 1999, ch. 12, sch.D; Licence Appeal Tribunal Act, S.O. 1999, ch. 12, sch. G; Ontario Lottery and Gaming Corporation Act, S.O. 1999, ch. 12, sch. L;

Statutes and Regulation Act, S.O. 1998, ch. 18, sch. C; Ministry of Health Appeal and Review Boards Act, S.O. 1998, ch. 18, sch. H).

9 The study was called the Speaking Out Project, and it was funded by the Atkinson Charitable Foundation and run through the Caledon Institute of Social Policy. I was one of four research associates on the project (which also included Louise Noce, Anne O'Connell, and Fraser Valentine). The project was headed by two senior scholars (Michael Mendelson and Sheila Neysmith) and was managed by Susan McMurray. For further details about the study and its methodology, see McMurray 1997; Bezanson 2006; and Neysmith, Bezanson, and O'Connell 2005.

10 The total number of individuals and households interviewed changed slightly over the three years of the study. When adult household members separated, each was interviewed separately in her or his new household, thus adding to the total number of households interviewed, though not always increasing the number of adult participants. Changes in household membership sometimes added to the number of total participants. In two cases, single adult participants could not be found to be reinterviewed, and in these cases, new participants were sought. Many children who remained co-resident with parents over the three years became "adults," that is, they moved from under 18 to over 18 during the course of the study. In 1997, members of thirty-eight households were participating in the study; in early 1998 there were thirty-nine; in late 1998–early 1999 there were forty; and in 2000 there were forty-one.

11 It should be noted, however, that although a household was chosen for specific characteristics, these did not determine and predict how members would discuss the effects of particular policies or even which policies they would emphasize. Cheryl and Paul, for example, a middle-income professional couple with strong ties to the field of education and children in the education system, spoke almost exclusively about health care for three of the four interviews as their parents entered the health-care system.

12 Statistics Canada's low-income cut-offs (LICOs) were used to define household income categories. LICOs vary by income, household size, and size of community. For 1998, they ranged from $11,839 for a single person living in a rural area to $43,634 for a family of seven living in a large urban centre. Families living below these income levels are considered to be in "straitened circumstances" (Statistics Canada 1999). "High-income" households were defined as those with more than double the average income for all families (average family income in 1995 was $55,247) – approximately $110,000. Households earning an income between the LICOs and $110,000 were defined as "middle-income."

13 Canada has a range of universal and targeted social programs. Funding for programs derives from complex federal-provincial transfers, straight federal administration, and provincial spending. Descriptions of selected income sources among the participating households follow.

| *Income Source* | *Description* |
|---|---|
| Ontario Works | part of the provincially administered social assistance/ welfare program |
| Ontario Disability Support Program | part of the provincially administered social assistance/ welfare program |
| Canada Child Tax Benefit | a non-taxable federal tax credit for working households |
| Ontario Student Assistance Program | provincial student loan program |
| Aid for Children with Severe Disabilities | needs-tested provincial program |
| Employment Insurance | federally administered contributory program |
| Workplace Safety and Insurance Board (WSIB) | employer-funded program for job-related injuries |
| Old Age Security | federal income supplement |
| Canada Pension Plan | contributory public pension |

14 This is figure slightly below national data, which indicates that 80 per cent of family income in Canada came from earnings in 2000 (Statistics Canada 2003c).

15 When income enters households, it is not always evenly distributed among members. Gender power imbalances between men and women often affect women's access to money (see Pahl 1984). The case study suggests that other factors also create resource inequalities within households. For example, adult children who moved in with a parent often felt they had to put more money into general household consumption and less toward meeting their or their children's needs.

16 This finding is consistent with national data, which indicates that women in Canada receive 18 per cent of their total income from government transfer payments, while men receive about 10 per cent of their total income from government (Statistics Canada 2000, 140).

17 Many of the women in this study who had left abusive relationships had low incomes. In many cases, this was due to their primary responsibility for young children and their position in the labour market, combined with the

failure of men to pay alimony or child support. Many of the women receiving social assistance in this study had left abusive partners.

18 In the case of a sole-support father with a young daughter, living in his parents' home and receiving child-care and financial support meant that he was not solely responsible for his child's care or costs. He also had subsidized daycare for his daughter and a flexible work schedule. The level of unpaid work that he performed, although high, did not approximate the levels managed by many female-headed households in this panel.

19 This data reaffirms findings in development literature (see Elson 1998, for example) that women are clients of the state, but that programs and services are generally targeted in gender-neutral ways that result in women's needs, especially regarding raising children, not being met.

20 It is important to note that the Canadian federal government plays a substantial role in transferring funds to provinces for the delivery of social programming, including health care. Education and social service spending have been lumped together as a transfer to the provinces, and health is now the only policy-specific transfer area, giving the provinces significantly more discretion in spending. The federal government throughout the 1990s adopted a neo-liberal approach and redrew the face of Canadian social policy. It cut the total cash transfer to the provinces by a third in 1995, and although the 2000 health-care agreement between the first ministers and the federal government promised to restore transfers for health care, federal cuts have had a significant effect on the provinces' ability to deliver health-care services (Browne 2000, 23–6).

21 Community-based care encompasses a range of services and supports. Home-care services are most often associated with community-based care, but this sector also includes homemaking services, professional services (nurses, physiotherapists), day programs for seniors, supportive housing, Meals-on-Wheels, and attendant services for people with disabilities, along with more formal long-term care services such as nursing homes and homes for the aged and for people who require twenty-four-hour on-site nursing services. Community Care Access Centres (CCACs) coordinate access to services to people at home and provide some long-term care placement (Bezanson and Noce 1999).

22 Funding for health care was significantly reorganized in Ontario after 1995. Provincial spending on long-term care, for example, increased, but between 1995 and 2000 hospitals lost a significant amount of funding ($575 million in 1997–98 alone), which put increased pressure on the long-term care system. Cutting hospital funding and beds without having long-term care

services available led to far fewer resources and, for many families/households, a crisis in accessing care, evidenced by very long waiting lists for long-term care services (Bezanson and Noce 1999.

23 In Ontario the private market sector expanded its involvement in the health-care field, supported by a provincial discourse about a lack of federal transfers to provinces for the funding of health care as well as a philosophy of private sector management. Ontario did not follow a wholesale privatization program in the field of health care; rather, it shifted public costs toward the private sector by contracting out various services and courting private financing. The primary ways that households experienced this dual process of privatization was increased unpaid work along with increased expenses in hospital, out-of-hospital care for additional home-care services or for drugs, increased waiting periods associated with medical testing (which was almost completely privatized), and decreased quality for in-hospital services such food services, which were contracted out.

24 These findings are consistent with the excellent research on health care done by Armstrong et al. (2001).

25 In 1998, of 129 people (63 adults, 66 children and youths), 30 had a connection with primary school education, 17 with secondary, 9 with post-secondary, 3 with adult education, 7 with a connection related to their jobs, and 9 with future plans, while 54 had no direct connection to education.

26 For participants with children with special needs, changes in classroom funding, standardized testing, and teacher preparation time meant that the education system became a "one-size-fits-all" model, which allowed much less room for children with specialized needs. According to a 1998 survey done by an organization called People for Education (1998), out of 642 elementary schools surveyed, 2,377 students were waiting to be tested and identified for special education.

27 According to Statistics Canada (2005b), between the academic years 1995/96 and 2001/02, tuition fees in Canada rose 80 per cent in law and 160 per cent in medicine, tripled in dentistry, and rose by about 50 per cent in all undergraduate disciplines. Fees in professional programs in Ontario were deregulated in 1998. During this period, recent university graduates from the most well-educated families, whose parents held a graduate or professional degree, became much more likely to pursue professional degrees.

28 I am grateful to Susan McMurray for her collaboration in developing a list of household coping strategies.

29 Ensuring that the daily and generational reproduction of people is done and that the poverty of the poorest does not provoke public outcry and political protests to demand more support and resources requires a good

deal of social control (Corrigan and Sayer 1985; Picchio 1992; Little 1998). This control is most clearly evident in the reorientation of state policies and practices with regard to the poorest members of society receiving social assistance.

30 One outcome of the kind of restructuring that the province undertook was an increase in property taxes for many, especially urban households. The province downloaded responsibility for a range of services to municipalities and set up a new system of property assessments. In order to meet the costs of new services, many municipalities raised taxes.

31 This strategy of going after former social assistance recipients for overpayments emerged in a number of household stories. While I could not find documentation confirming an escalation in the employment of collection agencies, anecdotally it appears that the Harris government attempted to use this avenue (in addition to a focus on fraud) to increase provincial revenues.

32 Data for Canada show that 68 per cent of all people in Canada aged fifteen or older moved at least once between 1985 and 1995. Couples with children were very likely to move (74 per cent) and to be "better off" as a result. Lone parents with children were even more likely to move (84 per cent), but only about half of these households were made better off. More than one in ten lone parents moved in search of more affordable accommodation (Kremarik 1999).

33 According to Statistics Canada, the median net worth of Canadian families in the fifty-five and older age group was over $200,000 in 1999, compared to under $100,000 for those thirty-five to forty-four and $81,000 for the population as a whole (Statistics Canada 2001c). This pattern means that parents in this study were more likely to have access to assets such as a home than were their children. However, for those families with incomes under $30,000 (44 per cent of family units in Canada), median net worth was less than $15,000.

34 Canadian data on three-generation households indicate that the number of these households has risen 39 per cent between 1986 and 1996 (Che-Alford, Hamm, and Hamm 1999). The most common type of three-generation households (31 per cent) consisted of a home shared by one grandparent, two parents, and any number of children. The next two most common arrangements were those centred around a single parent and children, with either two grandparents or one grandparent. The majority of three-generation households (44 per cent) were found in Ontario. While reasons for cohabitation and the number of earners in households varied, in households with only one "maintainer" (principal person who covered housing and utilities expenses), it was the grandparent in 59 per cent of cases. These data

reveal the effects of precarious employment on younger workers and the unequal distribution of assets across generations.

35 The writing of household profiles was a collective effort involving, at different stages, all members of the Speaking Out Project. See Neysmith, Bezanson, and O'Connell 2005; Bezanson and McMurray 2000; Bezanson and Noce 1999; O'Connell and Valentine 1998; Noce and O'Connell 1998; and Bezanson and Valentine 1998.

36 In 1997, the provincial government introduced the *Tenant Protection Act* (S.O. 1997, c.24). This legislation partially decontroled rents by removing rent control from vacant units and from new buildings, and making it easier to evict tenants. This legislation significantly affected those on low income and was compounded by the province's withdrawal from non-profit and co-operative housing (see S.O. 2000, Ch. 27). No new social housing was built in Ontario between 1995–2000, and in 1999, the Ontario Housing Corporation announced that it plans to sell off 5,800 units of social housing (Bezanson and McMurray 2000).

37 The subtitle for this conclusion is borrowed from Broomhill and Sharp (2003).

# 8

# Someone to Watch over You: Gender, Class, and Social Reproduction

SUSAN BRAEDLEY

Care for the populace is a central concern of Canadian public policy (Jenson 1997). Since the 1970s a shift toward neo-liberal approaches to public policy has facilitated an emphasis on budget deficit and debt reductions. At the same time, questions of who provides care to whom, who gets access to various levels and kinds of care, how care is provided, and who pays have become key considerations in policy implementation (McDaniel 1999; Jenson and Jacobzone 2000). Canadian governments at all levels have re-examined their roles as providers of social welfare and as regulators of the economy, of institutions and of individuals (Shields and Evans 1998, 36–7). When compared to changes in revenue generated by tax breaks and debt-servicing costs, increases in public expenditures appear to have played a secondary role in producing deficits (Bakker 1996, 5). Yet deficit reduction and budget-trimming exercises have been used to justify public spending restraints that entailed state withdrawal from social welfare programs and from direct service provision. These changes have facilitated a corresponding transfer of care work from state-operated and/or state-funded institutions to individuals and families (Jenson 1997; Brodie 2003; Maxwell 2003), increased informalization of the care work involved in social reproduction, and increased the burden on the individuals, mostly women, who provide this care. However, governments have not abandoned their roles as regulators. Indeed, I argue that this role has become an important aspect of continued state involvement in social reproduction. At every level of state intervention, there has been a shift from attempts to ameliorate or reduce social problems to practices that manage social problems. Unwaged care work in Canada, and specifically in Ontario, has intensified *and* has come under increasing surveillance, as a result of these changes to state involvement in social reproduction. At the same time, any notion of gender is disappearing under the cloak of "family" and a presumption that households and communities should and will actively provide services formerly offered by the state or third-sector organizations is becoming embedded.

In this discussion, the definition of social reproduction is not synonymous with care, although care is one component. Social reproduction is the work involved in biological reproduction, the reproduction of human labour, including education and training, and the reproduction of provisioning and care needs (Bakker 2003b). This work, whether provided as waged or unwaged labour, is performed primarily by women, but the unwaged aspect of this work is particularly interesting in that it is performed by women *in addition* to their waged employment. The unwaged aspects of care work, then, provide a case study in which the changing dynamic between governments and social reproduction can be examined in terms of its gendered implications.

The management, intensification, and surveillance of unwaged care work results, I suggest, from neo-liberalism's reconstitution of the relationship between the state and its subjects. Neo-liberal ideology assumes that care work is a family responsibility, and this notion is deeply and increasingly embedded in public policy discourse and practice. This "family responsibility paradigm" (Beauvais and Jenson 2001) reflects an individualization and familialization of social reproduction in which the responsibility to ensure well-being through the life course is placed in the private sphere of home and family and is excised from the sphere of state responsibility. The role of the state within this paradigm is to get involved only when families "fail" and to intervene in ways that "enforce the individualization of social costs"(Brodie 1999, 43).

The dominance of this discourse does not mean that it is the only one operational in Canadian public policy. Citizens have been resistant to accepting governments' short-term fiscal restraints, justified by the need to reduce deficits, as a permanent policy direction. They have increasingly called for reinvestment in social programs (Brodie 1999, 38). A growing body of research supports this call with empirical evidence that investments in social reproduction produce positive outcomes. This research argues that public investment in social reproduction will enhance a nation's competitive position in the world as a supplier of highly productive and skilled labour to capital markets (McCain and Mustard 1999; Heckman 2000). These studies and recommendations interlock with the dominant neo-liberal policy direction, which is driven by a belief that changes are necessary in order to maintain Canada's competitive position in world markets (O'Connor et al. 1999, 1–2, 9). Notions such as "investing in children," which have increasingly appeared in policy documents (Beauvais and Jenson 2001), have led to policies such as the federal government's National Child Benefit (Canada 2000). However, this program and others continue to reflect and maintain the notion of family responsibility for social reproduction by funding families, rather than other social institutions, to care. Federal policies set both the tone and many structural limitations for provincial governments' health, education, and social welfare provision through policies that de-emphasize national standards and decrease transfer payments (such as the replacement of the Canada Assistance Plan [CAP] with the Canada Health and Social Transfer and subsequently with the Social Union Framework Agreement). Thus convergences between the family-responsibility paradigm and "investment" discourses emanating from activists, economists, business interests, and researchers constitute a climate in which neo-liberal policies and programs have developed at multiple levels.

There are two apparently conflicting perspectives here: a neo-liberal approach, which maintains social reproduction as a private individual or family responsibility, and a social investment perspective, supported by research evidence that looks for state investment in social reproduction. These perspectives mix with a third factor: the application of administrative and management techniques to public policy, administration, and practice in ways that directly impact on women's unpaid labour (Brodie 1999, 43). These methods emphasize individualization, a particular concept of "risk," and an overriding concern about the fair distribution of scarce resources (Shields and Evans 1998, 79). This "new privatization" (Jurik 2004) of government services is also characterized by a burgeoning of practices by state agents, such as schools and social services, drawn from for-profit business methods and applied in a belief that these practices will enhance accountability and cost-effectiveness in the public sector (Rose 1999, 150).

The application of these various processes of management to interventions in unwaged care construct a private sphere that is considered to be self-maintaining, but is all the while maintained as "self-maintaining" by strategies of management. It is as if a private sphere of social reproduction were suspended as a discrete bubble within the public sphere, increasingly penetrated by rationalities and techniques of management that have developed in the surrounding public sphere of production. This management constitutes social reproduction in particular ways and keeps it always under the gaze of the public sphere.

Canadian governments have historically intervened to ensure that social reproduction supports an economic and social environment that nurtures private enterprise. However, there has been variation in the ways in which this regulation of social reproduction is enacted. First, Canadian governments at all levels have intervened through laws and/or licensing, such as those that criminalize child assault and those that regulate marriage and divorce. A second kind of intervention has been the deployment of rules such as the infamous "spouse in the house" proscription of Ontario, which denied social assistance to women who had adult male cohabitants (Ontario Works Act, 1997), that operate as another form of regulation. This form draws upon the power of the state to control access to its social benefits. Third, taxes, allowances, and subsidies have a regulatory impact, drawing upon the power of the state to tax and to redistribute wealth. A fourth type of regulation is found in the use of quantification and measurement, which regulates social reproduction through definitions, such as what is meant by a "household" or a "child" as expressed in the laws, policies, and practices of state governance.

However, state involvement in constituting and maintaining a private unwaged sphere of social reproduction, while drawing on all these forms of regulation and modes of power, has taken a significant turn during the past two decades. Through the implementation of tools of assessment, surveillance, and monitoring, the powers of the state, through its agents, to invoke "expertise" have been mobilized with the explicit goal of producing specific behaviours in its subjects. This management has produced a set of obligations, sometimes enforced through a variety of coercive means (Dean 2002). This analysis locates this move to regulation through management within the discursive climate of neo-liberal state formation, in which "all aspects of *social* behaviour are now re-conceptualized along economic lines" (Rose 1999, :141; emphasis in original). If we draw upon Foucault's notion of governmentality (1991) and Lemke's valuable discussion of the as-yet-unpublished Foucault lectures on neo-liberalism (2001), these discourses and their related practices of management can be viewed as aspects of the emergence of neo-liberalism as an understanding of social reality – an understanding that constitutes specific forms of intervention as it creates the social reality that is its object.

The shift in government involvement in social reproduction associated with this turn to neo-liberalism has left many gaps to be filled by individuals and families. Schools expect parents to be more active in their children's education; health services expect individuals and families to provide more of their own care; social services expect parents to deal with their children's special needs. Middle-class households have accommodated these changes by hiring private help, purchasing services through markets, organizing their labour-force participation in order to work less than full-time hours (usually women's participation because of their lower wages and traditional involvement with social reproduction), and organizing their household life to accommodate extended family. Working-class households, on the other hand, have fewer options. The work-life balance discussed in government documents (CAALL 2002; Ontario Human rights Commission 2005; de Wolff this volume) is, for many people, a very simple care versus money dilemma. If labour-force participation is reduced in order to provide necessary care, then household income will not meet the expenses of daily life. If care is not provided in sufficient quantities or quality, there is a risk not only that a family member may suffer but also that the state will intervene in an attempt to ensure that the care is accomplished by the household. Therefore working-class households tend to experience more surveillance and management control by the state. In addition, the lack of gender analysis at both policy and practice levels means that the differential effects of these changes on women and men is unexamined and unacknowledged in government discourse, although clearly it is women, and most often working-class women, who are most affected. In discussing the situation of old women, Sheila Neysmith writes, "'Being managed' is the price these women pay if for any reason they cannot define themselves into the privileged category of managing, with its image of competence, and independence, and not making demands on public resources" (2000, 15).

I argue that "being managed" is rapidly becoming the experience of those who are involved with state-operated social services. Further, this management is achieved through a monitoring process that simultaneously intensifies and masks gender relations inside households and labour markets. This turn to management is evidence of a shift in the rationale of governing. It seems that Canadian governments less frequently perceive social problems as potential targets for social policies designed to eliminate or ameliorate the social conditions which give rise to these problems. Rather, they tend to view social problems as the failure of individuals and families to cope with social conditions adequately. Thus this analysis paints the boundary between public and private, between production and social reproduction, as a site of contestation. These contours emerge in peoples' lives, as they become directly affected by services.

## SOCIAL REPRODUCTION: MANAGEMENT, INTENSIFICATION, AND SURVEILLANCE IN WOMEN'S LIVES

Evidence of the management of care and its intensification/surveillance dynamic emerged in a multi-generational qualitative study I conducted in 2001, in which I interviewed three generations of women in five families about their caregiving and care-receiving experiences throughout the life course. The generational cohorts showed some differences in marital status, labour-force participation, and numbers of children, all of which had significant implications. The oldest cohort, comprised of people who were young adults during the Second World War, had all been married with two to five children, and the majority had been engaged in some form of waged employment during their child-rearing years. Their daughters, however, had experienced more years of waged employment, more years of unwaged care provision, fewer long-term relationships, and fewer children. The youngest cohort had been providing care to children and others only briefly at the time of the study, but were all engaged in full-time employment, although not always with a single employer. These generational differences point to a broad range of social conditions that interact in ways which intensify unwaged care. The strand of state involvement, however, is particularly interesting. These interviews revealed a shift in the ways in which different generational cohorts described their interactions with government-funded services regarding the provision of care. They also expose some of the ways in which the practices of neo-liberal governments have made the labour involved in social reproduction more fraught, more anxious, and more materially difficult for the women who perform it.

The interviews revealed a significant and incremental intensification and surveillance of unpaid care work. First, there was a dramatic difference in the number of times the three generational cohorts mentioned doctors, nurses, teachers, social workers, psychiatrists, psychologists, and the like. Each successive generation mentioned these professionals more often, either as presences in their lives or as sources of expertise on caregiving. Second, there was a difference in the nature of the involvement with these types of supports and services. Although many public services were mentioned in interviews, including mental health, social assistance, pensions and insurances, child care, child tax credits, and more, this discussion focuses on specific stories that involve contact with health care, education, child protection, and disability services, as these stories directly relate to the distribution of care work.

One woman of the oldest cohort recounted her experiences with the health-care system after her mother suffered a debilitating stroke. Her mother was hospitalized for a continuous period of eleven years at a Toronto-area hospital, ending only at her death in the 1970s, and this high-quality care was fully funded from 1969 by the Ontario Health Insurance Plan (OHIP). The respondent indicated that she visited her mother once weekly throughout this period. This account contrasted sharply with Marie's situation in 2001. This forty-seven-year-old was providing daily care for her mother, Giselle, since Giselle's discharge from hospitalization for a number of serious chronic health concerns. Marie was providing basic needs for her mother, including meal preparation, dressing, bathing, and medication administration. Marie and Giselle had accessed support through the local Community Care Access Centre (CCAC) in their area and were working with a nurse, who was providing "case management" services (OACCAC 2001). Community Care Access Centres were set up by the Ontario Ministry of Health in 1996 to provide access to secondary and tertiary health-care services on a needs/risk basis as a mechanism to open health-care provision to the private sector and to minimize government spending on health-care services, including hospital-stay frequency and duration (Ontario 1994). Four months post-discharge from hospital, Giselle's case manager had requested significant medical and financial information from the family, had required them to attend a number of appointments and to host home visits, and had also failed to provide them with any on-going caregiving or housekeeping support. Marie reported that the case manager had commended her on her excellent care, which had reduced her mother's risk of future hospitalization significantly. In fact, since subsidized service was being allocated on a prioritized basis, Marie and Giselle had to wait longer for service because other people were more in need. In addition, the case manager suggested that Marie consider purchasing a mobile phone in order to be more readily available to her mother in an emergency. It is almost beside the point to mention that Marie worked shift work as a cashier at a grocery store, and her mother lived in straightened circumstances.

How did care for the frail elderly person or the sick person, which has traditionally been part of women's domestic labour but which was previously supported by health-care services, become transferred into the unwaged labour sector and *still* remain managed? Notice that Marie had been subjected to processes common in labour/management relations, produced through discourses of support, risk, and need. Her labour is, in fact, being overseen, measured, recorded, and included in statistical aggregations used to define rather than reflect norms and margins (Foucault 1991). The family-responsibility paradigm, so deeply entrenched in government policy and practice, is insufficient to account for this management of social reproduction. Rather than social reproduction simply being reprivatized to households, care work is being commodified through these processes of surveillance and described as a public "investment." By measurement and assessment, women's unpaid care work is transformed into an equivalent of market-based products and services that have a definable monetary value. Bakker argues that neo-liberal policy changes have reconfigured government in ways that "shift toward a citizenship based on individuals as consumers and taxpayers rather than one characterized by citizens who are politically engaged and active"(1996, 70). In the case of the populace's need for care, decisions regarding who provides care and under what circumstances are reframed to conform to market considerations regarding the costs of care and who pays for care. Thus state-funded involvement in care is not conceived as a social benefit of citizenship, or as a social safety net to buffer society from economic downturns, or as a stabilizing involvement in social reproduction. State-funded care has been transformed into a short-term residual social welfare measure that will manage individuals into taking up or resuming independence and self-sufficiency.[1] Paradoxically, government discourse ignores the fact that all so-called independence and self-sufficiency relies on the processes and relations involved in social reproduction, and at the same time, governments provide services that transfer the responsibility for care to women in households through disciplinary processes under the guise of "support" or "investment."

In addition, gender neutrality is embedded not only in policy formation but in the practices of CCAC workers, who must manage (primarily) women's unwaged care work as if the expansion of one's capacity to care is a matter of choice and efficiency and as if a caregiver's gender is coincidental. Thus these processes render invisible the inequitable burden of care borne by women.

This relationship between social reproduction and the state reveals the imagined boundary between public and private spheres as a shifting, socially constructed terrain, where markets and state apparatuses interact with the private sphere of households and families to reconfigure and reconstitute the boundaries between production and social reproduction. The lie of a private space containing uncommodified relations of social reproduction, juxtaposed with a discrete and separate public space of production, is exposed. Instead, the state is actively engaged in constructing a private sphere by "indirect techniques for leading and controlling individuals without at the same time being responsible for them" (Lemke 2001, 201).

Intensification and surveillance processes proved to be similar for those caring for children and adults with special needs. Diane, a woman in her late fifties, was the parent of an adult child with pronounced learning disabilities and emotional disturbance. She described how during the course of raising her child, she was continually held responsible for his behaviour by educators, psychologists, and medical professionals whenever she and her husband went for help. Diane said that the public school repeatedly refused to provide her child with the support needed, and she bore the burden for this refusal. For example, she regularly stayed with her child throughout the day at school and advocated for her child throughout his educational career. She was subjected to surveillance through countless assessments, treatment modalities, communication books with teachers, and Ontario School Record reports that suggested her insufficiencies as a mother were responsible for the challenges her child faced. She reported that her own intelligence and education level were queried as a potential cause for her child's disturbance. Diane both contested her surveillance and cooperated with it by providing her unwaged labour. But there is more. At the time of our interview, she was still providing almost daily support to her now adult child, who struggled to live independently. She had regular contact with her son's "case manager" from the local provincially funded Association for Community Living, who oversaw his "independence." Diane's cooperation with this service meant that her caregiving labour was subjected to continued surveillance and management as a normalized aspect of her son's access to publicly funded service. She had been, in fact, conscripted.

In earlier decades, it is likely that Diane's son would have been institutionalized at the province's expense. I do not advocate long-term institutionalization of either the frail elderly or those with disabilities. My intention is to illustrate that there has been a shift of care to a reconstituted unwaged labour sector, maintained by a corresponding and increasing management and surveillance emanating from the public sphere. Note, too, that Diane performed unpaid care work for her son within the walls of a public school, where other workers were paid to provide one-to-one support for other students with disabilities. Her case furnishes a clear example of the interpenetration between public and private spheres, where the unwaged care work of a mother for her child, which is usually associated with the private sphere, took place in the public sphere of a school setting in which other adults work for wages, participate as staff members, and have representation through collective organizations such as unions.

A consequence of this management of unwaged care is that women and some men are increasingly subjected to conflicting management strategies or regimes of rule. They are managed in their paid labour-force participation and in their unpaid labour-force participation in ways likely to create conflicts. Crystal was a twenty-four-year-old single mother whose jobs as a retail clerk and as a counter staff person at a coffee shop required her to negotiate a frequently conflicting work schedule in which her hours of work at each job were posted only one week at time. As a result of her unpredictable work schedule, daycare for her child was difficult to arrange, and Crystal used four different carers in order to cover evenings, weekdays, and weekends. She came into contact with child protection services when neighbours called about her child crying at night. Crystal felt that her status as a young, single, low-income mother made her an object of surveillance not only for child protection services but also for her fellow community members. Once involved, child protection services suggested that there were too many carers involved with her child and that Crystal's erratic schedule, as experienced by her child, was not in her child's best interests. At the time of our interview, she had not been able to address these issues. She revealed that she constantly worried about her daughter's fussiness, cleanliness, and well-being, for fear of attracting further surveillance. She found herself altering her behaviour as a parent and as a worker out of fear that child protection services would intervene.

The most disturbing part of Crystal's story, however, was that just a year before our interview she had quit a better paying full-time job with health benefits and opportunities for future advancement, in order to take these two jobs. She made this decision because of her former employer's requirements that she work an irregular schedule, including significant overtime, which was creating overwhelming conflict with Crystal's parenting responsibilities. She had opted for less money and security in hopes of increased flexibility for parenting. The conflicting regimes of her waged labour and unwaged parenting labour, combined with her status as a low-income, young, single mother, had constituted Crystal as a subject of surveillance.

These factors demonstrate that state intrusions into social reproduction not only have gendered effects, because of the continued division of labour that assigns care-work to women, but are differential on the basis of class. Lower-income women have fewer options for supports and services. They cannot afford to hire others to support their unpaid caring or other unpaid social reproduction. They cannot afford privately available professional services. They are less likely to have employer-sponsored health insurance plans for their families or to have employment that offers paid leave for family care. They are more likely to have employment with inflexible hours and working conditions. Thus they are more likely to have increased contact with the state and to experience higher levels of management and intensification of their social reproduction. The impact of neo-liberal policy orientations regarding care work has placed a double burden on low-income women, who not only bear the gendered responsibility for unwaged care in their families but have fewer buffers to mediate the conflict between waged employment and this care work. The state's former, albeit partial, mediation of conflicts between women's social reproduction and paid labour-force participation has been transformed into the facilitation of market values and discipline to care. It is arguable that market-driven governance necessitates these tighter social controls, and "the state, having been put to death, [is] resurrected when it is the matter of socially regulating women"(Lamarche 1999, 70).

A further significant consequence of this management of unwaged care work is that the only way to avoid conscription and subjugation to these regimes is to circumvent public systems of care altogether, an option difficult and expensive to exercise, if imaginable at all when you have a child with acute health or developmental needs or when you have an ailing parent. Yet, in avoiding these systems of care, individuals avoid only the direct intervention of the state, while still experiencing "management," in that they have taken on the very responsibility which the state is engaged in shifting to individual shoulders. One family in this study had accommodated to its members' needs for care by sharing a common household. Three generations of adults lived in one rambling house in a small Ontario town. It is important to note that the two main wage earners in this household had secure, full-time, unionized jobs with Ontario government-funded services. This fact, together with a stable marital relationship, meant that Patricia, the "sandwich generation" woman in this family, had been at home full-time with her young children and then worked part-time in order to provide care without compromising her ability to return to full-time work at other life points.

This family's multi-generational living arrangement was precipitated by two bouts of poor health experienced by Magret, the grandmother, a woman in her early eighties. Her children lived several hours away and needed her closer to them in order to provide care. Magret did not need institutional care but required regular social contact, help with basic living tasks such as grocery shopping, and monitoring of her well-being. The family decided that it would be easier to provide care if she moved in with her daughter, Patricia, and family. Jenny, aged twenty, was Patricia's daughter; she had not moved out of the family home because of her own health problems. The pressure to care and support clearly resided with Patricia and her husband. Patricia indicated that this household arrangement facilitated care while allowing her to maintain full-time work. This middle-class family had significant responsibilities, but its members coped because of their secure, well-paid employment and their willingness to cohabitate. Even so, the burden of caring and working full-time had taken its toll on Patricia, who described periods of severe stress, worry, and time pressure. She noted that she would work more years than her husband in order to accumulate pension contributions foregone during the years in which she provided care at home.

Patricia and her family have used few government-funded supports, but have taken on responsibility for themselves. Doing so has only been possible because of their stable and flexible employment relationships in the public sector. However, the increasing number of three-generational households in Canada, which rose 39 per cent between 1989 and 1996 (Che-Alford, Hamm, and Hamm 1999), demonstrates one way in which Canadian families are trying to cope. The stress that Patricia reported, and which could potentially have longer-term implications not only for her own health but for her care of others, is a gender-related consequence of this strategy.

This "cost" to women is hidden from public view by the depiction of the private sphere of care as a "family" or a "household" responsibility. Marie, Barbara, Crystal, and Patricia were not "families" but women in families whose unwaged care was necessary to ensure the well-being of others. Yet through the management of a carefully constructed private sphere, its inequitable burden on women vanishes as a social problem and is transformed into a family matter beyond the purview of the state.

My own career as a clinician and manager in publicly funded children's mental health services provides yet another example of the modes in which the state manages caregiving labour. Children's mental health services, like health, child protection, and disability services, are provided to ameliorate social ills on an individual or family basis. While children's policy documentation and research sometimes describe the social conditions that produce mental health problems (Offord 1991; Lipman et al. 1994), services are usually based on individualized treatment models (Steinhauer 1995). The family-responsibility paradigm, with its inevitable consequences for women, is evident and intact.

The demand for children's mental health service consistently and dramatically exceeds supply. In order to address this problem, one strategy has been to increase the efficiency and effectiveness of mental health treatments through a movement to evidence-based practice (Children's Mental Health Ontario 2001; Drake et al. 2003; Kazdin and Nock 2003). Another strategy has been to allocate services on the basis of "need" – defined as the absence of family resources to provide other alternatives – and "risk," which refers to potential risks of death, hospitalization, incarceration, or more costly forms of treatment, such as residential care (Bennett et al. 1998). Complex risk and functioning assessments based on epidemiological research have been devised in order to facilitate these strategies.[2] Children's access to mental health services depends on the extent to which their primary caregiver, usually their mother, is willing and able to cooperate with the social services system. Caregivers must make and attend appointments, provide information that includes detailed family background, fill out most of the forms for need, risk, and functioning assessments, work on interventions with their child, and help the child cope with all appointments and treatments. Their caregiving labour is not only essential to accessing help for their children; it is under surveillance and subjected to repeated "assessment" to see if treatment can be concluded. This information is, in turn, aggregated and used to provide "evidence" for future interventions via the repeated application of assessment tools.

These practices manage caregiving by constructing appropriate parental involvement as the pill to cure children's mental health and behavioural problems. The women who present their children for treatment are effectively erased as subjects in assessment processes, and the social conditions that impact on their children's well-being and on their own caregiving are minimized and treated as individual circumstances. The expertise located in assessment tools cannot measure what it does not recognize or query, and so the social nature of children's mental health problems has become subsumed under a barrage of behavioural interventions intended to bolster families, increase parenting capacities, and enhance coping through surveillance of primarily mothers' caregiving. These practices have developed in the climate of neo-liberalism, constructing the very reality that neo-liberalism takes as its object. Social problems are relocated to private households not merely through the withdrawal of the state but through deliberate strategies of management that fix and hold care in this private sphere, while all the time remaining blind to the women's lives that overflow with responsibility to care.

The changing nature of social services delivery has other implications for women. Women form the majority of workers in health care, social services, and education. These workers are affected by the dominance of these neo-liberal paradigms in their paid employment. As state-operated services, transfer payment agencies, and non-profit organizations have positioned themselves within an increasingly privatized and competitive market environment, they have used for-profit business management models both in operating their services and in providing service (Mintzberg 1996). This move has been made in order to survive organizationally in a transformed social services environment. There has been an increasing division of labour between employees who "assess and manage" through technology such as computers and phones, using provincially mandated "risk" tools, and those who do physical or face-to-face work with clients. When I called a case manager at a Community Care Access Centre to check the veracity of one research participant's story, she described her first day at work as a case manager. She had walked into a case managers' meeting where the women assembled were, in my informant's opinion, nurses and social workers who had excelled in previous jobs because of their exceptional skills in working with people. These women now spent most of their working days on the phone and in front of a computer screen. Employed by the non-profit centre, they made good wages in permanent positions with weekday hours of work and full benefits. The women who actually provided face-to-face care work were employed by for-profit firms that had contracts with the CCAC. These women were not well compensated, worked on contract and so were without employee benefits, and worked irregular hours. All the workers in the system were monitored through the collection of complex and detailed work and resource-allocation statistics. In this system, the care work of social reproduction is pushed out of the domain of state-operated and funded resources, while at the same time it is commodified and managed in keeping with market mechanisms. Management, however, remains with the state.

## CONCLUSION

These examples suggest that neo-liberal governance has increasingly shifted social reproduction to a reconstituted private sphere. This shift has been orchestrated and managed through the introduction of market-based principles in public services at the levels of policy and practice. I suggest that the mentality of rule here is one that regards social reproduction as both the responsibility of private families and important to Canada's long-term economic future as a supplier of a highly productive and skilled labour force to capital markets. Although there might appear to be a divide between a "social investment" and a "family responsibility" discourse in government policy, neo-liberal governance strategies encompass both discourses through techniques of management in which various levels of the state have switched from services that share responsibility for social reproduction to services that discipline women in their provision of unpaid care through specific kinds of surveillance. This change, increasingly evident in the stories of women who have been parenting in the last two decades, alters the material conditions within which reproductive labour is performed and transforms the nature of the work itself. It also creates further dissonances in women's lives between their unpaid reproductive labour and their paid labour-force participation, while at the same time transforming these dissonances from a social problem related to sexual inequality to a private responsibility with which households must cope.

In order to develop understandings of the ways in which the interactions between and among individuals and groups, structural factors, and processes and institutions operate, there is a need to consider gender and class as interactive categories of analysis within historically specific local contexts (Bakker 1996, 8–9). This analysis has pointed to the gendered and classed effects of neo-liberal paradigms operating at the level of the state. Here the concepts of gender and class have been lenses through which to examine the shifting terrain of social reproduction, the role of the state, the configurations of power, and the ways in which these aspects shape women's experiences. In revealing the fluidity of these social arrangements, including the interpenetration of the public and private spheres, I have attempted to demonstrate that social reproduction is politically contested and contestable territory. The challenge is to develop alternative possibilities for the future organization of this work based on the goals of social justice and sustainability within a discursive political terrain in which economic rationale has become nearly ubiquitous and in which political and social action are considered marginal and suspect. In order to develop these possibilities, it is a necessary step, among others, to counter the recasting of social and moral good in economic terms by challenging and deconstructing neo-liberal practices of power at the level of state governments.

## NOTES

1 Case management is to "support clients in their efforts to achieve optimal health and independence in a complex health, social and fiscal environment" (OACCAC 2001). Informal and family care providers are not mentioned in this document.

2 In Ontario Children's Mental Health Centres, standardized instruments such as the Brief Child and Family Telephone Interview (available at www.sevolution.com/bcfpi) and the Child and Adolescent Functional Assessment Scale (available at www.cafasinontario.ca/html) have been implemented with the financial support of the Ontario Ministry of Community, Family and Social Services.

# 9

# Motherhood as a Class Act: The Many Ways in Which "Intensive Mothering" Is Entangled with Social Class

BONNIE FOX

The work that mothers do for their children every day is the foundation of social reproduction. The practices, social relations, and ideology of motherhood are also central to women's subordination. Of course, the impact of motherhood on women's lives depends upon how gender, race, and social class intersect, as well as upon a range of other factors (including social policies affecting families). The careful exploration of the intersectionality of gender, race, and class with respect to motherhood has only recently begun however (Arat-Koç 1989 and this volume; Bakan and Stasiulis 1997; Blum 1999; Blum and Deussen 1996; Glenn 1992, 1999; Glenn et al. 1994; Hondagneu-Sotelo 2001). And as the study of diverse forms of mothering proceeds, it is overshadowed by the attention being given to ideas, especially in the American literature, where work on ideologies and images of motherhood dominates (see Bassin, Honey, and Caplan 1994 for a discussion of this literature). Perhaps because of the strength of the latter current or because common-sense notions about motherhood are so strong, there remains an unexamined assumption that the majority of mothers in Canada (and the United States) have very similar mothering practices. Rarely are the daily practices of mothering examined. This chapter aims to examine the mothering practices of a group of working-class and middle-class women in relation to the hegemonic ideology about how to do good mothering.

I begin with a brief discussion of the historical development of modern practices and ideologies of motherhood. In reviewing this history, I address the question of the relationship between capitalism and privatized social reproduction – that is, the fact that families hold the responsibility for meeting the basic subsistence needs of children. I argue that motherhood is a "class act" in that its practices were developed in the nineteenth century by middle-class women responding to a crisis in social reproduction that was caused by the development of capitalism – specifically, the problem of how to prepare their children for adulthood. In many ways, motherhood as we now conceptualize it was an invention of the middle class in the nineteenth century.

Social class continues to shape the practices of mothering. In the greater part of the chapter, I explore the ways in which it does. First, I argue that mothering in accord with current ideals of good mothering – what Hays (1996) has labelled "intensive mothering" – entails middle-class resources. Second, drawing on in-depth interviews with first-time middle-class and working-class mothers, I describe the variety of ways in which social class shapes mothering practices. In developing this argument, I also indicate something of how women's paid work shapes their experience of motherhood, especially in its impact on their experience of time. Finally, I suggest ways in which motherhood reproduces social class.

## ON THE HISTORICAL CREATION OF MOTHERHOOD

Families play a critical role in social reproduction. They care for and socialize the next generation; they sustain adults and thus the labour force (Luxton 1980). It seems, then, that families' assumption of responsibility for social reproduction is an essential part of a capitalist economy – that is, an economy in which employers rarely provide food, clothing, and shelter, much less emotional support. Yet working-class history – and the inhumane conditions of nineteenth-century industrial work, as well as those in sweatshops then and now (especially in the Third World) – indicates that, by its logic, a capitalist economy leaves no room for family and personal life.[1]

As capitalism transformed economic relations and the labour process in the nineteenth century in England, it was only because of persistent campaigns by organized labour and successive pieces of state legislation that the length of the workday was shortened enough to make family and personal life possible for the working class (Marx 1954). Only after many decades of campaigns by organized labour calling for a "family wage" and eventual slow rises in men's wages did working-class women begin to acquire the means to care adequately for their children (Humphries 1977; May 1985; Reeves 1913). As Jane Jenson (1986, 15) has argued, "capitalist states frequently compelled capital to inhibit its tendencies toward unduly rapacious behaviour, in the interests of guaranteeing the continued existence of the current generation and the appearance of the next." Thus working-class families as we know them were not sustained in, much less produced by, the development of capitalism. Family, for working-class people, was instead made possible by collective action demanding limits to the ravages of the developing capitalist economy and state legislation that protected the population (and thus the stock of soldiers [Davin 1978]).

Proletarianization, wage levels typically insufficient for family survival, and the precarious employment characteristic of the industrial revolution shook the foundations of labouring families throughout the nineteenth century. The demise of "household economies," in which women had contributed substantially to subsistence, produced their economic dependence on men and thus undermined the built-in cooperation between men and women that was essential to the family well-being of independent commodity producers in pre-industrial economies (Hill 1989; Stansell 1987; Tilly and Scott 1978). Moreover, the low wages paid to all but skilled craftsmen, which undermined men's household authority, promoted misogyny and violence toward women at a time when gender roles were being renegotiated in families (Gittins 1986; Stansell 1987). In addition, because working-class married women needed to earn money as well as manage arduous and necessary domestic work, their ability to care sufficiently for their children was compromised. In short, both husband-wife relations and mother-child relations – the core of families – were precarious for the working class as capitalism evolved in England, Canada, and the United States in the nineteenth century.

At the same time, many working-class families endured the ravages of the emerging industrial-capitalist economy because of family ties – because of cooperation and support among kin that extended beyond the nuclear unit, as well as ongoing reciprocity within nuclear families (Gittins 1986; Hareven 2000). So, for example, because sharing housing was such a common way to "stretch" earnings, extended-family households were more common in England during the nineteenth-century industrial revolution than at any time before or after (Anderson 1971). Nuclear families, in turn, pursued a collective family survival strategy that involved individuals prioritizing family over personal interests. For instance, the wages of teen and adult sons and daughters were critical to family survival, though daughters were sometimes needed more to help their mothers with their domestic labour (Bradbury 1993; Hareven 2000; Tentler 1979). On both sides of the Atlantic, grown children postponed marriage until their wages could be spared. In some families, a daughter might be denied the possibility of marriage in order to ensure that parents would be cared for in their old age (Gittins 1986).

Family relations were critical to the nascent working class, but it was only after prolonged campaigns for a shorter workday, a family wage, and even protective legislation that the material basis of stable family was secured (May 1985). What these struggles make clear is capital's historic indifference to the need for "personal life," much less an ideal of nuclear family based on a gendered division of labour. Only after decades of struggle for higher wages, benefits, and entitlements such as unemployment insurance and workers' compensation was it possible for working-class people to live in families that involved men as breadwinners and women as responsible for the domestic sphere.

For the middle class, the development of family life centred on emotional fulfillment in intimate relationships as well as basic care had a number of sources. Historians have argued that the construction of a familistic ideology, involving a celebration of domesticity, was central to the identity of this class as it emerged. Middle-class people in both England and North America, in the early nineteenth century, developed the notion of the home as a haven and seat of virtuous and loving behaviour, in contrast with the cruel, immoral capitalist economy (Cott 1977). The ideal's roots in religious imagery reflect the solace and support that middle-class people found in evangelical movements (Davidoff and Hall 1987; Ryan 1981). In turn, historians argue, the domesticity that became such a popular middle-class ideology in the nineteenth century became a badge of class, an emblem of moral strength that distinguished the middle class from (in its view) the profligate rich, the intemperate working class, and the lazy poor. This ideology anchored men's and women's identities in family roles.

Meanwhile, the nature of family life changed as the centre of market-oriented production moved out of the household. With the demise of household economies, the material basis of men's household authority – involving their ownership of land (in the case of farmers), their ownership of the business (in the case of artisans), and their role as managers of household production in both cases – weakened, allowing for the renegotiation of gender relations in marriage. One of the arenas in which middle-class women struggled to gain greater control of their lives was sexuality. Women were increasingly concerned to exert some control over the number of children they would bear. In fact, birth rates declined through the second half of the nineteenth century, for middle-class women. And as the nature of the household changed, time developed for "personal life," which meant that emotionally rewarding relationships were increasingly possible for middle-class couples (D'Emilio 1983).[2] Lower birth rates were in part a response to the changing material situation of the middle class. A key feature of their changed material conditions was a crisis of social reproduction. This crisis promoted the development of the ideals and practices of motherhood.

In an economy in which fathers could no longer guarantee the adult livelihoods of their children (e.g., by giving them land) and in which the skills necessary to success were continuously changing, it was not clear how to ensure social reproduction. The solution to this problem of how to prepare children for successful adulthood – and one most likely derived by women themselves – involved keeping children home and out of paid work and giving them long years of informal socialization and formal education (Coontz 1988; Ryan 1981). In essence, the solution was that mothers would assume responsibility for the long process of "raising" children, ensuring that they received the formal and informal education necessary to adult success. In so doing, women replaced men as the parents chiefly responsible for children's welfare (Coontz 1988; Margolis 1984). In short, motherhood as currently defined was fashioned by middle-class women in response to the problems of social reproduction that arose as capitalism developed.

If motherhood was produced by middle-class households' efforts to cope with the changing conditions of social reproduction, those efforts were in turn influenced by dominant ideologies that reflected changing conditions. In the United States the ideology of republican motherhood that developed in the period after the American Revolution glorified the role of mothers as creators of the new nation and simultaneously imposed a huge responsibility on them (Stansell 1987). Expressing concerns about the quality of the citizenry of the new republic, the ideology also addressed anxieties about the role of women that arose as household economies declined, eroding women's central role in the production of family subsistence (Margolis 1984).

By the late nineteenth century, mothers were defined as responsible for their children's care and well-being and, more specifically, responsible for ensuring their adoption of the values, attitudes, and behaviour that would suit them well in the world (Hays 1996). This solution to the nineteenth-century "crisis in social reproduction" not only served to bring about proper socialization of the labour force in the developing economy (in which employers no longer provided apprentice training); it also created a role for women that tied them to the household and guaranteed their economic dependence on men.

While the responsibilities of motherhood have been clear since then, how mothers should fulfill those responsibilities has been the subject of "experts'" advice since the early part of the twentieth century. The content of that advice has changed over time, reflecting changes in the economy and ongoing concerns about women's abilities as mothers. In the post–Second World War period, women's continuing attachment to paid employment generated concerns about their commitment to motherhood. John Bowlby's argument that anything short of full-time mothering constituted "maternal deprivation" was only the most prominent in a chorus of messages about babies' need for their mothers twenty-four hours a day, seven days a week (Eyer 1992; Margolis 1984).[3] This theme is at the heart of the ideology Sharon Hays (1996) has called "intensive mothering."

## INTENSIVE MOTHERING IN CONTEXT

In recent decades, expectations about the work needed to raise a child successfully have escalated at a dizzying rate: the bar is now sky-high. Aside from weighty prescriptions about the nutrition essential to babies' and children's physical health and the sensitivity required for their emotional health, warnings about the need for intellectual stimulation necessary for developmental progress are now directed at mothers. This stimulation is expected to begin in utero, increase with each "milestone" in baby development, and eventually include some assortment of music lessons, swimming lessons, organized sports, help with homework, and parents' involvement in the school (Wall 2001, 2004; Wrigley 1995). It is interesting that this inflation in mother work corresponds with a rise in the credentials needed for white-collar jobs, as well as mothers' increased commitment to the paid labour force.

Heightened expectations of mothers have come at a time of profound change in the economy. The decline of men's real earnings and thus their ability to provide for their families single-handedly, the increased precariousness of employment, and the rise in the need for two income earners in families with children have meant changes in family life and the life cycle of individuals. Young women are postponing marriage and child-bearing and having fewer children, and there are increasing numbers of lone-parent families. Cutbacks in social services mean even less community support for raising children. Arguably, it is getting more difficult to raise children – harder for women to devote the kind of time they might have in the 1950s and harder to know how to prepare them for the labour market. Intensified public concern about ensuring women's devotion to social reproduction is not surprising, then; nor is the development of a new ideal of good mothering that addresses that concern and tightens the social control to which women are subject.

Mothering a baby in the way that women are now expected to involves expenditures of physical and emotional energy that surpass those called for in earlier times. According to Hays (1996: 8), the ideal of "intensive mothering" involves "the assumption that the child absolutely requires consistent nurture by a single primary caretaker and that the mother is the best person for the job"; elevation of the child's needs above the mother's, and recognizing and responding to the child's every apparent need and desire; and the belief that the child is "priceless" and deserving of very special treatment. Hays argues that the ideology of intensive mothering is hegemonic and understood by the majority of American mothers to be "proper," even though they do not always follow it.[4] Meanwhile, many second-wave feminists have assumed that the "predominant image of the mother in white Western society" as "ever-bountiful, ever-giving, self-sacrificing" is key to women's oppression in this society (Bassin, Honey, and Caplan 1994, 2). Socialist feminists argue that the problem lies in the conjunction of the ideal and a dearth of social support for mother work and mothers' responsibility.

Motherhood ideals may be hegemonic, but the everyday practices that mothers develop to care for their children are less clear. Feminists studying motherhood have increasingly tended to pursue cultural analyses – of the ideologies and representations of motherhood. And focusing on the ideology of motherhood leaves the impression of a uniform pattern of everyday practices. Yet mothers care for their children in particular conditions, with varying social, emotional, and material resources, and in negotiation with their partners (if they are coupled). Given their different social locations, mothers develop different ways of caring for their children. Studies of the experiences of women with young children show clear social-class differences (Boulton 1983; Gavron 1966; McMahon 1995), as do studies of how women socialize their children (Walkerdine and Lucey 1989). Rare in this feminist literature is research on the transition that women and their partners make as they become parents and the practices they develop as they do so. Yet this transition and these practices are of special interest to feminists because research has shown that, for heterosexual couples, becoming parents makes for a significant intensification of the gendered division of household work and responsibility (Cowan and Cowan 1992; Fox 2001; Walzer 1998). Arguably, then, the practices that couples develop as they become parents, especially those involving the giving and receiving of care, are key to the reproduction of the gender order (Connell 1987: 140). We turn to these practices.

## DIFFERENT MOTHERING PRACTICES

The study on which this discussion is based involved a series of indepth interviews with forty heterosexual couples and one single woman living in Toronto, as they made the transition to parenthood for the first time. All were recruited in childbirth classes; so they may have been more enthusiastic about and psychically invested in parenthood than is common. The men especially may have been more involved in the pregnancy than most men. The couples should not be seen as representative of first-time parents, then, but the ways in which they deviated from the norm were likely advantageous for my research: there was more diversity among them in terms of gender patterns (e.g., men's involvement in household tasks and their assumption of responsibility) than would be true of the general population, and so I was able to study diversity among the couples.

Ten couples were interviewed between 1992 and 1994 in a pilot project, and thirty couples (and the single woman) were interviewed between 1995 and 1997 in a larger project involving essentially the same questions. The women were interviewed five times and the men four times, between the women's pregnancy and the end of the first year of parenthood. Nine of the forty couples were working-class (as defined by their education, income, occupation, and whether or not they owned a home), thirty-one of the couples were middle-class; and the single woman was working-class.[5] Aside from social class, other differences among the couples were minimal because fluency in English was essential for participation in the study. Only two couples were immigrants from non-English-speaking countries. And most participants were white: four people (two women, two men) were African Canadians, all married to white Canadians.

We interviewed these forty-one women and forty men (separately) during the pregnancy and at two months and a year after the birth.[6] Shortly after the birth, we interviewed the women alone; and at the six-month point, we interviewed the women and men together. Interviews were based on a structured questionnaire, but all questions were open, and people were encouraged to talk extensively about their lives and whatever else they thought important.

All of the women who participated in the study were aware of the experts' advice on how to care for babies, and all but a few seemed to agree with the theme of prioritizing babies' needs, at least in the first six months (e.g., picking babies up whenever, and as soon as, they cry; letting babies set their schedule instead of imposing one on them).[7] There were, however, a few women who held different beliefs (mostly driven by concerns about "spoiling" their babies); all but one of the four women who rejected the tenets of intensive mothering were working-class. Of course, in some ways all of the women in the study – including those with different beliefs, practised intensive mothering, in that for much of the first several months of their babies' lives, they prioritized caring for them and did other things only when they fit into a schedule that was largely built around their babies' needs. Only two women in the study returned to paid work before their babies were six months of age, and sixteen of the women stayed home all year. What was most clear from the interviews with all of these women was the extent to which they had devoted much of their energy over the course of the first year of motherhood to meeting the perceived needs of their babies. Only three of the men in the study cut back their paid work to be home with their babies, one of them truly sharing the baby care with his partner, day and night, and the other two caring for their babies during the day once their partners returned to their paid jobs.

Even though all of the women prioritized their babies, there were differences among them in terms of the intensity of their mothering. Eight of the forty-one women in the study developed *very* intensive mothering practices, in that they literally prioritized their babies as much of the time (over the course of twenty-four hours) as they were able. These women prioritized their babies' needs to such an extent that they picked them up at the slightest indication of need or desire on the part of the baby. For instance, Kate[8] said she "wore" her baby all day; others talked about "never" putting their babies down unless they (the babies) were asleep; and many nursed and held their babies to put them to sleep, both at night and during the day (Kate referred to this as "parenting" the baby to sleep).[9] Even when the babies were older and able to be left alone for brief periods without upset, these women tended to be in near-constant contact or interaction with them.

Another eight women also followed intensive mothering practices, but were a bit easier on themselves. By the time their babies were two months of age, these mothers were starting to distinguish their cries and sometimes let them cry a bit if they were sure the baby was all right and if they themselves were busy. They put their babies down more than the very intensive mothers, though they nearly always were in their presence. In short, there was a slight difference between these two groups of women, all of whom were doing intensive mothering. (I call these sixteen women "intensive mothers.")

The other twenty-five mothers in the study followed their babies' apparent desires less faithfully, periodically letting them cry unless they seemed to be in pain or very hungry in order to finish something they were doing. Moreover, while the intensive mothers were working to ensure that their babies were "stimulated" as well as cared for, the less-intensive mothers were less concerned about stimulation and, indeed, at times aimed to get their babies used to sitting alone. It was this objective that most distinguished these women from the intensive mothers. When asked about the percentage of time their babies were awake and left alone to entertain themselves, the women who were not adhering to the tenets of intensive mothering indicated sizable portions of the time (e.g., 20 per cent at two months; much more at a year). In contrast, the intensive mothers typically disliked the idea of *not* having their babies in their arms, in a sling at their side, or in a baby seat within a few feet of them, even when the babies were a year old.

The sixteen intensive mothers' descriptions of mothering make clear the intensity of their practices. When her baby was two months old, Jeanne said, "That's what my life is ... It's like this endless twenty-four-hour ribbon. Like there's no night and day – well, I mean, there is difference because she does sleep better at night ... But still it's all I do; it's just all I do all day long. I take care of her." Jeanne also slept downstairs with her baby so that her husband (whose health was not strong) could get undisturbed sleep; this sleeping arrangement lasted all year. Several other intensive mothers slept with their babies and in different rooms from their partners; many others had their babies sleep with them and their husbands. Another intensive mother, Irene, summarized her first year as a mother by saying: "Your life changes. It's just that she's a priority. You adhere completely to her time, and you give up your free time, and she becomes your project." When her baby was two months old, Irene said, "Two hundred per cent of my time is hers. And, you know, it's like I've been saying to my friends, 'If you are not willing to completely give up what you are doing and redefine what is a normal day for you, don't have a kid.'" While the attention the babies received declined a bit over the course of the year, these women continued to do intensive mothering all year. When her baby was a year old, Debra answered a question about how much of the time her baby was put down while the parent(s) did something else by saying, "Very rarely. We've encouraged her by stimulating. She's very used to having a lot of attention. She demands it, we give it and encourage it."

The way a mother's responsibilities are defined in intensive-mothering discourse creates very high demand on a woman's time. Echoing the women quoted above, Lisa explained that she fed her baby every hour (during the day) for the first two months, and that "we don't put her down for long; there's always interaction." On the question of how she and her husband handled crying, Lisa said, "We pick her up immediately, if not before." Lisa's husband was a very involved parent, but like most of the other fathers, his employment meant that he was away from home for about ten hours every day, five days a week. So Lisa was very busy.

The extent to which some of these women were willing to sacrifice their own needs in order to meet their babies' needs was clearest in the description of a woman on maternity leave from a highly demanding professional job. When interviewed two months postpartum, Jennifer said, "I've never had more demands on my time in my life, yet the demands are peculiar in that, for example, the demand might be to sit still in a chair for an hour with a baby on me [sleeping]." For Jennifer, sitting still was extremely difficult.

Another woman's remarks made clear how lofty were her expectations of herself. When her baby was two months old, Carla said that she felt not only that she alone should handle all her baby's fussiness but also (echoing Lisa) that "I want it to be quality time, not quantity time. That's my only concern. I want to make sure that every day that there's something." This for a two-month-old baby! In contrast, the twenty-five women who were not adhering closely to the tenets of intensive mothering talked about learning to distinguish different cries, so that they could judge how important it was to pick up their babies. At two months postpartum, the pressures of undone housework led Caitlin (who was middle-class) to modify the way she handled her baby: "I do really try to put her down like in the playpen because I want her to get used to half an hour by herself." It was fairly typical of these less-intensive mothers that they let their babies cry a bit because they often felt a stronger need to finish what they were doing – and often that was housework. In fact, the compulsion to do housework seemed to be the strongest pull away from intensive mothering. Caitlin and her husband had the most gender-divided household pattern in the study: Caitlin did the housework and child care, in addition to holding a full-time paid job; Matt worked on building his business.

While most of the sixteen women doing intensive mothering were by themselves for much of the day, in one family both parents were home full-time for the first two months of parenting, worked part-time only for the rest of the year, and were equally devoted to caring for their baby. For this couple, Sam's involvement in baby care enabled Rosa to be an intensive mother. When their baby was two months old, Rosa explained the importance of responding immediately to a baby when she was asked whether she thought babies should be picked up the minute they cry. She said, "Absolutely ... I just think it's absurd to let babies cry ... If they're crying, they're crying because they want something, and if the wanting is that they want to be held, then they should be held." When asked if she practised her beliefs, Rosa said,

> Ya, well because there're two of us. I mean I think a lot these days about what it would be like to have a baby this age on your own, and – I lose it sometimes ... I just get exhausted and when I get exhausted I get depressed and then I feel like I just don't want to do it. Like I just don't want to pick him up. But that never gets very far because there's always the two of us, or if there's not, if there's some stretch of time and [Sam's] away, then I know in three hours he's going to be back, and I just hold it together for three hours and then you're off duty, you know. So I would say, ya absolutely, we've been able to carry it through.

As a result, their baby was intensively mothered, but only because his parents were both caring for him.

The women who were not as intensive in their mothering practices seemed to be providing their babies with the care they needed. Some of the mothers I have not labelled "intensive" were so wrapped up in mothering – its joys and their love for their babies – that they stayed home with their babies all year, instead of returning to paid jobs as they had planned. One woman even decided (with her partner) to move to a cheaper home so as to allow her to stay home and care for her child full-time. In myriad ways, all of these women prioritized mothering. Nevertheless, it is useful to distinguish those doing very intensive mothering from the rest of the mothers because examining the differences among them increases the likelihood of gaining some perspective on the factors affecting the practices involved in intensive mothering.

## INTENSIVE MOTHERING AS A CLASS ACT: ITS PREREQUISITES

Given the nature of intensive mothering, middle-class circumstances and resources seem to be prerequisites for its accomplishment. In fact, all of the sixteen women in the study who practised intensive mothering were middle-class. Being home all year was conducive to intensive mothering, but it was neither sufficient nor necessary for the practice. The women who practised intensive mothering retained their child-centred focus (when at home) even after returning to their paid jobs, and the majority of women who stayed home for the entire year did not develop intensive-mothering practices. More important to the intensive mothering of these women than being home all year was that they be free of the economic pressures and financial worries that would pull them back into work outside the home in the early months of motherhood.

Overall, material security seemed to be essential to the ability of the women in the study to muster the huge amounts of energy, patience, and mental and physical resources necessary to adhere to the tenets of intensive mothering. Having either a partner who earned enough to support the family for a while or sizable replacement earnings while on maternity leave seemed to be necessary to the intensive mothering of the women in the study.[10] The middle-class men were more likely than the working-class men to have earnings sufficient to support women being at home, and the middle-class women were more likely than the working-class women to have paid maternity leave. All except one of the intensive mothers were either on maternity leave in their first six months of motherhood or had husbands with stable jobs and substantial earnings.[11] In contrast, only three of the nine women who had the least intensive mothering practices fit that financial profile; in fact, half of these women and their partners were struggling on very low incomes. The women who had been working as part-time clerks in Walmart stores, movie theatres, or small businesses were in a very different position from women who were on maternity leave from jobs as journalists, high-level administrators, teachers, and successful businesswomen.

All of the women in the study who were driven back to paid work, or at least to job hunting, by financial pressures mothered less than intensively. One indicator of the connection between women's experiences of pressure to return to paid employment and their mothering practices was the length of time they breast-fed their babies. In at least one way, breast-feeding is central to intensive mothering: most obviously, it is the only way to respond instantaneously (without delay) to a baby's need for sustenance or (with some babies) comfort.[12] The only women in the study who did not exclusively breast-feed their babies for a number of months at least were working-class.

There are a number of reasons why breast-feeding itself is more likely to be a middle-class activity, many of them explored in Linda Blum's *At the Breast.* Blum (1999, 116) argues that breast feeding is a middle-class project because it requires that women have some comfort with and control over their bodies, as well as private space in the home, factors that are not as common to working-class women as they are to middle-class women. The issues affecting breast-feeding that seemed significant in this study varied from individual characteristics such as self-confidence and a general sense of efficacy to environmental factors such as general peace and quiet in the home. Tracy (who was very young, unmarried, working-class, and lived on a low income) gave up her efforts to breast-feed as soon as she got home from hospital because of lack of support, help, and information (including knowledge of the lactation clinics that so many of the other women visited); Joanne (who was working-class) supplemented her milk with formula, somehow believing that her own milk was inadequate and thus ensuring that it would be inadequate; Barbara (also working-class) gave up trying to breast-feed after initial difficulties largely because she was having to cope with noise, dirt, and lack of privacy caused by the renovation of her house, as well as worries engendered by her husband's unstable work habits.

How long these women breast-fed was clearly related to how long they were home full-time. Those working-class women who did breast-feed typically did so for shorter periods than the middle-class women. Not only did some begin looking for jobs after a few months and return to employment well before six months – the earliest any of the middle-class women returned to employment – but they also had to prepare themselves and their babies for their return to work. Most obviously, this meant weaning them and thus withholding quick response to their babies' needs early on. Often the weaning occurred over several weeks before the woman's return to work. Nevertheless, the women who practised intensive mothering were more likely to continue to breast-feed their babies after they returned to paid work than to wean them, unlike the other women in the study. This persistence underscores the need to probe further the reasons why some women practised intensive mothering.

Having a partner is also a virtual prerequisite of intensive mothering, especially because of the help he (or she) can provide, if only in the evenings. Even relatively uninvolved partners typically shop for food and other necessities – relieving women of the need to go shopping during the day with the baby – and provide some help with the baby in the evening (even if that only involves playing with the baby). Most important, partners come home every night. It is hard to imagine a woman doing intensive mothering without daily help. Of course, people other than partners can provide essential help on a daily basis. In fact, a solid support network made up of people committed to a woman but not living with her could provide better support than a live-in partner, who is typically gone much of the day: several people are better than one. Partners are important largely because people's lives are so time-stressed that inter-household support is more difficult. The only single mother in this study dealt with her baby significantly differently from most of the partnered women. Most obviously, she left the baby unattended – in another room – for pretty long periods of time, out of necessity. While a very good mother (with a contented baby), she was the least intensive of the mothers in the study.

It seemed especially important that men be home for a couple of weeks following their baby's birth. Susan's husband took two weeks of vacation over that period, and her description of parenting a year after the birth was "I feel we've really learned how to care for [baby] absolutely together. At the heart of it was spending the initial two weeks of [baby's] life together. We both came out of that knowing the exact same amount." The fathers in the study who failed to learn how to care for their babies right away seemed to feel more marginal than others, and they tended to be less involved in the care of their babies than fathers who cared for their babies from the start.

More is at issue than the presence of a partner, however. A woman who wishes to do intensive mothering needs her partner to be supportive of her complete devotion to her baby and her neglect of the usual attention and care she gives him. Intensive mothering is dependent on a partner's "consent" – that he forego having his own needs met by the woman (Fox 2001). According to Blum (1999: 165), breast-feeding alone inhibits, constrains and sometimes even precludes men's involvement with their babies: intensive mothering may seem to the man to bind a mother and her baby in a way that marginalizes him. Indeed, some of the men in the study indicated that they felt marginalized.

Many of the working-class men in the study seemed more in need of the women's care than many of the middle-class men, and more affected by the redirection of women's caregiving. In the case of one working-class couple, for instance, even though Simon agreed with the tenets of intensive mothering, his own need for Nancy's attention drove him to insist of her that their "sex life" return to "normal" when his baby was under two months of age. He changed his objections to imposing a schedule on their very young baby and accepted Nancy's accommodation, which involved putting their baby to bed at 9:00 every night, even though the baby typically cried for some time (see Fox 2001).

The middle-class men seemed more likely to be able to handle having all of women's caring work directed at the baby – a situation Joe felt "marginalized" him – possibly because they derived a greater sense of satisfaction and accomplishment, and perhaps even companionship and support, from their paid work. Perhaps more is going on, however. Charles explained how he felt about Susan staying home full-time all year: "My attitude is that I'm very happy that [Susan] is willing and able to do this [full-time mothering], and I think that it is best for the child." A successful businessman who frequently talked about his ambitions for career and financial success, as well as his fear that he might lose his drive, Charles was clearly delighted at the way his son was being cared for. According to Susan, he was "thrilled to pieces that

I want to [do full-time mothering]." Charles talked about full-time mothering as if it were equivalent to an expensive private school education. Perhaps the middle-class men's greater acceptance of their partners' absorption in baby care rests on their greater long-term commitment to child-rearing practices that seem likely to be "successful." Susan's full-time mothering was also a sign of Charles's success as a provider. One woman in the study commented that mothers being home full-time was "the new sign of being middle-class."

Additionally, women's position vis-à-vis their husbands affected their likelihood of doing intensive mothering. Women who had to divide their attention between their partners and their babies could not do intensive mothering. And those women who were completely dependent financially on their partners were less able to withdraw their attention from meeting these men's needs. This obstacle to intensive mothering was apparent as early as the first few days following childbirth, when some women in the study were making an effort to *protect* their partners. At a time when the women themselves were badly in need of rest, if not recovery, some were protecting their partners' sleep (Kelleher and Fox 2002). What often propelled these sleep-deprived women to protect their husbands' sleep when their babies woke to be fed at 2 a.m. was concern about the men as breadwinners. That concern and the protective behaviour were more common among the women who were economically dependent on their partners, and the likelihood of being in this position was greater among the working-class women than the middle-class women in the study.

There is another set of requisites of intensive mothering, which has to do with women's personal strengths and seems related to their social class and material circumstances. First, in order to do intensive mothering, a woman must put her own needs "on hold." The women in the study who seemed able and willing to do so indicated (in an early interview) that they had a sense of achievement, or at least satisfaction, with what they had "accomplished" in their lives before becoming mothers.[13] The difference between the middle-class women in this position and the other middle-class women, who had not yet found their place in the world of paid work, was most apparent in the case of Susan, who was firmly committed to the tenets of intensive mothering but very concerned about being out of the labour force. Over the course of the year, she described being stuck in a perpetual dilemma over whether or not to stay home with her baby or return to paid work;

she mulled over the question daily, reading "everything written on the subject." Susan had not yet figured out what kind of career she wanted to pursue, and clearly this was a big issue for her. She attempted to take a correspondence course to upgrade her credentials while her baby was young, but ended up quitting the course for lack of time. Two years after her baby's birth, in discussing the care she gave her second baby, Susan confided that she thought she had given the first baby pretty little "special" attention beyond providing basic care. Differences in a sense of accomplishment distinguished the middle-class women in the study and seemed to affect their mothering practices.

To do intensive mothering, still more is required of a woman than that she be able to neglect some of her own and her partner's needs for a time.[14] The ability to respond continuously to a baby seems to require a general sense of confidence and even efficacy in the face of a huge and vaguely defined responsibility without any clear measure of success and for which women have little preparation. The common experience is that mothers feel completely unprepared for the task they face after they give birth and are initially overwhelmed by the challenge; they must scramble to climb what one woman said was a "very steep learning curve." New mothers have to cope with the fact that babies' needs are initially inscrutable, which means persisting in their efforts at care without any sense of competence, accomplishment, or control. It means persisting in spite of uncertainty about whether they are doing the right thing – in the most important responsibility of their lives.

Most of the women in the study talked at some point in the two-month postpartum interview about their uncertainty about whether they were giving their babies good care and how hard they found that uncertainty. After two months of mothering, for instance, Jennifer, who was a very successful and clearly competent professional, said that what was hardest about mothering a baby who frequently cried inconsolably in the early weeks was that "I was always worried that I was doing it wrong. I couldn't tell if he was happy or unhappy." She explained, "I'm used to feeling in control of everything, and I'm not in control of him. He's in control of me ... This is something that I never experienced before – not knowing at all, really, what to expect, what's normal, and what's okay." About the crying (apparently the result of gas pains), Jennifer said that she just "had to learn that there's nothing anybody can do, except do what you can." Learning that lesson, she remained a very intensive mother.

Barbara provided a stark contrast with Jennifer. A working-class woman, Barbara clearly showed her lack of confidence and low self-esteem in the first interview, when she was pregnant. In the weeks following her baby's birth, her response to persistent problems with breast-feeding was to abandon her attempt to do so. Generally, Barbara's mothering practices were the most unusual in the study. Her marital relationship was also the most unusual. When her baby was two months old, she answered a question about whether motherhood was as she had expected it to be by saying, "I didn't think it would be this hard, actually ... She's very hard to please." Barbara said that she played with her baby when the baby was "in a good mood," but regularly put her down when she cried. Asked why she did that, she said, "'Cause everything I try to do she won't stop." (Question: So even if you hold her it doesn't work?) "'Cause she's in the crying mood and that's it; she doesn't want to stop ... Sometimes you have to just forget about her cries." It was possible, though not apparent, that this baby cried more often and inexplicably than the others, but it was also the case that Barbara's husband, Fred, required more of her emotional energy than was true of the other marriages. Fred was periodically suspended from his job following altercations with his boss or co-workers, and Barbara felt the need to placate him at home in order to improve the likelihood that he would hold onto his job. Therefore, while lack of confidence and patience were entangled sources of her response to her baby's needs, so was the fact that she was in the most volatile marriage in the study, with a man who had persistent problems at work. None of these factors are unrelated to the working-class status of this couple.

The importance to intensive parenting of a personal sense of confidence about one's abilities – something likely related to class – was articulated most clearly in the case of Simon, a working-class man who had a troubled family background. He entered parenthood as excited as any of the fathers in the study: he was perhaps more involved in the pregnancy than any other father in the study, and he persisted in reading the monthly issues of two parents' magazines through the entire year. Simon saw fatherhood as a chance to do for his child what he had missed in his childhood and somehow to mend a few of his own childhood scars. Nevertheless, he found the realities of caring for a baby often (not always) to be too much, just as he found it too difficult to allow Nancy to neglect his sexual needs for very long. When his baby was two months old, he explained that he could not deal with the baby's crying: "[crying] gets me really bad 'cause it feels like I'm *useless.* I can't help him with what he's experiencing because I don't know what he wants." Faced with an experience that made him feel powerless, Simon typically handed the baby over to Nancy and left the room. Several other fathers expressed the same sense of helplessness and inadequacy in the face of their crying babies; all were working-class and all responded with decreased involvement with their babies.

Intensive mothering requires a strong sense of efficacy, a sense that one is doing the right thing in a task with huge consequences but almost no indicators of success and few sources of a sense of achievement. So, aside from the material conditions that clearly favour middle-class women in this endeavour, it seems likely that middle-class women who enter motherhood already feeling a sense of accomplishment and competence in their lives are more likely to take on – and persist in – the considerable challenges of intensive mothering.

Material resources, a consenting partner, and a general sense of accomplishment and confidence all enable women to do intensive mothering, and all are likely related to social class. There is another set of factors that contribute importantly to women's ability to do intensive mothering. The amount of support they receive from their partners and from people outside the nuclear unit strongly influences the practices that women develop to care for their children. All of the fathers who were very involved in the daily care of their babies, and who shared with the women the responsibility for their babies, had wives who were doing intensive mothering. Similarly, a few men's refusals to involve themselves fully with baby care seemed to weaken the intensity of the women's mothering.

While these mutual influences are about more than social class, it may be that middle-class men are more likely to have the confidence it takes to overcome the feeling of incompetence that is common to many men around their new babies. It is interesting that all of the intensive parents were middle-class, and only three of the nine women in the study who were least intensive in their mothering practices were middle-class. One of the latter was married to a man who was often away on business, and another was married to a man who was unemployed despite having a PhD. The latter, in fact, pushed his wife to follow intensive-mothering practices, but he failed over the course of the year to influence how she handled the baby and was himself insecure about handling their baby. It is tempting to connect his difficulties as household provider with his weak influence on his wife (who returned to part-time paid work before their baby was three months of age).

Just as men's support of women had an effect on how the women mothered, so did the amount of support women received from their larger circle of family and friends. More of the women who developed intensive mothering practices not only had very involved partners but also mothers or mothers-in-law, and some friends, who were very actively helping and supporting them than did the other mothers. At the same time, there were some women with very strong support from their mothers who were not doing intensive mothering. The impact of support from outside the couple relationship was, in fact, complicated. In the case of those women who were doing intensive mothering, relatives and friends both supported and (in some cases) helped to enable the men's active involvement, as well as giving the women help, support, and positive encouragement. In the case of those women mothering less intensively, however, sometimes the women's mothers' behaviour served to marginalize the men: they gave the women so much help that they both removed the women's need for their partners' involvement and made the men feel marginal. This outcome seemed to set up tension between the women and their partners which made intensive mothering less likely. These patterns were not related to class differences.

## THE "UNIVERSAL MARKET" AND THE COLONIZATION OF TIME

My argument has been that because middle-class women are more likely to have the material and personal resources necessary to give themselves over completely to mothering, they are more likely than working-class women to develop intensive-mothering practices. This consideration of resources raises questions about a resource not yet discussed – time. Women's relationship to time as a resource will either enable them to do the kind of mothering they wish or inhibit them in that endeavour. Most obviously, mothers of babies often feel as if they have no control over time, given the strong and unpredictable demands inherent in mothering a baby. Considering mothering as social reproduction, which highlights the relationship of family work to work done for the market, however, raises questions about how women experience time in other respects. Because they are home, do they feel a kind of ownership of time, such that they are able single-mindedly to do mothering (however little control they have while their babies are very young)? Or do mothers feel driven somehow to be productive in more visible ways and to accomplish things more tangible than baby care? That is, does the market somehow spill over into the household, in a sense colonizing time?

It appears that our time has been increasingly colonized by what Braverman (1974) called the "universal market," as women have been more and more involved in paid work in a way that resembles men's involvement. Not only are individuals putting in longer hours of paid work, but because both parents are now in the labour force, their time at home is also more pressured, as paid work spills over into personal time (aided most obviously by e-mail). There are resulting pressures on parents to "speed up" their children as they go through their daily routines, minimize definitions of children's needs, and so on (Hochschild 1997). The question I ask here is different from, but related to, those raised about two-earner couples and their time at home. The question is whether women who are home caring for their babies feel free of pressures to accomplish things that are more tangible than caring for a baby. Do they feel driven to be "productive" even though they are temporarily out of the labour market?

One woman in the study, Susan, suggested this question in the course of explaining that since becoming a mother, she now did "one-stop shopping." Her explanation was that "my time is money." Coming from Susan, this notion was somewhat surprising because she was a full-time mother for the entire year and had been a full-time homemaker before her pregnancy. Because the marketplace had no direct claim on her labour, it was puzzling that she felt commodified in this way. In contrast, Jane, who was home on maternity leave, talked about how she was "giving freely of my time" in mothering her baby. It seemed that these two women experienced their time differently.

As was true of Susan and Jane, the women in the study seemed to have two experiences of time. Some of them displayed a sense of *ownership* of their time, such that they were able to *spend* their time on their babies. These were women with careers or good jobs who seemed psychically able to relinquish their desires to use time to "get things done" and instead spend their time caring for their babies. They seemed not to feel the need to account for how they spent their time – almost as if the time they had invested in their paid work had earned them the right to this time for mothering. These women seemed to feel both more entitled to spend the time and less in need of using time to get their own needs met. This relationship to time was not automatic, but something that these women usually had struggled to achieve in their early weeks of motherhood. Nevertheless, they displayed a sense of ownership of time, as long as it was spent on the baby.

The other experience of time was that of being torn between babies' demands and the compulsion to "get things done". This relationship to time, common to some women, involved constant pressure to *use* the time productively. These women, who often did not have good jobs, or careers, seemed to feel accountable for using their time productively. They seemed more caught in a daily "time bind" than the other women. They displayed no sense of ownership of time. Both groups of women, however – and, indeed, all women in the study – felt they had no time "for themselves."

Jane (who was middle-class) illustrates the pattern of women who, without a huge amount of stress, were spending time they felt was theirs on their babies. When her baby was a few weeks old, Jane said, "I can't believe how much time I spend just looking at him!" A couple of months later, she said, "I wouldn't describe him [the baby] as demanding because, you know, I feel like I'm sort of giving freely of my time. But I give him most of my time. So he gets a lot of time." While clearly able to give her time to her baby, Jane had struggled initially to achieve such a sense of ownership of the time. Looking back on her first two months of motherhood, she said, "You sort of plan out what you're gonna do in your day, and then [with a laugh] it took me not too long to realize that it may get done, it may not; so if it does, it does, and if it doesn't it doesn't."

Although she spent time freely on her baby, Jane was conscious of how valuable her time at home was, given that she would return to paid work. When her baby was six months old, she said, "I'm trying to do everything I know I won't do when I start working again, or that I couldn't do when I was working. You know, you don't have time to do everything." So she was spending her time wisely and enjoying the period at home with her baby. All the same, Jane did not feel that she had time to spend on herself. She felt that she had to tell her husband, who was home all summer and still fairly uninvolved with the baby, that she would "need some time" for herself. That is, instead of taking time from the baby, she insisted upon taking it from her husband. As someone who normally contributed about half of the household income, she was in a good position to insist that her husband "give" her some time – and she did.

Susan (who, like Jane, was middle-class) is typical of women who had the second kind of experience of time as they became mothers. Looking back on her first two months of motherhood, she commented, "I can't get over how little I can get done ... You never thought you couldn't get your teeth brushed till noon." And, "I was almost getting nervous in my mind, thinking, 'Oh, you've gotta do this; we've gotta get it done' ... I was sort of like a woman possessed." What Susan felt driven to "get done" was not baby care, in its many dimensions, but a range of household chores and tasks not directly related to motherhood, such as creating a pleasant home and developing her career. She claimed that she had overcome her expectations about getting much housework done, but it was clear from her description of her daily activities that she felt driven both to create a comfortable home life for herself and her husband and to get her career underway. Accordingly, Susan contradicted herself in describing her attempts to overcome her feeling of being driven: "I've learned now not to sort of set myself up for not getting things done. I just sort of manage to *accomplish* bit by bit" (my emphasis).

In turn, Susan's experience of time had an impact on her mothering practices, which were less intensive than those of the sixteen "intensive mothers." "There's some times when he's crying and I think there's no reason why he should be, I will let him cry ... I leave him alone, and that's only because [otherwise] I'd never get anything done." When her baby was six months old, Susan talked about getting the baby up as "late" as 7 a.m. because in the morning, before then, "I have to do stuff." She was one of the few mothers in the study who was looking forward to her baby's independence of her, glad that "it [infancy] will not last forever." She started introducing formula and weaning the baby before six months, in order that someone other than she could feed him, and she explained that she was "trying increasingly more to give us sort of our independence." Susan was the woman who was conflicted about whether or not to return to the labour force and, most important, concerned that she had not yet begun a career (as had all her friends), and she was the woman who felt her time was "money." She was clearly struggling to find time for herself, partly to tackle the question of her future in the labour force. She also felt driven to create a comfortable home as well as a career.

The contrast between Jane and Susan – and the other women like each of them – indicates a strong impact of the market on mothers' experience of time. Past and (likely) future accomplishment in the labour market somehow gave the women who had them (such as Jane) ownership of time, which allowed them to devote their energies to motherhood. Their own needs and their husbands' seemed to intrude on this focus much less than either did for the other women: their labour-force accomplishments seem to have provided them both bargaining power in the relationship with their husband and personal rewards sufficient to carry them through a period in which many of their own needs were either "on hold" or being satisfied by the very different kind of work entailed in mothering. In contrast, women such as Susan seemed compelled to be productive – despite the demands of motherhood – in ways that would both give themselves a feeling of accomplishment and contribute to the household in ways their partners would recognize. Somehow, their time was "colonized."[15]

The other experience of time for these new mothers is a predictable one: the mothers who returned to paid work before the year's end typically experienced major time pressures. Their days were tightly scheduled, both inside and outside the home, with no time left for themselves or to spend with their partners. These women experienced time pressures that created serious stress in their lives. Indeed, the contrast for these women between the period in which they were home with their babies and when they were back at their paid work suggests that their experience of time at home in the postpartum period was partly one of relief from the travails of full-time paid work. Jane and some others of these women talked about being home with their babies as a "vacation." The feeling that they owned their time at home was probably partly due to the contrast with the way they experienced time in their paid jobs.

For all of the women, time was a scarce resource over which they had little control. Some of the women, who were "accomplished" in the labour force and not financially dependent on their partners, felt entitled to spend their time on the baby and able to overcome feelings that they needed to accomplish more than baby care. These women's labour-market position affected their mothering: they were likely to do intensive mothering. They felt entitled not to be "productive" in visible ways and to prioritize their babies' needs over their husbands' needs. They did not feel sufficiently entitled to spend time on themselves, however.

In contrast, the women who had not achieved any security in the labour force tended to be very torn between the need to attend to their babies, on the one hand, and the need to accomplish certain goals beyond baby care over the course of the day, on the other. They acted as if they did not have the right to spend their time just on baby care, which perhaps reflected the fact that their bargaining power in their marriage was weaker than the other women's. Much of what they felt driven to accomplish was housework, and thus the creation of a home comfortable enough to be pleasant (and rewarding) for the breadwinner. As well, they seemed to require time for themselves. They were less likely to do intensive mothering and more likely to devote some time to meeting their partners' needs, as well as their own.

## MOTHERING AND SOCIAL REPRODUCTION

Aside from the question of how social class influences mothering practices, the question of how mothering practices reproduce social class is an important one to explore. When one of the mothers in the study, Rhonda, remarked that "having a woman at home full-time is the new sign of being middle-class," she was probably referring to the privileges of being middle-class. Middle-class couples are better able to afford a single income earner, and I have argued that middle-class mothers are more likely to develop intensive-mothering practices. But the effects of full-time mothering and intensive mothering (which are somewhat related) on social class are much less obvious.

It is possible that intensive mothering directly reproduces social class, in that babies cared for in this manner are somehow better prepared for success later in life. Certainly, babies and toddlers who receive good-quality care that includes a program of stimulating activities are significantly better prepared intellectually for school, and thus for success in the early grades of school. The research that shows the benefits of early intellectual stimulation applies to children who have been in daycare or nursery-school programs, however, and involves a contrast with children who were at home in their early years (Clarke-Stewart 1993). One can only suspect that mother care that involves constant attention to babies' needs, plus greater interaction and thus stimulation, will similarly give babies a boost in their cognitive (though not social) development, especially if that attentiveness continues over the next few years of the child's life. The theoretical and empirical grounds on which to build such a case are not at all obvious. Yet I suspect that this is one of the key assumptions made by the middle-class parents in the study who, like the working-class parents, firmly believed that babies' needs are best met by full-time mothering.

It seems unlikely that intensive mothering constitutes a "badge" of middle-class status. Invisible by nature, women's intensive mothering is unlikely to garner recognition by anyone other than their partners and other very close family and friends. Many of the women in the study pointed out that their partners were the only people in the world who understood how much work they were doing and how hard it was. Women whose husbands did not seem fully to appreciate the way they were caring for their babies were doubly troubled by that oversight. However, breast-feeding, which is an important part of intensive mothering, may bolster a woman's – and even a couple's – class status in the eyes of others. Moreover, when one distinguishes women's and men's status, another possibility becomes clear: while being home with a baby and doing intensive mothering may detract from women's class status, given how much more recognition paid work is regularly shown, it may bolster men's status. Intensive mothering may signify men's ability to support dependants and something of the quality of the family he supports. In that respect, it may support a man's class status.

Reflecting on his experience of fatherhood, Jane's husband, Tom, indicated something of the privilege – and perhaps added status – that he had enjoyed because Jane was home all year when he noted that "it's a luxury having a wife at home." Given his situation, Tom must have been talking about more than status. After the early months of mothering, women at home typically were doing relatively more of the housework than they had done before becoming mothers, which meant that the men were enjoying the benefits of that work. The men did relatively less of the housework than they had before becoming fathers, and, more important, they benefited from having someone at home who could plan dinner, meet repairmen, and so on. Many men came home to a nice dinner, in fact. As well, when women stayed home, they were likely to be considerably less stressed than those who were trying to combine paid work with mother work and housework, and as a result, they were likely to put less pressure on their partners to do baby care and housework.

Many men in the study expressed gratitude that their wives were willing to do the kind of mothering they were doing and that their babies were given what they saw as the best care possible. While intensive mothering itself largely deprived these men of their wives' attention, the increased energy they spent at work after becoming fathers also meant some sacrifice. But both might have been seen as ways of undergirding their family's class position.

## SOME FINAL THOUGHTS

There is more than one way to care for a baby. What is clear in this study is that different social locations provide women with different capacities and resources, which in turn promote different ways of mothering. The women in this study who were more likely to do the kind of intensive mothering that is now advocated by "the experts" were middle-class, while the working-class women and other middle-class women were caring for their babies without dropping what they were doing every time the babies whimpered or even cried.

It is interesting to speculate about the impact of different mothering practices on babies. Perhaps there is no long-run impact. Possibly babies who are mothered intensively develop cognitively more quickly than those babies whose mothers care for them less intensively. Babies who are intensively mothered might also become less independent of adults, and more eager to please, as they mature (and if their mother maintains her style of mothering). Jessica Benjamin (1988) has argued very persuasively that healthy child development requires that a mother maintain a balance between addressing the needs of the child and asserting her own needs, so that the child experiences a give-and-take (i.e., healthy) relationship, learning to recognize the needs of others as she or he develops his or her sense of self. But we can only speculate on the impact of different mothering practices on babies.

Somewhat less speculative is the impact of intensive-mothering practices on mothers themselves. Ruth summarized most succinctly what many women in the study who were doing intensive mothering seemed to feel. "I'm not most important now", she said, in the course of explaining why she might abandon her career plans. Somehow women who were either successful in the labour market or at least comfortably middle-class were more likely to subordinate themselves to the rigours of intensive mothering. They were quicker to deny their own needs than other women in the study. As a result, sheer exhaustion was typically the mark of an intensive mother, unless she had extremely good support. The women who returned to their paid work were especially worn ragged by the demands on them.

Why middle-class women are more likely to subordinate themselves in this way is not clear. What is worth considering is that nearly all the women practising intensive mothering had achieved some success in paid employment – that is, in a world built for men (i.e., people without family responsibilities). As we saw, this success seemed to give them a sense of ownership of their time at home that enabled them to do intensive mothering. Those women who had not succeeded in the labour market were struggling to do so. When they thought about how to best care for their babies, two issues may have assumed priority for the women practising intensive mothering: first, a clear sense of the barriers to women's success in a man's marketplace and, second, anxiety about giving their babies good care when planning to combine motherhood with employment. Interestingly, all except one of the eight women who practised *very* intensive mothering had baby girls – an indication that concern about the long climb their daughters faced may have been a subtle (and probably unconscious) ingredient in their fastidious attention to their babies.

Guilt about their imminent return to paid work may also have been operating. Eyer (1992) has suggested that the popularity of the notion that mothers can "bond" instantly with their newborn babies if they have a half-hour of skin-to-skin contact with them following their birth derived in part from guilt about mothers' involvement in the labour force. The bond symbolized a kind of guarantee that things would be fine between mother and child, whatever the future. In a similar way, intensive mothering may also be some women's way of both trying to ensure their babies' quick development and high IQ, and thus future success, and assuaging their guilt about less-than-full-time mothering after six months.[16] In short, women may be trying to ensure the reproduction of social class across the generations.[17]

## NOTES

The research reported here was made possible by a grant from the Social Sciences and Humanities Research Council of Canada. I thank Meg Luxton, Kate Bezanson, Judith Taylor, and Barrie Thorne for helpful comments on an early draft of this chapter, as well as Diana Worts and Christa Kelleher, whose insights have contributed significantly to my analysis of the interviews reported here.

1 Of course, mass production requires mass consumption, and ideals of "family life" have become central to mass marketing, especially in North America. But corporate capitalism continues to eat away at people's time away from work: hours of work have increased in recent decades to such an extent that many people have little time for family life (Hochschild 1997;

Jacobs and Gerson 2004). To paraphrase Arlie Hochschild (1997, 198–9), in the battle between "work and home," work is winning.

2 Companionate marriage did not simply emerge as an ideal, however. There is an interesting historical conjunction of fears about "the family" engendered in the early twentieth century by declines in the birth rate, coupled with increases in divorce rates, on the one hand, and new ideals of self-fulfillment in marriage, including the notion that women as well as men should find sexual satisfaction in marriage, on the other hand (Katz 1995). It is out of that climate, and partly because of popularization by Hollywood, that modern expectations of companionate marriage seem to have developed. Some argue that a backlash against the gains made by women was behind the new ideals about marriage, which captured and co-opted a sense of optimism women felt about the possibilities they faced and steered it in the direction of seeking fulfillment in marriage (Rapp and Ross 1986).

3 John Bowlby is a British psychiatrist who relied on studies of children institutionalized during the Second World War to argue that the problems they manifest were due to "maternal deprivation" and not the absence of social, emotional, and physical stimulation and sheer contact with human caregivers. During the 1950s he developed "attachment theory," which assumed an instinctual attachment of infant to mother (Eyer 1992). His ideas were very popular in the 1950s and 1960s, when he advocated women's full-time mothering.

4 Hays (1996) reports that a 1981 study found that 97 per cent of American women had read at least one child-rearing manual. She asserts that women are generally very aware of what the experts consider appropriate.

5 With the exception of one couple, the women and their male partners were of the same social class; so I was able to classify the couples as a unit. With respect to the couple that was the exception, the woman had an MA and a professional job, while the man had only a high school education and a low-status white-collar job. Because he was from a middle-class family and seemed to have not moved on in school primarily because of his countercultural life style, and because this couple owned a house and had an income over $60,000, I classified them as middle-class. Joan Acker (1999) has argued that class is something people "do," and I think it significant that this couple hired a babysitter for their baby and a woman to clean their home after the woman's maternity leave ended.

6 Research assistants Diana Worts and Sherry Bartram, who were graduate students at the University of Toronto, interviewed twelve of the couples.

7 How a woman cares for her baby is an issue on which the stakes are high. Women are continually judged by how well they approximate motherhood

ideals, as well as expectations about womanhood, and the two are bound together (Walzer 1998). More important, mothers are held responsible for the well-being of their children. What is at stake, then, as parents decide how to care for their babies, is clear. But beyond that, almost nothing is very clear. The specific *way* a woman mothers her child is her own, and in part her partner's, decision.

In advocating very labour-intensive mothering, the popular ideal assumes a completely selfless woman who is at the same time naturally suited to mothering and fully in need of clear directives. Intensive-mothering ideals advocate a mode of selfless responsiveness to babies, yet this child-centred approach contradicts the fact that caring for a new baby calls for heads-up problem-solving on a regular basis. Moreover, practising intensive mothering – submerging oneself fully in motherhood – in a culture where market success is what carries value and care work merits little esteem can be a lonely enterprise. Even more immediately problematic is the assumption that a woman can give never-ending care regardless of how well her own needs are being met.

At the same time, making choices about baby care that allow a woman some time to meet her own needs (e.g., deciding to bottle-feed her baby rather than breast-feed) risks condemnation by others and a good deal of "mother guilt" (Eyer 1996). In short, women face impossible decisions about how to do mothering, a "damned if you do, damned if you don't" situation. (I thank Judy Taylor for pointing this dilemma out to me.)

8 The names are fictitious, of course.

9 Kate was following the advice of William Sears and Martha Sears, authors of *The Baby Book,* who base their advice on John Bowlby's "attachment theory." See Diane Eyer (1992) for a discussion of Bowlby and his influence.

10 In the years during which these women were interviewed, women could take seventeen weeks of maternity leave, fifteen of which were paid if the women were entitled to benefits through Unemployment Insurance (at 60 per cent of usual wages/salaries, as replacement earnings). Women could also take parental leave of ten weeks, also paid through UI. Employers frequently "topped up" UI payments.

11 Rosa was the exception, and she had educational credentials that enabled her to find paid work easily.

12 Beth described how she had to let her baby cry often because if he was hungry, considerable time was occupied heating up his bottle.

13 When the women were pregnant, I asked them a question about how "satisfied" they felt about what they had so far accomplished or where they were in terms of any life goals.

14 For very good fictional descriptions of what motherhood means for accomplished middle-class women, in terms of the cost to women's status, sense of accomplishment, need fulfillment, and so on, see Jackson 1992, Lazarre 1976, and Wolf 2001. For an excellent study of postpartum depression and the grassroots self-help movement in the United States that has developed to help mothers, see Taylor 1996.

15 This finding of mothers' increased ability to devote themselves to their babies when they were at home on maternity leave from a paid job is another benefit of maternity-leave provisions that would pay women generously. Payments to Canadian women now are low, relative to those in Europe.

16 In Ontario, conservative provincial government messages and programs stressing the importance of the "early years" for children's intellectual development and school success have served to increase pressure on mothers, underlining their responsibility for their children's school success (Wall 2004).

17 Women's intensive mothering has an interesting effect on their relationship with their partner. Although parenthood typically promotes more-unequal gender relations in couples, intensive-mothering practices seem to test a man's commitment to the relationship and the woman (who has little energy for anything but the baby) and strengthen unions in which a man supports and helps the woman. In this study, intensive mothering also frequently increased men's respect for women. Indeed, several men in the study expressed their greater sense of respect for their wives, and several of the women mentioned feeling clearly appreciated by their partners. Gary, for example, talked about his new-found "respect for women ... I have a respect for motherhood that I mean I just never realized before." Women may, then, improve their position in their family when they mother intensively.

# 10

# Friends, Neighbours, and Community: A Case Study of the Role of Informal Caregiving in Social Reproduction

MEG LUXTON

Feminist political economy has mobilized the concept of social reproduction as a way of insisting that the activities involved in establishing and maintaining households and families are central social and economic processes. Defining social reproduction as the processes and activities involved in ensuring the survival of individuals and the population as a whole, they have insisted that its activities, occurring in three spheres – states, markets, and households – are essential to the daily and long-term life of capitalist societies (Picchio 1992, 2003). Most work informed by a social reproduction perspective has focused either on one of these spheres or on their interactions (Luxton this volume).

While states, markets, and households may be the main institutional centres for social reproduction, an array of community organizations and networks have always played important parts in ensuring social reproduction. For centuries, formal religious, philanthropic, self-help, and activist organizations have provided emergency support for people in crisis. Single-issue services such as food banks, rape crisis centres, or HIV/AIDS support groups emerge in response to specific needs and typically either expand into more formal organizations or decline as needs change and/or participants' enthusiasm dwindles.[1] The importance of the voluntary or third sector to social reproduction is increasingly recognized and investigated (Statistics Canada 1998a; Brock 2003). However, informal communities and personal social ties, inevitably less publically visible and typically more limited in scope and duration, are harder to identify, less well-known, and, to date, largely ignored in the social reproduction literature.

The potential importance of such relationships was sharply posed when, in 1995, the newly elected Conservative government in Ontario implemented dramatic, neo-liberal policy changes significantly based on cuts to taxes and social services. Government MPPs urged people in Ontario to accept the cuts to social services, exhorting them to rely less on government services and more on informal, personal ties with families, friends, and neighbours and on community groups (*Toronto Star* 1995a; 1995b). Between 1999 and 2002 I conducted a study in the Greater Toronto Area (GTA) designed to investigate what happens when people do turn to informal personal ties for caregiving, particularly in a large urban centre. Here I report on one part of the study that explores the ways in which informal volunteers – neighbours, co-workers, acquaintances, and friends – facilitate social reproduction by engaging in various kinds of caregiving for people who have experienced an unexpected medical emergency (see appendix for details). The study asked, What kinds of help can be mobilized, by whom, and for whom? How are caregiving relationships shaped by race and ethnicity, class, gender, and family? What makes it more or less likely that people will volunteer, and how important is their help to the individuals involved and to the larger society, particularly to the health-care system? What costs are absorbed by such volunteers? What is the importance of informal "community" and interpersonal ties to social reproduction?[2] What are the consequences if social policy is actually based on the assumption that such help is available, and what policies might facilitate it? Finally, how viable is a social policy predicated on the assumption that people can rely less on government services and more on their informal ties?

The premise of this part of the study is that when someone has an unexpected medical emergency, which means they need help beyond what they normally require in their day-to-day life, they can ask for help from, or make demands of people without incurring the usual social obligations for reciprocity. The emergency nature of the situation means that others are often willing to offer help on a short-term basis to people they would not normally consider part of their caregiving responsibilities. Since such caregiving is usually an important aspect of ensuring the patient recovers, it contributes to the social reproduction of that individual. Where volunteer informal caregiving takes up household and caregiving responsibilities the patient cannot meet, such as child care, it contributes to the social reproduction of the patient's dependents and household. In that way, such caregiving contributes to the social reproduction of the larger society.

## THE STUDY

I interviewed thirty-one individuals (eighteen women and thirteen men of eighteen years of age or older) who had had an unexpected medical emergency that incapacitated them for at least two weeks, during which time they were not in hospital or any other formal caregiving facility. I did second, follow-up interviews at least six months later with thirteen of them (twelve women, one man). These "patients" identified a total of 104 people who had provided informal care. While the larger study investigated the reliance on family as well as others, one of the unexpected findings was that many of the people interviewed did not rely on family for help, even when they had family members in close geographic proximity who, in theory, could have provided care. Equally unexpected was the fact that while some of the care providers had been close friends of the patients, more were acquaintances with only casual ties prior to the emergency.[3] Here I focus on informal caregiving provided by non-kin, friends, neighbours, co-workers, and other acquaintances.

I interviewed forty-two of the care providers (thirty-seven women, five men) and did follow-up interviews with twenty-nine (twenty-six women, three men). Two of the patients had no one. Only seven relied solely on kin to look after them. Ten relied on both kin and others, and twelve depended entirely on friends, neighbours, co-workers, or others. The care providers included sixteen spouses and partners (heterosexual: six women and seven men; lesbian and gay: two women and one man), eight other relatives (three mothers, three sisters, one aunt, one married daughter), thirteen neighbours (eleven women and two men), fifteen co-workers (ten women and five men), and fifty-two friends (thirty-six women and sixteen men).

All but three of the thirty-one patients had been in hospital for some time before their period of recuperation at home. All were under medical care for most of the time they were at home. The medical emergencies that triggered the need for unusual assistance from informal caregivers included seven car accidents, six falls, three heart attacks, two cases of breast cancer, and one each of flu, blood poisoning, toxemia, abdominal surgery, gall bladder surgery, stroke, scarlet fever, malaria, burst appendix, suicidal depression, and miscarriage with complications, and two workplace accidents: one where a worker was pushed through a glass door and suffered serious cuts, another where a worker's hair and arm were caught in machinery.[4] During the period they were recuperating at home, most were bedridden and unable to do the basic work needed to ensure daily survival, such as making meals. Many required help with personal activities, such as going to the toilet, and more than half needed some medical help, such as changing dressings or injecting medicines. More than half also had ongoing responsibilities for other people, elderly parents and children in particular, and so needed someone else to take over those obligations as well. In every case, the patient required care that was not readily available from the formal health-care or social services systems, and typically, it was their responsibility to arrange such care.

## THE IMPORTANCE OF INFORMAL CAREGIVING

The health-care system in Canada provides medical care for those (covered by health insurance) who can alert emergency services. Many of the people interviewed spoke highly of the prompt response from emergency services, the quality of care they received from emergency personnel, and the medical care they received in hospital. A woman described the care her husband received: "Everyone was great! From the minute I made the call [to 911], they were just so ... The operator stayed on the phone talking to me till the ambulance arrived. The ambulance guy held me all the way to the hospital and just talked, telling me what to expect. He was so kind. And Emergency and the nurses and doctors, they were all unbelievable – so good." However, her example underscores the potential importance of intimate social ties for survival. Her husband received prompt care because she was there when he was taken ill and she was able to mobilize professional medical assistance on his behalf.

Perhaps nothing illustrates more vividly the importance of such networks as their absence.[5] A man who was taken seriously ill very suddenly was too sick to make a phone call; so he spent three days alone without care: "It was only after, when I realized how sick I had been, that I got scared. I was helpless. I didn't eat or drink ... I couldn't get out of bed to go to the bathroom, so the bed was soaked and stank. It was awful. I could have died and no one would have known." A woman who fell down a flight of stairs and broke her leg was similarly unable to reach a phone. She spent the night alone and in pain and was only rescued when the letter carrier heard her cries. "It was about 7 p.m. when I fell. I remember watching the windows go dark and thinking I wouldn't be alive in the morning. I passed out several times, but the good Lord looked after me because I was conscious when the mailman came. I heard him and I just screamed, 'Help! Help! Help!' and God made sure he heard me." The woman's religious explanation reveals her belief that marriage offered the best protection from the vulnerability of living alone: "The nurse in the hospital said how lucky I was the mailman come. But you know, it wasn't luck. God was protecting me. God took my husband from me. That's why I was all alone, and He knew I needed looking after, special like. I was a good wife, you know, and I was alone just because God took my husband."

Another woman with a similar experience offered a very different sociological interpretation. She too fell, injured her back, and spent hours unaided until pounding on a shared wall roused her neighbours. She blamed her isolation on the way Canadian society is organized, contrasting it with her experience elsewhere: "Here everyone is supposed to live in little families, all alone, so private. Not like home [Jamaica] where we live in a community and all look out for each other. Sure, everybody knows your business, but alone and hurt for so long – that would never happen. This Canada is too lonely, everyone expected to look out for their own selves. That's just not a right way to live." These examples demonstrate how vulnerable people are if they do not have other people regularly involved in their daily lives. In each case, a sudden injury or illness left them unable to call for help in a context where no one was likely to check on them. Their social isolation put their lives at risk.

A contrasting example shows how the activities of people who provide informal support can sometimes play a vital role in helping not just an individual but a household to survive. A woman with three small children (aged six, three, and ten months) was already finding it difficult to manage her domestic situation and her job as a secretary in a real estate office during the three months her husband was away. When she came down with a serious case of the flu, she collapsed:

> I was so lucky. My next-door neighbour just took over and arranged everything. She called the daycare centre and told them to find someone who could take the baby. The mother of one of the other infants came immediately, picked him up, and kept him for two weeks. And every day she dropped off a

note telling me how he was, what he'd been doing. Then [the neighbour] called the school and got the principal to find someone to look after the oldest one. She found another neighbour on our street willing to take the middle one. She packed their bags, drove them, and even made the children feel like it was a big adventure so they weren't scared. Then she talked to my doctor and got a home visit (I think she threatened to call an ambulance if they didn't come to see me). She got all the neighbours on the street to each make one day's meal. In fact, people were so generous I had enough food for more than a month.

Several things about this woman's experience are striking. Her neighbour knew her and the children well enough, first to find out that she was ill and then to know what daycare and school the children attended and how to move the children without frightening them. She had the confidence necessary to approach the professionals and insist that they help out. She also relied on institutions, assuming that the daycare supervisor and the school principal could find trustworthy care providers. When asked to provide food for a day, the neighbours all responded generously. The woman recounting these events recognized that her circumstances were unusual and depended on the presence of a neighbour willing and able to make such arrangements: "I was blessed to have such a good neighbour. Not many would do what she did, but I couldn't have managed without her."

It is widely assumed that family, particularly women, will look after those who need care at home. The social reproduction literature has documented the extent to which women's (and men's) caring work in the home acts as a residual labour, expanding and contracting as much as possible to offset the impact of market forces, state practices, or changing family circumstances (Bezanson 2006, Luxton this volume). One of the trends of the past decades has been the reduction of publicly funded and regulated health care and social services. The availability, quality, and duration of available medical care have all been reduced since the late 1970s, when neo-liberal policies came to dominate governments, resulting in major restructuring of health-care services (Armstrong et al. 1994; Braedley this volume). As Armstrong and Armstrong noted, "And finally we have the privatization of care itself, as more of the caring work is sent home to the private household where women are expected to do the work without pay" (Armstrong and Armstrong 1996, 147).

Increasingly, formal medical care relies on informal, usually family, caregivers to take care of patients, both during their hospital stay and after. The current organization of health care assumes that informal caregivers will be available and puts pressure on patients and their families and friends to reduce the responsibility of the medical system for patients. The recent Romanow report, for example, takes for granted that families will provide most home care (Romanow 2002).

But during that same period, significant changes make that solution more difficult to implement. As women's labour-force participation has increased, they are less able to provide such care. As family ties become more fluid and fractured, through divorce and changing values about kinship obligations, family members may be less willing or available. Finally, single-person households are the most rapidly increasing household form; more and more people are living alone and may not have close kin to call on. This dynamic leaves most vulnerable those who do not have such networks to draw on.

I suggest that we are currently going through a transition, where family ideologies still hold sway, especially around caregiving, even though actual family practices are changing rapidly. This contradiction gets played out in negotiations around care provision and is one of the reasons that non-kin ties are so important. The continuing hegemony of family ideologies acts as a block to some who want to provide care and generates resistance in others to receiving care from non-kin. Care providers typically deferred to family members, both of the patient and of their own. Single people are vulnerable both to isolation and to invasion.

Unlike the demands on kin to provide care which are comparatively well-established (although always requiring negotiations), the expectations of friends, co-workers, neighbours, or others in informal social relations are not clear-cut. In each situation, the individuals concerned have to negotiate how much they can ask of, or offer to, each other. One man provided his insight into these dynamics: "Asking friends to help me was like being on the dating circuit again, a delicate dance of tentatively making eye contact, offering a small smile, poised to leap back if the response isn't positive but always hopeful."

A woman who, in contrast, insisted her strategy was forthright and clear hinted at a similarly equivocal practice: "I just said right out, 'This is what I need. Can you help me?' And I was very clear. I expected them to be just as straight with me, yes or no. Whatever they decide is okay. Of course, I didn't want to put anyone on the spot or make them feel obligated, so I made sure they had an out. I said, 'You know I already have lots of help so don't worry if you can't be part of it.'"

A man who had been looking after a neighbour made a more general point that most people interviewed would agree with: "I guess it's really hard to ask for help and just as hard to accept it gracefully. There's so much at stake. Does the other person value me enough? What will I have to do in return? What if I can't do it? Plus, it means giving up time and energy for other things. But the worst for me is what if someone helps me out and feels resentful?"

Giving and accepting care and assistance in an emergency situation evoke all the complex dynamics of obligation and rules of reciprocity involved in gift exchange. Entangled with the emotional complexities of friendship and the neediness of the patient, the lack of recognized normative expectations and practices creates an intricate social situation in which every interaction must be negotiated and assessed. A woman who had spent a lot of time caring for a co-worker described the implications of the lack of clarity and the power of family ideologies and obligations: "When people realized how much time I was spending here, lots of them were surprised and asked why. It seems everywhere I have to explain, even justify, helping a friend. Even my husband, he doesn't get it, thinks I'm nuts and is even annoyed because I am spending time here rather than at home with him. If it were family, everyone would take it for granted I should be there, but friends just don't count."

A woman who had been involved in helping her close friend made an observation that shed light on such dynamics: "Friends is so unclear, isn't it? Like, what you can ask of friends, it's not clear. It's easy to ask too much. Then you piss your friends off and they want to run away. But friends want to help too. It feels good, even important, like look at me, I am such a good person. But not if I start feeling ripped off. Then I just want to get the heck out of there." Many people pointed out the difference between helping kin and helping others. "Family's different. There you've got an obligation, don't you? That's what family is. You just have to do it. But someone who isn't family, well, there's certainly no obligation, so why would you do it?"

The answer most care providers offered to that question stressed the individual and idiosyncratic quality of their decision: "It was just something I wanted to do because I like her." While each situation generated its own specifics, and each individual brought her or his own particular predispositions, certain patterns emerged. It is not easy for most patients to ask for help. Adult dependency has negative connotations in most liberal welfare states (Fraser and Gordon 1997). Most of the patients confirmed that becoming dependent and having to ask for help were difficult and sometimes humiliating processes: "Suddenly, I couldn't manage. It felt like being a kid again. I felt so helpless. It was an awful feeling."

At the same time, patients also described how, in addition to receiving needed care, they also felt cared for and loved, their value as a friend affirmed by the attention they received. The rewards for providing care were obvious to most people. Care providers described feeling useful, needed, valued, and respected. Most derived considerable satisfaction from seeing themselves as generous and socially responsible. Both care providers and patients recognized that caregiving and receiving entails something more for both parties, as they inevitably became more involved in each other's lives. One of the more dramatic instances of such involvement was described by a woman who, having witnessed her co-worker's accident, became a regular caregiver: "I don't know, I can't explain it really, but you know, it was, like so intense, so intimate. You're holding someone in your arms. They're dying and I was panicking and yelling at him, 'Live, god damn it! Live!' So I can't just walk away once he does. It's kind of like forever, what I feel about him now."

A man whose stroke had kept him bedridden for several months attributed his recovery to the devoted care provided by a co-worker, two neighbours, and six friends. He offered an insight into what care involves: "Well now, it's a very complicated thing, isn't it, because it gets to the heart of our lives. If we're sick like I was, we need that care to live. But if you are asking someone to help you live, you are also asking him to give up some of his life for you. Now, don't you think that is a great deal to ask of someone, that they give you some of their life? And if they want to live, they have to make sure they don't give up too much."

Because these relationships were informal, most people assumed their decisions to invite or offer care were based on their individual relationship with the other person and reflected their personal preferences, moral values, and individual proclivities. "It's not like family or the health-care system, is it? I mean, she's just a friend, a neighbour who lives down the street. So it's just up to her and me. Like it's strictly individual, if we choose to do something for each other. Nothing affects us except what we choose to do." However, there were other social patterns, particularly relating to race, ethnicity, class, gender, and familial ideology that noticeably moulded practices relating to care and affected who provide care and why.

## PATTERNS OF RACE, ETHNICITY, CLASS, AND GENDER IN CAREGIVING PRACTICES

### *Race and Ethnicity*

Participants came from a range of racial and ethnic backgrounds (see appendix). When asked about racial identity, only one of the thirty-four whites recognized that he was a member of a racialized group, responding, "Yeah, well, I'm white with all the privilege that goes with that." The rest had some difficulty with the question; a number of them said they were not part of a racialized group. As one said, "There are lots of different races living in Toronto and that's good. But I'm not one. I'm Canadian." Another said, "I'm nothing, just an ordinary Canadian." This unproblematic sense of being in a cultural mainstream is part of the dynamic of racism that allows the dominant group to escape being identified as racialized. In contrast, all those who identified as black or of colour and three who identified as Asian, volunteered comments about their experiences of racism. All six patients who identified as people of colour and one who identified as black described racist experiences they had with the formal medical system. Three insisted that their treatment was adversely affected as a result.

Many of the care providers who identified as visible minorities were immigrants who gave their experiences as an explanation for their involvement in caregiving. There appeared to be, for some, a relationship between experiencing the pain of racism and their willingness to help out across the divides of race and ethnicity. One black woman, helping her white neighbour, gave a clear statement of this position: "I've lived with racism all my life. It's ugly, ugly. So when I can, I lend a hand, rub away some of the ugly, I do."

Most of the recent immigrants gave their experiences on arrival as an explanation for their caregiving practices. Some described being welcomed warmly, given lots of help, finding people in Toronto to be friendly. In return, they claimed, they were giving help as a way of reciprocating. Others cited their lonely or hostile reception as an explanation: "No one should go through what I went through. It's such a big city, and everyone's angry if you need help. I want to make it different."

Some people claimed that dedication to helping others and providing care is a specific ethnic characteristic: "the Chinese way," "people from the islands," "what we First Nations people do." Several contrasted their ethnic way with less attractive "Canadian" or "Toronto" ways: "Where I come from [West Africa], people are kind and help each other, not like this cold heartless city." A First Nations woman said: "My people take very seriously their obligation to look after one another. Not like you Canadians with your 'me first' values."

Quite a few immigrants said that they had been used to participating in the responsibilities and obligations of extended family networks before they migrated and they missed those ties. They implied that by volunteering to help friends or acquaintances, they were to some extent replicating those ties and hoping their contribution might help create a new community for them in Toronto. A Filipina woman said: "At home in the Philippines I have my mother and aunties and uncles and sisters and brother and cousins and nephews and nieces, just lots of people in and out of my life, looking after me, me looking after them. Here is so lonely. I think I look after [the patient] because, while it's not so good as at home, it's something. I begin to have people in my life here."

A small incident suggests the importance that a race- and ethnic-sensitive perspective can have. The West African who looked after an injured white co-worker, in part because he was offended by the cold, unfriendly way of life he found in Toronto, had experienced a number of racist incidents at work. As their relationship developed, the white co-worker came to understand racism in new ways. When he recovered, he forced their union to take up issues of racism, a struggle that resulted in the formation of a race relations committee and new contract language. The white worker attributed his activism to the experience of learning first-hand about racism: "Racism was always something out there. It didn't affect me until I watched it work on someone I knew well and who I owed a lot to. Then I suddenly understood how it actually affected me too." The West African offered a more sophisticated insight: "I just helped out because it seemed right. But I realize that when people of different races or backgrounds actually have a chance to get to know each other, then you can confront our differences and explore what's similar and then you've a basis for forming alliances. His activism on anti-racism has changed me. It's made things better at work. More important, I'm not so angry and I don't think this is such a heartless city to live in. I'm beginning to feel like me and my family belong here."

## *Class*

While race and ethnicity were explicitly acknowledged by people of colour as factors shaping caregiving practices, only a few people recognized class differences either among patients or among care providers in both their willingness to help and the kinds of help they provided. However, while all patients accepted care, there were some differences that appear to be class-based in the kinds of care they preferred and in the ways they accepted care. There were also noticeable differences in both the costs care providers were willing to sustain and their attitudes toward caregiving.[6]

There was a clear, although not simple, correlation between class location and access to resources. Access to material resources obviously made it easier for people to ask for and offer caregiving. While few patients could afford to hire full-time nursing and housekeeping services, the upper- and middle-class patients already had modified services in place that covered their basic housekeeping. Most had cleaners who came to the house on a regular basis. They were used to ordering in food and sending out laundry. They hired babysitters on a regular basis. Patients with service providers already in place found it relatively easy to increase such services for the duration of their illness. What they needed in addition was personal care and replacement help for the caregiving they normally provided for others.

Care providers with resources obviously had an easier time too. Those with cars could get around more easily; those with money could afford to buy supplies, such as takeout meals, that reduced the demands on their time. Those whose jobs permitted a certain flexibility or whose hours were regular found it easier to provide care than those whose hours were unpredictable or who risked censure or loss of pay for taking time off. A working-class woman working split shifts, who only knew her schedule two days in advance, described the choices she faced: "I asked for time off for when [the patient] was sent home. But they told me 'No way.' So I asked for my sick days time but he said, 'You're not sick. No.' So I could have skipped but I knew he'd be on my case. He'd fire me like a shot if I gave him the chance. But then [the patient] was so sick. So I moved me and the kids into her house so at least I was there a bit. Of course, it meant two hours on the bus both ways to get the kids to school. But what else could I do?"

Upper- and middle-class people tended to offer care that involved adding work for the patients to what they were already doing for themselves. They volunteered to shop and pick up takeout meals; they ran errands, such as dropping off or picking up laundry or collecting prescriptions. They tended to prefer specific tasks with well-defined expectations. Many assumed that it was the patient's responsibility to inform them about what needed doing. Most importantly, upper- and middle-class caregivers were less likely to disrupt their own lives in order to provide care. A wealthy lawyer explained: "I'm glad to lend a hand. I pop in on my way home from work every day. Now I don't usually know what time that will be, so I phone first, check what shopping she needs and then pick it up on the way. It's something definite I know I can commit to doing." Another professional woman described her contribution: "I stop in every other day for about an hour. I explained to her that I could give her an hour. I will do whatever needs doing during that time."

In contrast, many of the working-class people were willing to be more flexible about what they offered. Few assumed the patient should or would tell them outright what needed doing. Many took for granted that offering help would significantly disrupt their lives and might interfere with their work. A sales clerk described her contribution: "Well, like my hours, I don't know except a day in advance, so I can't plan anything. But when I get off, I stop by and visit for as long as I can. Usually after a while, I get a sense of what she needs and then I go do it – like shopping or the laundry or whatever. You can't just ask someone what they want because they might be too embarrassed or, well, it might seem rude, wouldn't it?"

A woman who had two friends providing care gave her perspective on class differences: "[My working-class friend] is careful at first. She sort of checks things out then just rolls up her sleeves and gets to work. [My middle-class friend] is quite direct. 'Just tell me what to do,' she'll say. It's kind of easier with [the working-class friend] because she just does it. I feel uncomfortable asking people to do my laundry or clean up the kitchen. I don't like to ask. So it's such a relief when she just goes ahead and does it."

*Gender and Familial Ideologies*

In contrast to patterns shaped by race, ethnicity and class, gender differences were universally recognized and explicitly discussed, often in ways that naturalized them and only occasionally in ways that problematized them. As gender differences are central to family ideologies, and as heterosexual family caregiving practices are anchored by gendered divisions of labour, gender differences in caregiving practices were significantly linked to family ideologies.

There were notable gender differences in who provided care and for whom; men and women had quite different types of support. Not surprisingly, I found that the majority of care providers were women. That finding replicates international trends identified by the United Nations and national trends documented by Statistics Canada. Canadian studies since 1960 show that women consistently do about two-thirds of all unpaid work, including caregiving. Even as teenagers, women do more domestic labour than men (Statistics Canada 2000, 97). The 2001 census reported that women were 2.5 times more likely than men to spend more than thirty hours a week looking after children without pay, 2.9 times more likely to spend more than thirty hours a week on unpaid housework, and 2 times more likely to spend ten or more hours on unpaid caregiving to seniors (Statistics Canada 2003a).

Perhaps more unexpectedly, gendered patterns of care seem to leave men more socially vulnerable than women. Men appeared to rely almost exclusively on their spouse or partner. Only four men, none of whom had a spouse, drew on other people. The two people with no care providers at all were both men. In a follow-up interview, one man described what happened when his marriage, already strained before he was injured, finally ended, leaving him without care. At the time, he was relying on government services: "For six months she did everything. She took good care of me, but it was too much and finally she left. That's when I finally had to face up to how I was all alone in the world. I had no one, but I couldn't do it on my own and now I'm here. There are people who come, in but it's just a job for them. I'm barely managing."

Comments by those providing care to the single men offer some insights into ways in which gender and family ideologies re-enforce men's isolation. One woman explained why she was involved in looking after an injured co-worker: "I feel bad because he's alone. If he had a wife, I would not have offered at all. I'd feel like I was interfering. But with no family, well, I thought I should help out." Another gave a similar interpretation of her involvement with her ill neighbour: "He's just a young guy, not married yet and all on his own, so I just pop in to check and do whatever I can. I feel sorry for men who don't have wives. There's really no one to look after them, is there? And when they are sick like that, well, they end up with no one."

In contrast, women drew on a wider range of people and were more likely to rely on friends, neighbours, and others. Only two women relied solely on kin and those were women (both relied on their mothers, one on an aunt, the other on a sister). While seven of the eleven women who relied on kin identified their male spouse or partner, they also all identified one or more other care providers, almost all of whom were women. The presence of a spouse did not act as a deterrent to others in the case of women. In fact, prevailing gender ideologies re-enforced the notion that even when men are willing and able care providers, other women should be involved.

The majority of patients and caregivers agreed that women were preferable to men as caregivers, generally assuming that women are capable and men are less so. Some simply declared that women were better at it. A woman offered an explanation for her preference for her women friends over her husband: "Women are just better at that sort of thing. Men can try, but they just don't know how. Women don't fuss, but men get all anxious and want you to tell them how great they are doing."

The men, for the most part, offered similar views on the gender specificity of caring capacities: "Women are just better at looking after people. I'd rather a woman any day." The one gay man affirmed a similar perspective, arguing that the devoted and skilled care provided by his male partner was specific to gay men and, in his partner's case, learned from women: "[My partner] is just so lovely, but then that's gay men for you, isn't it? And anyway, he had lots of older sisters and a wonderful mother, so he was taught well."

The widespread assumption that men were less-skilled care providers than women was complemented by gender-specific expectations about care provision. Men who offered only minimal care typically received extensive praise for their efforts, while women's care provision, even when extensive, was less noteworthy. Several patients, both women and men, were effusive in their thanks to men who had stopped by to visit. One woman's comments after her male co-worker had visited for half an hour were typical: "Isn't he just so wonderful? What a terrific guy! He's so caring and so generous. Imagine him dropping in to see how I am. He's just so fantastic." Of her female co-worker who also stopped by at the same time, having done a week's grocery shopping, and who stayed for over three hours to put the groceries away, prepare a meal for the patient, do the laundry, fold and put the clean clothes away, and change the bed linen, the same patient gave a more muted assessment: "She's a great help. I certainly appreciate all she does for me. It's very kind of her."

The frequency with which the role of women in caregiving was presented as natural and inevitable, as well as socially necessary, was striking. Unprompted, fifty-one of the seventy-three people interviewed made some assertion to that effect; twenty-eight actually used the phrase "woman are naturally." The complementary assumption, that men are indifferent care providers at best, occurred frequently. A woman who, despite the extensive and exhausting demands of her high-stress job and several young children, was spending several hours a day looking after her friend commented: "Sometimes I think I just can't go over there. I am almost at breaking point myself and my kids need me. Sure, I know he's [the husband] doing a terrific job, but I just think, well, you know, a woman just ..."

Such gender ideologies and stereotypes appeared to dominate even when the actual practices contradicted them. In six cases, men were providing care that the women patients described as excellent. Yet in each of those cases, at least one of the women who were also providing care volunteered the opinion that women were better caregivers. A man who had provided excellent care for his wife was one of the few to identify the sexism involved that may sometimes act to discourage men:

> It's like they all assume because I'm a guy, I can't look after her right, but at the same time they also are, like, so impressed that I do stuff, they make a big fuss. It's sort of like what happened to that Kim Campbell who became prime minister for a while, remember? Like, no one thought she could do the job, so when she did it they were more than impressed, but they still wouldn't let her do it for long. I think it's sexist they think I can't look after her because I'm a guy.

As accepted family obligations and responsibilities change, and as more women are in the labour force, family-based care can no longer be taken for granted, but deeply held familial ideologies and gendered assumptions still shape practices in ways that may undermine care.

### THE IMPACT OF KINSHIP AND FAMILIAL IDEOLOGIES ON CAREGIVING

Hegemonic values about the importance of family influenced many of the caregiving situations and often undermined the possibility of receiving help from non-kin. A woman who broke her leg insisted that her adult children and particularly her daughter should provide care, despite the fact that both had young children and full-time employment and that the daughter lived over three hundred kilometres away. Her demands were clear: "They must come here to stay with me. That's what family does. I know she has a job and her children but she could make arrangements. I am her mother. She must come here." This woman's son visited her every two days for three weeks. Her daughter came for a three-day visit and phoned daily. But both children resisted her demands that they move in with her. She was hurt and angry: "How can they be so selfish? I need them now, here. What have I done to deserve such treatment?"

Two neighbours, both single, retired women who were free to do so, offered to move in with her for the duration and provide full-time care. Despite the actual support she received from these neighbours, however, her desire for evidence of her children's devotion blinded her to what she had: "[My neighbour] moved in here and took good care of me. [My other neighbour] shopped and did the laundry, and yes, I was well looked after but it isn't family." Months later, after she had fully recovered, she was still bitter, overwhelmed by her sense of rejection, and unable to appreciate the excellent care she had received: "Well, yes, it's true [my neighbour] was very generous but she shouldn't have had to be. My children failed me. That is a terrible thing."

A number of care providers indicated that they deferred to kin and felt that the presence of kin restrained or hampered their interventions: "I really wanted to look after my friend. I love her. But her husband was always there, so I held back." Another confirmed the same point: "I could have done way more, but with her mother and sister there, I felt like I was intruding." The overwhelming dominance of kin overshadows friendship and community relations and often undermines informal relationships: "At first my husband was supportive. He said it was a good thing I was doing. But after a few days, he said he thought I had done enough. Like, he thought I should just do a little bit because she is just a friend. If I did more, it was too much."

### LIMITS TO INFORMAL CAREGIVING

Many people are willing to extend impressive amounts of time and energy, and extensive resources, to those needing care. But there are also real limits. Friends and acquaintances were often willing to provide care as a stop-gap measure; long-term demands were of a different order. While many of the care providers made contributions that required considerable sacrifice on their part, all of them acknowledged that their participation was bounded. People were more willing to become engaged when they were sure that it would be for a short-term commitment. If they thought that some involvement would open them to further demands, they were likely to withdraw and offer less help. For example, when a woman was initially diagnosed with breast cancer, several neighbours accompanied her to doctors' appointments and looked after her following her initial surgery. As her illness shifted from a short-term medical emergency to a long-term illness, her demands increased beyond what the neighbours were willing to provide: "Like, we all felt bad for her. It's an awful disease. And no one should go through it alone. But it got to be too much. Going to one appointment, that's fine. But then she needed way more than we were able to give. We had other obligations. I couldn't just drop everything for her." They were afraid that if they continued to be involved with her, they would be pressed into a greater commitment. The neighbour, who carried on offering limited care, explained:

> I'm willing to help out someone who needs it. A little help now and then, we can all manage that. But I'm not ready to take over looking after someone like that. I feel trapped now. I can't completely walk away. After all, she's right next door and she can see me out the window coming and going. I couldn't just refuse to pop in now and then for a bit and maybe fetch her a drink or even pick up some shopping. But it's awful because I know she needs so much more and I feel guilty all the time. And I resent it.

In general, the more support patients had, the more additional people were prepared to join in and the more involved caregivers were prepared to be.[7] Six months later the cancer patient was more incapacitated, but she had professional home care from social services, who came in daily, took care of all medical treatments, gave her baths, and did basic housecleaning. In response, her neighbours had rallied and dropped in regularly to visit. The neighbour who had previously expressed resentment said: "It's okay now. It's manageable. I feel great dropping in each day just to say hi and make tea and straighten her bed and bring her books and stuff."

Most were comfortable asking for or providing emotional support and visiting. Many were also willing ask for or provide a certain amount of domestic labour, such as the day-to-day activities of shopping, cooking, cleaning, and running errands. When patients had young children they were unable to care for, care providers rallied. All of the patient parents agreed that they found it relatively easy to ask others to take care of their children. One mother suggested why this might be the case: "Well, kids need care. Everyone knows that. And I can't look after them, so I just have to ask someone else." The imperatives of child care also meant that providers were sometimes willing to agree even when it involved a major imposition. One care provider explained her decision: "There wasn't really any choice. Those children had to be looked after. So would we let the Children's Aid take them away? No way. Yes, it was very hard. Some days I didn't think I would cope at all, but I had to. She was smashed up and her children needed looking after. It was that simple."

In contrast, responsibilities for other people were far easier for care providers to ignore. Several patients had responsibilities for adult dependents, but few care providers took up that work. One woman articulated a general sentiment: "We're friends, so I will do it for her, but it's enough already that I am looking after [the patient]. I can't look after her mother as well, though I don't know what her mother will do. I can help look after my friend, but I can't take over her life."

Patients and caregivers described limits to familiarity, such as helping patients with intimate bodily functions. As one woman explained, "Well, it's nothing to take her a drink or make a meal. I do that in normal times, don't I? But taking her to the bathroom, that's a bit much. I don't like to do that." Only one person presented a different approach, affirming collective social responsibility, which she attributed to her First Nations cultural values. Already burdened by heavy demands in her own life and looking after her co-worker, who had been seriously injured in a car crash, this care provider also took over the patient's obligations to her elderly mother and a neighbour with a disability. For two months, the care provider phoned the mother weekly and sent her money each month. She also shopped weekly and prepared two dinners each week for the neighbour: "It just has to be done, that's all. Because [the patient] can't do it, someone has to, and if I am looking after her, part of looking after her is looking after the people she looks after. That's just the way we do things in my community."

This person went on to offer suggestions for strengthening caregiving more generally:

> In Canada you people are so limited. You think you just are responsible for yourselves. You don't have a sense of how you belong to your community. Maybe it's time for you to learn from us and change your values. We all share this earth together and what happens to you affects me. Maybe your government should start educating you in new ways to take care of each other – like those campaigns for no drinking and driving, or no smoking. I can see the posters in the bus shelters now, can't you? Caring for Canada? Help your neighbour and make the world a better place? Well, someone could figure out how to make it catchy!

In the majority of cases, the willingness of friends, neighbours, co-workers, and other acquaintances to provide care is significantly shaped by their sense of being able to provide meaningful and helpful assistance without becoming overwhelmed by increasing demands for greater involvement or for types of care they deem inappropriate or too intimate. When they are confronted with demands they consider too much, they tend to withdraw.

## CUTBACKS AND DOWNLOADING IN HEALTH CARE

The combination of funding cuts to the health-care system and policies that promote private responsibility for care puts new pressures on patients and on their friends and acquaintances. The more the health-care system relies on informal caregiving to supplement formal care, the more individuals have to mobilize their own resources. This process produces major inequalities in the care available to patients and leaves those without such networks vulnerable. A man was due for release from hospital while he was still unable to walk alone:

> There I was. They were ready to send me home and I couldn't even stand up by myself. The hospital social worker walked in all cheery to ask when my family was coming to get me. I had to say I had no one to come and get me. Do you have any idea how painful that was to say? Then, it was like I was a bad person because I didn't have someone to look after me and I was such a problem because they had to find services for me.

Downloading health care may impose inappropriate expectations on patients and their friends or acquaintances, driving away the very support patients hope to rely on. A woman who had visited her co-worker in hospital detailed the pressure she experienced from hospital personnel. Friends at work, they had never visited each other's homes. As the hospital was across the street from their office, the co-worker visited the patient daily:

> suddenly, everyone seemed to assume I would take her home and look after her. One day her doctor says, to her and me, she was going home the next day and how lucky she was to have such a good friend to take her home. She says, 'I'm not going home with her!' But the doctor ignored her and told me the nurse and social worker would tell me how to look after her. Later, the nurse came in to ask her when I would come in to talk to them. When she said I wasn't, they got mad! When I dropped in that evening, the nurse was quite rude to me.

The patient reported that the nurse had actually chastised her visitor: "Here [the visitor] had been so great, coming to see me every day, keeping me up on office gossip and cheering me up. And that nurse had the nerve to say she wasn't a good friend to me!" The visitor commented on the impact of these expectations: "It's sure made me think twice about visiting people in hospital. It's pretty crazy if you can't visit someone without it being like you owe them for life."

Her experience was not unusual. A number of care providers said they were pressured to administer medical treatments, a breaking point for most of them. A woman described her decision to withdraw from providing care to her neighbour:

> So I'd been helping out while she was in hospital by going in every day and doing a little housework. Before she came home, I shopped and put clean sheets on her bed, and her first day home I dropped by to make her tea and

bring her some cookies. While I was there, the home-care nurse showed up. So this nurse, she starts to empty [the patient's] drain and all the while she is chatting away about what you have to do, and I suddenly realize that she is telling me how to empty the drain! In fact, she even said that she would come by the next day to make sure I was doing it okay and then she could leave it to me! Well, I got out of there fast. I was okay to help, but I'm not a nurse.

An irony noted by several people is that one of the most basic premises of formal medical practice is that doctors should not treat people they are intimately related to as their patients. With the downloading of health care onto individuals, more and more people are under pressure to do precisely that. As one man said, "My doctor would never expect to have to treat his own son, but he expects my son to treat me!"

When health-care provision is organized on the unrealistic assumption that patients have their own resources, it can generate situations that end up imposing greater costs on the system than would have been incurred had appropriate services been available initially. A woman recovering from a major car accident was housebound for six weeks after a week in hospital. Immediately following the accident, the authorities proposed arranging with Children's Aid to put the children (aged four and two) in foster care. Outraged by that suggestion, one of her co-workers took the children in and kept them for the first three weeks. Once the patient returned home, she received some formal health care from a visiting nurse, who came twice a week for three weeks; a home-care visitor came weekly for six weeks to give her a bath and wash her hair. Initially, she needed full-time help for personal care and housekeeping. After the third week she also needed child care. According to her, once she had left the hospital, it was almost impossible for her to get the help she needed: "It was like they were so relieved once I was home, they really didn't have to do anything for me anymore. I was someone else's problem. Except there wasn't someone else."

While two of her friends and three of her co-workers rallied and provided some care, none of them was willing or available to provide the extensive complex and full-time care she needed. One day she collapsed, physically and emotionally unable to cope with the anxieties and pressures she was under. She ended up back in hospital with her children in foster care (which intensified her anguish and panic). Months later she observed: "I'm the thing that holds it all together. Without me, it's chaos and crisis. So when I was in crisis, it all fell apart and I had no one to help me. And I couldn't fall apart until it got so bad I just lost it altogether. There's something wrong there. We all need backup systems and they ought to just be there."

## THE LACK OF SUPPORT FOR INFORMAL CAREGIVING

As this case study suggests, some people rely on informal non-kin ties, and many friends and acquaintances are willing to provide care. However, existing policies and practices often undermine potential caregiving among friends and acquaintances. The lack of social support and recognition for such care often subverts its provision. A woman whose friend was suffering from major depression expressed her willingness to provide care: "I would do anything for that man, anything at all. When I first came to Toronto, he helped me so much. He is just wonderful. And in my culture we look after our friends. I will stay with him, make sure he takes his medication, hold him close when he feels so despairing, and just look after him till this passes." But then she went on to reveal the discrepancy between her values and wishes and the actual resources available to her: "But then I find out the doctors will not speak to me about him because I am not family. And I cannot get time off work because he is not family. And our union just lost our unpaid leaves what we had before. And I cannot quit this job to care for him because I don't think I can get another." Although this patient had four people deeply concerned about him and willing to help, the constraints they faced reduced their involvement, undermined their effectiveness, and ultimately left him without the care he needed. As is so often the case when people do not get the care they need, his subsequent crisis was more serious than his original illness and required greater intervention by both health care and social-service agencies.

The lack of social support for informal relationships such as friendship was confirmed for many by the difficulties they encountered when trying to offer care. Several care providers noted that they were entitled to paid or unpaid leaves from work to care for family members but not for friends or co-workers. A single, childless co-worker of a woman injured on the job expressed her outrage: "She nearly died because of what happened and it was management's fault. But would they give me time off to stay with her? No! The foreman said leave is only for family. 'Well,' I said, 'Let her be family to me.' I will never take a leave for family, so why I should not get it for her."

Others reported on the lack of support from their own family and friends for their efforts to look after a friend or neighbour: "When I told my friends I was looking after her, they all told me how wonderful I was, like it was surprising I would do it. And none of them would help me out so I could help her." One woman noted that precisely because she was not a family member, her contribution to the patient's care was ignored and dismissed by the health-care professionals. Although she had provided daily care for the three weeks after the patient returned home, including personal care in the first two weeks, and although she was in the house putting away groceries she had just bought, doing the laundry, making a meal, and tidying the house, the visiting nurse consoled the patient for not having "anyone" to look after her. The patient reported: "That nurse, she outright says, 'Well, isn't it a shame you don't have no one to come look after you.' So I say my neighbour has been great and aren't I lucky. That nurse says back "You are so brave to make the best of it, to put up such a strong face when you have no family to look after you.'" As her care-providing neighbour observed, "It's like I don't exist because I'm not her family. It doesn't matter what I actually do here. If I'm not family, I don't count."

Most patients were clear that the more involved their friends and acquaintances were in caring for them, the more loved they felt. They confirmed that such affection was vitally important, strengthening their sense of well-being and self-esteem. But they were also aware of the limits of such care. Almost all of them agreed that the ideal solution would be for them to have the services they needed from professionals, so that friends and others could spend their time visiting rather than working: "I have a great set-up now. I have a housekeeper who does all the shopping, meals, and cleaning and laundry even. A nurse comes daily to change the dressings and check me over. So my friends who want to help, they take turns keeping me company. They read to me or we chat." Patients noted that relying on formal professional relationships was much less stressful since the obligations inherent in informal gift giving and receiving are minimal. With professional caregivers, patients can express their wants more directly, in ways not easily done with friends: "It was so much easier when the hospital started sending the nurse in. It was all straightforward. It was her job, not like my friends who were helping me. I didn't have to feel grateful and I could tell her off if she did things I didn't like. My friends, I was just so happy they were there that I just kept saying, 'Thank you, thank you.'"

However, a number of patients who had received limited assistance through the health-care system complained that they were uncomfortable receiving care from workers who were paid so badly and whose working conditions were both exploitative and precarious: "All the women who come to look after me are pleasant but I know that have to travel all over the city on the bus, they don't get breaks, they get paid peanuts. How can I feel good about getting a bath, having my drain checked by immigrant women workers who are underpaid and overworked?" Three patients complained that while nurses and home-care providers did their best, they were rushed, limited in what they could do, and often uninformed about their client's medical condition. They said that they were unwilling to complain about problems with such care providers for fear of costing these workers their jobs.

One of the main solutions promoted by advocates of neo-liberal economic policy is that people should purchase care through the market. But that option is not available to the majority of people, who simply cannot afford to hire care. Most patients and caregivers envisioned a health-care system that would screen, train, and treat with respect employees who would ensure that patients received appropriate care in their own homes: "Then I could relax and ask my friends to drop by for a visit. I could ask them to help out with little things, knowing I wasn't putting my friendships at risk."

## CONCLUSIONS

The organization of daily life in capitalist societies such as Canada depends significantly on the unpaid and unrecognized labour of adults who manage their own day-to-day subsistence and provide care for their children, partners, and other family members. The various provisions of the Canadian welfare state have generally been designed to complement that care to only a limited extent (Brodie 1996; Christie 2000; Porter 2003). The health-care system was built on, and continues to rest on, the assumption that families, particularly women, will provide basic health care. The long tradition of relying on unpaid work in the home, usually by women, with its related practices of low status and low pay for employees who provide paid home care, has subsidized health-care systems in most welfare states for decades.

Neo-liberalism has strengthened such assumptions as governments and health-care institutions expect people to rely increasingly on their families and the prevailing discourses take for granted that family will be available, willing, and able to take over full caregiving responsibilities. And they often are: families, predominantly women, do provide the greater part of unpaid care in Canada. But as numerous studies have shown, women's caregiving capacities are not infinite, and changing gender relations and women's labour-force participation have made such reliance more precarious (Maushart 2001; Picchio 2003). Furthermore, not everyone has family available to help, and access to care should not depend on having available family members; nor should family members be subject to "compulsory altruism," pressured to help loved ones because no alternative support is available. The social capacity to ensure social reproduction on a daily and more long-term basis for greater numbers of people depends on new ways of providing care.

This study suggests that there is a pool of other potential caregivers – friends, neighbours, co-workers, and others – who are often drawn into caregiving and whose contributions could be as valuable as those provided by family members. Such non-kin caregivers supply substantial work, often at considerable cost to themselves and their own families, for at least short periods of time. Informal relations can offer essential support of material resources and services and, perhaps more importantly, a sense of well-being, of belonging to community that strengthens reciprocal commitments.[8] However, their involvement is more unpredictable, inconsistent, and precarious than that prompted by kinship and family obligations. Informal non-kin relationships are fragile, easily disrupted by priority demands of formal organizations and especially kinship hierarchies, often undermined by both the lack of official recognition and support for their efforts, and easily destroyed if the demands on them are too heavy.

More people would be willing and able to offer voluntary care to their friends and acquaintances if they were assured that providing some help would not implicate them in more-extensive obligations and if their efforts were recognized as at least equally valuable as family care and supported appropriately. Given the extent to which many people count on such caregiving relationships, their well-being depends on the capacity of such relationships to handle the demands on them. If health-care policy continues to assume that unpaid caregiving is part of the total care system, it will fail unless related policy changes are introduced to make informal care provision more viable. A more-effective system of mobilizing such care would require new policy initiatives that take account of the dynamics involved in informal caregiving. Some of the policy changes implied in people's assessment of what helps or hinders the provision and acceptance of informal care are quite simple. Changing policies to recognize all caregiving, rather than privileging familial relations, is relatively straightforward. For example, union contracts that allow employees paid or unpaid leaves can easily permit employees to choose the people they take time off to care for, rather than specifying particular kin relations (de Wolff this volume). Changing practices and social values to accord informal relationships the same respect as family ties might be harder, but public education has changed attitudes on equally difficult topics. Such support and recognition would strengthen the capacity of friends, neighbours, and communities to provide informal care. However, such care is even less elastic than that provided by family members, and neither can adequately substitute for public health-care services. Over the long term, neo-liberal policies based on informal care provision leave patients vulnerable, impose heavy burdens on informal caregivers, and potentially undermine the very social relations that patients rely on.

# APPENDIX
# THE MEDICAL EMERGENCY: INTERVIEWS CONDUCTED IN TORONTO, JANUARY 1999 – JANUARY 2002

*Individuals needing care*

31 individuals (18 years of age or older)
- who had experienced an unexpected medical emergency as a result of which they required short-term help (such as getting around the house, shopping, cooking, errands, and medical treatment)

Total: 31 interviews: 18 women, 13 men
Follow-up: 13 interviews: 12 women, 1 man

*Individuals providing care*

42 caregivers (for 29 of the individuals who needed care)
- 1 caregiver for 20 individuals (19 women, 1 man)
- 2 caregivers for 5 individuals ( 8 women, 2 men)
- 3 caregivers for 4 individuals (10 women, 2 men)

Total: 42 interviews: 37 women, 5 men
Follow-up: 29 interviews: 26 women, 3 men

| *Ethnicity* | *Men* | *Women* |
|---|---|---|
| Canadian | 4 | 10 |
| American | 1 | 2 |
| Caribbean | 0 | 4 |
| British or Irish | 0 | 3 |
| Southern European | 0 | 3 |
| Eastern European | 0 | 2 |
| Vietnamese | 0 | 2 |
| East African | 0 | 4 |
| Chinese | 0 | 4 |
| First Nations | 0 | 1 |
| West African | 0 | 1 |
| Philippines | 0 | 1 |

| *Class* | *Working-class* | *Middle-class* | *Upper-class* |
|---|---|---|---|
| Patients | 13 | 17 | 1 |
| Caregivers | 23 | 17 | 2 |

## NOTES

1 Rape crisis centres, food banks, and AIDS support groups all began when small groups of activists recognized a need, organized ways of responding to that need, and over years of providing services, developed into formal organizations that eventually became part of provincial and national coalitions (Rebick 2005, 59–85).

2 "Community" is widely used and has a range of definitions. Here I use the term to refer to the various loose networks of association to which people feel they belong, beginning with close social ties with family, neighbours, co-workers, and friends and including a range of informal ties (e.g., the casual congregation of dog walkers in the park), formal organizations (such as religious centres, unions, or sports teams), and larger provincial, national, and international networks (for example, the Coalition for Better Child Care, the international feminist movement, or the Irish diasporic community) based on common interests and activities. In this chapter, I am exploring only informal ties, focusing on friends, neighbours, and the informal wider associations typically identified as "community." The more formal community institutions are often vitally important in supporting social reproduction, but they are not the subject of this study.

3 For the most part, few patients drew on previously established networks; care providers typically had individual ties to the patient but did not know each other until they got involved.

4 The diagnosis reported here is what the patients told me. In a few cases (abdominal surgery, toxemia) I was unable to clarify what the exact medical diagnosis was.

5 The dire consequences for people who are not part of supportive networks was illustrated by the tragedies in France when over 10,000 people died during a heat wave in August 2003. Authorities assumed that, because most people were on holiday during August, those who were elderly or ill were unusually isolated. People who might normally check in on them were holidaying elsewhere. President Jacques Chirac said: "Many fragile people died alone in their homes. These dramas again shed light on the solitude of many of our aged or handicapped citizens" (*Time* magazine, Canadian ed., 1 September 2003, 11).

6 Using education, occupation, and level and sources of income, I classified people as upper-, middle- or working-class. The wealthiest were the three upper-class women, two of whom had enough income from investments to live without employment, although one worked as a lawyer. The third ran her own business. About a third (thirteen) of the thirty-four middle-class

people had incomes below the national average of $25,000 for women and $38,000 for men, but their occupations – for example, as graduate students (three), artists (two), actors (two), a writer, a feminist publisher, and a lawyer working as an activist for an environmental group – and the educational qualifications they had warranted a middle-class location. The other twenty-one middle-class people had incomes above the national average. Twenty-five of them were on salary, and many could take time during a workday or a full day off work without losing pay. All but three owned their own homes and cars. In contrast, over 70 per cent (twenty-six) of the thirty-six working-class people had high school completion or less and incomes below the national average; most were either self-employed or paid an hourly wage (see appendix).

7 This research confirms earlier findings (Finch 1989; Finch and Mason 1993) that the more support a recipient has, the more likely others are to contribute.

8 The importance of social ties to individual survival has been confirmed by medical studies, which show that, for example, older men who have few personal relationships may have an increased risk of heart disease. In a study examining factors that influence successful aging, researchers found that among a group of men in their seventies, social isolation was linked to increased levels of C-reactive protein (CRP), interleukin-6, and fibrinogen in the blood. These blood components are elevated during inflammation. Recent research has suggested that inflammation in the body is a risk marker for cardiovascular disease. People with elevated CRP and fibrinogen have higher risks for heart disease and stroke (http://www.americanheart.org/presenter.jhtml/identifier=3016890).

# Works Cited

Abele, Frances. 1997. "Understanding What Happened Here: The Political Economy of Indigenous Peoples." In *Understanding Canada: Building on the New Canadian Political Economy*, ed. Wallace Clement. Montreal and Kingston: McGill-Queens

Abella, Rosalie. 1984. *Equality in Employment: A Royal Commission Report: General Summary.* Toronto: Commission on Equality in Employment

Acker, Joan. 1999. "Rewriting Class, Race and Gender: Problems in Feminist Rethinking." In *Revisioning Gender,* ed. Myra Marx Ferree, Judith Lorber, and Beth Hess. Thousand Oaks: Sage

Adams, Tamara, and Xijan Liu. 2001. *ESCAP II: Evaluation of Lack of Balance and Geographic Errors Affecting Person Estimates.* Executive Steering Committee for A.C.E. Policy II (ESCAP II), Report 2. Washington: US Census Bureau. Available at http://www.census.gov/dmd/www/ReportRec2.htm.

Adamson, Nancy, Linda Briskin, and Margaret McPhail. 1988. *Feminist Organizing for Change: The Contemporary Women's Movement in Canada.* Toronto: Oxford University Press

Advisory Council on the Status of Women. 1994. *101 Statistics on Work and Family, 1994.* Ottawa: Government of Canada

Akyeampong, Ernest B. 2002. "Unionization and Fringe Benefits." *Perspectives on Labour and Income,* 3 (8). Ottawa: Statistics Canada

Allnut, Chris. 2003. Affidavits in the Supreme Court of British Columbia in Reference to Plaintiffs: The Health Services and Support-Facilities Subsector Bargaining Association, The Health Services and Support-Community Health Bargaining Association, The Nurses' Bargaining Association, The

Hospital Employees' Union, The British Columbia Government and Service Employees' Union, The British Columbia Nurses' Union, Josephine Chauhan, Janine Brooker, Amaljeet Jhand, Leona Fraser, Marguerite Amy McCrea, Sally Lorraine Stevenson and Sharlene G.V. Decilla; and Defendant: Her Majesty the Queen in Right of the Province of British Columbia

Anderson, Bridget. 2002. "Just Another Job? The Commodification of Domestic Labor." In *Global Woman: Nannies, Maids and Sex Workers in the New Global Economy*, ed. Barbara Ehrenreich and Arlie Russell Hochschild. New York: Metropolitan Books

– 2001. "Reproductive Labour and Migration." Transnational Communities Programme Working Paper Series, ed. Ali Rogers. Available at www.transcomm. ox.ac.uk/working_papers.htm

– 2000. *Doing the Dirty Work? The Global Politics of Domestic Labour.* London, New York: Zed Books

Anderson, Kim. 2001. *A Recognition of Being: Reconstructing Native Womanhood.* Toronto: Sumach Press

Anderson, Michael. 1971. *Family Structure in Nineteenth Century Lancashire.* Cambridge: Cambridge University Press

Andrews, Caroline, ed. 2003. *Studies in Political Economy: Developments in Feminism.* Toronto: Women's Press

Aramark and IWA Local 1-3567. 2003. Partnership Agreement, 17 July

Arat-Koç, Sedef. 1989. "In the Privacy of Our Own Home." *Studies in Political Economy* 28

Arat-Koç, Sedef, with Fely Villasin. 2001. *Caregivers Break the Silence: A Participatory-Action Research on the Abuse and Violence, Including the Impact of Family Separation, Experienced by Women in the Live-in Caregiver Program.* Toronto: INTERCEDE

Armstrong, Hugh, et al. 2001. *Unhealthy Times: Political Economy Perspectives on Health and Care.* Don Mills, Ont.: Oxford University Press

Armstrong, Pat, and Hugh Armstrong. 2003a. "Beyond Sexless Class and Classless Sex: Towards Feminist Marxism." In *Studies in Political Economy Developments in Feminism*, ed. Caroline Andrews, Pat Armstrong, Hugh Armstrong, Wallace Clement, and Leah Vosko. Toronto: Women's Press

– 2003b. "Production and Reproduction: Feminist Takes." In *Studies in Political Economy Developments in Feminism*, ed. Caroline Andrews, Pat Armstrong, Hugh Armstrong, Wallace Clement, and Leah Vosko. Toronto: Women's Press

— 1996. *Wasting Away: The Undermining of Canadian Health Care.* Toronto: Oxford University Press

— 1994. *The Double Ghetto: Canadian Women and Their Segregated Work.* 1978. 3rd ed. Toronto: McClelland and Stewart

Armstrong Pat, Hugh Armstrong, Jacqueline Choiniere, Gina Feldberg, and Jerry White. 1994. *Take Care: Warning Signals for Canadian Health Care.* Toronto: Garamond

Armstrong, Pat, and M.P. Connelly, eds. 1999. *Feminism, Political Economy and the State: Contested Terrain.* Toronto: Canadian Scholars' Press

Armstrong, Pat, et al. 2002. *Exposing Privatization: Women's Health Reform in Canada.* Aurora: Garamond

*Atlantis.* 2004. *Transphobia and Transactivism.* Vol.29, (1), fall/winter. Special issue.

Auditor General of Scotland. 2000. "A Clean Bill of Health? A Review of Domestic Services in Scottish Hospitals." April. Available at www.audit-scotland.gov.uk

Ayliffe, G., J. Babb, and L. Taylor. 1999. *Hospital-Acquired Infection: Principles and Prevention, 3rd ed.* Oxford: Butterworth-Heinemann

Bacchi, Carol Lee. 1983. *Liberation Deferred? The Ideas of the English Canadian Suffragists, 1877–1918.* Toronto: University of Toronto Press.

Bakan, Abigail B., and Daiva Stasiulis. 1997. "Foreign Domestic Worker Policy in Canada." In *Not One of the Family: Foreign Domestic Workers in Canada,* ed. Abigail B. Bakan and Daiva Stasiulis. Toronto: University of Toronto Press

Bakker, Isabella. 2003a. "Neo-liberal Governance and the Reprivatization of Social Reproduction: Social Provisioning and Shifting Gender Orders." In *Power, Production and Social Reproduction,* ed. Isabella Bakker and Stephen Gill. Basingstoke, UK: Palgrave MacMillan

– 2003b. "Ontology, Method, and Hypotheses." In *Power, Production and Social Reproduction,* ed. Isabella Bakker and Stephen Gill. Basingstoke, UK: Palgrave MacMillan

– 2001. "Neoliberal Governance and the Reprivatization of Social Reproduction." Paper presented at the International Studies Association Annual Convention, New Orleans, 23–27 March

– 1996. "Introduction: The Gendered Foundations of Restructuring in Canada." In *Rethinking Restructuring: Gender and Change in Canada,* ed. Isabella Bakker. Toronto: University of Toronto Press

– 1989. "The Political Economy of Gender." In *New Canadian Political Economy,* ed Glen Williams and Wallace Clement. Montreal: McGill-Queen's University Press

– (ed). 1996. *Rethinking Restructuring: Gender and Change in Canada.* Toronto: University of Toronto Press

– (ed). 1994. *The Strategic Silence: Gender and Economic Policy.* London: Atlantic Highlands, NJ: The North-South Institute, Zed Books

Bakker, Isabella, and Stephen Gill, eds. 2004. *Power, Production and Social Reproduction: Human In/security in the Global Political Economy.* London: Palgrave Macmillan

Bakvis, Herman, and Grace Skogstad, eds. 2002. *Canadian Federalism: Performance, Effectiveness and Legitimacy.* Don Mills, Ont.: Oxford University Press

Bannerji, Himani. 2000. *The Dark Side of the Nation.* Toronto: Canadian Scholars Press

– 1991. "But Who Speaks for Us? Experience and Agency in Conventional Feminist Paradigms." In *Unsettling Relations The University as a Site of Feminist Struggles.* ed. Himanni Bannerji et al. Toronto: Women's Press

Barbeau, Carole. 2001. *Work-Related Child-Care Centres in Canada – 2001.* Ottawa: Human Resources Development Canada

Baril, Robert, Pierre Lefebvre, and Philip Merrigan. 2000. *Quebec Family Policy: Impact and Options.* Montreal: IRPP

Barrett, Michele. 1992. "Words and Things." In *Destabalizing Theory: contemporary feminist debates,* ed. Michele Barrett and Anne Phillips. Stanford, Calif.: Stanford University Press

– 1991. *The Politics of Truth: From Marx to Foucault.* Stanford, Calif.: Stanford University Press

Bashevkin, Sylvia, ed. 2002. *Women's Work is Never Done: Comparative Studies in Caregiving, Employment, and Social Policy Reform.* New York: Routledge

– 1998. *Women on the Defensive: Living through Conservative Times.* Toronto: University of Toronto Press

Bassin, Donna, M. Honey and M.M. Kaplan, eds. 1994. *Representations of Motherhood.* New Haven: Yale University Press

Beauvais, C., and J. Jenson. 2001. *Two Policy Paradigms: Family Responsibility and Investing in Children.* Ottawa: Canadian Policy Research Network

Beechey, Veronica. 1987. *Unequal Work.* London: Verso

Benjamin, Jessica. 1988. *Bonds of Love: Psychoanalysis, Feminism, and the Problem of Domination.* New York: Pantheon Books

Bennett, K.J., et al. 1998. "Do Measures of Externalizing Behaviour in Normal Populations Predict Later Outcome? Implications for Targeted Interventions to Prevent Conduct Disorder." *Journal of Child Psychology and Psychiatry* 39(8)

Bennett, R.B. "The Premier Speaks to the People, January 2, 1935." In *First among Equals: The Canadian Prime Minister in Life and Politics: The Right Honourable Richard Bedford Bennett.* National Archives of Canada. Available at http://www.nlc-bnc.ca/2/4/h4-4049-e.html. Accessed 31 January 2004

Benston, Margaret. 1969. "The Political Economy of Women's Liberation." *Monthly Review* 21 (4)

Bezanson, Kate. 2006. *Gender, the State and Social Reproduction: Household Insecurity in Neo-liberal Times.* Toronto: University of Toronto Press

Bezanson, Kate, and F. Valentine. 1998. *Act in Haste ... The Style, Scope and Speed of Change in Ontario.* Ottawa: Caledon Institute of Social Policy

Bezanson, Kate, and L. Noce. 1999. *Costs, Closures and Confusion: People in Ontario Talk about Health Care.* Ottawa: Caledon Institute of Social Policy

Bezanson, Kate, and S. McMurray. 2000. *Booming for Whom? People in Ontario Talk about Income, Jobs and Social Programmes.* Ottawa: Caledon Institute of Social Policy

Bittman, Michael. 2002. "The Visible and the Hidden: States, Markets and Non-Market Activity." Melbourne: RMIT University

Blum, Linda. 1999. *At the Breast: Ideologies of Breastfeeding and Motherhood in the Contemporary United States.* Boston: Beacon Press

Blum, Linda, and Theresa Deussen. 1996. "Negotiating Independent Motherhood: Working-Class African American Women Talk about Marriage and Motherhood." *Gender & Society* 10

Blumberg, Rae Lesser. 1978. *Stratification: Socioeconomic and Sexual Inequality* Dubuque, Iowa: Wm Brown and Co.

Boismenu, Gérard, and Jane Jenson. 1998. "A Social Union or a Federal State? Intergovernmental Relations in the New Liberal Era." In *How Ottawa Spends 1998–99: Balancing Act: The Post-Deficit Mandate,* ed. Leslie A. Pal. Toronto, Oxford, and New York: Oxford University Press

Bottomore, Tom, Laurence Harris, V.G. Kiernan, and Ralph Miliband, eds. 1983. *A Dictionary of Marxist Thought* Oxford: Blackwell

Boulton, Mary. 1983. *On Being a Mother: A Study of Women with Pre-School Children.* London: Tavistock

Bowlby, G. 2000. "The School-to-Work Transition." *Perspectives on Income and Labour.* (Statistics Canada), Spring

Boychuk, Gerald William. 1998. *Patchworks of Purpose: The Development of Provincial Social Assistance Regimes in Canada.* Montreal and Kingston: McGill-Queen's University Press

Bradbury, Bettina. 1993. *Working Families: Age, Gender, and Daily Survival in Industrializing Montreal.* Toronto: McClelland & Stewart

Brand, Dionne. 1999. "Black Women and Work: The Impact of Racially Constructed Gender Roles on the Sexual Division of Labour." In *Scratching the Surface: Canadian Anti-Racist Thought,* ed. Enakshi Dua and Angela Robertson. Toronto: Women's Press

Braverman, Harry. 1974. *Labor and Monopoly Capital: The Degradation of Work in the Twentieth Century.* New York: Monthly Review Press

Brenner, Johanna. 2000. *Women and the Politics of Class* New York: Monthly Review Press

Brenner, Johanna and Barbara Laslett. 1991. "Gender, Social Reproduction and Women's Self-Organization: Considering the U.S. Welfare State." *Gender and Society* 5(3)

Brock, Kathy, ed. 2003. *Delicate Dances: Public Policy and the Nonprofit Sector.* Montreal: Published for the School of Policy Studies, Queen's University by McGill-Queen's University Press

Brodie, Janine. 2003. "Globalization, In/Security, and the Paradoxes of the Social". In *Power, Production and Social Reproduction,* ed. Isabella Bakker and Stephen Gill. Basingstok, UK: Palgrave MacMillan

– 1999. "The Politics of Social Policy in the Twenty First Century". In *Citizens or Consumers: Social Policy in a Market Society,* ed. D. Broad and W. Antony. Halifax: Fernwood

– 1995. *Politics on the Margins: Restructuring and the Canadian Women's Movement.* Halifax: Fernwood

– 1994. "Shifting Public Spaces: A Reconsideration of the Role of Women in the State in the Era of Global Restructuring." In *The Strategic Silence: Gender and Economic Policy.* ed. Isabella Bakker. London: Zed Books

– (ed). 1996. *Women and Canadian Public Policy.* Toronto: Harcourt Brace

Brooks, S., and L. Miljan. 2003. *Public Policy in Canada.* Toronto: Oxford University Press

Broomhill, R., and R. Sharp. 2003. "A New Gender (Dis)order? Neo-liberal Restructuring in Australia." In *Decommodifying Public Life: Resisting the Enclosure of the Commons,* ed. G. Laxer and D. Soron. London: Zed Books

Brown, Rosemary. 1989. *Being Brown.* Toronto: Ballantine Books

Browne, P.L. 2000. *Unsafe Practices: Restructuring and Privatization in Ontario Health Care.* Ottawa: Canadian Centre for Policy Alternatives

Burawoy, Michael. 1980. "Migrant Labour in South Africa and the United States." In *Capital and Labour: Studies in the Capitalist Labour Process,* ed. Theo Nichols. London: Athlone

Butler, Judith. 1990. *Gender Trouble: Feminism and the Subversion of Identity.* London: Routledge

California Advocates for Nursing Home Reform. 2001. "Staffing in California Nursing Homes: A Continuing Crisis in Care." Available at www.canhr.org/publications

Calixte, Shana, Jennifer Johnson, and Maki Motapanyane. 2005. "Liberal, Socialist, and Radical Feminism: An Introduction to Three Theories about

Women's Oppression and Social Change." In *Feminist Issues: Race, Class and Sexuality*, ed. Nancy Mandell. Toronto: Pearson, Prentice Hall

Cameron, Barbara. 2006. "Accounting for Rights and Money in Canada's Social Union." In *Poverty: Rights, Social Citizenship and Governance*, ed. Susan Boyd et al. Vancouver: UBC Press.

– 2004a. "A Legislative Framework for a Pan Canadian System of Child Care Services: A Discussion Paper Prepared for the Child Care Advocacy Association of Canada." Available at http://www.childcareadvocacy.ca/resources

– 2004b. "The Social Union, Executive Power and Social Rights." *Canadian Woman Studies* 13(3/4)

– 2002. "The Chrétien Legacy and Women's Equality," *Canada Watch* 9 (3/4)

– 1999."A Framework for Conflict Management." *Constitutional Forum Constitutionnel* 10 (4)

– 1997. *Rethinking the Social Union: National Identities and Social Citizenship.* Ottawa: Canadian Centre for Policy Alternatives

Canada. 2005. "Chapter 4 – A Productive, Growing and Sustainable Economy." In *Federal Budget 2005: Securing Our Social Foundations.* Ottawa: Department of Finance

– 2004. "Chapter 4 – Moving Forward on the Priorities of Canadians: The Importance of Learning." In *Federal Budget 2004: New Agenda for Achievement.* Ottawa: Department of Finance

– 2003. *Multilateral Framework on Early Learning and Care.* Ottawa: Ministry of Supply and Services. Available at www.socialunion.gc.ca/ecd-framework_e.htm

– 2002a. "Appendix 7 – The National Child Benefit Governance and Accountability Framework." Available at http://www.nationalchildbenefit.ca/ncb/NCB-2002/a7.html

– 2002b. *Federal/Provincial/Territorial Early Childhood Development Agreement: Report on Government of Canada Activities and Expenditures 2001–2002.* Ottawa: Minister of Public Works and Government Services

– 2002c. *The Well-Being of Canada's Young Children: Government of Canada Report.* Ottawa: Minister of Public Workers and Government Services

– 2001. *Federal/Provincial/Territorial Early Childhood Development Agreement: Report on Government of Canada Activities and Expenditures 2000–2001.* Ottawa: Minister of Public Works and Government Services

– 2000. *National Child Benefit Reinvestment Report.* Ottawa, Government of Canada

– 1999a. *A Framework to Improve the Social Union for Canadians. An Agreement between the Government of Canada and the Governments of the Provinces and Territories.* Ottawa

– 1999b. *Public Report: Public Dialogue on the National Children's Agenda: Developing a Shared Vision.* Ottawa

– 1997. *Background Information on the National Children's Agenda.* Available at http://www.socialunion.gc.ca/nca/nca1_e.html

– 1985. Royal Commission on the Economic Union and Development Prospects for Canada. *Report.* 3 vols. Ottawa: Minister of Supply and Services Canada

– 1943–44. Advisory Committee on Reconstruction. Subcommittee on Post-War Problems of Women. *Final Report, November 30, 1943.* Ottawa: King's Printer

– 1940. Royal Commission on Dominion-Provincial Relations. *Report.* Book 2. *Recommendations.* Ottawa: King's Printer

Canada-Ontario. 2005. *Moving Forward on Early Learning and Child Care: Agreement-in-Principle Between the Government of Canada and the Government of Ontario.* Available at www.sdc.ac.ca. Accessed 15 August 2005.

Canadian Association of Administrators of Labour Legislation (CAALL). 2002. *Work-Life Balance: A Report to Ministers Responsible for Labour in Canada.* Social Development Canada. Available at http://www.sdc.gc.ca

Canadian Auto Workers. 2004. "CAW Lesbian, Gay, Bisexual and Transgender (LGBT) History." Available at http://www.caw.ca/whatwedo/pride/lgbthistory.asp. Accessed 19 July 2005

Canadian Child Care Federation (CCCF). 2001a. "Across Canada: Early Childhood Development Agreements." *Interaction* 15 (3)

– 2001b. "Early Years Centres." Unpublished brief

Canadian Labour Congress (CLC). 2005a. "CLC Constitution: In Clear Language." June. Available at www.canadianlabour.ca/updir/constitution

– 2005b. "Employment Insurance Fairness." Available at http://www.canadianlabour.ca/index.php/Employment_Insurance Accessed 19 July 2005

– 2003. *Falling Unemployment Insurance Protection for Canada's Unemployed.* Ottawa: CLC

Canadian Union of Postal Workers. 2003. *Moving Mountains: Work, Family and Children with Special Needs.* Ottawa: Canadian Union of Postal Workers

Carby, Hazel. 1982. "White Women Listen! Black Feminism and the Boundaries of Sisterhood." In *The Empire Strikes Back: Race and Racism in Britain,* ed. Centre for Contemporary Cultural Studies. London: Hutcheson

Cardinal, Linda. 1992. "La recherche sur les femmes francophones vivant en milieu minoritaire: Un questionnement sur le féminisme." *Recherches féministes* 5 (1)

Cardinal, Linda, and Cécile Coderre. 1990. "Reconnaître une histoire: Le movement des femmes francophones hors Québec." *Femmes d'action* 19 (3)

Carty, Linda. 1993. "Combining Our Efforts: Making Feminism Relevant to the Changing Society." In *And Still We Rise: Feminist Political Mobilizing in Contemporary Canada*, ed. Linda Carty. Toronto: Women's Press

Castles, Stephen, and Godula Kosack. 1973. *Immigrant Workers and Class Structure in Western Europe*. London: Oxford University Press

Chang, Grace. 2000. *Disposable Domestics: Immigrant Women Workers in the Global Economy*. Cambridge, Mass.: South End Press

– 1992. "Disposable Nannies: Women's Work and the Politics of Latina Immigration." *Radical America* 26 (2) (published in 1996)

Che-Alford, J. Hamm, and B. Hamm 1999. "Under One Roof: Three Generations Living Together." *Canadian Social Trends* (Summer)

Child Care Advocacy Association of Canada. 2005. "The Federal Budget and the Child Care Promise: Promise Made but Not Yet Kept." Unpublished brief. Available at www.childcareadvocacy.ca

Children's Mental Health Ontario. 2001. *Evidence-Based Practices for Children and Adolescents with Depression*. Toronto: Children's Mental Health Ontario

Chow, Olivia. 2003. "A New Deal for Child Care in Toronto: Selling Children Short." *Toronto Star*. Available at www.cit.toronto.on.ca/children/campaign/_ochow_staraprio3.htm

Christie, Nancy. 2000. *Engendering the State: Family, Work, and Welfare in Canada*. Toronto: University of Toronto Press

Clarke, L. 2000. "Disparities in Wage Relations and Social Reproduction." In *The Dynamics of Wage Relations in the New Europe*, ed. L. Clarke, P. Gijsel, and J. Jannssen. London: Kluwer Academic Publishers

Clarke-Stewart, Alison. 1993. *Daycare*. Rev ed. Cambridge, Mass.: Harvard University Press

Clement, Wallace. 1997. "Whither the New Canadian Political Economy?" In *Understanding Canada: Building on the New Canadian Political Economy*, ed. Wallace Clement. Montreal and Kingston: McGill-Queen's University Press

Clement, Wallace, and Leah Vosko, eds. 2003. *Changing Canada: Political Economy as Transformation*. Montreal: McGill-Queen's University Press

Cleveland, Gordon, and Michael Krashinsky, eds. 2001. *Our Children's Future: Child Care Policy in Canada*. Toronto: University of Toronto Press

Coffey, Charles, and Margaret Norrie McCain. 2002. *Commission on Early Learning and Child Care for the City of Toronto: Final Report*. Toronto: City of Toronto. Accessed at http://www.city.toronto.on.ca/children/report/elcc.pdf

Cohen, Marjorie Griffin. 2001. *Do Comparisons between Hospital Support Workers and Hospitality Workers Make Sense?* Vancouver: Hospital Employees' Union. Available at http://www.sfu.ca/~mcohen/publications

– 1988. *Women's Work, Markets, and Economic Development in Nineteenth-Century Ontario.* Toronto: University of Toronto Press.

Colen, Shellee. 1995. "'Like a Mother to Them': Stratified Reproduction and West Indian Childcare Workers and Employers in New York." In *Conceiving the New World Order: The Global Politics of Reproduction,* ed. Faye D. Ginsburg and Rayna Rapp. Berkeley: University of California Press

Comfort, D., K. Johnson, and D. Wallace. 2003. *Part-time Work and Family-Friendly Practices in Canadian Workplaces.* The Evolving Workplace Series, 6. Ottawa: Statistics Canada and Human Resources Development Canada

Communication, Energy and Paperworkers Union of Canada. 2004. *Shorter Hours of Work Campaign.* Ottawa: CEP. Available at http://www.cep.ca/swtime_e.html. Accessed 14 July 2005

Connell, R.W. 1987. *Gender & Power.* Stanford: Stanford University Press

Connelly, Patricia. 1978. *Last Hired, First Fired: Women and the Canadian Work Force.* Toronto: The Women's Press

Connelly, Patricia, and Pat Armstrong, eds. 1992. *Feminism in Action Studies in Political Economy.* Toronto: Canadian Scholars Press

Coontz, Stephanie. 1988. *The Social Origins of Private Life: A History of American Families, 1600–1900.* New York: Verso

Coontz, Stephanie, and Peta Henderson, eds. 1986. *Women's Work, Men's Property: The Origins of Gender and Class.* London: Verso

Corrigan, P., and R.D. Sayer. 1985. *The Great Arch: English State Formation as Cultural Revolution.* Oxford: Blackwell

Cossman, Brenda, and Judy Fudge, eds. 2002. *Privatization, Law, and the Challenge to Feminism.* Toronto: University of Toronto Press

Cott, Nancy. 1977. *The Bonds of Womanhood: Women's Sphere in New England, 1780–1835.* New Haven: Yale University Press

Courtice, Ian. 2000. "Redistribute Funds and Privatize Non-essential Services Says BCMA President." *Sounding Board* (Vancouver Board of Trade) 39 (8)

Cowan, Carolyn, and Philip Cowan. 1992. *When Partners Become Parents: The Big Life Change for Couples.* New York: Basic

Creighton, Donald. 1940. "The Economic Objectives of Confederation." In *British North America at Confederation: Report of the Royal Commission on Dominion-Provincial Relations,* book 3, appendix 3. Ottawa: King's Printer

Daly, M., and J. Lewis. 2000. "The Concept of Social Care and the Analysis of Contemporary Welfare States." *British Journal of Sociology* 51 (2)

Dancer, J.S. 1999. "Mopping up Hospital Infection." *Journal of Hospital Infection* 43 (2)

Davidoff, Lenore, and Catherine Hall. 1987. *Family Fortunes: Men and Women of the English Middle Class, 1780–1850.* Chicago: University of Chicago Press

Davin, Anna. 1978. "Imperialism and Motherhood." *History Workshop Journal* 5

Day, Shelagh, and Gwen Brodsky. 1998. *Women and the Equality Deficit: The Impact of Restructuring Canada's Social Programs.* Ottawa: Status of Women Canada

Dean, M. 2002. "Liberal Government and Authoritarianism." *Economy and Society* 31 (1)

de Beauvoir, Simone. 1952. *The Second Sex.* 1949. Trans. H.M. Parshley. New York: Alfred A. Knopf

Dehli, K. 1994. *Parent Activism and School Reform in Toronto.* Toronto: Ontario Institute for Studies in Education, Department of Sociology in Education.

– 1993. "Subject to the New Global Economy: Power and Positioning in Ontario Labour Market Policy Formation." *Studies in Political Economy* 41

D'Emilio, John, 1983. "Capitalism and Gay Identity." In *Powers of Desire: The Politics of Sexuality,* ed. Ann Snitow, Christine Stansell, and Sharon Thompson. New York: Monthly Review Press

de Wolff, Alice. 2003. *Bargaining for Work and Life.* Toronto: Ontario Federation of Labour

– 1994. *Strategies for Working Families.* Toronto: Ontario Coalition for Better Child Care

Discussion Collective No. 6. 1972. *Women Unite! An Anthology of the Canadian's Women's Movement.* Toronto: Canadian Women's Educational Press

Doern, Bruce G., and Mark MacDonald. 1999. *Free Trade Federalism: Negotiating the Canadian Agreement on Internal Trade.* Toronto: University of Toronto Press

Doherty, Gillian, Martha Friendly, and Mab Oloman. 1998. *Women's Support, Women's Work: Child Care in an Era of Deficit Reduction, Devolution, Downsizing and Deregulation.* Ottawa: Status of Women Canada

Drache, Daniel. 1978. "Introduction." In *The New Practical Guide to Canadian Political Economy,* ed. Daniel Drache and Wallace Clement. Toronto: Lorimer

Drake, R.E., et al. 2003. "Strategies for Implementing Evidence-Based Practices in Routine Mental Health Settings." *Evidence-Based Mental Health* 6(1)

Drolet, Marie. 2002. "The Male-Female Wage Gap." *Perspectives on Labour and Income* 14 (1)

Dua, Enakshi, and Angela Robertson, eds. 1999. *Scratching the Surface: Canadian Anti-Racist Feminist Thought.* Toronto: Women's Press

Dumont, Micheline, Michele Jean, Marie Lavigne, and Jennifer Stoddart. 1987. *Quebec Women: A History.* Toronto: Women's Press

Egan, Carolyn. 1987. "Toronto's International Women's Day Committee: Socialist Feminist Politics." In *Feminism & Political Economy: Women's Work,*

*Women's Struggles*, ed. Heather Jon Maroney and Meg Luxton. Toronto: Methuen

Ehrenreich, Barbara, and Arlie Russell Hochschild. 2003. "Introduction." In *Global Woman: Nannies, Maids, and Sex Workers in the New Economy.* New York: Metropolitan Books

Eichler, Margrit. 1997. *Family Shifts: Families, Policies and Gender Equality.* Don Mills, Ont.: Oxford University Press

EKOS Research Associates. 2001. *Survey on Canadians' Attitudes Regarding Their Workload.* Ottawa: Canadian Union of Public Employees

Elson, Diane. 1998. "The Economic, the Political and the Domestic: Businesses, States and Households in the Organisation of Production." *New Political Economy* 3 (2)

– ed. 1995. *Male Bias in the Development Process.* 2nd ed. Manchester and New York: Manchester University Press

Engels, Frederich. 1972. *The Origin of the Family, Private Property and the State, in the Light of the Researches of Lewis Henry Morgan.* 1884. New York: International Publishers

Equality for Gays And Lesbians Everywhere (EGALE). 2005. "Moore v. Canada (Treasury Board)." Available at http://www.egale.ca/index.asp?lang=F&menu=1&item=36&version= FR. Accessed 19 July 2005

Evans, Mary. 2003. *Gender and Social Theory.* Buckingham: Open University Press

Eyer, Diane, 1996. *Motherguilt: How Our Culture Blames Mothers for What's Wrong with Society.* New York: Random House

– 1992. *Mother-Infant Bonding: A Scientific Fiction.* New Haven: Yale University Press

Fairey, David B. 2003. *An Inter-Provincial Comparison of Pay Equity Strategies and Results Involving Hospital Service & Support Workers.* Vancouver: Trade Union Research Bureau

– 2002. "HEU's Wage Equity Bargaining History." Unpublished paper for the Trade Union Research Bureau, Vancouver

Fanon, Frantz. 1963. *The Wretched of the Earth.* New York: Grove Press

Ferge, Z. 1997. "The Changed Welfare Paradigm: The Individualization of the Social." *Social Policy and Administration* 31 (1)

Finch, Janet. 1989. *Family Obligations and Social Change.* Cambridge: Polity Press

Finch, Janet, and Jennifer Mason. 1993. *Negotiating Family Responsibilities.* London: Tavistock/Routledge

Firestone, Shulamith. 1970. *The Dialectic of Sex: The Case for Feminist Revolution.* New York: William Morrow

First Ministers (Canada). 2000. "First Ministers' Communique on Early Childhood Development. "Available at http:/www.childcareadvocacy.ca

Forget, Claude E. 2003. "Towards a Consensus on Continuing Chaos." *C.D. Howe Commentary*, February

Foucault, M. 1991. "Governmentality." In *The Foucault Effect: Studies in Governmentality*, ed. G. Burchell, C. Gordon, and P. Miller. Chicago: University of Chicago Press

Fox, Bonnie. 2003. "Becoming Parents: The Relational Dynamics that Produce Mothers and Fathers." Paper presented at the 3rd annual Carework Conference, an ASA pre-conference, Chicago, August

– 2001. "The Formative Years: How Parenthood Creates Gender." *Canadian Review of Sociology and Anthropology* 38(4)

– 1988. "Conceptualizing 'Patriarchy.'" *Canadian Review of Sociology and Anthropology* 25 (2)

– (ed). 1980. *Hidden in the Household: Women's Domestic Labour under Capitalism.* Toronto: Women's Press

Fraser, Nancy, and Linda Gordon. 1997. "A Genealogy of 'Dependency': Tracing a Keyword of the U.S. Welfare State." In *Justice Interruptus: Critical Reflections on the "PostSocialist" Condition*, ed. Nancy Fraser. New York: Routledge

Friendly, Martha. 2001. "Child Care and Canadian Federalism in the 1990s: Canary in a Coal Mine." In *Our Children's Future: Child Care Policy in Canada*, ed. Michael Krashinsky and Gordon Cleveland. Toronto: University of Toronto Press

Friendly, Martha, J. Beach, and M. Turiano. 2003. *Early Childhood Education and Care in Canada: 2001*. Toronto: Childcare Resource and Research Unit, University of Toronto

Fudge, Judy. 1999. "Legal Forms and Social Norms: Class, Gender, and the Legal Regulation of Women's Work in Canada from 1870 to 1920." In *Locating Law: Race/Class/Gender Connections*, ed. Elizabeth Cormack. Halifax: Fernwood Publishing

– 1997. *Precarious Work and Families.* Toronto: Centre for Research on Work and Society, York University

Fudge, Judy, and Brenda Cossman. 2002. "Introduction: Privatization, Law, and the Challenge to Feminism." In *Privatization, Law, and the Challenge to Feminism*, ed. Brenda Cossman and Judy Fudge. Toronto: University of Toronto Press

Fudge, Judy, and Leah F. Vosko. 2003. "Gendered Paradoxes and the Rise of Contingent Work: Towards a Transformative Feminist Political Economy of the Labour Market." In *Changing Canada: Political Economy as Transformation*, ed. Wallace Clement and Leah F. Vosko. Montreal and Kingston: McGill-Queen's University Press

Fuller, Sylvia. 2001. *The Case for Pay Equity*. Vancouver: Canadian Centre for Policy Alternatives. Available at http://www.policyalternatives.ca

Furedi, Frank. 2002. *Culture of Fear*. London and New York: Continnum

Gannage, Charlene. 1986. *Double Day, Double Bind: Women Garment Workers*. Toronto: The Women's Press

Gardiner, Jean. 1997. *Gender, Care and Economics*. London: Macmillan

Gavron, Hannah. 1966. *The Captive Wife: Conflicts of Housebound Mothers*. London: Routledge & Kegan Paul

Georgetti, Kenneth V. 2003. Letter to Dave Haggard at the Industrial, Wood and Allied Workers of Canada (IWA), 17 September

Gibson, Gordon. 2003. *Fixing Canadian Democracy*. Vancouver: Fraser Institute

Giles, Wenona, and Sedef Arat-Koç, eds. 1994. *Maid in the Market: Women's Paid Domestic Labour*. Halifax: Fernwood

Ginsburg, Faye D., and Rayna Rapp. 1995. "Introduction." In *Conceiving the New World Order: The Global Politics of Reproduction*. Berkeley: University of California Press

Gittins, Diana. 1986. "Between the Devil and the Deep Blue Sea: The Marriage and Labor Markets in Nineteenth-Century England." In *Women in Culture and Politics: A Century of Change*, ed. Judith Friedlander, B.W. Cook, A. Kessler-Harris, and C. Smith-Rosenberg. Bloomington: Indiana University Press

Glenn, Evelyn Nakano. 1999. "The Social Construction and Institutionalization of Gender and Race: An Integrative Framework." In *Revisioning Gender*, ed. M.M. Ferree, J. Lorber, and B. Hess. Thousand Oaks: Sage

– 1992. "From Servitude to Service Work: Historical Continuities in the Racial Division of Paid Reproductive Labor." *Signs* 10

Glenn, Evelyn Nakano, Grace Chang, and Line R. Forcey, eds. 1994. *Mothering: Ideology, Experience, and Agency*. New York: Routledge

Gorz, Andre. 1970. "Immigrant Labour." *New Left Review* 61

Gottleib, Amy. 1993. "What about Us? Organizing Inclusively in the National Action Committee on the Status of Women." In *And Still We Rise: Feminist Political Mobilizing in Contemporary Canada*, ed. Linda Carty. Toronto: Women's Press

Greenwood, John. 2003. "Forest Union Fighting to Remain a Player." *Financial Post*, 6 October

Guest, Dennis. 1997. *The Emergence of Social Security in Canada*. 3rd ed. Vancouver: UBC Press

Gutierrez, Martha. 2003. *Macro-Economics: Making Gender Matter*. London: Zed Books

Hahnel, Robin. 2005. "What Mainstream Economists Won't Tell You about Neoliberal Globalization." *Socialist Studies: The Journal of the Society for Socialist Studies* 1 (1)

Hamilton, Roberta, and Michele Barrett, eds. 1986. *The Politics of Diversity.* London: Verso

Hareven, Tamara. 2000. *Families, History, and Social Change: Life-Course & Cross-Cultural Perspectives.* Boulder: Westview Press

Hartmann, Heidi. 1979. "The Unhappy Marriage of Marxism and Feminism: Towards a More Progressive Union." *Capital and Class* 8

Hays, Sharon. 1996. *The Cultural Contradictions of Motherhood.* New Haven: Yale University Press

Heckman, J. 2000. *Fostering Human Capital.* Chicago: Harris School of Public Policy, University of Chicago

Heisz, A., A. Jackson, and G. Picot. 2002. *Winners and Losers in the Labour Market of the 1990s.* Analytical Studies Branch Research Paper Series 184. Ottawa: Statistics Canada, Business and Labour Market Analysis Division

Hekman, Susan. 2000. "Beyond Identity: Feminism Identity and Identity Politics." *Feminist Theory* 1 (3)

Hennessy, Rosemary, ed. 1997. *Materialist Feminism: A Reader in Class, Difference, and Women's Lives.* New York: Routledge

Hennessy, Rosemary, and Chrys Ingraham. 1997. "Introduction: Reclaiming Anticapitalist Feminism." In *Materialist Feminism: A Reader in Class, Difference, and Women's Lives,* ed. Rosemary Hennessy. New York: Routledge

Heyzer, Noeleen, et al. 1994. *The Trade in Domestic Workers: Causes, Mechanisms and Consequences of International Migration.* Kuala Lumpur: Asian and Pacific Development Centre; London and Atlantic Highlands, NJ: Zed Books

Higgins, Christopher, and Linda Duxbury. 2001. *National Work–Life Conflict Study.* Ottawa: Human Resources Development Canada

– 1999. *An Examination of the Costs of Work-Life Conflict in Canada.* Ottawa: Health Canada

Hill, Bridget. 1989. *Women, Work & Sexual Politics in Eighteenth-Century England.* Oxford: Basil Blackwell

Hochschild, Arlie Russell. 2003. "Love and Gold." In *Global Woman: Nannies, Maids and Sex Workers in the New Economy,* ed. Barbara Ehrenreich and Arlie Russell Hochschild. New York: Metropolitan Books

– 1997. *The Time Bind: When Work Becomes Home & Home Becomes Work.* New York: Metropolitan Books

Hogg, Peter W. 2003. *Constitutional Law of Canada.* Student ed. Scarborough, Ont.: Carswell

Hondagneu-Sotelo, Pierrette, 2001. *Doméstica: Immigrant Workers Cleaning and Caring in the Shadows of Affluence.* Berkeley: University of California Press

Hontagneu-Sotelo, Pierrette, and Ernestine Avila. 2000. "'I'm Here, but I'm There': The Meanings of Latina Transnational Motherhood." In *Gender Through the Prism of Difference,* ed. Maxine B. Zinn, Pierrette Hontagneu-Sotelo, and Michael A. Messner. 2nd ed. Boston: Allyn and Bacon

Horowitz, Gad. 1968. *Canadian Labour in Politics.* Toronto: University of Toronto Press

Hospital Employees' Union. 2005. "More Compass Workers Vote to Join HEU." 8 August

Human Resources Development Canada. 2003. "A National Child Care Strategy: Investing In Employment, Securing Our Future." Unpublished memorandum to Cabinet. 31 January

Human Rights Internet. 2003. *Singapore: Thematic Reports.* Available at http://www.hri.ca/fortherecord2003

Humphries, Jane. 1977. "The Working-Class Family, Women's Liberation, and Class Struggle: The Case of Nineteenth-Century British History." *Review of Radical Political Economics* 9

Hurley, James Ross. 1996. *Amending Canada's Constitution.* Ottawa: Supply and Services.

Hurley, Mary. 2005. *Sexual Orientation and Legal Rights.* Ottawa: Law and Government Division, Library of Parliament. Available at http://www.parl.gc.ca/information/library

Iyer, Nitya. 2002. *Working through the Wage Gap: Report of the Task Force on Pay Equity.* Victoria: Government of British Columbia

Jackson, Andrew. 2003a. *"In Solidarity": The Union Advantage.* Ottawa: Canadian Labour Congress

– 2003b. "Is Work Working for Women?" Research Paper no. 22. Ottawa: Canadian Labour Congress

Jackson, Andrew, and Sylvain Schetange. 2003. *Solidarity Forever? An Analysis of Changes in Union Density.* Ottawa: Canadian Labour Congress

Jackson, Marni. 1992. *The Mother Zone: Love, Sex, and Laundry in the Modern Family.* New York: Henry Holt and Co.

Jacobs, Jerry, and Kathleen Gerson. 2004. *The Time Divide: Work, Family and Gender Inequality.* Cambridge, Mass.: Harvard University Press

Jamieson, Kathleen. 1979. "Multiple Jeopardy: the Evolution of a Native Women's Movement." *Atlantis* 4

Jenson, Jane. 1997. "Who Cares? Gender and Welfare Regimes." *Social Politics,* Summer

– 1990. "Gender and Reproduction, or Babies and the State." *Studies in Political Economy* 20

Jenson, Jane, and Stephane Jacobzone. 2000. *Care Allowances for the Frail Elderly and Their Impact on Women Care-Givers.* Labour and Market Policy Occasional Papers No. 41. Paris: Organisation for Economic Co-operation and Development

Jenson, Jane, Rianne Mahon, and Susan D. Phillips. 2003. "No Minor Matter: The Political Economy of Childcare in Canada." In *Changing Canada: Political Economy as Transformation,* ed. Wallace Clement and Leah Vosko. Montreal and Kingston: McGill-Queen's University Press

Johnson, K. 1997. *Shiftwork from a Work and Family Perspective.* Ottawa: Human Resources Development Canada, Applied Research Branch

Joseph, Gloria. 1981. "The Incompatible Menage a Trois: Marxism, Feminism and Racism." In *Women and Revolution: A Discussion of the Unhappy Marriage of Marxism and Feminism,* ed. Lydia Sargent. Boston: South End Press

Jurik, N.C. 2004. "Imagining Justice: Challenging the Privatization of Public Life." *Social Problems* 51 (1)

Katz, Cindi. 2001. "Vagabond Capitalism and the Necessity of Social Reproduction." *Antipode* 33 (4)

Katz, Jonathan Ned. 1995. *The Invention of Heterosexuality.* Harmondsworth: Penguin

Kazdin, A.E., and M.K. Nock. 2003. "Delineating Mechanisms of Change in Child and Adolescent Therapy: Methodological Issues and Research Recommendations." *Journal of Child Psychology and Psychiatry* 44(8)

Kelleher, Christa, and Bonnie Fox. 2002. "Nurturing Babies, Protecting Men: The Unequal Dynamics of Women's Postpartum Caregiving Practices." In *Child Care & Inequality: Rethinking Carework for Children & Youth,* ed. Francesca Cancian, Demie Kurz, Andrew London, Rebecca Reviere, and Mary Tuominen. New York: Routledge

Kempadoo, Kamala.2004. "Globalizing Sex Workers' Rights." In *Race, Class and Gender: An Anthology,* ed. Margaret L. Andersen and Patricia Hill Collins. 5th ed. Belmont, Calif.: Wadsworth Thomson

– 2003. "Transnational Migrations and the 'Problem' of Trafficking." Theorizing Transnationality, Gender and Citizenship: Institute of Women's Studies and Gender Studies Public Lecture, 7 February.

Kent, Tom. 1988. *A Public Purpose: An Experience of Liberal Opposition and Canadian Government.* Kingston and Montreal: McGill-Queen's University Press

Kremarik, F. 1999. "Moving to Be Better Off." *Canadian Social Trends,* Winter

Kuhn, Annette, and AnnMarie Wolpe, eds. 1978. *Feminism and Materialism: Women and Modes of Production.* London: Routlege and Kegan Paul

Kwavnick, David, ed. 1973. *The Tremblay Report: Report of the Royal Commission of Inquiry on Constitutional Problems.* Carleton Library no. 64. Toronto: McClelland and Stewart

Lamarche, L. 1999. "New Governing Arrangements, Women and Social Policy." In *Citizens or Consumers? Social Policy in a Market Society,* ed. D. Broad and W. Antony. Halifax: Fernwood

Laslett, Barbara, and Johanna Brenner. 1989. "Gender and Social Reproduction: Historical Perspectives." *Annual Review of Sociology* 15

Lazar, Harvey, ed. 1997. *The State of the Federation 1997: Non Constitutional Renewal.* Kingston, Ont.: Institute of Intergovernmental Relations

Lazarre, Jane. 1976. *The Mother Knot.* Boston: Beacon Press

Leacock, Eleaner. 1972. "Introduction and Notes" in F. Engels *The Origin of the Family, Private Property and the State, in the light of the researches of Lewis Henry Morgan* New York: International Publishers

Lemke, T. 2001. "'The Birth of Bio-Politics': Michel Foucault's Lecture at the Collège de France on Neo-Liberal Governmentality." *Economy and Society* 30 (2)

Lerner, Gerda. 1986. *The Creation of Patriarchy.* New York: Oxford University Press

Lewis, Jane. 1998. *Gender, Social Care and Welfare State Restructuring in Europe.* Aldershot: Ashgate

Lipman, E.L., et al. 1994. "Relation between Economic Disadvantage and Psychosocial Morbidity in Children." *Canadian Medical Association Journal* 151

Little, M. 1998. *"No Car, No Radio, No Liquor Permit": The Moral Regulation of Single Mothers in Ontario, 1920–1997.* Toronto: Oxford University Press.

Livingstone, David, and Elizabeth Asner. 1996. "Feet in Both Camps: Household Classes, Divisions of Labour, and Group Consciousness." In *Recast Dreams: Class and Gender Consciousness in Steeltown,* ed. David Livingstone and Marshall Mangan. Toronto: Garamond Press

Luxton, Meg. 2002. *Feminist Perspectives on Social Inclusion and Children's Well-Being.* Toronto: Laidlaw Foundation

– 2001. "Feminism as a Class Act: Working Class Feminism and the Women's Movement in Canada." *Labour/Le Travail* 48

– 1998. *Families and the Labour Market: Coping Strategies from a Sociological Perspective.* Ottawa: Canadian Policy Research Networks

– ed. 1997. *Feminism and Families: Critical Policies and Changing Practices.* Halifax: Fernwood

– 1980. *More than a Labour of Love: Three Generations of Women's Work in the Home.* Toronto: Women's Press

Luxton, Meg, and Heather Jon Maroney. 1992. "Begetting Babies, Raising Children: The Politics of Parenting." In *Socialism in crisis? Canadian Perspectives,* ed. Jos Roberts and Jesse Vorst. Winnipeg and Halifax: Society for Socialist Studies/Fernwood Publishing

Luxton, Meg, and June Corman. 2001. *Getting By in Hard Times: Gendered Labour at Home and on the Job.* Toronto: University of Toronto Press

Luxton, Meg, and Leah F. Vosko. 1998. "Where Women's Efforts Count: The 1996 Census Campaign and 'Family Politics' in Canada." *Studies in Political Economy* 56

McBride, Stephen. 2001. *Paradigm Shift: Globalization and the Canadian State.* Halifax: Fernwood Books.

McBride-King, Judith, and K. Bachmann. 1999. *Is Work-Life Balance Still an Issue for Canadians and Their Employers? You Bet It Is.* Ottawa: Conference Board of Canada

McCain, Margaret Norrie, and J. Fraser Mustard. 2002. *The Early Years Study Three Years Later.* Toronto: The Founders' Network of the Canadian Institute for Advanced Research

– 1999. *Reversing the Real Brain Drain: Early Years Study Final Report.* Toronto: Canadian Institute for Advanced Research

McDaniel, S.A. 1999. "Untangling Love and Domination: Challenges of Home Care for the Elderly in a Reconstructing Canada." *Journal of Canadian Studies* 34 (2)

McDowell, Linda. 1991. "Life without Father and Ford: The New Gender Order of Post-Fordism." *Transactions of the Institute of British Geographers* 16

McFarlane, Lawrie, and Carlos Prado. 2002. *The Best-Laid Plans: Health Care's Problems and Prospects.* Montreal: McGill-Queen's University Press

McIntyre & Mustel Research Ltd. 2002. *HEU Member Profile Survey.* Vancouver: McIntyre & Mustel

McKeen, Wendy. 2004. *Money in Their Own Name: The Feminist Voice in Poverty Debate in Canada, 1970–1995.* Toronto: University of Toronto Press.

McKeen, Wendy, and Ann Porter. 2003. "Politics and Transformation: Welfare State Restructuring in Canada." In *Changing Canada: Political Economy as Transformation,* ed. Wallace Clement and Leah Vosko. Montreal: McGill-Queen's University Press

McMahon, Anthony. 1999. *Taking Care of Men Sexual Politics in the Public Mind.* Cambridge: Cambridge University Press

McMahon, Martha. 1995. *Engendering Motherhood: Identity and Self-Transformation in Women's Lives.* New York: Guilford Press

McMurray, S. 1997. *Speaking Out: Project Description, Research Strategy and Methodology.* Ottawa: Caledon Institute of Social Policy

McPherson, Kay. 1994. *When in Doubt, Do Both: The Times of My Life.* Toronto: University of Toronto Press

McRoberts, Kenneth. 1997. *Misconceiving Canada: The Struggle for National Unity.* Toronto: Oxford University Press

Malatest, R.A. 2003. *The Aging Workforce and Human Resource Implications for Canada's Sector Councils.* Ottawa: Alliance of Sector Councils

Marche mondiale des femmes/World March of Women. 2005. "Women's Global Charter for Humanity." International Committee of the World March of Women, Supporting Document 1. Available at www.marchemondiale.org

Margolis, Martha. 1984. *Mothers and Such: Views of American Women and Why They Changed.* Berkeley: University of California Press

Maroney, Heather Jon. 1992. "'Who Has the Baby?' Nationalism, Pronatalism and the Construction of a 'Demographic Crisis' in Quebec, 1960–1988." *Studies in Political Economy* 39

Maroney, Heather Jon, and Meg Luxton. 1997. "Gender at Work: Canadian Feminist Political Economy, after 1988." In *Building on the New Canadian Political Economy,* ed. Glenn Williams and Wally Clement. Montreal-Kingston: McGill-Queen's University Press

– 1987. "From Feminism and Political Economy to Feminist Political Economy." In *Feminism & Political Economy: Women's Work, Women's Struggles,* ed. Maroney, Heather Jon and Meg Luxton. Toronto: Methuen

Marshall, Katherine. 2003. "Benefiting from Extended Parental Leave." *Perspectives on Labour and Income* (Statistics Canada) 4 (3)

Marx, Karl. 1954. *Capital.* Vol. 1. Moscow: Progress Publishers

– 1976. *Capital.* Vol. 2. 1867. Harmondsworth: Penguin

Marx, Karl, and Frederick Engels. 1976. *The German Ideology* [1845]. In Karl Marx and Frederick Engels, *Collected Works,* vol. 5, 1845–47. New York: International Publishers

Mattingly, Doreen J. 1989. "Making Maids: United States Immigration Policy and Immigrant Domestic Workers." In *Gender, Migration and Domestic Service,* ed. Janet H. Momsen. London and New York: Routledge

Maushart, Susan. 2001. *Wifework: What Marriage Really Means for Women.* London: Bloomsbury

Maxwell, J. 2003. *The Great Social Transformation: Implications for the Social Role of the Government in Ontario.* Ottawa: Canadian Policy Research Networks

May, Martha. 1985. "Bread before Roses: American Workingmen, Labor Unions and the Family Wage." In *Women, Work, and Protest: A Century of US Women's Labor History*, ed. Ruth Milkman. Boston: Routledge & Kegan Paul

Milton Community Resource Centre. 2003. "Ontario Early Years: Resources for Parents and Caregivers." Available at http://www.mcrc.on.ca/familyframes.html. Accessed 1 March 2003

Mintzberg, H. 1996. "Managing Government, Governing Management." *Harvard Business Review* 74 (3)

Mitchell, Juliet. 1971. *Women's Estate*. Harmondsworth: Penguin

Molyneux, Maxine. 1994. "Women's Rights and the International Context: Some Reflections on the Post-Communist States." *Millennium* 94 (2)

– 1979. "Beyond the Domestic Labour Debate." *New Left Review* 116

Momsen, Janet Henshall. 1999. "Maids on the Move: Victim or Victor." In *Gender, Migration and Domestic Service*, ed. J.H. Momsen. London and New York: Routledge

Moody, Louise. 2002. "A New Vision for FRPs in Ontario: Early Years Centres." *Play and Parenting Connections*, Winter. Available at http://ww.frp.ca/g_Article.asp/ArtilceID=59

Moore, Henrietta. 1988. *Feminism and Anthropology*. Minneapolis: University of Minnesota Press

Morgan, Robin. 1970. "Introduction." In *Sisterhood Is Powerful: An Anthology of Writings from the Women's Liberation Movement*, ed. Robin Morgan. New York: Vintage

Morris, Lydia. 1990. *The Workings of the Household*. Cambridge: Polity Press

Morton, Peggy. 1972. "Women's Work Is Never Done." In *Women Unite! An Anthology of the Canadian's Women's Movement*, ed. Discussion Collective No. 6. Toronto: Canadian Women's Educational Press

Mosher, J. 2000. "Managing the Disentitlement of Women: Glorified Markets, the Idealized Family, and the Undeserving Other." In *Restructuring Caring Labour: Discourse, State Practice, and Everyday Life*, ed. S. Neysmith. Toronto: Oxford University Press.

Murphy, Janice. 2002. *Literature Review on Relationship between Cleaning and Hospital Acquired Infections*. Vancouver: Hospital Employees' Union

Muszynzki, Alicia. 1996. *Cheap Wage Labour: Race and Gender in the Fisheries of British Columbia*. Montreal: McGill-Queen's University Press

National Action Committee on the Status of Women in Canada (NAC). 1995. *A Decade of Deterioration in the Status of Women in Canada: A Summary Report*. Toronto

Neysmith, S. 2000. "Networking across Difference: Connecting Restructuring and Caring Labour." In *Restructuring Caring Labour: Discourse, State Practice, and Everyday Life*, ed. S. Neysmith. Toronto: Oxford University Press

Neysmith, S., K. Bezanson, and A. O'Connell. 2005. *Telling Tales: Living the Effects of Public Policy.* Halifax: Fernwood

Noce, L., and A. O'Connell. 1998. *Take It or Leave It: The Ontario Government's Approach to Job Insecurity.* Ottawa: Caledon Institute of Social Policy

O'Connell, A., and F. Valentine. 1998. *Centralizing Power, Decentralizing Blame: What Ontarians Say about Education Reform.* Ottawa: Caledon Institute of Social Policy

O'Connor, J.S., et al. 1999. *States, Markets, Families: Gender, Liberalism and Social Policy in Australia, Canada, Great Britain and the United States.* Cambridge: Cambridge University Press

O'Connor, James. 1974. *The Corporations and the State: Essays in the Theory of Capitalism and Imperialism.* New York: Harper & Row

Offord, D.R. 1991. "Growing Up Poor in Ontario." *Transitions,* June

Ontario. 2005. "Strengthening Ontario by Investing in People: Early Learning by Investing in People: Early Learning, Education, Postsecondary Education, Health and Infrastructure." In *2005 Ontario Budget: Investing in People, Strengthening Our Economy.* Toronto: Ministry of Finance Information Centre

– 2004. *Ontario Early Years Centres: Implementation Review of Ministry of Children and Youth Services.* Prepared by Harry Cummings and Associates Inc., Guelph Ont.

– 2003. *Ontario's Early Childhood Development Investments and Outcomes: 2002–2003 Report.* Ontario: Ministry of Community and Social Services

– 2002–03. "Ministry of Community, Family and Children's Services: 2002–2003 Business Plan." Accessed at http://www.cfcs.gov.on.ca/CFCS/en/busPlan/default.htm

– 2002. *Ontario's Early Years Plan.* Ontario: Ministry of Community and Social Services

– 2001. *Ontario Early Years Centres: Guidelines for Communities.* Ontario: Ministry of Community and Social Services

– 1994. *Bill 173: An Act Respecting Long Term Care.* Toronto.

Ontario Association of Community Care Access Centres (OACCAC). 2001. *The Case for Community Care Access Centre Case Management.* Scarborough, Ont.

Ontario Ministry of Finance. 1996. *Your Budget, Your Future: 1996 Ontario Budget Highlights.* Toronto: Queen's Printer for Ontario

Ontario Coalition for Better Childcare. 2005. "Build It Right! Ontario Coalition for Better Child Care Response to Best Start Plan." Available at www.childcareontario.org

– 2003. "Moving towards Better Child Care in Ontario: A Presentation to the Standing Committee on Finance and Economic Affairs, Government of Ontario." January

Ontario Federation of Labour. 1997. *No Longer Silent.* Toronto: Ontario Federation of Labour

Ontario Human Rights Commission. 2005. *Human Rights and the Family in Ontario.* Toronto: OHRC.

Ontario Secondary School Teachers' Federation. 1998. 'Issues in Ontario Education.' Background Paper on Bill 34. Toronto: OSSTF

Organisation for Economic Co-operation and Development (OECD). 2005. *Babies and Bosses: Reconciling Work and Family Life.* Vol. 4. Paris: OECD.

– 2004. *Early Childhood Education and Care Policy: Canada.* Paris: OECD

Orloff, Ann. 1996. "Gender and the Welfare State." *Annual Review of Sociology*

Pahl, J. 1984. "The Allocation of Money within Households." In *The State, The Law and the Family: Critical Perspectives,* ed. M.D.A. Freeman. London: Tavistock

Palmer, Vaughan. 2001. "NDP Policies Depleted the Health System." *Vancouver Sun,* 15 January

Panitch, Leo, and Donald Swartz. 2003. *From Consent to Coercion: The Assault on Trade Union Freedoms.* 3rd ed. Toronto: Garamond Press

Parrenas, Rhacel Salazar. 2003. "The Care Crisis in the Philippines: Children and Transnational Families in the New Global Economy." In *Global Woman: Nannies, Maids and Sex Workers in the New Global Economy,* ed. Barbara Ehrenreich and Arlie Russell Hochschild. New York: Metropolitan Books

– 2001a. *Servants of Globalization: Women, Migration and Domestic Work.* Stanford: Stanford University Press

– 2001b. "Transgressing the Nation-State: The Partial Citizenship and 'Imagined (Global) Community' of Migrant Filipina Domestic Workers." *Signs* 26 (4)

Pathe, Victor. 2003. Decision of Impartial Umpire, ID # 207/2003: Allegations of Violations of the Canadian Labour Congress (CLC) Constitution, Canadian Union of Public Employees (CUPE) vs Industrial, Wood and Allied Workers of Canada (IWA). 17 September

Peck, J. 2001. *Workfare States.* New York: Guilford Press

Peel Early Years. 2003. "Early Years Challenge Funded Projects for Peel." Available at www.pealearlyyears.com/msword.pdf. Accessed 2 March 2003

People for Education. 1998. *1998 Elementary Survey.* Toronto: People for Education.

Perry, Chris. 2003. "Cleanliness Matters!" Presentation at Vancouver General Hospital, 10 March

Peterson, Spike. 2002. "Rewriting (Global) Political Economy as Reproductive, Productive and Virtual (Foucauldian) Economies." *International Feminist Journal of Politics* 4 (1)

Pettman, Jan Jindy. 1999. "Globalization and the Gendered Politics of Citizenship." In *Women, Citizenship and Difference*, ed. Nira Yuval-Davis and Pnina Werbner. London and New York: Zed Books.

– 1996. *Worlding Women: A Feminist International Politics.* London and New York: Routledge

Philipps, Lisa. 2002. "Tax Law and Social Reproduction: The Gender of Fiscal Policy in the Age of Privatization." In *Privatization, Law, and the Challenge to Feminism*, ed. Brenda Cossman and Judy Fudge. Toronto: University of Toronto Press

Philips, Susan D. 1989. "Rock-a-Bye, Brian: The National Strategy on Child Care." In *How Ottawa Spends, 1989–90: The Buck Stops Where?* ed. Katherine A. Graham. Ottawa: Carleton University Press

Picchio, Antonella. 2003. *Unpaid Work and the Economy: A Gender Analysis of the Standards of Living.* London: Routledge

– 1992. *Social Reproduction: The Political Economy of the Labour Market.* Cambridge: Cambridge University Press.

Pierson, P. 2000. "The Limits of Design: Explaining Institutional Origins and Change." *Governance* 13 (4)

Piven, Frances Fox, and Richard A. Cloward. 1993. *Regulating the Poor: the Functions of Public Welfare.* New York: Vintage Books

Porter, Ann. 2003. *Gendered States: Women, Unemployment Insurance, and the Political Economy of the Welfare State in Canada, 1945–1997.* Toronto: University of Toronto Press

Porter, Marilyn, and Ellen Judd, eds. 1999. *Feminists Doing Development: A Practical Critique.* London: Zed Books

Prentice, Alison, Paula Bourne, Gail Cuthbert Brandt, Beth Light, Wendy Mitchinson, and Naomi Black. 1996. *Canadian Women: A History.* 2nd ed. Toronto: Harcourt Brace and Co.

Public Service Alliance of Canada. 2003. "Meeting Member's Needs: Negotiating Family Care." *Issues* (Public Service Alliance of Canada) 6

Quebec Liberal Party. 2001. Special Committee on the Political and Constitutional Future of Quebec Society. *A Project for Quebec: Affirmation, Autonomy and Leadership. Final Report.* Quebec: QLP

Rampling, A., S. Wiseman, L. Davis, A.P. Hyett, A.N. Walbridge, G.C. Payne, and A.J. Cornaby. 2001. "Evidence that Hospital Hygiene Is Important in the Control of Methicilloin-Resistant Staphylococcus Aureus." *Journal of Hospital Infection* 49 (2)

Ramsey, Cynthia. 1995. *Labour in the Hospital Sector.* Vancouver: The Fraser Institute

Rapp, Rayna, and Ellen Ross, 1986. "The 1920s: Feminism, Consumerism, and Political Backlash in the United States." In *Women in Culture and Politics*, ed. Judith Friedlander, C.W. Cook, A. Kessler-Harris, and C. Smith-Rosenberg. Bloomington: Indiana University Press

Razack, Sherene. 1991. *Canadian Feminism and the Law: The Women's Legal Education and Action Fund and the Pursuit of Equality.* Toronto: Second Story Press

Rebick, Judy. 2005. *Ten Thousand Roses: The Making of a Feminist Revolution.* Toronto: Penguin

– 2004. "We've Come Part Way, Baby." *Globe and Mail*, 11 March, A21

Rebick, Judy, and Kiki Roach. 1996. *Politically Speaking* Toronto and Vancouver: Douglas and McIntyre

Reeves, Pember. 1913. *Round about a Pound a Week.* London: G. Bell & Sons

Rochon, Charles Philippe, ed. 2000. *Work and Family Provisions in Canadian Collective Agreements.* Ottawa: Human Resources Development Canada

Rodriguez, Robyn M. 2002. "Migrant Heroes: Nationalism, Citizenship and the Politics of Filipino Migrant Labor." *Citizenship Studies* 6 (3)

Romanow, Roy J., commissioner. 2002. *Building on Values: The Future of Health Care in Canada: Final Report.* Saskatoon: Commission on the Future of Health Care in Canada.

Rose, Joseph B. 2003. Affidavits in the Supreme Court of British Columbia in reference to Plaintiffs: The Health Services and Support-Facilities Subsector Bargaining Association, The Health Services and Support-Community Health Bargaining Association, The Nurses' Bargaining Association, The Hospital Employees' Union, The British Columbia Government and Service Employees' Union, The British Columbia Nurses' Union, Josephine Chauhan, Janine Brooker, Amaljeet Jhand, Leona Fraser, Marguerite Amy McCrea, Sally Lorraine Stevenson and Sharlene G.V. Decilla; and Defendant: Her Majesty the Queen in Right of the Province of British Columbia

Rose, N. 1999. *Powers of Freedom: Reframing Political Thought.* Cambridge: Cambridge University Press.

Rosenberg, Harriet. 1987. "Motherwork, Stress and Depression: The Costs of Privatized Social Reproduction." In *Feminism and Political Economy*, ed. Heather Jon Maroney and Meg Luxton. Toronto: Methuen

Rosenberg, Sharon. 2005. "An Introduction to Feminist Poststructural Theorizing." In *Feminist Issues Race, Class, and Sexuality*, ed. Nancy Mandell. Toronto: Pearson Prentice Hall

Rothman, Laurell. 2001. "Reflections on the Social Union Framework Agreement and the Early Childhood Development Services Agreement: Are We

Moving in the Right Direction for Young Children?" *Canadian Review of Social Policy* 47

Rowbotham, Sheila. 1992. *Women in Movement: Feminism and Social Action.* London: Routledge

– 1989. *The Past Is Before Us: Feminism in Action since the 1960s.* London: Pandora

– 1983. *Dreams and Dilemmas: Collected Writings.* London: Virago

– 1973. *Woman's Consciousness, Man's World.* Harmondsworth: Penguin

– 1972. *Women, Resistance and Revolution.* London: Penguin

Rubin, Gayle. 1975. "The Traffic in Women: Notes on the 'Political Economy' of Sex." In *Toward an Anthropology of Women,* ed. Rayna Reiter. New York: Monthly Review Press

Ryan, Mary. 1981. *Cradle of the Middle Class: The Family in Oneida County, New York, 1790–1865.* Cambridge: Cambridge University Press

Ryerson, Stanley B. 1973. *Unequal Union: Confederation and the Roots of Conflict in the Canadas, 1815–1873.* 2nd ed. Toronto: Progress Books.

Sargent, Lydia, ed. 1981. *Women and Revolution: A Discussion of the Unhappy Marriage of Marxism and Feminism.* Boston: South End Press

Sassen, Saskia. 2002. "Global Cities and Survival Circuits." In *Global Woman: Nannies, Maids and Sex Workers in the New Global Economy,* ed. Barbara Ehrenreich and Arlie Russell Hochschild. New York: Metropolitan Books.

– 1996. *Losing Control? Sovereignty in an Age of Globalization.* New York: Columbia University Press.

Scott, J. 1995. "Using Household Panels to Study Micro-Social Change." In *Women in Canada: A Statistical Report.* 3rd ed. Ottawa: Statistics Canada.

– 1986. "Gender: A Useful Category of Historical Analysis." *American Historical Review* 91

Seccombe, Wally. 1993. *Weathering the Storm: Working-Class Families from the Industrial Revolution to the Fertility Decline.* London: Verso

– 1992. *A Millennium of Family Change: Feudalism to Capitalism in Northwestern Europe.* London: Verso

– 1974. "The Housewife and her Labour under Capitalism." *New Left Review* 83

Segal, Lynne. 1987. *Is the Future Female? Troubled Thoughts on Contemporary Feminism.* London: Virago

Sen, Gita. 1994. "Reproduction: The Feminist Challenge to Social Policy." In *Power and Decision: the Social Control of Reproduction.* Cambridge: Harvard School of Public Health. Available at http://www.hsph.harvard.edu/rt21/globalism/SENFeminist_Challenge.html

Shields, John, and B. Mitchell Evans. 1998. *Shrinking the State: Globalization and Public Administration "Reform."* Halifax: Fernwood

Shillington, C. Howard. 1972. *The Road to Medicare in Canada*. Toronto: Del Graphics

Singleton, J.W. 2000. "Urban Shared Services Corporation: Implementation of Shared Food Services." *Manitoba Provincial Auditor's Value-for-Money Audits*, June.

Skeggs, Beverley. 2004. *Class, Self, Culture*. London: Routledge

Smith, Dorothy. 1989. "Feminist Reflections on Political Economy." *Studies in Political Economy* 30

Social Development Canada. 2002. *Addressing Work-Life Balance in Canada*. Ottawa: Social Development Canada

Sonpal-Valia, Nilima. 2001. "Staff Turnover in Rehabilitation Services in Alberta for 2001." *Rehabilitation Review* 13 (5)

Spivak, Gayatri. 2000. "Thinking Cultural Questions in 'Pure' Literary Terms." In *Without Guarantees: In Honour of Stuart Hall*, ed. Paul Gilroy, L. Grossberg, and A. McRobbie. London and New York: Verso

Stanford, Jim. 1999. *Paper Boom: Why Real Prosperity Requires a New Approach to Canada's Economy*. Ottawa and Toronto: The Canadian Centre for Policy Alternatives and James Lorimer and Co.

Stansell, Christine. 1987. *City of Women: Sex and Class in New York, 1789–1860*. Urbana: University of Illinois Press

Stasiulis, Diva. 1997. "The Political Economy of Race, Ethnicity, and Migration." In *Understanding Canada Building on the New Canadian Political Economy*, ed. Wallace Clement. Montreal and Kingston: McGill-Queen's University Press

Statistics Canada. 2005a. "Births and Birth Rate, by Province and Territories." Accessed at http://www.statcan.ca/101/cst01/demo04a.htm

– 2005b. "Study: Access to Professional Programs Amid the Deregulation of Tuition Fees, 1995 to 2002." *Daily* (Statistics Canada) 27 September.

– 2004. "Labour Force Characteristics by Age and Sex." *CANSIM II*, Table 282-0002. Ottawa: Statistics Canada

– 2003a. *Census of Canada 2001*. Ottawa: Ministry of Industry, Science and Technology. Accessed at www12.statcan.ca/english/census01/products/analytic/companio n/paid/canada.cfm

– 2003b. *The Changing Profile of Canada's Labour Force 2001*. Ottawa: Statistics Canada

– 2003c. *Income in Canada 2001*. Ottawa: Statistics Canada.

– 2003d. "Number of Persons Aged 15 and Over, by Number of Unpaid Hours Doing Housework, Canada, 1996 and 2001." In *2001 Census, Release 6*. 11 February. Ottawa: Statistics Canada

– 2003e. "Number of Persons Aged 15 and Over, by Unpaid Hours Providing Care or Assistance to Seniors, Canada, 1996 and 2001. In *2001 Census, Release 6*. 11 February. Ottawa: Statistics Canada

– 2003f. "Number of Persons Aged 15 and Over, by Unpaid Hours Looking After Children, Canada, 1996 and 2001." In *2001 Census, Release 6.* 11 February. Ottawa: Statistics Canada

– 2003g. *Profile of Canadian Families and Households: Diversification Continues, 2001 Census.* Ottawa: Statistics Canada

– 2002a. "Immigrant Status and Period of Immigration by Labour Force Activity." Catalogue Number: 97F0012XCB01001. Ottawa: Statistics Canada

– 2002b. *Profile of the Canadian Population by Mobility Status: Canada, a Nation on the Move.* 2001 Census: Analysis Series. Ottawa: Statistics Canada

– 2001a. "Births." *Daily* ( Statistics Canada), 10 December

– 2001b. "Distribution of Earnings in 2001 Constant Dollars, by Sex, for All Earners, Annual." CANSIM Table 202–0101. Ottawa: Income Statistics Division.

– 2001c. *Income in Canada 1999.* Ottawa: Statistics Canada.

– 2000. *Women in Canada 2000: A Gender-Based Statistical Report.* Ottawa: Minister of Industry

– 1999. *Low Income Cut Offs.* Ottawa: Statistics Canada.

– 1998a. *Caring Canadians, Involved Canadians: Highlights from the 1997 National Survey of Giving, Volunteering and Participating.* Ottawa: Statistics Canada

– 1998b. "Earning Characteristics of Two-Partner Families," *Daily* (Statistics Canada), 23 October

Statistics Canada and Status of Women Canada. 1994. *International Conference on the Measurement and Valuation of Unpaid Work: Proceedings.* Ottawa: Ministry of Industry, Science and Technology

Steinhauer, P. 1995. "The 'Whys' and 'Hows' of Mental Health Promotion for Children." Paper presented at Child Health 2000 International Conference, Vancouver, Voices for Children

Stinston, Jane. 1999. "Ontario Pay Equity Results for CUPE Services Workers in Ontario Hospitals: A Study of Uneven Benefits." MA thesis, Carleton University

Strong-Boag, Veronica Jane. 1976. *The Parliament of Women: The National Council of Women of Canada, 1893–1929.* Ottawa: National Museums of Canada.

*Taipei Times.* 2003. "Outsourcing Played Role in Outbreaks: CDC Head." 10 June

Taylor, Malcolm G. 1978. *Health Insurance and Canadian Public Policy: The Seven Decisions that Created the Canadian Health Insurance System.* Montreal: McGill-Queen's University Press

Taylor, Verta, 1996. *Rock-a-Bye-Baby.* New York: Routledge

Teelucksingh, C., and G.-E. Galabuzi. 2005. *Working Precariously: The Impact of Race and Immigrants Status on Employment Opportunities and Outcomes in Canada.* Toronto: Centre for Social Justice

Tentler, Leslie Woodcock. 1979. *Wage-Earning Women: Industrial Work and Family Life in the United States, 1900–1930.* New York: Oxford University Press

32 Hours. 2000. "Action for Full Employment/Shorter Work Time Network." *Better Times,* March 1998–February 2000. Available at http://www.web.net/32hours/ betterti.htm. Accessed 17 July 2005

– 1999. "CLC Work Time Pledge." *Better Times,* 10 (September 1999). Available at http://www.web.net/32hours/btsept99.htm. Accessed 17 July 2005

Threlfall, Monica, ed. 1996. *Mapping the Women's Movement: Feminist Politics and Social Transformation in the North.* London: Verso

Tilly, Louise, and Joan Scott. 1978. *Women, Work & Family.* New York: Holt, Rinehart and Winston

Toronto. 2003a. "Financial Pressures Related to Local Service Realignment of Child Care, Social Housing & Ontario Works." Report no. 2 of the Community Services Committee, 4–6 February. Accessed at http://www.city.toronto.on.ca/children/pdf/financial_pressure.pdf

– 2003b. "Preserving Child Care in Toronto: The Case for New Ontario Government Funding." Accessed at: http://www.toronto.ca/children/pdf/risk_jan2003.pdf

– 2003c. *Toronto Report Card on Children: Update 2003.* Vol. 5. Toronto: City of Toronto. Accessed at http://www.city.toronto.on.ca/children/report/repcard5/rep5_ execsum.pdf

– 2002. *Toronto Report Card on Children.* Vol. 4. Toronto: City of Toronto. Accessed at http://www.city.toronto.on.ca/children/report/repcard4/repca rd4_sec4a.pdf

– 2001. "Minutes of the Community Services Committee Meeting No. 11, Thursday, November 15." City of Toronto City Clerk's Division. Accessed at http://www.city.toronto.on.ca/legdocs/2001/minutes/committee s/cms/cms011115.pdf

Toronto First Duty Research Team. 2004. *Toronto First Duty: Progress Report.*

*Toronto Star.* 1996. "Nothing Sacred in Review: Harris." 5 April, A1

– 1995a. "Find Your Own Sitters Working Moms Told." By Kelly Toughill. 18 September, A1

– 1995b. "Welfare Not Set Up to Feed the Kids: Harris." By Kelly Toughill. 28 September, A14

Tougas, Jocelyn. 2002. *Reforming Quebec's Early Childhood Care and Education: The First Five Years.* Occasional Paper 17. Toronto: Childcare Resource and

Research Unit, University of Toronto

United Nations. 2002. "Number of World's Migrants Reaches 175 Million Mark." Press release, 28 October. Accessed at http://www.un.org/News/Press/docs/2002/pop844.doc.htm

United Nations Development Program. 2003. *Human Development Report 2003: Millennium Development Goals: A Compact Among Nations to End Human Poverty.* New York: United Nations

Ursel, Jane. 1992. *Private Lives, Public Policy: 100 Years of State Intervention in the Family.* Toronto: Women's Press.

Vaillancourt, Yves. 1994. "Quebec and the Federal Government: The Struggle over Opting Out." In *Canadian Society: Understanding and Surviving in the 1990s,* ed. Dan Glenday and Ann Duffy. Toronto: McClelland and Stewart.

Vickers, Jill, Pauline Rankin, and Christine Appelle. 1993. *Politics as if Women Mattered: A Political Analysis of the National Action Committee on the Status of Women.* Toronto: University of Toronto Press

Vogel, Lise. 1983. *Marxism and the Oppression of Women: Toward a Unitary Theory* London: Pluto Press

Vosko, Leah F. 2002a. "Mandatory 'Marriage' or Obligatory Waged Work: Social Assistance and the Single Mother's Complex Roles in Wisconsin and Ontario." In *Women's Work Is Never Done: Comparative Studies in Care-Giving, Employment, and Social Policy Reform,* ed. Sylvia Bashevkin. New York: Routledge

– 2002b. *Rethinking Feminization: Gendered Precariousness in the Canadian Labour Market and the Crisis in Social Reproduction."* A monograph prepared for the Annual Robarts Lecture, John P. Robarts Centre for Canadian Studies, 11 April

– 2000. *Temporary Work: The Gendered Rise of a Precarious Employment Relationship.* Toronto: University of Toronto Press.

Vosko, L., N. Zukewich, and C. Cranford. 2003. "Beyond Non-standard Work: Towards a Typology of Employment." *Perspectives on Income and Labour* (Statistics Canada), Fall

Walker, Tom. 2002a. *Profile of Aramark Worldwide Corporation.* Vancouver: Hospital Employees' Union

– 2002b. *Profile of the Compass Group, PLC.* Vancouver: Hospital Employees' Union

– 2002c. *Who is Sedexho?* Vancouver: Hospital Employees' Union

Walkerdine, Valerie, and Helen Lucey, 1989. *Democracy in the Kitchen: Regulating Mothers and Socializing Daughters.* London: Virago

Wall, Glenda. 2004. "Is Your Child's Brain Potential Maximized? Mothering in an Age of New Brain Research." *Atlantis* 28 (2)

– 2001. "Moral Constructions of Motherhood in Breastfeeding Discourse." *Gender & Society* 15 (4)

Walzer, Susan, 1998. *Thinking about the Baby: Gender and Transitions into Parenthood.* Philadelphia: Temple University Press

Waring, M. 1988. *If Women Counted: A New Feminist Economics.* San Francisco: Harper and Row.

Webb, Patricia G. 1994. *The Heart of Health Care: The First 50 Years.* Vancouver: Hospital Employees' Union.

Weedon, Chris. 1987. *Feminist Practice and Poststructuralist Theory.* Oxford: Blackwell

White, Julie. 2002. "A New Look at Shorter Hours of Work in the Communications, Energy and Paperworkers Union." *Just Labour* 1. Available at http://www.yorku.ca/julabour/volume1/index2.htm. Accessed 20 July 2005

– 1993. *Sisters and Solidarity: Women and Unions in Canada.* Toronto: Thompson Educational Publishing

White, Linda A. 2002. "The Child Care Agenda and the Social Union." In *Canadian Federalism: Performance, Effectiveness, and Legitimacy,* ed. Grace Skogstad. Don Mills, Ont.: Oxford University Press

Wolf, Naomi. 2001. *Misconceptions: Truth, Lies, and the Unexpected on the Journey to Motherhood.* New York: Anchor Books

Wrigley, Julia. 1995. *Other People's Children: An Intimate Account of the Dilemmas Facing Middle-Class Parents and the Women They Hire to Raise Their Children.* New York: Basic

Yalnizyan, A. 1998. *The Growing Gap: A Report on Growing Inequality between the Rich and Poor in Canada.* Toronto: Centre for Social Justice.

Zarembka, Joy M. 2002. "America's Dirty Work: Maids and Modern-Day Slavery." In *Global Woman: Nannies, Maids, and Sex Workers in the New Global Economy,* ed. Barbara Ehrenreich and Arlie Russell Hochschild. New York: Metropolitan Books.